A PLAUSIBLE MAN

Also by Susanna Ashton

Collaborators in Literary America, 1870–1920

A PLAUSIBLE MAN

THE TRUE STORY OF THE ESCAPED SLAVE WHO INSPIRED *UNCLE TOM'S CABIN*

SUSANNA ASHTON

THE NEW PRESS

NEW YORK
LONDON

Published in the United States by The New Press, New York, 2024
Distributed by Two Rivers Distribution

ISBN 978-1-62097-819-1 (hc)
ISBN 978-1-62097-866-5 (ebook)
CIP data is available

The New Press publishes books that promote and enrich public discussion and understanding of the issues vital to our democracy and to a more equitable world. These books are made possible by the enthusiasm of our readers; the support of a committed group of donors, large and small; the collaboration of our many partners in the independent media and the not-for-profit sector; booksellers, who often hand-sell New Press books; librarians; and above all by our authors.

www.thenewpress.com

Book design and composition by Bookbright Media
This book was set in Times New Roman and Gotham

Printed in the United States of America

2 4 6 8 10 9 7 5 3 1

CONTENTS

Introduction ix

Prelude: The Man Who Came Back—W.P.A Interview with Jake McLeod (1936) xviii

Chapter 1: "Feloniously Inveigling"—A Judgment on the Kidnapping of Doctor (1821) 1

Chapter 2: The Reverend Lowery's Story Based on Facts (1911) 26

Chapter 3: "Speaks Plausibly"—The Reverend and His Runaway Advertisement (1847) 44

Chapter 4: Henry Foreman's Boarding House Census Report of 1850 62

Chapter 5: "A Genuine Article"—Harriet Beecher Stowe's Letter to Her Sister (1850) 96

Chapter 6: Race: United States—The New Brunswick Census of 1851 132

Chapter 7: *The Experience of a Slave in South Carolina* by John Andrew Jackson (1862) 160

Chapter 8: *The White Preacher and the Black Slave Lecturer* (1865) 194

Chapter 9: "One Thousand Acres"—A Letter to General Howard (1868) 214

Chapter 10: "Hard Labor"—Court Minutes from Surry County, North Carolina (1881) 252

Acknowledgments 269

Notes 275

Image Sources 323

Index 325

A PLAUSIBLE MAN

INTRODUCTION

I

In December 1850, a faculty wife in Brunswick, Maine, who had a modest sideline in magazine writing, hid a fugitive in her house. A friendly neighbor had sent the man over, and so it was that the little-known writer and harried mother Harriet Beecher Stowe opened her door.

It was bitterly cold, and Stowe's house was crowded with children. Her husband was away. And yet she opened the door—a criminal act, in 1850.

The man stayed for only one night, but he made an impression upon both Stowe and her children, singing and entertaining them all and telling Stowe about his hardships. In a space apart from the children, no doubt, he bared his back and showed her his scars from whippings he had received in a slave labor camp. We might imagine he spoke, too, of his wife and child he had left behind: "He was," she later wrote to her sister, "a genuine article from the "Ole Carliny State."

Drawing from this experience, some seven weeks later, in 1851, Stowe began to write *Uncle Tom's Cabin*, a novel that helped inspire the most consequential social revolution in the history of the Western world: the overthrow of modern slavery.

Stowe never named the man who was fleeing to Canada. It is possible he didn't even share his name with her. Yet he was, indeed, "a genuine article." He went by John Andrew Jackson, and his encounter with Stowe was only one pivotal incident in his rich and complicated career. And while there is a good argument to be made that his life story inspired some parts of *Uncle Tom's Cabin*—even serving as a model for a crucial chapter that portrays a fugitive being welcomed into a Northern senator's home, a house unprepared for hosting a freedom seeker—the more significant story he created was his own.[1] Through determination and canny charisma, Jackson reclaimed what it was to be genuine, not according to the condescending assessment of white America, but through his savvy self-fashioning.

Born enslaved sometime around 1820, Jackson endured the suffering expected for a man in bondage until his wife, Louisa, and young daughter he called "Jinny" were sent away from him. Then, facing heartbreak beyond endurance, Jackson fled on horseback across the dangers of the South Carolina terrain until reaching the coastal port of Charleston. Once there, he engineered a harrowing escape, hiding between bales of cotton aboard a northbound vessel. Over the next years, in the comparative freedom of the Northern states and later Canada and Great Britain, he carved out a life for himself and constructed a destiny of broad, strange horizons.

Jackson's life reflects an era of new possibilities for a generation of African American authors arising out of bondage. His particular experiences in first engineering an escape from slavery and then building a life in freedom are powerful, to be sure. But once out of the South, his experiences are uniquely telling. He navigates an international lecturing career initially under the mercurial patronage of powerful British Baptist Evangelicals who assist him in publishing his memoir, *The Experience of a Slave in South Carolina* (1862).

Yet, in another striking turn, once that relationship grew sour, Jackson returned to the United States for some thirty-five years of independent operations as an advocate for freed people, collecting donations, lecturing across postbellum America, and promoting ill-fated social experiments. He even attempted to purchase back his enslaver's family land to resettle forty Black families in a utopian plan for communal farming. Jackson faced failure regularly but somehow kept at his dreams. Implausibly and yet truly, when in 1880 he was arrested in North Carolina and sentenced to hard labor on a convict work gang, this man in his midfifties somehow managed to escape. Again, Jackson was not going to be kept down.

Unlike most other extant narratives of slavery and freedom, Jackson's tale is one of independent negotiations and survival. His is a tale of individual hustle; separate from most established Black and white organizations, he would almost always go it alone.

Ultimately, *A Plausible Man* is a tale of a remarkable but overlooked American figure who challenges what we might think of as the history of fugitivity and, in particular, how the Reconstruction-era lives of these freedom seekers arose from their earlier experiences in slavery. His story spans generations and lingers today with his family descendants in South Carolina.[2]

At the same time, this story is a tale of the archive and its vacillating richness and scarcity: How do we tell a tale of the nineteenth century and of people who sought to disappear? Of a person whose color meant that his history was ultimately relegated to the folk knowledge of his neighbors?

Jackson's story is about the archive of the marginal, the folklore of the underground, and the truths of the forgotten networks that make up how we see our histories and our communities.

II

In telling Jackson's story, I have chosen to depart from the biographical practice of using archival documentation simply as fodder for fact-checking and footnotes. Rather, each chapter here focuses on one particularly telling historical document that frames a perspective not merely upon Jackson's life activities, but upon notions of what can and cannot be recorded.

The first chapter, "'Feloniously Inveigling'—A Judgment on the Kidnapping of Doctor," for instance, weighs interpretative possibilities around an assault charge leveled between two white men in 1821. One of these white men accused the other of stealing or "inveigling" away from his personal property, property which happened to be, according to the Sumter County Court records, a man named "Doc." A physical altercation between the white men ensued.

While "Doc" is referenced in the county records of this case, he is not called to witness or testify about the events. This enslaved man held the full name of "Doctor Clavern,"* according to his own family, at least.[3] His story was at the core of the court record, and yet it only glancingly acknowledges his presence in the case. Doctor was Jackson's father, and my examination of this document launches the book not merely to provide context for the violent world Jackson was born into but also to highlight how its passing reference to "Doc" reminds us how certain stories are allowed to survive.

A court record embodies a kind of archival assault. That is to say, the

* Doctor was referred to variously as Dock, Doctor, Dr. and Doc in different documents but for purposes of consistency I refer to him as "Doctor" or "Doctor Clavern."

practice of retaining and indexing this kind of legal conflict, registering the white names of the dispute but deliberately ignoring the experience of the man listed within the document's core, is an aggressive act in and of itself. In this instance, as in the case of the other documents that provide a threshold of entry for each chapter that follows (a runaway slave advertisement, a newspaper clipping, a family letter, an addendum page to a census report, a self-published pamphlet, a solicitation letter, a census map, and a property deed), such historical documents cannot be understood as solely a background to one man's life. Rather, these documents demonstrate how Black presence and identity bleed through the otherwise obfuscatory nineteenth-century ledger lines.

The name of "Doc" eventually connected what started as a largely historical study to a twenty-first-century world. As I struggled to figure out who Jackson's descendants might be and why he had been named "Jackson" at all, I realized that his father's first name, "Doc," was a name to follow. And indeed, it was his father's first name that led me to the living members of the Clavon/Clabon/Clyburn family.[4] While it doesn't appear that any

Photo of Dock Clavon, a descendant of the original Doctor Clavern, with the author.

direct descendants of Jackson survived, children of his sisters and brothers did, and they sweetly continued to honor their patriarch "Doc" with generation after generation naming at least one child "Doctor," "Dock," or "Doc."

This modern family of Clavons*, which is perhaps disproportionately rich with clergy, salespeople, and vibrant personalities, embodies the hustle, talent, and collective love which enabled Jackson to survive.[5] The Dock Clavon pictured here, is not the man at the heart of the 1821 court dispute, but as a holder of a doctorate degree from George Washington University, in engineering, he is, as of 2022, Dr. Doctor Clavon. This is an achievement that would embody the dream of his enslaved and embattled ancestor who fought hard for his own education, John Andrew Jackson.

III

Stories of escape and survival can be celebrations of unimaginable individual achievement. But those people carried tremendous burdens of guilt and loss.

Jackson's survival and escape were, of course, unfathomably brave. There was also a cost, likely a terrible cost, to the families he left behind. There are indeed no records with details on what happened to the Clavon/Jackson family immediately after Jackson fled. And yet, it would have been tragic but typical for remaining enslaved family members to be punished or tortured to find out where freedom seekers such as Jackson might have gone. We shouldn't be surprised that much of Jackson's narrative thus dances between the tension of providing testimony about his achievements and establishing himself as a speaker on behalf of others. Fortunately, records of his life go far beyond his testimony in his memoir. It is the other ephemera that flesh out the story of his life, particularly in the four decades after he wrote his book, and that suggest to us how he may have balanced out this flashy and heroic persona that allowed him to survive and succeed alongside a quieter regret and responsibility to the people he had left behind.

---

* While spelling variations occur across generations, the name "Clavern" is the one Jackson uses for his father and thus I shall also do so when referencing that individual. Most of the other family members after Emancipation refer to themselves as Clavon or other variations and thus I refer more generally to the Clavon family.

The questions that plagued Jackson remain relevant today. The notion that only virtuous citizens deserve freedom is one he struggled with. He was accused of lying, misrepresentation, exaggeration, and fraud on various occasions throughout his life. It is certainly possible, even probable, that on occasion these accusations had some truth behind them. He hustled, for sure. He collected money for years on behalf of others, and while we have evidence that some of his collections made their way to their destination, it is not clear that they always did. Certainly, he would have used some collected funds for his survival and support, perhaps in either an honest or an underhanded way.

The historical records that provide us with incomplete knowledge, therefore, are especially ripe for scrutiny, though—as in various chapters where I reference the runaway slave advertisements or solicitations for the freemen, or interviews with people who knew him—the historical record appears to check out. Thanks to digital tools of the modern age, I've been able to cross-reference addresses, newspaper notices, government records, and census data that support a contention that he was usually, if not always, who he said he was.

This question about documentation and reliability was a notion coded and inflected with racist assumptions about character. Jackson's enslavers posted an advertisement in their local paper, the *Sumter Banner*, in March 1848, three months after he fled—a notice that warned against listening to him, because he "speaks plausibly."[6] Cautioning white readers against the duplicitous nature of fugitives was a relatively common rhetorical technique in advertisements.[7] This language served the dual function of heightening suspicion about this garrulous and clever man and implicitly reminding audiences that sincerity of character was rarely found in Black people—particularly those who had the effrontery to steal themselves. In the eyes of many powerful people at that time, self-theft was a serious property crime. Warning readers about the inherent untrustworthy nature of even the most well-spoken or persuasive runaways had the additional effect of reminding newspaper audiences that words, logic, skill, and even truth had no precedence over the color of one's skin.

While a close reading of the *Sumter Banner*'s runaway advertisement of 1848 in all its particulars is a core part of chapter 3, how Jackson renders himself "plausible" is the heart of my entire project. It is not the copious documentation compiled that "authenticates" his life story. Jackson would never have given pieces of paper that kind of power.

Instead, it is Jackson's assertion of his manhood, his place in the world, and even his status as an "advocate for the freeman" that undergird any documents. Not the other way around. He subverted the casual assertion of slaveholders and turned the notion of "plausibility" in on itself. His identity was to be on his terms and articulated in books he would write, pamphlets he would author, and speeches he would deliver. Without much of a white amanuensis or editor, what we know of Jackson's life is largely on his own terms. As readers, our choice to assess his witness as plausible or not is up to us. But Jackson lays out his tools and the criteria for such assessment.

The following chapters tell a difficult tale that resists designation as a triumph narrative despite occasional moments of happiness. Even his greatest moments, such as when he escaped from South Carolina, were tinged with bittersweet knowledge about those he had left behind. The location of Jackson's grave is unknown. He may have died with friends and family, but he certainly died in poverty. Few of his dreams came true for himself or his community; he never established or built a church, he never appears to have built a home for the aged freedmen, and he wasn't able to bring any orphaned children north. He had dreamed of creating a Black utopia on his ruined enslaver's property. But it was not to be.

And yet, Jackson's spectacular self-creation allowed him to travel the world. His confidence allowed him to speak to thousands about the most consequential social movements of the modern age. He was able to build and rebuild a family. He managed to reconnect with a devastated community, deliver supplies to the starving, escape from a chain gang, and ensure his voice would survive. He spent the last decades of his life traveling between New England and the rural South, trying to fulfill the promise of a post–Civil War Union. He had friends, for sure, but as an independent operator in a world that demanded Black people stay quiet, he was a self-promoter and self-proprietor.

Jackson's bold self-fashioning as a man of substance pushes back against the paternalistic affirmations he often was met with by white people—after all, Stowe appointed herself as arbiter by asserting he was the "genuine article" with some bemused racism. And his enslavers put out advertisements for him, cautioning that he "speaks plausibly" and should not be trusted. They were right.

Jackson hectored and lectured. He sang and scolded. He was quick to speak truths but he'd hustle with lies. The story of his survival was always linked to the survival of his stories.

History's judgment on what is real might be only an assessment of what is or what we think is *plausible*—as we consider which truth fits our predictions, our preconceptions. Jackson's story eluded scholars until now precisely because his clear-spoken claims about who he was, what he did, and how he moved through the world didn't fit the subservient, unctuously grateful, truth-telling role in, indeed, the Uncle Tom model.[8]

Jackson instead built a life in which he could be plausible according to the whims of his mercurial patrons or enemies. Being plausible could buy Jackson time. It could allow him to elude pursuers and detractors alike. Being plausible didn't mean he was a fraud. It simply meant that other people couldn't read him as well as they thought they could.

For Jackson, being plausible gave him space.

Notes on structure

This book is organized chronologically but also concerns itself with memory and witness. Honoring Black memory here, which is rarely in perfect concert with archival documentation, allows for some shifting perspective throughout the chapters. Looking at historical paperwork afresh asks us to reframe what is "plausible."

Studying and writing about enslaved people demands a degree of thoughtful speculation to get out of the trap of simply endlessly seeking more and more documentation, which often won't exist. And if we stop our study because, say, a certain name is not listed in an inventory list of human beings, such as in an antebellum slave schedule that was enumerated for the political representation of white people and attendant taxation purposes, we not only impoverish a project but we re-create and bolster up a system of archival work that allows only for some kinds of cultural recognition.[9] By quitting when information doesn't present itself to us in the traditional form of paperwork, we fail our subjects. And so, in this book, I try to consciously draw upon my notions in general terms about relationships and the context of life as I try to place Jackson in a world that can make sense to us, even when the traditionally understood historical production of an archive fails us and him.[10]

To travel through Jackson's life, we must return again and again to the community that he carried and which carried him. This means that the heroic figure he sometimes liked to pose as needs to be understood not against but *alongside* his neighbors in New Haven, his comrades in Saint John, Black worshipers at Southern revival camp meetings, his sisters and brothers left behind in South Carolina, his peers on the British lecture stage, or his fellow lodgers in a Black sailors' boarding house. This is their archive, too.

PRELUDE: THE MAN WHO CAME BACK

W.P.A Interview with Jake McLeod (1936)

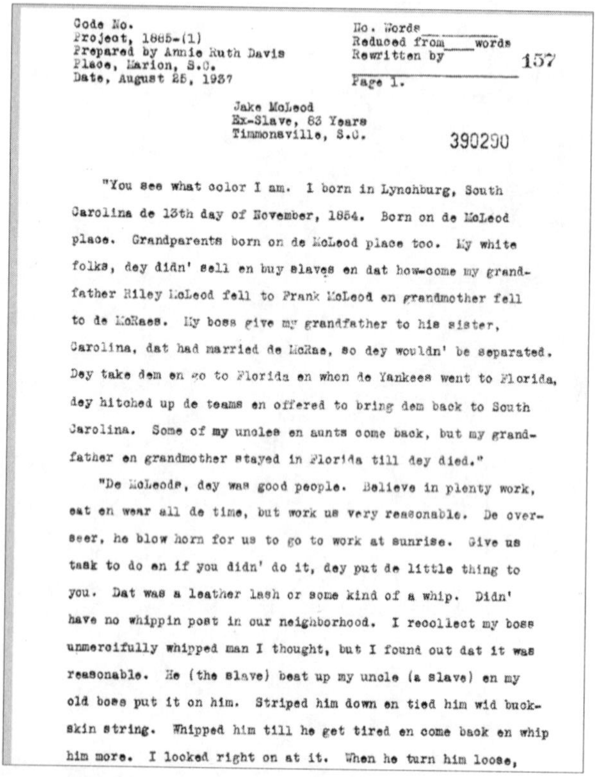

Code No.
Project, 1885-(1)
Prepared by Annie Ruth Davis
Place, Marion, S.C.
Date, August 25, 1937

No. Words ______
Reduced from ___ words
Rewritten by ______ 157

Page 1.

Jake McLeod
Ex-Slave, 83 Years
Timmonsville, S.C.

390290

"You see what color I am. I born in Lynchburg, South Carolina de 13th day of November, 1854. Born on de McLeod place. Grandparents born on de McLeod place too. My white folks, dey didn' sell en buy slaves en dat how-come my grandfather Riley McLeod fell to Frank McLeod en grandmother fell to de McRaes. My boss give my grandfather to his sister, Carolina, dat had married de McRae, so dey wouldn' be separated. Dey take dem en go to Florida en when de Yankees went to Florida, dey hitched up de teams en offered to bring dem back to South Carolina. Some of my uncles en aunts come back, but my grandfather en grandmother stayed in Florida till dey died."

"De McLeods, dey was good people. Believe in plenty work, eat en wear all de time, but work us very reasonable. De overseer, he blow horn for us to go to work at sunrise. Give us task to do en if you didn' do it, dey put de little thing to you. Dat was a leather lash or some kind of a whip. Didn' have no whippin post in our neighborhood. I recollect my boss unmercifully whipped man I thought, but I found out dat it was reasonable. He (the slave) beat up my uncle (a slave) en my old boss put it on him. Striped him down en tied him wid buckskin string. Whipped him till he get tired en come back en whip him more. I looked right on at it. When he turn him loose,

Typed transcript of Jake McCloud's WPA interview

In 1936 Jake McLeod, a poor Black man of eighty-three years, agreed to be interviewed by two white federal agents seeking to speak with survivors of slavery. Why he agreed is not clear. Was he lonely? Intimidated? Seeking to curry some favor from the government during the Great Depression? Simply hoping to share some testimony and wisdom from his life?

It is hard to say. But he let them enter his home in Timmonsville, South Carolina, and agreed to speak with these government workers so that they might transcribe his memories.

One and probably both of his interviewers were, like him, native South Carolinians, but there any similarities surely ended. They had much to learn from what McLeod could tell them. As a survivor of slavery, a survivor of the violent backlashes against Reconstruction, and a witness to decades of racial oppression, McLeod likely had stories they wouldn't have been able to hear well, no matter how hard they listened. Nonetheless, he tried to speak his truth, and they took down his words in a rough and racist transcriptive dialect.

Many of the people employed and working as agents of the Federal Writers' Project of this era were anthropologists, journalists, artists, or scholars hired to do cultural work and, in this case, local folklore research.[1] The two agents assigned to this region, however, brought with them different skills and interests. The lead agent was H. Grady Davis, a veteran who had sustained injuries from his service in World War I. As a disabled man seeking work in the Depression of the 1930s, he must have been grateful for the opportunity to earn a steady, albeit small, salary from this jobs program of what was known as the Works Progress Administration. He had been living in Johnson City, Tennessee, for some years but returned to South Carolina for the opportunity to go door-to-door collecting interviews with elderly citizens who had survived childhoods in state-sanctioned bondage.[2]

Davis's partner for the McLeod interview was Mrs. Lucile Young. What role she played is not clear, and her identity even less so. Was she an equal questioner? Was she there, as a woman, to help the elderly Black subjects feel less intimidated? Was she the transcriptionist or stenographer while Davis led the questioning? Certainly, they had worked out a careful partnership and had a plan. Easy questions to start and then move into harder, bolder topics. What might they have expected of Jake McLeod in this conversation, where their race and class status, not to mention their role as representatives of the government, surely created a barrier to easy conversation? And what might Jake McLeod have expected from them?

McLeod was careful. He sprinkled his interview with repeated references to how kindly his particular enslavers, the white McLeod family, were: "Dey was good people," he affirms.[3] But he then doesn't hold back from talking about the pervasive violence they had used on men, women, and children. And he emphasizes the omnipresent nature of community control in which patrollers and, really, any white person could call out for violence and enforcement on any Black transgression.

As McLeod put it, "De community have man den call patroller en dey business was to catch dem dat run away."

Learning to fear capture and its consequences was ingrained early. As a child, Jake McLeod had once, in what was likely desperate terror, run away. "Somehow another," as the old man recalled, the overseer knew where to find him, and he was caught and whipped by his mistress "til de whip broke."

We cannot read the exact questions in this transcript, only the answers, but we can infer that the interviewers persisted and wished to know more. Running successfully to freedom must have seemed almost impossible in a landscape menaced by patrollers, monitored by the overseers, and endlessly surveilled by white people, who, solely by their racial status, could detain and interrogate anyone they wished. But McLeod knew it could and had happened. And so he told his interviewers:

> I hear tell bout one man runnin away from Black Creek en gwine to Free State. Catch ride wid people dat used to travel to Charleston haulin cotton en things. He come back bout 15 years after de war and lived in dat place join to me. Come back wid barrels en boxes of old second hand clothes en accumulated right smart here. Talk good deal bout how he associated wid de whites. Don' know how-come he run away, but dey didn' catch up wid him till it was too late.

McLeod recounts the tale of an unnamed Black Creek man who achieved what McLeod had only dreamed of: getting "to Free State."

Then, in an act perhaps even beyond the extent of McLeod's dreams, this Black Creek man returned in freedom with goods and tales of a different world, a world in which Black and white people could have, in a way that might have strained credibility, "associated" with one another.

Finally, in what might have been the oddest of all to McLeod, this bold, strange man moved right back to where he had run from—and came to settle in Lynchburg, "joined" to McLeod.

Even fifty years later, the story of the Black Creek man who came back was so remarkable that McLeod felt it needed to be recorded, a memory that needed to be shared.

This runaway was John Andrew Jackson, a man who achieved almost mythical status in Black memory even while he was effectively erased from history by many of his former white friends and allies.

In 1846, Jackson had fled a slave labor camp near the area of Lynchburg, South Carolina, close to the Black River (or what McLeod calls the "Black Creek"). And, after the Civil War, Jackson returned with barrels and boxes of secondhand goods, just as McLeod had said. Federal Freedmen's Bureau records itemize receipts for barrels of donations of used clothes and food Jackson arranged to be shipped south from Northern communities after the war. Jackson went back and forth from South Carolina over the decades that followed. By 1881, as McLeod attested, Jackson bought a lot in the tiny town of Lynchburg, close to the crossroads where he had once lived back when he was enslaved by Robert English and, as Sumter County property records demonstrate, immediately adjacent to McLeod's small parcel of land.[4]

Jackson was remembered in a different way, too, beyond his friends' memories. For Jackson had altered how stories about slavery could be told, not just by inspiring or instigating Stowe to launch her book but by claiming and performing his own story again and again. As McLeod knew: no one could catch up to him until it was too late.

CHAPTER ONE

"FELONIOUSLY INVEIGLING"—A JUDGMENT ON THE KIDNAPPING OF DOCTOR (1821)

Lynchburg, South Carolina (1821–1846)

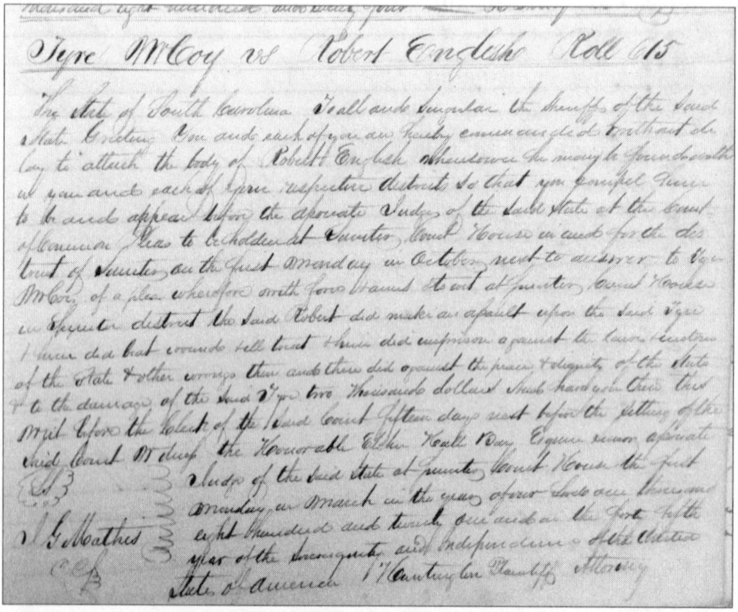
Tyre McCoy vs Robert English Roll 615

The State of South Carolina To all and singular the Sheriffs of the said State Greeting You and each of you are hereby commanded that without delay to attach the body of Robert English wheresoever he may be found within your and each of your respective districts so that you compel him to be and appear before the associate Judges of the said State at the Court of Common Pleas to be holden at Sumter Court House in and for the district of Sumter on the first Monday in October next to answer to Tyre McCoy of a plea wherefore with force & arms to wit at Sumter Court House in Sumter district the said Robert did make an assault upon the said Tyre & him did beat wound & ill treat & him did imprison against the laws & customs of the State & other wrongs then and there did against the peace & dignity of the State & to the damage of the said Tyre two thousand dollars And have you then there this writ Before the Clerk of the said Court fifteen days next before the sitting of the said Court Witness the Honorable Elihu Hall Bay Esquire senior associate Judge of the said State at Sumter Court House the first Monday in March in the year of our Lord one thousand eight hundred and twenty one and in the forty fifth year of the Sovereignty and Independence of the United States of America

J. G. Mathews C.C.P.

[illegible] Plaintiff's Attorney

This Sumter County courthouse case record of *Tyre McCoy vs. Robert English* chronicles a violent altercation between two neighbors in 1821. The man at the heart of the story, Doctor, is mentioned only fleetingly, but this experience for him may have launched a chain of events that would alter the future for generations of Black and white people in Lynchburg, South Carolina.

How did a young man, raised to think he was nothing, come to believe in himself so powerfully that he could not only escape from slavery but try to change the world with his words? The story of John Andrew Jackson is that of a self-made man in many ways. It's a story told through his words and the words of others. Court documents, gravestones, receipts, highway plaques, family histories, and crumbling storefronts all work in concert to tell their overlapping truths. But Jackson's tale is also one of the worlds he carried with him, the people who lifted him up, and the people he left behind.

I

On a hot afternoon in September 1821, in an inland hamlet of South Carolina, two white men got into a fight. It was vicious. The younger man, Tyre McCoy, was beaten badly. The older man, Robert English, walked away from the brawl without injury. English, however, persuaded a local justice of the peace to issue a warrant to arrest McCoy and have him imprisoned. English was known across the county for violent and unpleasant behavior, but he was a well-connected citizen of the region, owning a large plantation labor camp and other landholdings.[1] McCoy, a man from a nearby homestead along the Black River, had run afoul of someone dangerous.

What had brought them to this point? The exact precipitating incident is unknown. It must have been ugly, though.

Whatever had happened initially, English accused McCoy of "feloniously inveigling" or attempting to "carry away" English's property. What was this property? It was an enslaved man in his prime, assessed by English as a man worth $1,000. It seems unlikely that McCoy was an abolitionist, as the McCoy family also ran a small plantation work camp operated by enslaved people. An attempt to steal or kidnap an enslaved man from a powerful neighbor, unless the plan was to smuggle the kidnapped man far away, would have been a reckless endeavor. So the mystery of why English thought McCoy intended to carry away the enslaved laborer remains.

While the events chronicled by the court records are a bit hazy, it is clear that English, who was never one to wait upon ceremony, decided McCoy was guilty and assaulted him with ferocity. English, then, using his power as a prominent citizen (in this town, which for a while was known as "English Cross Roads"), had the seriously injured McCoy cast into a local jail for some twenty days before the case was adjudicated.[2]

McCoy was eventually released. The court found no just cause to keep him. McCoy then turned around and sued English for some $2,000 in damages over false imprisonment and assault—a tremendous sum for the time and one which suggests more than umbrage over a conflict; it suggests McCoy understood the attack as attempted murder. Before his suit could go too far, though, McCoy dropped it, perhaps aware that slave theft was an offense eligible for execution, and he was lucky to have survived the accusation, however unfounded it may have been.[3]

Chronicling white people's problems of the 1820s tells us something about the culture of South Carolina at that time and how seriously the theft of human property was taken. This legal imbroglio also gives us a glimpse into the casual violence that was only occasionally checked by rural courts. Most of all, we see that Robert English was a man to be feared.

What this version of history doesn't tell us, however, is anything about the voice that has been lost from the center of this story. The enslaved man who may or may not have been "inveigled" away was known in the court records as "Doctor." More important, he had a full name known to his family: Doctor Clavern. He was a man of wisdom. He was a man of consequence. Doctor's father (who would have been Jackson's grandfather) had been kidnapped from Africa. It was from him that Doctor, as his family reported, "learned the African method of curing snake bites." He was thereby honored by the enslaved community in one of the few ways they had to bestow such respect: he became known first by them but later even by his enslavers as "Doctor."[4]

Doctor was also a husband, a survivor who outlived many of his enslavers, and a man who was later able to claim his right to vote.[5] He would survive both Robert English and his wife. Key to this story, though, is that Doctor Clavern was the beloved father to a child who grew to be known as John Andrew Jackson. Together, he and his son would triumph over Robert English and the structure of white supremacy that held the Clavon/Jackson family in bondage.

While Doctor's account is not told in court documents, since his testimony would have no standing, one wonders what he learned from the incident. What might he have gone on to teach his children about their enslaver? What would he have told them about the vagaries of white justice? Had Doctor agreed to go with McCoy? Did he pretend to be grateful for his "rescue" from McCoy? Or was he bitter over his return to English's control? We cannot know. But this case does illustrate the volatile environment that shaped the experiences of so many enslaved families.

Doctor had presumably witnessed English's assault upon McCoy. How did it compare to the horrors he had seen inflicted upon himself and other Black people under English's dominion? Indeed, Doctor learned that, if there had been any doubt before, English had the power of the law and the community on his side, so much so that English could thwart the law without repercussions. English's assault on McCoy was understood as a defense of property. And thus, as property, Doctor remained in bondage to the English family.

This courthouse document registers Doctor as worth $1,000. It utterly fails to assess how he was of value to his wife, parents, children, and friends, an assessment of what historian Daina Ramey Berry might term his "soul value."[6] The document silences his voice, but it cannot mute the story of his legacy. That would be recorded in memory for and by his children.

II

As was common for the era, the families of Robert English and Doctor Clavern were entwined by power, violence, and, quite possibly, blood connections. Unsurprisingly, the English family is well documented and well connected across the intermarried white family trees of Sumter County, South Carolina. The Clavern family had to fight for survival and connection, often in the face of horrifying circumstances and not always with success. Family members were lost to ill treatment, abuse, displacement, and murder. The shadow archive of the Clavern family—or, as it became more often known, the "Clavon" family—is thus most present in Jackson's 1862 memoir, *The Experience of a Slave in South Carolina*, along with a few sparse supplementary documents from the late nineteenth century. Still, together with the collective community memory, they frame a scaffold of being, confidence, and love that sustained and shaped Jackson's future.

Not surprisingly, documents about the births of enslaved children held in bondage by the English family are sparse. In 1821, at the time of the incident between McCoy and English, Doctor likely had a wife and at least one or two children, including Ephraim, Jackson's older brother. It is hard to imagine Doctor leaving his young family willingly. Then again, it is difficult to imagine how anyone who endured such bondage might not have gambled upon a better circumstance. In 1821, Doctor was probably in the prime of his life (perhaps his early twenties) and would therefore have been a valuable kidnapping victim. He would have been a powerful field hand for any enslaver seeking to run a massive cotton and livestock operation such as the one Robert English had established. And, of course, we cannot discount the entire situation as trumped up entirely by English, who was known as a hot-tempered neighbor and one who, not surprisingly, was especially brutal to the Black people within his power.

Doctor lived under the power of the English family for at least another forty-four years. He survived to raise his children and provide them with some stability, as much as was within the grasp of any fractured and embattled family unit under slavery. While Betty, Doctor's wife (and Jackson's mother), likely died sometime in the mid-1850s and several of Doctor's children did not survive to be emancipated, Doctor himself, as one of the elder patriarchs of the Black community, managed to outlive Robert English and most of English's children.

Remarkably, Doctor survived long enough to see himself emancipated and claim citizenship. Our last archival trace of Doctor is in 1868, when he shows up on a Sumter County voter registration list for the town of Lynchburg, South Carolina.[7] His exact date of death is not clear, but descendants of Doctor have featured several generations with sons named "Dock" and "Doctor." His *soul archive* has lived on.

III

Robert English had what he termed his "Mansion House" property built in the 1820s with wealth gained at the expense of the labor of Jackson's enslaved parents and grandparents. This large but relatively straightforward structure with many outbuildings demonstrated English's solid grip on the power and politics of the area. The building was dismantled in the early or mid-twentieth century. This undated image is likely from the 1890s, and the Black people in the photo are unidentified, while the white people are an assortment of English family descendants.

It started with a sketchy general store at a desolate crossroads in South Carolina, established around 1793. While one description of it is as a "lone store" located in a "veritable wilderness," Jackson recalled it primarily as "a liquor store" and one that funded the rise of a corrupt and brutal family.[8]

And what was this establishment? Not much, really. A brash and savvy twenty-year-old named Robert English (1773–1847) located it at a crossroads near Lynche's Creek—a stretch of land that followed Scottish and Scots-Irish immigrant settlements along the Black River of the region. It wasn't choice land. The area was filled with many uncultivable swamps, cypress trees, and pine forests. It was crisscrossed with small creeks, muddy flats, and rivers.[9] Most of the native people had been run off, and some of the most prominent white landowners had been displaced during the American Revolution. Their properties were newly available for rising generations of white people to acquire. The land between these swamps and rivers was flat and rich enough to support the burgeoning and ridiculously profitable crop of short-staple cotton. And this made it interesting for new settlers.

Before the invention and spread of the cotton gin in the 1790s, cotton grown on the Carolina coast (known as "sea island" cotton) could be quite profitable. Nonetheless, growing cotton inland required a different cultivar. Because of the more arid inland environment, in a county such as Sumter, one needed to plant what was known as short-staple cotton. This was a tricky crop to harvest and efficiently prepare for market. Unlike the coastal long-staple cotton, it had sticky seeds that took long hours to comb out. After the availability of a gin that could automatically comb out these sticky seeds, serious money could now be made. Assuming you had the labor of unpaid people, you could torture them with impunity—until they died, that is.

And so, white settlers started arriving in this Sumter County region of South Carolina. They would need supplies and provisions. Robert English's crossroads store was a long way, over seventy miles, from the settlement of what was to become the capital city, Columbia. And it was even farther afield from the cosmopolitan coastal world of Charleston—well over a hundred miles. But it seemed to be in a place that could grow.

English's business venture went well. A railroad didn't go through this part of Sumter County until the 1850s. Still, enough new white settlers and their enslaved laborers were coming in during the late eighteenth and early nineteenth centuries that locations between the Black River and the Lynches River area must have appeared to be a strategic locale for future investment. English, too, began to buy land.

Picking short-staple cotton by hand was a grueling task under the best circumstances. Cotton plants of this sort are usually about three feet high. Picking them requires constant stooping for any adult. The sharp edges of the cotton bolls could easily cut fingers and arms as one worked alongside them, not to mention when one would grab hold of the bolls to pull out the white fiber within. Stinging insects abounded in such fields during the pre-pesticide era. Snakes, too. The intense heat and sun of South Carolina would mean that temperatures would frequently be over 90 degrees well into the fall, and enslaved people were usually expected to work in the fields from sunup until sundown. While individual handfuls of cotton are light, enslaved adult workers could be expected to pick over 100 pounds—sometimes up to 300 pounds a day. This meant they would pick cotton and haul heavy bags behind them as they moved through the rows for hours and hours.

The English family prospered alongside other enslavers of the region, thanks to the crops and livestock raised by the labor of men, women, and children tortured to ensure compliance. Robert English began attending the nearby Salem (Black River) Presbyterian Church and met Elizabeth Wilson, the young daughter of one of the church elders.[10] They married in 1794 when he was twenty-one and she was just fifteen, and they went on to have eight children, seven of whom survived into adulthood.

IV

Marriage to Elizabeth Wilson brought English some measure of respectability. Better than that, though, as Jackson tells it, she brought at least a few enslaved people as assets into the marriage.[11] Betty and Doctor Clavern, Jackson's parents, may have been part of this human dowry. White people of that era frequently deeded enslaved people to white daughters as wedding gifts or in their wills. The operating assumption was that while daughters might not stay around to manage any land they inherited, enslaved men, women, and children would represent portable property that could be easily carried away, transferred, or sold as the whims of their daughter and her new husband might require.[12] Thus, with pooled resources and the enslaved as capital, Robert and Elizabeth English came together to raise a small dynasty.

Fifty-four men, women, and children were enslaved by Robert English, according to the 1840 census. There were some family groups in there, certainly. But there were also several lone individuals who had been ripped away from their families and friends and added to the work crews enslaved by Robert English to increase his wealth. Fifty-four may seem like a large number, but as the patriarch of a large family, English had indirect control and interest in easily over one hundred enslaved people distributed (often through informal loans and gifts) among his relatives.[13]

Despite his power, Robert English's place in the white community was socially precarious. The white community was aware of and wary of Robert English's violent temperament. Nearly beating a Black person might go unnoticed, but nearly killing another white man such as Tyre McCoy, for instance, would be remembered, if not condemned. English was rich, and money can buy a lot of tolerance. As one English family descendant observes, "in the early years of his life, . . . Robert English seemed interested only in increasing his wealth. His relationships with family and neighbors were anything but cordial."[14] His descendant John English Cousar Jr. chronicled multiple incidents where Robert English was sued by his neighbors for complications involving horse sales and endless property disputes with relatives and neighbors, many involving conflicts over human property such as we saw with Doctor.

This legacy of what was understood as such unpleasant and unneighborly behavior in the annals of white history played out quite differently for the Black people whose lives he led in his power. For them, the stakes were far higher. What might be unneighborly to fellow enslavers could be murderous to the enslaved.

By 1825, maps of the Sumter District show Robert English to be the owner of at least three significant properties, including one with a sawmill on it, and he continued to acquire land well after that date.[15] The crossroads store seems to have been relegated to a minor side venture, or it might have been sold. Instead, he raised hundreds of cattle and hogs and planted various crops to support his establishments. Cotton, however, became his primary focus, and he channeled his investments in human property to expend their strength and life force in cultivating, harvesting, and planting ever more cotton each year for the benefit of the English family. Robert English was determined to make as much money as possible from his advantages of marriage, white supremacy, capital, connections, and health.[16]

English's success rose steadily. Every decade he seems to have acquired more land in the area and even more Black people. While so many sales and property transfers in this community of intermarried white members make it hard to assess precisely how much land he owned or controlled at any given time, we can see that in 1823 he had enough property to freely deed 843 acres of land to his daughter, Ann J. English Law. As a later survey of 1857 suggests, his daughter alone owned most of what is now the town of Lynchburg, and his other properties were extensive.[17]

It is no surprise to learn that this town was briefly named "English Crossroads" during the 1820s and 1830s. Perhaps it was Robert English's unpleasant temperament and his poor relations with his neighbors, but for whatever reason, the name did not last. The more neutral and evocative names "Willow Grove" and also "Magnolia" were occasionally used to replace "English Crossroads" throughout the antebellum period and into the late nineteenth century. But the name that stuck for the growing hamlet was eventually "Lynchburg," named after the nearby Lynches River, which operated roughly parallel to the north of the Black River and was a common shorthand reference to describe the region. By 1859 the town was officially incorporated as "Lynchburg."[18] In 1902, county lines surrounding the city changed, and while what is now known as "Lee County" was carved out from the old boundaries of Sumter, Darlington, and Kershaw counties, shifting the township into the new county, the name Lynchburg has remained constant since.[19]

Robert English might have been an unpopular or unpleasant neighbor, but he was one to be reckoned with. By 1825, English owned valuable property in multiple locations across Sumter County, and as he grew wealthier, he continued to buy land. Much of it he held or deeded to his children and their families. Because several of his children married local landowners, the English family stayed tightly interwoven. More important, the people they enslaved were formally and informally shared, deeded, argued over, and shifted among various Sumter county sites. We might say that, if not interlaced, these families, Black and white, were coiled around one another. And their connections were all launched from the crossroads of tiny Lynchburg.

V

Today Lynchburg (and "South Lynchburg") is a quiet place. With a population of fewer than 400 inhabitants listed in the census of 2021 and an overall poverty rate of 54 percent, the town, as of 2021, had few operating businesses beyond the occasional in-home beauty parlor and funeral home, a tiny bank branch, and a gas station.[20] Cotton fields still occupy much of the land, although now they are industrially run. And corn stalks, too, rise in small and large plots alongside the roads of this area.

At Lynchburg's height during the late nineteenth century, when the Wilmington and Manchester Railroad lines were operable, stores and shops functioned along Lynchburg's Main Street. The 1870 census indicates that, at times, there were almost three times as many Black residents as white residents: roughly 566 white people and 1,432 Black people.[21]

Well into the mid-twentieth century a lively African American community inhabited Lynchburg, Mayesville, and the environs. It is hard to say whether its eventual decline was because of the railroad's closure, the consolidation of agribusiness that made it more challenging to survive on small farms, the boll weevil infestations, or a general decline in agricultural markets of the modern era. Still, in the early twenty-first century, the town is indisputably under challenging straits, with abandoned and collapsing buildings occupying almost the entirety of "downtown."[22] The regional churches, while largely segregated by race, are nonetheless surviving and clearly are one of the institutions holding the community together with love.

Jackson's life and legacy aside, other individuals loom larger in the popular memory of the area for reasons both good and ill. Early on, a South Carolina governor, Thomas G. McLeod (served 1823–1827) called Lynchburg home. By the early twentieth century, another of Lynchburg's native sons, Ellison D. Smith, later known as Senator "Cotton Ed" Smith, earned notoriety for his claim that "cotton is king and white is supreme."[23] Smith was repeatedly reelected on a platform of avowed white supremacy and was particularly known for opposing the antilynching bills of 1935. Smith's mansion still stands. Its prominent presence on the street powerfully illustrates how long the legacy of privilege and oppression in that area must have functioned.[24]

Another prominent local figure hailing from the area who had the luxury of a privileged education unimaginable to the Clavon family and who carried the family traditions of white supremacy somewhat uneasily was Senator Smith's nephew, the author and educator John Andrew Rice, who was born at his grandparents' home in Lynchburg and knew his uncle well. Bucking the conservative traditions of his family, he became a visionary founder of the experimental and progressive Black Mountain College outside Asheville, North Carolina, in the 1930s—a college nonetheless that was markedly slow to allow for the integration of Black students.

The mixed legacy of conflicting thoughts and cultures all harkening from the same tiny stretch of land was similarly embodied in the life of a prominent white missionary, John Leighton Wilson (1809–1885). Wilson was raised just down the road from Robert English and would have seen Jackson and his family laboring in the fields. While a much-honored and accomplished religious leader whose opinions on human bondage may have diverged from that of his neighbors, he never pushed the status quo too much. He was, after all, a Black River man: Wilson opposed slavery yet supported the Confederate cause.[25]

The most famous of all citizens from that area, though, was undoubtedly Mary McLeod Bethune (1875–1955), who left an oppositional legacy to that of the well-known white supremacists of Lynchburg. The educator and prominent political leader was born at least two generations after Jackson but, nonetheless, was raised by parents who had survived slavery within the same community. She started picking cotton as a child of five but left town for school at an early age, using her knowledge of deprivations and injustice that she had seen and experienced to fuel her career.

Lynchburg was tiny, but its troubled ambitions and impact packed a punch.

VI

To understand how the English family held its sway over Jackson, it is helpful to work through sketches of the central family members to see how they figured or, in some cases, loomed in Jackson's memory. He refused to let such memories confine or utterly define him, but he could not deny how they haunted him. And if those memories could be a tool to deploy in his writing to his advantage in the future, he was ready to walk through every bloody detail.

While all four of the English family's daughters were abusive, the one that stood out most in Jackson's mind was the youngest, Martha. The incident that haunted him was when she forbade one of Jackson's older sisters, probably Bella, from praying. When she continued to pray, Martha ordered her husband, whom Jackson called "Gamble McFarden" and who was almost certainly John Gamble McFaddin (1806–1861), to have the young woman whipped one hundred times. Jackson's sister never recovered and died about three weeks after McFaddin's whipping, leaving two very young children, a boy and a girl. Jackson never forgot about his sister's murder and her remaining children, his niece and nephew. In later years in England, he regularly spoke of them and worked unsuccessfully to raise money to buy them their freedom.

Other members of the English family also feature villainously in Jackson's narrative. Robert English's wife, Elizabeth, merited an entire chapter to herself in Jackson's memoir, perhaps because he felt her cruelty was so random and indicative of how the brutal power inherent in the culture of slavery shaped the psyche of the enslavers whether they be men or women, as much as it shaped the psyche of those held in bondage. He knew portraying her genteel evil might have an impact on his readers.

Jackson made it clear: "I had many whippings through her influence."[26] He wrote: "The sight which most delighted her eyes, was to see a slave whipped." Jackson's mother received "many a hundred lashes" from this mistress.[27]

By bitterly underscoring the particular truth of Elizabeth English's violence, Jackson might, to his audience at least, have painted a picture all the more horrifying, coming as it did from a seemingly gentle woman.[28] Yet, notably, it was Elizabeth English who was to inherit Jackson once her husband died. And even though Jackson had long since fled the state, she continued to pursue him. Even years later, while the family might have given up the hunt, she (or at least her estate) claimed Jackson as lost property with aggrieved self-righteousness. For decades, she and Jackson remained tied to one another in their bitter imaginations.

While Jackson was not directly under the power of James Wilson English, the oldest son of Robert and Elizabeth English, James's reputation meant that enslaved people throughout the region feared him. Jackson told of a man named Willis who was on an auction block and saw James Wilson English bidding on him. In terror at being owned by such a man, Willis jumped off the block and fruitlessly tried to flee, claiming, desperately, as he ran, "'Cause he's the baddest massa 'tween this an' hell fire."[29]

The middle and most successful of the English family's sons, Thomas Reese English, was only a few years older than Jackson and became a much-lauded Presbyterian minister. By the twentieth century, he was even assigned an honorary roadside plaque that still stands, touting his achievements.[30] He was, however, well known in the Black community, at least, as a brute. As Jackson put it, "The chip off the old block doesn't fall far from the stump."[31] According to Jackson, Thomas Reese English once whipped him merely to test a new whip. Jackson was only ten or twelve at the time.

That relationship between Thomas Reese English and Jackson was to prove lasting, with scars that would never heal.

Eli McFadden (known as "Mack"), the youngest son of Robert English, was, according to Jackson, "worse than either of the others." Mack's violence was seemingly unstoppable. Jackson recalls that Mack "knocked my mother down with the butt of his whip, while I stood by feeling as if I had been struck myself. . . .[32] And he ordered enslaved people to pick almost impossible amounts of cotton a day; Jackson remembered: "On their not presenting that amount of cotton at the machine, he gave them from twenty-five to fifty lashes each; so that during the cotton-picking season, the place was filled with screams of agony every evening."[33]

For some reason, Mack particularly hated Jackson's older brother, Ephraim. Jackson remembered young Mack boasting that his father was going to give him a plantation "and fifty niggers, and then I will buy a cowhide whip, well corded, five feet long, and I'll make all the niggers take Ephraim by force, and tie him to an oak tree, and I'll make Adam give him one of the hardest hundred lashes that ever man put on a nigger."[34]

Jackson wrote: "I, myself, was willed to that tyrant, but God had willed me to myself."[35]

In 1837, when Jackson was about twelve years old, Mack English died suddenly of an illness, and young Jackson felt his prayers had been "signally answered." He and Ephraim had had a lucky break.

VII

As we have seen, Jackson explained that his father, known as "Doctor Clavern," had been born to a man from Africa. And while Jackson himself was born on an English family property, Jackson's claim to his full name, "John Andrew Jackson," suggests that he was intent on having an identity entirely separate from that of both his father and of the English family. Adopting the name of one's former enslavers, whether out of convenience or fraught loyalty, was a common practice. That not only Jackson but his entire extended family appears to have distinctly *avoided* carrying the name "English" is telling.

The first instance we have of Jackson's name at a time when he could, presumably, assign a name to himself was in 1850, shortly after his self-emancipation. At that time, in an act of either brazen foolishness or courage—or perhaps it was beyond his control—Jackson gave his name to be listed in the federal census as living in a Boston boarding house for Black seamen. Let us underscore the astonishing nature of this record, lest it get buried in historic minutiae: even though a fugitive, having arrived in Boston fewer than three years earlier, *he was listed by name in the 1850 census.* At that moment, his name was shared for posterity by the census recorder as "Andrew Jackson." While there is much to unpack later involving this time when he hid in plain sight at a Boston boarding house, here we can assess it as the first moment when Jackson was allowed to identify himself on paper.[36]

Did he volunteer his name, or did his landlord, the boarding house proprietor, supply it? Since Jackson was on good terms with the proprietor—the Black abolitionist Henry Foreman—Foreman would undoubtedly have known about his illegal status. (As we shall see later, Foreman also, actively and at real risk, helped save Jackson from recapture.) We can assume, therefore, that either Jackson volunteered it to the census taker or the landlord, comfortable in the safety of the free Black community of Boston in 1850 before the passage of the Fugitive Slave Act later that year, thought sharing the name of the runaway wouldn't endanger anyone. Either way, Jackson lived there at least on and off in September 1850, and his name was freely registered.[37]

Now "Jackson" wasn't a name he had invented once arriving to freedom. We know that the English family knew him as "Jackson" before he fled to Boston: the first time it appears at all in any known historical record was in the series of runaway slave advertisements placed in the *Sumter Banner* by the Reverend Thomas Reese English in the spring of 1874. In the advertisements English was to place, he describes the runaway merely as "a negro man named Jackson."[38]

As a fugitive from slavery, Jackson would have been wise to jettison his name for strategic reasons. But unlike many other fugitives—most famously the young Frederick Bailey of Maryland, who changed his name to Frederick Douglass—the price of a name change was something Jackson was unwilling to pay. He was so intent on retaining that part of who he was that he was never willing to give it up, no matter the risk.

Throughout his life, he certainly shifted his name around: in the early days of his freedom, he used Andrew on few occasions, but he used "John Andrew Jackson" in full for his writing. And when it came time to write his memoir, he could have titled it as many formerly enslaved people did by integrating his claim to selfhood into the title itself—such as "As Written by Himself" or "Written by a statement of facts made by himself." Instead, he asserted his full name: "*The Experience of a Slave in South Carolina.* By John Andrew Jackson."

Unsurprisingly, the historical record is not entirely consistent. In various newspaper accounts, he is listed occasionally as John A. Jackson and J.A. Jackson. He seems to have also used "Andrew Jackson" from time to time, whether by choice or accident it is hard to say.[39] In each case, though, the name "Jackson" predominates. He never referred to himself as Clavern, Clyburn, Cliben, Clavon, or any derivative of his father's name, even though many of his own family adopted these names throughout later generations.[40] For John Andrew, the name "Jackson" evidently had a power to it and was one of the few constants in his life.

Was he named by his parents or his enslavers after President Andrew Jackson? It seems unlikely, although President Jackson was from that general region, born somewhere along the hazily defined border of South and North Carolina in 1767. [41] But President Andrew Jackson wasn't elected president until 1828, several years after John Andrew Jackson was born. Moreover, while it is true that Andrew Jackson was a nationally prominent military hero and politician in the mid-1820s around the time of J.A. Jackson's birth, it seems unlikely that he would have been the source of that name for a beloved baby born to Doctor and Betty.

Could John Andrew have been the child of a man named Jackson, whether Black or white, and his mother chose to give him that name to recognize his separate origins? It is certainly possible. But no obvious suspects come to light in the historical records. There were no major property holders by the name of Jackson in that region of Sumter County, and while there were some white men named Jackson in the area generally, and later a few Black individuals, there were no apparent families or neighbors who carried that name residing near the English holdings and who immediately present themselves as possible candidates for Jackson's namesake.

However he got the name, it appears within his immediate family circles to have been a significant one: none of Jackson's Black relatives that he mentions and who exist in the historical records (with the important exception of his wives and children) carry the name "Jackson" as a surname or first name. His name was another factor that made this charismatic man stand out from the crowd. Of course, his name should not belie the fact that he remained deeply tied to his extended Clavon family. Indeed, many of the

Current-day Clavon Street in Lynchburg, South Carolina.

determining decisions of his life were about maintaining those connections and rescuing those he had left behind.

VIII

Of Jackson's mother, we know little. But Jackson knew her, and that is something he didn't take for granted. Unlike many enslaved children, Jackson grew up with an intact family. Robert English enslaved his parents, and while some of his siblings may have been sold off or died when he was young, he grew up alongside several of them and remembered both his parents well. Indeed, he remembered his mother lovingly, although he supplied only sparse details about her life in his memoir or interviews.

There are clues, however, about some of the horrors she must have known under the tyranny of the English family. Her name was Betty, and she may have had up to eleven children, Jackson among them.[42] Robert English did not spare her in any way despite what enslavers of that time would refer to as "her increase" to his estate and what must have been a life of hard labor while enduring perpetual pregnancies.

Betty must have been someone special. Someone fearless. Someone who could model resistance and strength to her family. Someone, perhaps, with passions more fierce than wise. Once, Betty and another enslaved woman on the plantation came to terrible blows. What they fought over is unknown. But as Jackson told it, the English family would not stand for such a scene. Betty received ninety lashes.

What might ninety lashes mean to a human body? Variables such as what kind of whip was being used or how much force the person wielding the whip chose to use all made a difference. Even a few strikes could kill if applied with sufficient force, and people frequently died from fewer than ninety lashes. In the nineteenth century, when the slightest infection could turn septic and kill a person within a few days or hours, even one such blow could be fatal. But ninety lashes? This punishment was not far from a death sentence.

Betty managed to survive this incident but was eventually murdered by overwork and abuse at the hands of the English family. She did, however, leave a legacy for her own family. Betty was a woman who knew her honor and reputation mattered and were worth risking everything for. While Doctor's persistent strength may have given Jackson an inheritance of dogged stubbornness that allowed him to overcome many challenges, it may have been from his mother that he learned the power to claim his name, believe in his honor, and fight for what mattered.

It is unclear if Jackson, as a child, was forced to witness that particular assault. But he wrote of Robert English's wife, Elizabeth, standing by and goading it on: "And there was my mistress looking on and saying . . . 'that's right, put it to her, cut her all to pieces.'"[43] The psychodrama of such performative torment suggests fraught relationships played out or played upon the bodies of these young black women and which involved the mistress in some ugly and troubled manner. Why was Elizabeth English so particularly obsessed with torturing Betty? Had Betty caught the eye of Robert? Did Robert English father some of Betty's children? Or was Elizabeth English just fueled by more generalized hatred? Perhaps it doesn't matter. Betty was whipped just the same.

Jackson's love for his mother did not allow him to save her: the last time he saw her was during Christmas of 1846, when he bade her a silent farewell before his dash to freedom. Betty is listed in Robert English's will of January 1848, so she did at least live for a few years after Jackson's escape, doubtless praying for his safety all the while.[44]

In 1878, some thirty-two years after he first left South Carolina, Jackson and his wife had a baby girl named Anna Elizabeth Jackson. Sadly, the infant died within a year. A second daughter, named Elizabeth Jackson, was born in 1879 and appeared to have survived for at least some time.[45] Betty's life, cut short after savage abuse, was honored, with a version of her name continuing for future generations.

IX

While Jackson had several siblings, he doesn't speak of all of them in his memoir. It seems likely that most of them used the name "Claven" or some derivative of that, for at least one brother shows up after the war in the census of 1870 as "Ephraim Claven," living in Mayesville, a town immediately adjacent to Lynchburg. There are thousands of men and women, Black and white, using similar names who can trace their families back to the Lynchburg community.[46]

The three siblings who figured most prominently in Jackson's narrative were Bella, who had been murdered by the McFaddin family; William, one of his younger brothers; and Ephraim, his much-tormented eldest brother. Ephraim particularly enraged Robert English's son Mack, who at one point threatened him with "the hardest hundred lashes that ever man put on nigger."[47] Fortunately, Mack died before carrying out that particular threat, but Ephraim had a hard life thereafter. He was forced to leave the woman he loved and marry someone more conveniently owned by the English family. He was accused of stealing cotton and whipped with fifty lashes in front of his wife and children. He was a survivor, but the cost of surviving was hard. When Jackson was to meet with him after the war, Ephraim was beaten down, and while he was probably only a few years older than Jackson, their different lives in bondage and in freedom had taken an awful toll. In 1868

Jackson wrote, " Ephraim is a poor old man who has received a great deal of hard use and is not able to support himself."[48]

As noted earlier, Bella's death at the hands of Martha English McFaddin (Robert English's daughter) and her husband, John Gamble McFaddin, may have gone undocumented with the possible exception of any long-since-disappeared McFaddin family accounting records. Nonetheless, Jackson's account of her death in his memoir serves as a parallel shadow accounting of her life and loss. Years later, when lecturing in England, he repeatedly spoke of her murder and of her orphaned children. He was determined to raise money for their liberation. Bella's life and the circumstances of her death preyed on his mind and heart for the rest of his years.

Jackson's youngest brother, William, comes up only in a poignant incident mentioned early on in Jackson's memoir. William, as a child of only five or six, also fell afoul of Martha English, who, "from pure mischief," Jackson wrote, chased young William and hit him with stinging nettles on his naked body. When "at last he fell down through pain," Jackson, about ten at the time, ran at them to distract Martha's attention and allow his brother William to escape. Jackson remembered that when little William finally returned home, "he was covered with large lumps all over his body."[49] Sadly, William may not have survived to adulthood, for there seems to be no census trail or other clear documentation of him in later years, and Jackson didn't leave any clues about his fate.[50] Jackson wasn't going to let the memory go, though. His little brother's pain stayed with him. Jackson would continue to "run at" tormentors.

While what happened to young William is unclear, Ephraim's fate became known to Jackson after the Civil War. The two brothers reunited shortly after Jackson's return to the United States in 1865, and while Jackson could not bring Ephraim north, their lives again became intertwined. They exchanged letters to one another (done via dictation by Ephraim), and Jackson fought hard to find supplies and help for his brother.[51] Ephraim likely held a special place in Jackson's mind because it was Ephraim's life and fate Jackson would have probably shared if his own escape hadn't been successful.[52]

X

Robert English was a rich man with political power to be reckoned with. To show off this clout, he built a showcase property that was formidable enough for his family to know it as their "Mansion House." This property was sited a mile or so down the road from a property owned by the Wells family, a proximity that would soon be significant for Jackson's life. Thanks to many complex family intermarriages, the English family was related to nearly every prominent family in the region, including the Wellses. Robert English wasn't popular, but he was a formidable patriarch; hence, his family relationships were consequential.[53] What's vital for Jackson's story is that these white family ties had a parallel map of shadow connections for the enslaved families held in bondage. These connections may have been ignored or scorned by their enslavers but were real ties nonetheless.

While the English family would have defined their neighborhood by proximity to white households and landowning structures, the notion of Black neighborhoods was looser, and the geographic sensibilities were often quite different. Slave neighborhoods were defined by the enslaved people and not their enslavers.[54] These spaces were marked by the geography of memory and personal bonds, not necessarily easily limned by official property lines. In the case of Jackson, the structures of the Black community relationships of his "neighborhood" within Lynchburg enabled him to fall in love.

Jackson's first love, perhaps a teenage romance, was brutally ended. English purchased two sisters, Rose and Jenny Wilson, from a neighbor.[55] While Jenny Wilson and Jackson soon developed a relationship, and Jackson stated that she was "in love with me," English nonetheless forced both Rose and Jenny to "marry" other men he owned (one of the men, Adam, who initially resisted this, was subjected to "some hundreds" of lashes, according to Jackson). After such abuse, Adam was forced to concede. He and Jenny Wilson were forcibly yoked to be coerced into sex and procreation. Jenny Wilson was needed to breed children for the English family's profits.[56] English's propensity for forcing marriages between people he enslaved was a pattern. He had done so with Jackson's brother Ephraim, too. And Jackson would soon have to reckon with this cruelty again.[57]

While the horror and sadness of the forced break with Jenny Wilson stayed with Jackson, he nonetheless sought a way to control his future and find love as he could, this time even more acutely aware of the risks and the stakes. And, in time, he did find some solace in his suffering with a new love, Louisa, who was to become his wife.

The conflict between historical records and Jackson's testimony is essential here. Robert English might have been able to force Rose to "marry" someone. He could also separate Jackson from Jenny Wilson and compel Jenny to "wed" Adam. But English and his fellow enslavers could not entirely control the relationships people under their power sustained.

Jackson's accounts of this relationship with Louisa had some variations over the years, perhaps occasionally in deference to later relationships or perhaps because of his failing memory. Whatever the cause of his variable reminiscences, the basic traits remain steady: he chose to enter an intimacy that he knew full well was vulnerable. As he put it simply in his narrative: "I fell in love with a slave girl named Louisa, who belonged to a Mrs. Wells, whose plantation was about a mile off."[58] Their marriage had no official ceremony or recognition in the eyes of their enslavers.[59] As Jackson explained: "Do not let the reader run away with the idea that there was any marriage ceremony, for the poor slaves are debarred that privilege by the cruel hand of their fellow-man."[60]

Louisa led a shadowed, if parallel, life to what her enslavers planned—the kind that enslaved people tried to carve out for themselves with the few choices they had at their disposal. Louisa and Jackson created a bond, fully aware of its precarity. "How long could this last," they must have hated themselves for thinking. But how could they not wonder? And yet, they judged their longing for love worth its dangers. They knew their relationship would always be subject to violent severing according to a white man's whims and pocketbook. For, as court transactions in the area reveal, many of the sales of human beings in that area of Sumter County were not to chained and shuffling slave coffles destined for out-of-state locations but were, instead, often informal transfers among local white relatives and family members as their convenience and generosity dictated. Robert English had many cousins, children, siblings, and grandchildren who resided in Sumter County. It wasn't impossible to imagine that Louisa and Jackson began their relationship, hoping with some cautious optimism that they could remain near one another. After all, they had Jackson's relatively intact family as a model to aspire to.

Jackson and Louisa followed their hearts. Their choices and the high stakes attached to those choices are mapped out differently in different kinds of archival manifestations. In some ways, Louisa's conflicting paper trail is typical of the era. In other ways, we can read it closely and see the diversions between the official story and the story Jackson recounts. These quiet divergences, indicated by a mere word here and there in enslavers' paperwork, are outlined as follows. These transcriptive divergences suggest

Louisa was a woman of courage who managed to carve out some autonomy and independence in a world shaped to crush such dreams.

Louisa was likely born in the mid-1820s, but she first appeared in official white-sanctified documents in the 1830 will of Thomas Wells, who owned land in Lynchburg, close to English family property. And the contours of her life were shaped by the variable legal shifts that white ownership, white sales, and white whims necessitated.

It can be challenging, even dizzying for a modern reader to keep up with all the shifts in ownership and power demanded by the chattel slave system. For the Black people under that system, each loan, sale, mortgage, and subleasing was monitored to the last detail. It wasn't just dizzying for them; it would have been a state of steady anxiety and terror. They followed every scrap of information they could get. Who had power over you at any given moment was everything. They might not have been privy to the legalities, but they made it their business to know with whom they had to curry favor, whom they had to please, and whom they might strategically avoid or ignore. Enslaved people speculated, dreamed, fretted, and dreaded each shift coming their way. It wasn't anything they had control over, but it would have eaten at them every minute of their lives. When would they be separated from their friends, family, and world? Could they possibly fall into a better situation? Unlikely. But you never could know.

After Thomas Wells died in 1833, young Louisa became the property of Thomas Wells's widow, Margaret Wells. By 1840 Margaret Wells wrote up a will that listed Louisa and linked to her name an "&." This simple conjunctive marker in the antebellum South operated as an established code to indicate a family grouping, usually a mother and child. And here, attached to Louisa's name, was "& Jinny"—a name we can identify as the same child Jackson refers to as his own "little Jinny." Jackson and Louisa had begun a relationship sometime in the mid-1830s and little Jinny was born.[61] According to the state of South Carolina, the child was technically the property of the enslaver Margaret Wells, but she was truly Jackson and Louisa's dear little girl.

In 1841, shortly after writing her will, Margaret Wells died, turning over "Louisa & Jinny" to her granddaughter, Elizabeth, who then married Jared R. McKelvin Law. And so, Louisa's life was put into someone else's hands again. Jared Law came to be the owner of Louisa, Jackson's wife. Yet again, it was to be the vagaries of a white man whose mercurial fortunes launched a chain of events that forever altered Jackson's life.

As long as the Law family enslaved Louisa, Jackson wasn't far from her. The Jared Law house still stands, and it was, as Jackson claimed, only about a mile from English-owned land. Louisa lived near the western edge of an area known as "Elliott," close to Robert English's primary "Mansion House." In the 1840s, it would have appeared as a modest but prosperous house, obscuring the structural violence which built it. While outbuildings aren't visible anymore, in the nineteenth century, several sheds and structures, perhaps an outdoor kitchen or barn, would have been additional parts of this property. At least one of these modest outbuildings would have likely housed the enslaved people, Louisa and Jinny among them. We can imagine Louisa or even little Jinny forced to sweep off the porch and those wide stone steps regularly. Fires would need to be stoked and monitored by enslaved people for those three chimneys. Water would be brought in from the nearby waterways and wells. Today the house sits quietly on a rural road often speckled with white tufts of cotton that blow off the surrounding fields.

Despite the proximity of their locations at the English "Mansion House" property and the nearby Law family land, Louisa and Jackson were unlikely to have seen each other often. She may have worked in the fields picking cotton much as Jackson did or been employed domestically taking care of the household needs, or, quite likely, she might have worked both in the fields and in the house depending upon the demands of her enslavers. Either way, she would have lived under tight surveillance.

Not only would the duties required of both Louisa and Jackson have been heavy and the restrictions on their movement rigid, there were also worse challenges facing the young couple. English decided to oppose the marriage and was determined to end it. English was incensed by Jackson's audacity in choosing a woman enslaved by another (even if it was a relative of his), particularly since any children born to Louisa would increase Jared Law's wealth. According to Jackson: "My master was exceedingly angry when he heard of my marriage because my children would not belong to him, and whenever he discovered that I had visited my wife's plantation during the night, I was tied up and received fifty lashes."[62]

Jackson was not deterred. When he reflected upon the memory some eighteen years later, he did so with what might be characterized as a resigned yet still resistant kind of anger. As he wrote: "But no man can be prevented from visiting his wife, and the consequence was that I was beaten on the average, at least every week for that offense. I shall carry these scars to my grave." His scars were, of course, both internal and external, but he was able to deploy those physical scars to his advantage; in later years, he was able to invoke them as vital inscriptions of authenticity.

While taking whippings and regularly defying Robert English might not have been a sustainable plan, it was all Jackson had for a while, and perhaps for a few years it worked. He suffered so that they might love.

A turning point ws inevitable, and it came about when Louisa's enslavers decided to move. Records indicate that Jared and Elizabeth (Wells) McKelvin Law, along with people they held in bondage, including Louisa and little Jinny, all moved to Georgia.[63]

They didn't stay there long: the 1850 census shows the Law family back in South Carolina. By the end of 1851, though, in another complicated inter-family transaction, the Wells/Law family deeded three enslaved people back to another Law family member.[64] This time, however, Louisa's status had changed: the deed of trust between these white families records the transfer of "Enoch and his wife Louisa and a girl named Jinny."[65] Was this marriage with Enoch a relationship coerced by her enslavers such as those Robert English had repeatedly maneuvered? It seems likely. We can only hope that Enoch was kind to Louisa, who was surely grieving the separation from her husband.

In later years, Jackson didn't appear to resent Enoch too much. He even was to solicit Enoch's help in searching for Louisa. And some slight evidence suggests Louisa and Jackson may have met again after the Civil War.

But for Jackson, who couldn't see into the future during those hard months of late 1846, his wife and daughter had been taken away from him with no hope for return.[66]

To make it worse, Jackson knew that mother and daughter might not even be kept together for long. Little Jinny was no longer a baby; she was at least six or seven years old. A child could easily be sold away from her mother at that age. And perhaps the most painful realization was that Louisa was now even more vulnerable to abuse: she was farther from the only community she had known. He never had much power to protect his family, but at least while they lived close by, he could occasionally visit and comfort them. *I love you. We can get through it. Things will get better. We can pray*, they must have whispered to one another. Now, however, Louisa would be out of reach entirely. Jackson grieved and raged in his impotence.

By the fall, the demands of the local cotton harvest would be in full force. The daily labor of those months must have been excruciating, made all the harder because the world as Jackson had known it was over. He had reached his own crossroads. All this heartbreak and fury must have been discombobulating emotions, for his subsequent actions were to career from strategic to foolhardy.

The crisis Jackson now faced was going to be both internal and external—not just how to survive but also to decide: who he would *be* now that his beloved wife and child had been taken.

CHAPTER TWO

THE REVEREND LOWERY'S STORY BASED ON FACTS (1911)

Lynchburg, South Carolina (Fall–Winter 1846)

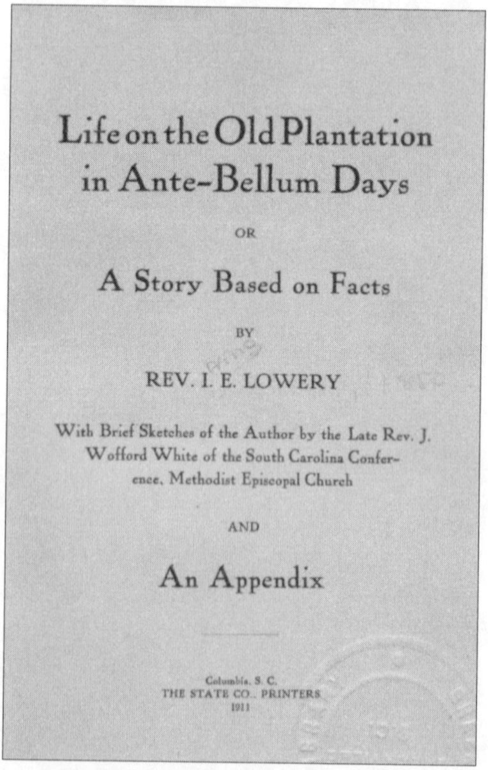

Life on the Old Plantation in Ante-Bellum Days

OR

A Story Based on Facts

BY

REV. I. E. LOWERY

With Brief Sketches of the Author by the Late Rev. J. Wofford White of the South Carolina Conference, Methodist Episcopal Church

AND

An Appendix

Columbia, S. C.
THE STATE CO., PRINTERS
1911

Lowery's memoir was published in 1911 and was a twentieth-century narrative of witness and conciliation. This was in stark contrast to the activist abolitionist narrative tradition, from which Jackson's 1862 memoir was written. And yet their narratives arising from the same community corroborate each other in often surprising ways.

Jackson's life had been shattered. His wife and child were taken away. Surely he raged and wept. But what to do with all that emotion? Praying might help. But would a prayer meeting? Would there be solace in community, or might he use that meeting for other purposes? For an answer to these questions and to understand what happened next, we have Jackson's version of events, but we also have an account from a neighbor of his, another survivor of bondage, the Reverend I.E. Lowery. Lowery's story serves up his competing truths about the Black community of Lynchburg.

I

When we were picking cotton, we used to see the wild geese flying over our heads to some distant land, and we often used to say to each other, "O that we had wings like those geese, then we could fly over the heads of our masters to the 'Land of the free.'"

John Andrew Jackson would recount his dreams in the memoir he published after his escape. Of course, Jackson's flight did not come on the wings of the geese that first inspired him but instead on the best conveyance he could commandeer after the loss of his wife and child: a purloined pony, one he was to ride into a white-sponsored religious camp meeting in 1846 as an act of spiritual defiance.

Jackson's audacious arrival into the camp astride a horse set tongues wagging. It would have been unusual to see an enslaved man on a horse in that region unless he was explicitly at authorized work. Jackson, whose proud and loud character surely was well known in his community, arrived at this gathering amid the tents, bonfires, and singing looking like a man of substance, a man of courage. While all would have known about his recent suffering, he would nonetheless have invoked awe, not pity. For the members of his community, Jackson's bold entrance made an impression.

How that impression played out and was to shape the events that followed can be understood a bit more richly because, in addition to Jackson's words and the historical record about how these camp meetings operated, we have the good fortune to access another kind of archive: that of Jackson's neighbor, who survived a childhood of slavery and wrote of that very same annual affair.

Enslavers surveilled Jackson, his family, and his community in ways that veered from terrifying at worst to cloyingly paternalistic at best. But as a community, the Black people of the Black River area near Lynchburg also watched one another with love and compassion. Jackson was to learn, many years in the future, that his neighbors remembered him and the choices he and his family made. That is not simply because he was able to return many years later; it is because his account of his life has some remarkable corroboration from another man who survived bondage in the same Black River neighborhood.

Some four years after Jackson faced his reckoning about Louisa and Jinny, another enslaved child was born in Sumter County and wrote his narrative about life within a few miles of English family land. And in his life story, a young Irving Lowery bore witness to an annual Lynchburg event that had changed Jackson's life. In Lowery's memoir, *Life on the Old Plantation in Ante-Bellum Days, or a Story Based on Facts* (1911), we see the events that next unfolded in Jackson's life—in particular, Jackson's decision to visit a religious camp revival meeting on a contraband horse and the consequences that unfolded after that.[1] While the two men's perspectives are often opposed, their comparative accounts of life for the enslaved communities in the Black River area of Sumter County provide a context and a sense of the reasoning for Jackson's foolhardy actions.

II

At the time that Louisa and Jinny were taken away to Georgia, the health of seventy-three-year-old Robert English was failing. He could no longer supervise his estates, his feuds, his family, or the people he held in bondage with the acute attention he had formerly invoked. This development was, no doubt, welcomed by the many people held hostage to his cruel behavior. Jackson, for one, observant of Robert English's decline, began to take advantage of the looser controls around the plantation.

Around this time, Jackson learned that another enslaved man in the area had surreptitiously acquired a pony, but a rumor of his activities returned to his enslavers. Owning a horse outright would have been impossible for an enslaved person who had no legal right to property. And possessing one under any circumstances (even if it was somehow borrowed or being independently cared for) would have been a noteworthy and troubling circumstance from an enslaver's perspective. A horse enabled mobility and a degree of freedom that, even for a person not planning an escape, could represent autonomy and liberty intolerable to local authorities.

Perhaps to skirt around a tricky explanation about what may have been a sketchy acquisition, Jackson wrote merely that "a slave on a neighboring plantation had a pony; it being discovered by his mistress, she ordered the overseer, the Rev. P. Huggin, to kill it."[2] This poor man with the pony was now in a bad situation. Threatened with punishment and the risk of losing his horse to the white people who planned to kill the animal rather than see a

Black man profit from it, this man had to move fast. He was desperate to rid himself of the incriminating pony, and he and Jackson, ever the hustler, were able to negotiate a quick deal; Jackson traded some chickens for the pony.

What exactly Jackson planned to do with this pony is not entirely clear. If he was planning an escape at this time, he did not mention it. As a savvy entrepreneur, though, he might have seen the pony as an investment in the kind of black-market trading we know was rife among the free and unfree in the community. But, regardless of his motives at that moment—and they may have been mixed—Jackson writes that he hid the pony in the woods for a few days, and then, "as my master had just then gone out of his mind I could keep it with greater impunity so that at length I went to a camp meeting on it."[3]

Had Jackson lost his judgment after the unbearable loss of his family? Had he, like English, "gone out of his mind"? It's hard to imagine what might have induced him to take such a risk. He was already known as a troublemaker, and appearing in public on a pony that he, too, would certainly be punished for possessing seems like a foolhardy decision at best.

Even worse, these religious gatherings, even though they were officially sanctioned events, could be fraught with danger for Black attendees. They often lasted several days, with, as Jackson explains, white people attending during the week and enslaved people allowed to participate on Saturday night.[4] Because these were authorized Black gatherings of groups from the region, it was known that white people would be keeping an eye on events and that nothing was truly private there. Moreover, it also meant that there were opportunities for abuse and violence. Jackson noted in his memoir that women were at risk of being attacked and raped by white "libertine scoundrels" who could visit such supposedly sacred gatherings after dark and "attend for the purpose of seizing and carrying off by force, for their own vile purposes the most beautiful slave girls they can see."[5] As Jackson saw it, these camps could be sites of terror.

And yet the risks were worth it. The lure of the camp revival meeting to be held at what was known as the "Tabernacle Camp Ground" in Lynchburg—a twice-annual event—was difficult for Jackson to resist.[6]

Such a gathering would have been a rare opportunity for community and diversion, commodities of solace all too uncommon amid the brutal burdens of daily life he endured. Perhaps he would have found comfort in the hymns, the sermons, or simply the fellowship.[7] It might have been an occasion to reconnect with enslaved family members that had been deeded, loaned, rented, or otherwise shared among local white families of the region, such as English's score of interrelated kinfolk. With his charismatic, confident swagger, Jackson might have assumed that, even if noticed on his horse by white people or other Black people, he would have a good shot at charming his way out of any difficulties. Or perhaps he no longer gave a damn.

The significance of the camp meetings for both Lowery and Jackson needs to be understood in conversation with the more coercive participation of enslaved people in the regularized and sanctioned white church culture in Lynchburg of that period. As with many small Southern towns, Lynchburg had several churches that enslaved people were often forced or encouraged to attend. The Black people enslaved by the English family were directed to the Salem Black River Church, where Robert English and his wife had first met. This Presbyterian church was led from 1827 to 1841 by the Reverend Robert Wilson James, who prided himself on exceptional attentiveness to the enslaved people in his congregation and was known, as some local historians report, for a "passion for ministry among the growing slave population."[8] He thereby presumably worked with local white families to ensure some degree of attendance by those who might otherwise choose to spend their time resting or simply existing under a bit less supervision for a few hours. Doc Clavon, his wife Betty, and their children and family members would certainly have been in at least semiregular attendance at the Salem Black River Church.

Once the Reverend James left the position in 1841, a Reverend Gregg followed him at the Salem Black River Church and similarly sought to minister to this mixed congregation. To the Black congregants, of course, he would preach on messages of piety as seen fit by the white Southern Presbyterians of that time. We cannot know how welcome these messages were or whether or not the enslaved people in attendance were there willingly. Either way, the Black population of that church was formidable. Statistics for congregants during Jackson's years are not available, but by the end of the Civil War, when admittedly fewer whites might have been around to attend church, the church membership boasted six times as many Black as white congregants. By 1866, for example, this church reported 100 white members worshipping in the main galleries. At that time, the balconies above were reserved for the 610 Black members—an astounding number in comparison.[9] Of course, those numbers might not be evidence of the church's popularity among the Black congregants; they may have attended by coercion as much as choice. But it does indicate that attendance at a white-directed church was an

Salem Black River Church, founded in 1759, was rebuilt in 1846 as the brick building seen here. The gallery for Black members is still intact. While a firm was hired to build it, it is not unlikely that Jackson and others in the local enslaved community were conscripted to assist. After the Civil War, the enslaved congregants immediately left to found their own church down the road, the Goodwill Presbyterian Church.

unavoidable part of the Black experience for the area during the first half of the nineteenth century. Jackson and his family would almost certainly have spent many hours listening to sermons there.

Enthusiasm by the enslaved for the Salem Black River Church may be hard to gauge from the antebellum period. Still, Black actions after emancipation leave no doubt for interpretation: the entire Black membership of that church, almost certainly including Jackson's immediate family, voted with their feet. Immediately after the Civil War ended, probably right after those statistics of 1866 membership were calculated, the newly emancipated Black congregants left Salem Black River Church en masse. By 1867 most of them came together to create an alternative gathering a mile or two down the road, which became known as the Goodwill Presbyterian Church in Mayesville.[10] There were no balconies in their new church.

With the antebellum expectations of forced attendance at Salem Black River Church in mind for comparison, we can see why Jackson would have been determined to attend a camp meeting, even, or perhaps especially, on a contraband horse.

Church services were highly surveilled and disciplined events for enslaved people to attend. But camp revival meetings, held over several days, and sited outdoors, could offer spiritual relief and solace in an entirely different way and could often be flexible in welcoming different denominations. We cannot discount the menace, especially for women, that Jackson recalled. These meetings were overseen by white spiritual leaders, of course, as such gatherings would never have been allowed to operate otherwise. But for the Black community, the appeal still held. Enslaved people were allowed to attend, first and foremost, to ensure the comfort of their enslavers. They might drive carriages, lay fires, serve picnics, erect tents, set up seating, and perform other such actions to benefit the white attendees. But, in addition to serving on the sidelines, separate days, fields, or sessions were usually set aside just for them.[11]

The nature of such gatherings, which often had evening events, allowed for opportunities to elude surveillance. This meant that enslaved people could carve out time and some degree of privacy to revive their bonds and their spirits.[12] They could woo and court one another. Laugh and share the news. Grieve or dispense advice. Gossip. They could see family they might only otherwise see once or twice a year. Maybe someone there could tell Jackson something about how Louisa and Jinny were faring in Georgia. For a bereft and grieving man, the event must have seemed impossible to resist. Jackson could show his community that he was, although beaten down, still a man of consequence.

A hand-colored engraving entitled "A Negro Camp Meeting in the South" was published in *Harper's Weekly* on August 10, 1872.

Jackson's act of appearing in public on a horse, particularly one he had only a precarious claim to, was a telling moment of resistance. He boldly claimed a presence and a way of being that was staunchly defiant of enslavers' conscriptions. Enslavers had taken away his family, but he was still a man whose audacity was itself to be a survival tool. We can only assess the risk if we imagine what the rewards of such a public act must have been to him.

III

Irving Lowery, who was some twenty-five years younger than Jackson, had also been enslaved nearby. Even though he was born soon after Jackson's flight, he knew many of the same people, very likely knew of Jackson's family, and recalled how the role of the camp meeting continued to be pivotal to the local Black experience, even after Jackson had left. From Lowery's witness, we can better understand what was at stake in these meetings. His fond tone in speaking of the camp may have been shaped by complicated attitudes within his narrative about his own past. Still, his recollections are largely consistent with other historical assessments.[13] As Lowery wrote:

> Everybody went to camp-meeting—white and colored. . . . [The tents] were built with several rooms, and with front piazzas. They formed a large circle, with the tabernacle, or church, in the center. Elevated scaffolds, about three feet square, with earth thrown up on them, and a bright lightwood blaze burning on the top, constituted the lighting system of the encampment. In addition to these scaffold lights, there were bonfires built on the ground in front and the rear of each tent.
>
> These camp-meetings were great occasions. They were the biggest occasions that came within the experience of plantation life, and were hugely enjoyed by all, white and colored, old and young, male and female.[14]

Lowery's memory of the local camp revival was likely shaped by the fact that he became a religious leader with the Methodist Episcopal Church and had a proprietary affection for such events. He makes no mention of the menaces that so troubled Jackson's memories. Moreover, he spent much of his later years praising local white patrons he saw as supporting Black

Frontispiece from Lowery's *Life on the Old Plantation in Ante-Bellum Days* (1911).

schools, church organizations, and individuals, so his tone was often conciliatory and warm in remembering the early years of his childhood under slavery.[15]

Lowery's family was connected with all the others in this Black "neighborhood" of the region, and he knew of the suffering others endured. In his own memoir, he does reference how, like Jackson, he was whipped and abused.[16] He was no stranger to suffering, and he understood the intricate and intertwined relationships of his world, including relationships that connected Lowery to the Clavon family: At one point, Lowery tells of a prominent Black conjurer from a nearby labor camp who was called upon to help an enslaved woman who had fallen ill.[17] Was that local conjure man Doctor Clavern from the English family labor camp—the local elder revered among the Black community in Lynchburg for knowing cures to snakebite? It seems probable, and Lowery's knowledge of Jackson's world is all the more convincing for that. The Frierson labor camp where Lowery lived and the English family properties where Jackson worked were only a few miles apart.

Lowery remembers camp revival meetings as loving sites for diversion, spiritual growth, community connections, and emotional release. Those were precisely the same reasons Jackson couldn't resist their allure. Lowery may have remembered the Black world of Lynchburg with a different interpretative agenda, but his memoir corroborates much of Jackson's story and builds a richer context for seeing why Jackson made the choices he did—even reckless ones.

IV

As almost anyone could have predicted, Jackson's decision to throw caution to the wind and brazenly attend the camp meeting on a dubiously owned horse proved to be a disaster.[18] He was spotted riding there by one of Robert English's grandchildren, who duly reported Jackson's audacity to Elizabeth English. Jackson had already returned by this time and hidden the pony in the woods. Presumably, he returned to his regular duties the next day. But nobody was fooled. His appearance at the camp meeting had created a stir. Everyone waited for the other shoe to drop.

What exactly it was about the action that infuriated his enslavers, we cannot know. Perhaps it was the gall of such an appearance or a sense that he had somehow broken some local order in trading or owning a black-market horse. Perhaps it enraged Elizabeth English because it came on the heels of previous clashes between Jackson and the English family, and she saw this provocation as a last straw. Whatever the cause, though, she was furious. She ordered the overseer, Ransom Player, to find and kill the pony and to give Jackson a hundred lashes—a punishment that could be difficult to survive. It was not far off from being a death sentence.

Ransom Player was a ferocious man by Jackson's account. But perspectives can differ. Lowery had known him, too. Lowery wrote of the same man that "he ["Rance" Player] was pretty strict in his discipline, but not cruel." But we've already seen that Lowery had a different approach and more conciliatory goal in compiling his "true story based on facts" in 1911—some forty-six years after emancipation. So perhaps the truth of Player's disposition can be understood as evolving or variable.

However, regardless of what Lowery thought about the elderly Ransom Player in later years, Jackson, at the time of his own struggles in 1846, knew a different sort of enforcer. He feared Player's wrath. At that time, Player was part of a team working for Robert English, a team that Jackson reported spent two hours a night regularly whipping Black workers who had brought in the least amount of cotton on a picking day: "At the setting of the sun each slave had to bring one hundred weight of cotton, which many of the weaker slaves could not do. In consequence of this, each night there were two hours whipping at the 'ginning house.'"[19]

In the 1840s, as Jackson saw it, Player's reputation and livelihood were predicated upon successful brutality. He knew that Player might well kill him.

Elizabeth English's punishment of Jackson did not go as planned. In a struggle to carry out orders and tie Jackson down, Player lost his grip, and Jackson was able to flee. Jackson eluded Player by swimming across a mill pond "full of alligators" and then hiding in the woods.[20] It was a temporary victory. Jackson had successfully escaped a whipping at that moment but was now stuck in the swampy woods without recourse, supplies, or a feasible plan for sustainable escape. And he knew if he returned, his defiance would not be forgiven.

Jackson's situation was dire, but it wouldn't have been an unfamiliar one to any of the parties involved. Popular conceptions of escapes commonly imagine people fleeing in the night with plans and supplies, connecting with underground railroad agents, arriving in the North, and then never returning to their families. This was almost never the case. While that might have been the dream of many enslaved people, it was not the reality.

Flight from violence was frequently instinctive and desperate; someone might slip out of an abuser's grasp and flee into the woods but return only a few days later when hungry and having calculated that they had no other options.

This frantic flight of Jackson was the kind of sometimes-planned and sometimes-impulsive acts that could upturn slave labor camp economies, reliant upon the steady exploitation of the workers. From the perspective of the aggrieved enslaved laborer, it allowed for a kind of nuanced autonomy. Moreover, such a short flight could even occasionally provide some bargaining power: an abused or terrified person might flee, but the absence mattered, and the cost of serious punishment or torture upon return could render that person unable to work for some time. Perhaps Jackson might be able to return once tempers had cooled, and he could argue his case.

While disappearance was a major offense, enslavers knew that punishing people who returned too harshly would deter others from ever seeking amnesty in a similar situation. From an English family perspective, the flight mattered in symbolic terms (indicating that the owners had lost control of their domain), and it also mattered simply in terms of the loss of their labor to the tasks at hand. Jackson's flight demonstrated the unjustness of Elizabeth English's decree and made a statement, too, to his peers.

The act of running away for short periods is often referred to by scholars as "petit marronage," or as essentially a "small escape." This phrase is useful because, while no less powerful an act of resistance than "grand marronage" or a larger flight that is intended, at least, to be permanent, "petit marronage" represented the kind of daily interaction and shifting power relations that characterized life in a society of enslavers and the enslaved.[21] This differentiation is handy to understand because it can help us get at the evolving plans in Jackson's mind. When Jackson initially escaped from the overseer Ransom Player, he was desperate and had no calculated scheme for survival beyond simply putting as much distance between himself and the hundred lashes. It is his bold return, however, that we must understand in terms of how the resistance of petit marronage could operate.

Petit marronage was a dangerous gamble, to be sure. Escape was dangerous under any circumstances, but when unplanned, it was especially so; one would have no provisions, no set strategy, and, except rarely, no long-term scheme. Nonetheless, by depriving an enslaver of their presence, even briefly, short-term fugitives often could restart some measure of negotiation.

Full escape, or "grand marronage," was, for an enslaved person in the deep inland South, a far rarer occurrence. Men and women who escaped might occasionally be able to survive on the outskirts of plantations or sometimes with bands of other fugitives hidden by swampland or wilderness. And there were certainly communities of "maroons" or escaped slaves that lived in remote areas of South Carolina beyond white control. But these communities in the United States (unlike many long-lasting ones in the Caribbean and South America) could rarely remain unmolested for long. These runaways would frequently need to interact with men and women still held in bondage who could betray them, and they would still not infrequently raid plantations and farms for food. They were rarely successful in escaping far or isolating themselves from the world of nearby enslavers.

Jackson had no plan to join even these tenuously free men and women surviving in the swamps, or if he did, he doesn't mention it in his memoir or later accounts. Enslavers and their accomplices knew well how petit marronage could play out, and they, too, gambled that aggrieved slaves would eventually return to their punishments and resume their old lives in bondage. It is not surprising that neither Elizabeth English nor Ransom Player immediately pursued him with much energy, and there is no mention by Jackson of a posse being sent out to track him down at this point.

As far as Jackson was concerned, his quick flight had been a gamble but not a suicide mission. And his venture was not ill-conceived. Jackson's labor was valuable: he was needed on the property, and one hundred lashes might well kill him. Buying time made sense: there was always a chance someone or something might intervene on his behalf. Perhaps his mistress would be distracted by something and forget her threats? That might be unlikely, but perhaps no longer in the heat of the moment she would change her mind. Moreover, by humiliating Player and challenging the authority of his mistress, Jackson had positioned himself as a powerful figure to be reckoned with, even if he were to return. Did he have even a sliver of bargaining power now? There was only one way to find out. Might he now create some sort of uneasy truce whereby Ransom Player might leave him be? It wasn't a great wager, but it was something. It was all he had.

As it worked out, Jackson's resistance and flight from Player saved his life and redirected his future entirely: this instinctive rebellion helped spur him to claim his freedom in a later act of full-on flight. Having practiced once, he was now ready to entertain a bolder venture. He was soon to liberate himself with no plan for return—no plan to return alive, that is.

V

After what must have been a terrible night hiding in the swamps, Jackson walked back to the English property the next day and calmly started to work again, waiting to see how everything would unfold. He wrote merely, "I kept a look out for them."[22] While Jackson surely knew his affront to Player and Elizabeth English's authority was grave, he banked upon the facts that Player couldn't subdue him, that Robert English was indisposed, and that Jackson's resistance had indeed bought some time. Jackson learned that Elizabeth English had counseled Player to hold off on any punishment until a larger group of enforcers, including her two sons-in-law, could be secured, saying to Player: "You can't whip that nigger yourself, wait till Rev. T. English, and Mr. M'Farden and Mr. Cooper are here, and then you can catch him in the barn."[23]

So, as it worked out, the isolation of the English slave labor camp had bought Jackson some time. Since there weren't enough nearby white men to capture and whip him, getting far away from this inland hell was now a challenge he was finally in a position to achieve. At this point, he had a pony still hidden in the woods. Even more significant, he had one other tool up his sleeve: knowledge of the route to Charleston and the opportunities this coastal port city might offer a freedom seeker.

Jackson had, in previous years, traveled to Charleston with English to sell horses. He knew the roads and the route. Most important, he knew that in Charleston he might have a chance at disappearing within the urban population and perhaps even finding his way out of the South.

And thus, although aware he was under special surveillance and operating essentially on probation until the anticipated arrival of Elizabeth English's relatives to whip him, he began to plan. Louisa and Jinny, his wife and daughter, had been sent away. He was likely to be whipped and tortured, perhaps to death, within the near future if he remained. He had a pony, although it might not remain alive and successfully hidden for much longer. He had now a brief opportunity—before the English sons-in-law were to visit—to operate with some impunity.

While the dates of all these events are a bit imprecise, it appears that the incident when Jackson was spotted on the pony at the Tabernacle Camp meeting happened late in 1846 and, as he wrote, "I kept the pony hid in the woods until Christmas."[24] Hence he had a few weeks to plan: rather than head west toward his wife and child, he weighed his chances and would go east. He would head for the coast and get out of the South entirely. The English family wouldn't see it coming.

Even a relatively small, inland town such as Lynchburg saw many visitors. The diverse commercial enterprises involving all the slave labor camps and white households in the area meant that peddlers, artisans, itinerant preachers, cotton brokers, merchants, judges, and slave traders would regularly come through. Thus even the "backcountry," as this South Carolina region was referred to well into the early nineteenth century, while hardly cosmopolitan, kept busy. This meant that enslavers could not entirely control the encounters or information their bondsmen had access to.[25] Whether through a Black grapevine of whispers or news overheard from gatherings of whites, no one was fully isolated from the world. This access to information was to prove more vital, for it was from outsiders that Jackson learned of the feasibility of freedom.

As Jackson later wrote: "The 'Yankees,' or Northerners, when they visited our plantations, used to tell the negroes that there was a country called England, where there were no slaves, and that the city of Boston was free; and we used to wish we knew which way to travel to find those places."[26]

England. Boston. He must have repeated to himself: *England. Boston.*

In one of Jackson's more reflective passages, and one that echoes a famous passage of Frederick Douglass's that recalled slaves staring out at the sails of boats on the Chesapeake wondering how their flight might take place,[27] Jackson wrote that the Yankee visitors gave form to the almost visceral and yet lyrical dreams of impossible freedom he and his fellow slaves shared:

> When we were picking cotton, we used to see the wild geese flying over our heads to some distant land, and we often used to say to each other, "O that we had wings like those geese, then we could fly over the heads of our masters to the 'Land of the free.'"

Jackson continued: "I had often been to Charleston—which was 150 miles distant from our plantation—to drive my master's cattle to market, and it struck me that if I could hide in one of the vessels I saw landing at the wharfs, I should be able to get to the 'Free country,' wherever that was."[28]

Jackson's plan was good, or at least as good as it could be. Despite the ridiculously long odds of his survival for a successful stowaway escape to Boston, the odds of escaping overland from South Carolina to a Northern free state would be absurdly dire. And while useful statistics on such escapes do not exist, at least a few men did manage to escape from South Carolina by ship or escaped to the swamps, escaped to Florida (before it, too, became a slave state), or otherwise made their way to freedom.

Many others certainly tried and became part of both the folklore and the powerful cultural language of the men and women who never had the ability or opportunity to flee. One former slave from South Carolina, Amie Lumpkin, for instance, testified in 1937 that she knew a man who "tried to steal a boat ride from Charleston. . . . He tell the overseer who questioned him after he was brought back: 'Sho, I try to git away from this sort of thing. I was goin' to Massachusetts, and hire out 'til I git 'hough to carry me to my home in Africa.'"[29] With such stories, we can see that Massachusetts, its freedom, and its short distance by sea were known even to the inland communities of bondsmen and women.

One instance that would have held great interest to Jackson if he had known of it was that of a fellow South Carolinian, James Matthews, who, in 1837, escaped through Charleston and made it to Boston and then up to Maine. Upon his arrival north, Matthews narrated his story to an abolitionist newspaper and told of smuggling himself amid cotton bales in the hold of a ship docked in the Charleston Harbor.[30]

To be sure, it seems almost impossible to imagine an abolitionist paper with Matthews's tale would have ever made it to the enslaved communities of Sumter County, but no enslaved person would ever be likely to forget such stories even if conveyed only in a whisper. Matthews's exact story might not have been known to Jackson, but other Black men and women in Charleston knew well that the more security around the harbor, the more evidence there was that some people had successfully managed to escape aboard ships. The ships in Charleston Harbor carried more than just cotton; they carried collective dreams for liberation.

Jackson put his plan in motion.

VI

Christmastime provided an opportunity that would happen only once a year. As Lowery asserted, the practice in that region was to give some truncated and controlled respite to the men, women, and children who had been laboring for the enslavers' profit all year: "Three days were usually given to slaves for Christmas. The day before, generally called 'Christmas Eve,' and the day after: hence the slaves thought of December 25th as the 'second day of Christmas' and the day after as 'the third or last day of Christmas.'"[31] At the site where Lowery was enslaved, hogs were butchered in anticipation of the holiday, and thus, food was more plentiful during this time. Moreover, as he recalled, the holiday was also a time when enslaved people were usually given their allocated shoes or clothing.

Frederick Douglass noted that Christmas was a time that enslavers knew they needed to allow some meager measures of comfort or flexibility to tamp down attempts at resistance or rebellion. Douglass wrote: "From what

I know of the effect of these holidays upon the slave, I believe them to be among the most effective means in the hands of the slaveholder in keeping down the spirit of insurrection. Were the slaveholders at once to abandon this practice, I have not the slightest doubt it would lead to an immediate insurrection among the slaves. These holidays serve as conductors, or safety valves, to carry off the rebellious spirit of enslaved humanity."[32]

We can therefore imagine that the English family and their overseers held to the general holiday customs of the region since it served their self-interest. Jackson reports that the enslaved people laboring for the English family were relieved of some work for several days, and there was a general tolerance for mobility during this time, which was to prove key to his schemes. And it is likely, thanks to holiday customs on the English properties, that Jackson may have had at least a good meal or two and perhaps a warmer jacket or shoes to take on the road with him by choosing this time. We cannot know whether he had any material gifts to take with him or not. Jackson doesn't say. Instead, he carried fears, prayers, and absolute resolve.

As Jackson told it, "The first day I devoted to bidding a sad though silent farewell to my people; for I did not even dare to tell my father or mother that I was going, lest for joy they should tell some one else." He held on to his secret for the evening, and "early next morning, I left them playing their 'fandango' play. I wept as I looked at them enjoying their innocent play, and thought it was the last time I should ever see them, for I was determined never to return alive."[33]

To run by day or by night? To flee on the road or in the woods? To rely upon subterfuge or unadulterated boldness? These were life-or-death decisions. Jackson made strategic choices for his survival, some of which he explains but others go unsaid. He must have gathered together the warmest clothes he could find and any supplies he could quietly obtain. He retrieved the pony he had hidden in the woods. The swampy wilderness was too tricky to navigate on horseback; thus, he planned to ride on several main roads, praying he could somehow talk his way out of any confrontations. He gambled on his charm. Most of all, he clung to faith in his ability to mislead others with his imagination. He crafted his own terrain.

CHAPTER THREE

"SPEAKS PLAUSIBLY"—THE REVEREND AND HIS RUNAWAY ADVERTISEMENT (1847)

Lynchburg-Charleston, South Carolina (December 1846–February 1847)

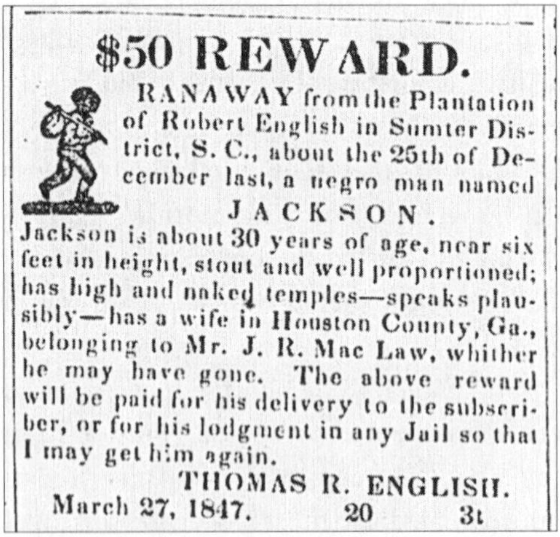

$50 REWARD.

RANAWAY from the Plantation of Robert English in Sumter District, S. C., about the 25th of December last, a negro man named

JACKSON.

Jackson is about 30 years of age, near six feet in height, stout and well proportioned; has high and naked temples—speaks plausibly—has a wife in Houston County, Ga., belonging to Mr. J. R. Mac Law, whither he may have gone. The above reward will be paid for his delivery to the subscriber, or for his lodgment in any Jail so that I may get him again.

THOMAS R. ENGLISH.

March 27, 1847. 20 3t

Published in the *Sumter Banner* on March 24, 1847. The date it first ran was March 24 and the date of March 27 indicates its weekly run.

Jackson's escape was surely discovered swiftly after the holidays, but the English family waited a few weeks before advertising for him. Why that was and why it matters is demonstrated in part by the particular language of the runaway advertisement the English family placed, a document that centers this chapter.[1]

Jackson had terrible choices to make about how to get himself out of Sumter County. He would need to rally all his skills and bravado to make it work. How he crossed this terrain and made his way to the coast, and, importantly, how he talked his way out of capture in Charleston is unpacked here thanks to his memoirs but also thanks to shipping records, artifacts of the "slave badge" system, and information about ship design. Jackson figured all of this out for himself because of his bold curiosity and knowledge of what might happen if he failed. The stakes were everything.

I

Spring was well underway by the time that Reverend Thomas Reese English rode down to the county capital from Lynchburg. Dutifully and perhaps with great irritation, he located the offices for the *Sumter Banner* and arranged on behalf of his parents to place an advertisement for a valuable fugitive. One or two advertisements for fugitives appeared in most issues of the newspaper during the 1840s, so the Reverend's request would have been common enough. The only thing out of the ordinary may have been how out-of-date the advertisement was.[2] Something was wrong.

Jackson had fled on Christmas, but it was several weeks before the English family understood that a major escape had happened and not merely an incident in which the runaway might quickly return. But that's not surprising. The English family was in some disarray when Jackson fled. Jackson had timed it well. Old Robert English was still alive at the moment of Jackson's escape (he was to pass away a full year later in December 1847) but he was all but bedridden and incapacitated. Jackson had described him, after all, as "out of his mind."

The Reverend paid for the advertisement to run for only a few weeks, perhaps confident that Jackson would soon be found—or perhaps ruefullly acknowledging that it was becoming less and less likely Jackson would be found in the state. It was worth a try, he must have figured. If they made an eventual insurance claim on the loss of property that Jackson's body represented, placing an advertisement would lend legitimacy to their claim.

To be sure, that didn't mean the English family would give up when the advertisements ran out. One of the family members, most likely the Reverend Thomas Reese English, later hired agents to trace and hunt down the fugitive up into Massachusetts. He was theirs to seize.

The English family was not one to cross. Jackson's escape and, later, his public prominence came to be seen as a personal insult to the honor of the English family and was not forgotten: Elizabeth English, in particular, refused to let the matter go. Some fourteen years after the escape, the aggrieved Elizabeth English still listed one man in his forties under the "Fugitives from the State" column on her official inventory of humans, known as the Slave Schedule of 1860.[3] Surely she was thinking of Jackson, the man who got away.

From reading the 1847 advertisement in the *Sumter Banner*, we can learn much about the English family's *perception* of Jackson at the moment of his flight, if little about the man himself.

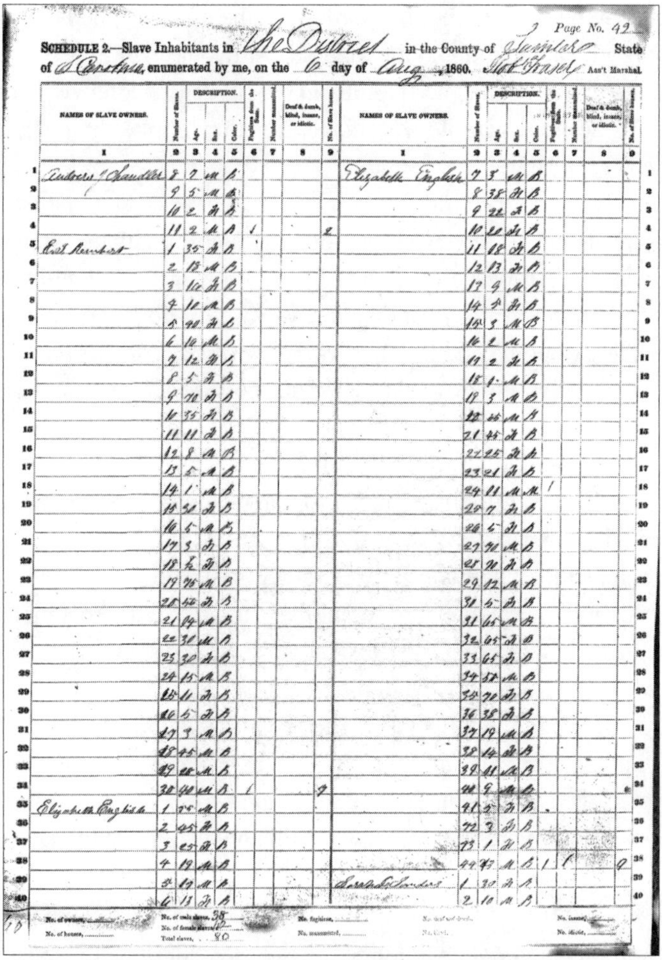

Page No. 42

SCHEDULE 2.—Slave Inhabitants in the District **in the County of** Sumter **State of** S Carolina, **enumerated by me, on the** 6 **day of** Aug, **1860.** [signature] **Ass't Marshal.**

	Names of Slave Owners	Number of Slaves	Age	Sex	Color	Fugitives from the State	Number manumitted	Deaf & dumb, blind, insane, or idiotic	No. of Slave houses
	1	2	3	4	5	6	7	8	9
1	Andrew J Chandler	8	7	M	B				
2		9	5	M	B				
3		10	2	F	B				
4		11	2	M	B	1			2
5	Est Rembert	1	35	F	B				
6		2	13	M	B				
7		3	16	F	B				
8		4	10	M	B				
9		5	40	F	B				
10		6	14	M	B				
11		7	12	M	B				
12		8	5	F	B				
13		9	70	F	B				
14		10	35	F	B				
15		11	11	F	B				
16		12	8	M	B				
17		13	5	M	B				
18		14	1	M	B				
19		15	32	F	B				
20		16	5	M	B				
21		17	3	F	B				
22		18	½	F	B				
23		19	75	M	B				
24		20	42	F	B				
25		21	14	M	B				
26		22	31	M	B				
27		23	30	F	B				
28		24	15	M	B				
29		25	11	F	B				
30		26	5	F	B				
31		27	3	M	B				
32		28	45	M	B				
33		29	28	M	B				
34		30	40	M	B	1			7
35	Elizabeth English	1	75	M	B				
36		2	45	F	B				
37		3	25	F	B				
38		4	19	M	B				
39		5	17	M	B				
40		6	13	F	B				

	Names of Slave Owners	Number of Slaves	Age	Sex	Color	Fugitives from the State	Number manumitted	Deaf & dumb, blind, insane, or idiotic	No. of Slave houses
	1	2	3	4	5	6	7	8	9
1	Elizabeth English	7	3	M	B				
2		8	38	F	B				
3		9	22	F	B				
4		10	22	F	B				
5		11	18	F	B				
6		12	13	F	B				
7		13	9	M	B				
8		14	4	F	B				
9		15	3	M	B				
10		16	2	M	B				
11		17	2	F	B				
12		18	1	M	B				
13		19	3	M	B				
14		20	26	M	B				
15		21	45	F	B				
16		22	25	F	B				
17		23	21	F	B				
18		24	11	M	M	1			
19		25	7	F	B				
20		26	5	F	B				
21		27	30	M	B				
22		28	11	F	B				
23		29	12	M	B				
24		30	5	F	B				
25		31	65	M	B				
26		32	65	F	B				
27		33	65	F	B				
28		34	57	M	B				
29		35	70	F	B				
30		36	38	F	B				
31		37	19	M	B				
32		38	14	M	B				
33		39	11	M	B				
34		40	9	M	B				
35		41	5	F	B				
36		42	3	F	B				
37		43	1	F	B				
38		44	43	M	B	1	1		9
39	Sarah Sanders	1	30	F	B				
40		2	10	M	B				

No. of owners, ... No. of houses, ... No. of male slaves, 38 No. of female slaves, 42 Total slaves, 80 No. fugitives, ... No. manumitted, ... No. deaf and dumb, ... No. blind, ... No. insane, ... No. idiotic, ...

This 1860 slave schedule shows Elizabeth English holding forty-four people in bondage listed across two columns, including one entry for a Black man aged forty-three near the very bottom on the right. As property, enslaved people were not reported with names—usually, only ages, skin color, and a few other details were listed. This individual had a tick in the column indicating he was a "Fugitive from the State" and thus still claimed as property by Elizabeth English or her heirs. This entry was undoubtedly referencing John Andrew Jackson, added there by Elizabeth English or her son, the Reverend Thomas Reese English, who was handling her affairs. Even though Jackson had escaped fourteen years previously, nothing appears to have been forgotten or forgiven.

First, they had accurately caught on to the day of his disappearance (December 25), whether by observation or by torture and threats to force information from his community we cannot know. The advertisement also demonstrates that they knew him as "Jackson" and didn't reference the name Clavon or Clavern, perhaps in casual disregard for his family unit.

We can also learn from the speculation that he may have fled to Georgia to look for his wife and child that the English family was tacitly acknowledging the relationships they had tried to compel him to deny. Moreover, by remarking upon his desire to reunite with his family, they implicitly recognized his tremendous suffering.

The fact that the Reverend English was ready to travel considerable distances as necessary to retrieve him from any holding jail also suggests that Jackson was of considerable value to them and that they thought he might have made it a substantial distance away. So, too, does the description of his youth and strong physique. They knew they had lost a powerful laborer.

The reward offer suggests that Jackson's value to the English family was significant, albeit not extraordinary. The advertisements for runaways in the *Sumter Banner* generally initially listed lower rewards and let them increase as weeks went by. While the $50 reward appears to be a bit on the high end compared with other such advertisements that had run in the same newspaper in previous months, it wasn't exceptionally high.

For comparison, let us examine another runaway advertisement on the same page of that issue. This other advertisement sought a man named Jacob, who was in his thirties. That notice offered a $100 reward for his capture. Earlier advertisements for Jacob had first appeared in December 1846 with a lower reward amount, suggesting that the practice was to raise the reward as the weeks went by and as the aggrieved enslaver got more and more frustrated. Reverend English was probably using $50 for Jackson only as his starting point.[4]

Would Jackson have known about this advertisement? That seems unlikely. The *Sumter Banner* was not going to be circulating in Massachusetts, where he was hiding at the time. But he knew how things worked. He would have known that an advertisement would be placed and leveraged against him. He was lucky the advertisement came out long after he was gone. If he had seen it, he probably would have felt insulted that the reward wasn't higher.

Deciding to place an advertisement wasn't an easy or obvious move, even when faced with such a significant property loss. By publicly allowing the loss of Jackson to be known in the broader white community, the English family weighed the possible hit to any reputation they might have imagined they held as kindly enslavers or effective managers as less significant than the benefit of regaining one of their workforce. But they had waited for him to come back on his own, and it hadn't happened. Serious measures now needed to be taken.

As clinical as advertisements might seem, they can hint at the personal or intimate relationships between the fugitives and the enslavers. And Thomas Reese English knew Jackson. They had grown up together. He knew Jackson was wily, clever, and desperate. With that in mind, he felt that he had to warn white readers of the *Sumter Banner* that Jackson "speaks plausibly."

What did he mean by this? In this phrase, which was a common one in such notices, we can detect something about the habits of mind that characterized the enslaving class. Indeed, it tells us how enslavers imagined Black people to be. In this construction, enslaved people faced impossible standards. Not only did the white ruling class assume that Black people were inherently less truthful than whites, it also assumed that duplicity was part of the intrinsic wily nature of Black people.

For runaways to "speak plausibly" implied they were slippery and persuasive enough to feign an intelligence they did not possess. Indeed, as the ads would have it, runaways were trying to be believable, to be plausible by the standards of a white world. Their inner selves held them to a higher standard, of course; for many, and for Jackson, the act of running away might have been the expression of the most authentic self he had. Any subterfuges these runaway individuals underwent to appear plausible to interrogators were irrelevant to their true sense of self.

For Jackson to be known as "plausible" meant, in the most direct sense, that he would have to overcome skepticism wherever he turned. However, the advertisement also indicates that the English family knew they had a formidable enemy operating out in the world who could match their moves, who could carry on with his tales of misuse, and who had already established an identity they could not control.

But time was not on the side of the English family. When this late-March advertisement appeared in the *Sumter Banner*, Jackson was long gone. At that point, he was almost nine hundred miles away, in Massachusetts, the "free country" he had dreamed of.[5]

II

Some fifteen years after his escape, Jackson finally wrote down the story of how he got away. Yet despite what must have been a journey of frenzied fear and experiences he might wish to forget, many of the details he recalled were precise. He named properties he passed, a hotel he stopped at, and even creek landings he crossed. Some of his recollections, though, suggest a hazy dreamscape of horror—a perspective blurred by fear. He knew the dangers, but, as he had acknowledged earlier, "I was determined never to return alive."[6]

As we have seen, Jackson's flight from South Carolina did not begin with the furtive acquisition of a pony that allowed him to traverse nearly 150 miles of roads, rivers, and swamps.[7] It started when he and his family and friends had picked cotton and observed the wild geese winging themselves to a "distant land." For Jackson, his escape plan began when he could first project himself into the bird and imagine the landscape from a bird's-eye view. Jackson could project a higher vision of his relationship to the land, mentally flying from South Carolina itself, which enabled his more physical flight.

He didn't run. He flew.

III

As noted earlier, Jackson had been to the coastal city of Charleston to drive Robert English's cattle to market on more than one occasion. He knew the route.

That didn't, of course, solve all his problems. His flight was still full of dangers. While he had not worked out the details of what he would do in Charleston aside from somehow hiding "in a vessel," traveling the roads toward the coastal city over a few days was going to be his greatest challenge.

On December 25, 1846, Jackson gathered up his possessions, including some coins and his hidden pony from the woods, and started down a public road. And, almost immediately, he had to assume the persona of a Black man legitimately on the road: "I met many white persons, and was hailed, 'You nigger, how far are you going?' To which I would answer, 'To the next plantation, mas're.'"[8]

Jackson's wry observation that followed, "But I took good care not to stop at the next plantation," reveals something about his sharp humor. It also demonstrates that he knew his own geographies were not the same as those of his white interrogators.[9] By the sheer force of his imagination, Jackson could know that "far" meant something entirely different to him.

Through a combination of bravado and luck, Jackson made it a good distance on the road until he arrived at the property of a "G. Nelson" and, avoiding the white folk there, mingled instead with the local Black celebrants. It wasn't unheard of for enslaved people to be allowed some mobility during these days around Christmas, so while his appearance must have been noted, it wasn't overly suspicious. Jackson used his charm and persuasive skills to again share the story that he was merely on leave for Christmas, and he was able to spend the night there without much notice.

It is hard to know which of several Nelson family properties in Sumter County Jackson visited, but southeast of the English properties was a cluster of sites owned by members of the Nelson family during the 1840s. It makes sense that Jackson would have arrived at holiday celebrations at one of those places near the intersection of the Black and Pocotaligo Rivers.[10] Again, when one considers that he wrote his memoir in England at least fifteen years after his escape, the scale of throwaway details that he shares with readers, down to the first initial of Nelson, is a testimony to his excellent memory. It also demonstrated the artful yet verifiable nature of the tale he wished to convey. He spoke the truth and was ready to provide receipts.

After hiding among the enslaved families of the Nelson property, Jackson continued south and east on his pony. He was now farther from what he knew.

How to move forward? Quietly. But not as if he was hiding. Ride steady. Don't hurry too much. Don't lurk in shadows but veer toward darker routes. Greet people on the road calmly and with respect, perhaps tip a hat. Don't look anyone in the eyes, even if you are of their height as an equal, up on a saddle. Be dull and unmemorable. Be forgotten.

After many anxious hours of hard riding, Jackson persuaded a man who ran a ferryboat on the "Sante [*sic*] River" (Santee River) to waive any usual scrutiny and allow Jackson and his pony aboard. As he put it:

> The negro who kept that ferry, was allowed to keep for himself all the money he took on Christmas Day, and as this was Christmas Day, he was only too glad to get my money and ask no questions; so I paid twenty cents, and he put me and my pony across the main gulf of the river. . . .[11]

Even with the purchased quiet of his ferryman, the landing of a Black man traveling alone astride a horse might attract unwelcome attention. The ferryman was no fool. He recognized the danger of helping Jackson but also the opportunity for himself. Jackson remembered, "He would not put me across to the 'Bob landing'; so that I had to wade on my pony through a place called 'Sandy Pond' and 'Boat Creek.' The current was so strong there that I and my pony were nearly washed down the stream; but after hard struggling, we succeeded in getting across."[12] Jackson didn't know it then, but this was the first of many times when he would make a difficult crossing only to find a more difficult landing.

Was the ferryman now going to turn around and turn him in? The possibility was real. He could claim to have seen Jackson in the area. He might assert that Jackson had threatened him and forced him to take him across. He could claim that Jackson had commandeered or stolen his boat. There could be a reward. Jackson wasn't likely to succeed anyway, and if he was going to be caught, shouldn't the ferrymen at least get something for himself out of it? The ferryman must have pondered his subsequent actions while Jackson and the pony splashed out of sight. Jackson pushed the pony hard to get as much distance between him and "Sandy Pond" as possible.

The last stage of Jackson's flight on the road was when he arrived at what he describes as a "hotel" of a "Mr. Shipman," where he rested until midnight.[13] As his ruse of a Christmas visit was going to be a lot less persuasive with every hour that went by, and perhaps having been a bit unnerved by the concerns of the ferryman from the day before, he thought it wise this time to take to the road in the middle of the night, hoping he might have fewer encounters with curious people. As he prepared to leave, though, he encountered perhaps the worst moment on his journey: his preparations caught the attention of Mr. Shipman. As Jackson explained, his imminent departure "roused Mr Shipman's suspicions, so he asked where I belonged to"—a question that was to recur at many points in Jackson's life.[14]

"I was scared," Jackson recalled, but he called upon his courage and answered with eminent plausibility:

> "Have you not seen me here with Jesse Brown, driving Cattle?" [Mr. Shipman replied] "Yes I know Jesse Brown well. Where are you going?" I answered him, "I am going on my Christmas holiday." This satisfied him. I was going to take a longer holiday than he thought for.[15]

And so Jackson survived that harrowing encounter. With what must have been a hard night and day of riding on the roads, Jackson noted: "I reached Charleston by the next evening."[16]

IV

The bustling city of Charleston was no easy haven for a fugitive. There were free people of color there, to be sure, and cities always provided access to different kinds of opportunities. There were many permanent refugees from slavery there, hiding in perpetuity as they walked among the urban crowds.[17] But different kinds of perils awaited as well. Free people of color often operated under constraints and control not far from slavery, and there was no guarantee that the person Jackson might confide in wouldn't turn him in for a reward. Nonetheless, he leveraged his charm and talked his way into the first true earnings.

Jackson doesn't explain much about how he managed things, but he notes that upon arrival in Charleston he found a Black man to help hide his pony and quickly worked out a way to join a work gang on the wharves. With this job, he started receiving "a dollar-and-a-quarter per day, without arousing any suspicion."[18] Jackson writes that many of the men on the work gang were locally enslaved men, operating as laborers for hire. The custom in Charleston at that time was for such men or, occasionally, women to hire themselves out for whatever work they might find; at the end of each week, they would need to turn over perhaps two and a half dollars to their

Black stevedores loading bales on the cotton wharf in Charleston, South Carolina, in the 1870s.

enslavers.[19] Jackson, who wouldn't have to turn over those extra days of salary to anyone, was suddenly in a position to save up a bit of money quickly and, while still in danger, get at least a bit of respite to plan his next step. He could catch his breath.

Jackson doesn't say much about these few weeks he spent in Charleston, but they would have been terrifying and heady days. He knew that this subterfuge wasn't sustainable. He could always build some relationships with charm and bonhomie, but casual friends couldn't be trusted with his secret. Someone was bound to turn him in later. He needed to learn the lay of the land and figure out the best strategy for smuggling himself aboard these closely monitored ships. He needed to be affable enough to get along with the work gang and learn places to sleep, eat, and how to hustle to survive during these cold weeks of January. He wouldn't have been able to relax for a moment.

Jackson thus kept to himself the best that he could. This was a time to watch and learn. He tried not to enjoy his precarious freedom too much. He needed to collect coins for his labor, for the first time, without letting satisfaction show on his face. Play it calm.

Jackson had a lot to do during these weeks. He needed to gather information carefully without seeming too inquisitive. Keep it casual, he must have told himself. His primary mission would have been to find out which ships would be heading as directly as possible to the correct destination and what kind of hiding situation they might offer a stowaway, depending on the cargo they carried. He needed, too, to save some money and gather supplies for his plans. There was the question, too, of whether he would need to go this alone or if he might find a trustworthy ally to smuggle him aboard.

These delicate and high-stakes maneuvers could not be rushed, yet time was not on Jackson's side. He would have known that the ports were regularly canvassed for runaways. Every day that went by, he was liable to be found out. And the thing that made him most vulnerable at this time was that he lacked the most potent and protective currency for an enslaved person in Charleston: a slave badge.

Slave badges were used during the eighteenth and nineteenth centuries as part of a surveillance system particular to a handful of coastal port cities in the southern United States. The practice was most widespread and long-lasting in Charleston, and so far, only badges manufactured in Charleston have ever been authenticated.[20] Enslavers would swear an oath of responsibility and pay a fee to have an official badge—generally good for a calendar year—registered and assigned to a specific individual under their control. These copper badges would allow an enslaved person a fair amount of free movement within the city environs. If a person were to be apprehended or detained by officials, the number on the badge would enable the enslaver to be contacted. Women who might be hired out as domestics would generally wear badges on their clothing or on their person that would say "servant," while men seeking work on the docks would have held badges engraved with "porter."[21]

Jackson was a canny and intelligent man, but he was still a young and unsophisticated laborer from the backcountry, unfamiliar with the logistics of Charleston port life. He was shocked when another Black dockworker asked him about his badge—something he had not known about before—and he panicked and realized that now was the time for quick action.

An 1848 Charleston copper slave badge with chamfered corners. It is stamped as "Porter No. 401." This particular badge would have been worn by an enslaved person hired as a day laborer, performing such jobs as loading and unloading ships.

> One morning, as I was going to join a gang of negroes working on board a vessel, one of them asked me if I had my badge? Every negro is expected to have a badge with his master's name and address inscribed on it.[22] Every negro unable to produce such badge when asked for, is liable to be put in jail. When I heard that, I was so frightened that I hid myself with my pony, which I sold that night for seven-and-a-half dollars, to a negro.[23]

By this time, Jackson had learned about a ship anchored in port that was Boston bound. He now understood the danger of not having a badge. It was time. He took his money from the pony sale and, with it and the money he had saved from the wages he had earned from loading and unloading cargo, he immediately bought some supplies. He quietly purchased a cloak for warmth. He bought bread, water, a gimlet for boring holes, and two knives.

The knives were everything. If he had to fight, he was ready.

Jackson's plan for smuggling himself on a ship would require good decisions and a lot of luck—he had identified the vessel he needed, but how to get aboard? And how to make sure he could be adequately hidden? He had little knowledge of trading vessels aside from what he might have learned in those few weeks of January spent helping load cargo. Every ship was different, and it would be hard to know whom to trust.

Hiding amid bales of cotton on a northern-bound vessel wasn't unknown, although it was almost inconceivably dangerous. Southern slaveholders and civil authorities made it clear they were almost frantic with concern about the matter.[24] By the 1850s, laws were passed in many Southern states that required searches for stowaways to be conducted before any ships bound for the North could clear Charleston's harbor.[25] Moreover, new systems of aggressive fumigation for departing ships were developed using noxious substances such as tar, vinegar, and brimstone (sulfur). These could be pumped into ships to force fugitives to reveal themselves.[26] Jackson was fortunate the ship he chose was not subjected to such fumigation, but, as his narrative goes on to show, the deprivations and conditions of his hiding place nearly killed him anyway.

V

Donning his cloak, with all of his "rattletraps," as Jackson called his jostling bags of supplies, underneath, he approached a Boston-bound ship that was scheduled to leave the following Wednesday morning. With the confidence of a man now accustomed to walking on and off gangplanks, he went on board.[27] He cautiously approached a cook, a free Black man, struck up a conversation, and then finally, with great trepidation, asked for help. The cook, while sympathetic, was nervous about helping a stowaway. As the cook explained to Jackson, free Black sailors were required by local ordinance to spend the night in jail whenever their vessels were docked in Charleston to keep them from mingling with enslaved people. The cook may have been let out of jail to prepare food aboard the ship in preparation for its next day's departure. The cook wasn't eager to be put in jail again. He was afraid of Jackson betraying him: greed, desperation, and collaboration could go either way. What if Jackson had been sent as a plant by white men to ferret out which Black seamen couldn't be trusted?

"Can't you stow me away?" said I.

"Yes," said he, "but don't you betray me! Did not some white man send you here to ask me this?"

"No."

"Well," answered he, "don't you betray me! for we black men have been in jail ever since the vessel has been here; the captain stood bond for us yesterday and took us out."

"What did they put you in jail for?" said I.

"They put every free negro in jail that comes here to keep them from going among the slaves. Well, I will look out a place to stow you away, if you are sure no white man has sent you here."[28]

It must have been with great hope that Jackson returned the following day. Unfortunately, and perhaps not surprisingly, the cook had second thoughts:

> "Walk ashore, I will have nothing to do with you; I am sure some white person sent you here." I said, "No, no one knows it but me and you." "I don't believe it," said he, "so you walk ashore"; which I did.[29]

Refusing to give up, Jackson waited until the cook had returned to his duties and then slipped on board. A white ship's mate assumed he was part of the work crew designated to load supplies and cargo. Jackson started following orders and moving things about as if he knew what he was doing until the regular Black work gang appeared. They must have been suspicious, for they observed him closely and asked him some pointed questions.

> They asked me, "Are you going to work here this morning?" I said, "No." "Aren't you a stevedore?" I said, "No."[30]

And then one of the gang remarked that his cloak gave him away: "I know better, I know by that cloak you wear." Surely intuiting that he was a fugitive, he asked Jackson, "Who do you belong to?"

What to do? That question summed it all up. He had to belong. He didn't belong.

In a bit of a panic, Jackson replied with biting obfuscation: "I belong to South Carolina."[31] Later, in his memoir, he remembered that moment with some satisfaction: "It was none of their business whom I belonged to; I was trying to belong to myself."[32] And with that line, he effectively claimed his place in a landscape of freedom that exceeded any other authority.

The Charleston work gang left him alone and debarked without signaling to anyone that they had seen him below. Jackson then worked on burrowing among the cotton bales. He maneuvered himself between two bales, but then someone pushed an additional bale around him so that he was "shut-in . . . a space about 4-ft. by 3-ft. or thereabouts" and left in "total darkness."[33] Fortunately, although the air was stifling, there was a board between him and a sleeping space for sailors that was pushed out or broken in some way, allowing precious air to pass.

VI

After a few weeks of working the docks, Jackson knew a bit about how to read the ships—which were heading down south to Florida or even around the continent toward New Orleans; which were slated to stay in port for only a few days; and which were pulling in for long-term repairs or rest. Most important, he learned to identify which were heading north. Studying the kind of cargo, the number of masts, and the type of crew was as important as figuring out the destination. Could he even ask around, discreetly, about the reputation of the captain? It was worth trying. The chance that he would be discovered at some point was fairly certain. Gambling on the temperament of an unknown captain could be a terrible mistake, a deadly mistake. But asking too many questions could be equally fatal. Jackson watched everyone around him closely and tried to gather what information he could. Eventually, though, he just had to take his best guess and make a choice.

While it isn't absolutely certain because he doesn't name the ship, the vessel Jackson appears to have chosen was the barque *Smyrna*, as indicated by the schedule of comings and goings of cotton trade ships in the Charleston-Boston route for that week in February. A "barque" or "bark" was a medium-to-small ship with three masts that could operate with a fairly small crew but maneuver with some speed up and down the coast. They were one of the most common kinds of ships of this era. The *Smyrna* was a typical workhorse, no different from thousands of similarly constructed vessels moving in and out of ports on the eastern seaboard. Jackson had wagered well with the kind of vessel he had selected. Similar ships would be plying a route to New York, not Boston. And New York was not nearly as welcoming to fugitives as Boston might be. The *Smyrna* made sense. But what of the captain and the crew?

The *Smyrna*, led by a young captain named George Scott of Wiscasset, Maine, was equipped to carry bales of cotton or any other cargo. Key for Jackson: it was not simply that it was Boston-bound; it was based out of a northeastern port. It thus happened to have a crew of Black and white sailors not inclined to go to much trouble to follow Southern laws unless they had to. Having been in jail the night before, under such Charleston regulations, would not have endeared the Black sailors of the *Smyrna* to South Carolina's mores. He might not have known it then, but he was fortunate in his choice.[34]

As the *Smyrna* pulled out of the harbor, and from between the bales, Jackson could hear Black seamen singing "their farewell songs." He briefly rejoiced with a sense of freedom at leaving South Carolina behind but quickly felt seasick and suffered tremendously from the ship's motion. Within a few days, he had run out of water, and the thirst became unbearable. He finished his bread all too quickly. He became weaker. But every minute he remained hidden took him farther away from Charleston.

Was it seven days and nights that went by? He wasn't sure. But, in great desperation, he finally used the gimlet he had brought to bore two holes in the boards separating him from the deck.[35] He later remembered that the sight of stars above comforted him: "I cast my eyes up through the gimlet holes and saw the stars," he wrote, "and I thought that God would provide

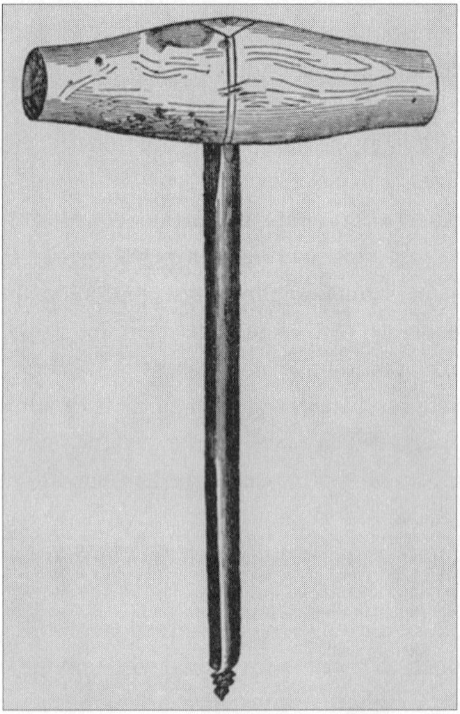

This picture of a gimlet is from Jackson's 1862 memoir and is presumably a picture of the facsimile tool he used as a prop during his lectures. When a stowaway on the *Smyrna* he had used such a tool to bore a hole in the deck.

for me, and the stars seemed to be put there by Him to tell me so; and then I felt that He would care for me as He did for Jonah in the whale's belly, and I was refreshed."[36]

A sailor eventually spotted the gimlet holes, and Jackson, throwing caution to the wind, called to him for water, crying, "Pour me some water down, I am most dead for water."[37] After some initial confusion (because the sailor wasn't sure where the voice had come from and thought it might be a ghost), Jackson was discovered. The sailor fetched the captain, who, echoing the cook's concerns, asked Jackson if he had been planted there by a white man to get the captain "in trouble." Jackson assured him that he had hidden on his own accord. He was sawed out from his hiding place and pulled onto the deck.[38]

The next few days must have been a blur of horror for Jackson. He was saved from immediate death from suffocation, hunger, or thirst, but the fear of being returned to Charleston must have been excruciating. Captain Scott persisted in believing that Jackson had been put aboard the ship as part of a scheme of white men trying to frame him. The captain threatened to turn Jackson over to any southern-bound vessel they might encounter. To Jackson's great good fortune, though, they met no other ships, and within a few days, the *Smyrna* pulled into Boston's harbor.[39]

Jackson's dangers were not over. He still needed to get off the *Smyrna*, for one thing, which, with Captain Scott's irritation and inclination to turn him in, was not going to be easy. But even with all that weighing on him, he knew his arrival in Boston was a moment, an achievement that would change his life.

Years later, Jackson was able to remember that moment with precision: "At nine o'clock on the evening of the 10th of February 1847, I landed at Boston, and then indeed I thanked God that I had escaped from hell to heaven, for I felt as I had never felt before—that is, master of myself, and in my joy, I was as a bouncing sparrow."[40]

CHAPTER FOUR

HENRY FOREMAN'S BOARDING HOUSE CENSUS REPORT OF 1850

Boston, Salem, and Western Massachusetts (February 1847–November 1850)

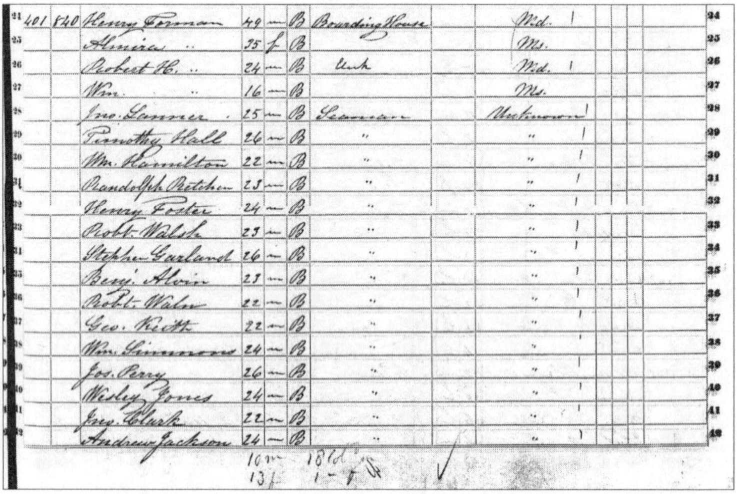

401	840	Henry Forman	49	—	B	Boarding House	Md.	1	24
		Almira ..	35	f	B		Ms.		25
		Robert H. ..	24	—	B	Unk	Md.	1	26
		Wm. ..	16	—	B		Ms.		27
		Jno. Lanmer .	25	—	B	Seaman	Unknown	1	28
		Timothy Hall	26	—	B	"	"	1	29
		Wm. Hamilton	22	—	B	"	"	1	30
		Randolph Ritchen	23	—	B	"	"	1	31
		Henry Foster	24	—	B	"	"	1	32
		Robt. Walsh	23	—	B	"	"	1	33
		Stephen Garland	26	—	B	"	"	1	34
		Benj. Alvin	23	—	B	"	"	1	35
		Robt. Walw	22	—	B	"	"	1	36
		Geo. Keith	22	—	B	"	"	1	37
		Wm. Simmons	24	—	B	"	"	1	38
		Jos. Perry	26	—	B	"	"	1	39
		Wesley Jones	24	—	B	"	"	1	40
		Jno. Clark	22	—	B	"	"	1	41
		Andrew Jackson	24	—	B	"	"	1	42

10m 18B
13f 1-F

This page from the 1850 Census shows Henry Foreman and his family living at the Boston boarding house along with a list of Black men in their twenties, all with the profession of "Seaman" and of "unknown" place of birth. "Andrew Jackson" is listed on the very last line.

Jackson's arrival in Boston wasn't an easy triumph. He needed to find friends, and he needed to find schemes—most of all, he needed to get off that ship. A handful of Black sailors had saved him and would point him toward some temporary havens in Boston and beyond. But merely surviving was one thing; figuring out how to now save Louisa and little Jinny was an entirely different kind of challenge. He didn't have the luxury of going "underground." For it was in Massachusetts that he began to build a network of activists ready to work on his behalf. But how much could he outsource this work when the stakes for his family were so high? And how could one logistically negotiate for someone's freedom with bad-faith actors, slow mail, erratic bank practices, and little room for error?

A census from 1850 helps us build out a portrait of a community that allowed Jackson the sanctuary and security he needed to advance his cause. Just when the dream of reuniting his family was beginning to seem possible, disaster struck. The Fugitive Slave Act had passed, and all of Jackson's carefully laid plans were shattered. What had he learned in Massachusetts that could help him now?

I

Snow flurries made the decks slippery, and it was certainly cold on Wednesday, February 10, when the *Smyrna* pulled into Boston Harbor, or at least it must have felt so to a South Carolinian.[1] And how had the crew dealt with the stowaway during the trip? After being discovered, Jackson had probably been kept in confinement, likely still huddled in his cloak and divested of his gimlet, knives, and money. Weak. Shaking. But did he have the energy to be hopeful, too? And what about helpful?

An extra pair of hands would have been useful on a busy vessel. Was he forced or encouraged to work at something useful for the final days of their voyage to earn his keep? The cook might have used a hand in peeling potatoes or stoking the cooking fires. And a strong man could always help haul, pull, clean, or hoist something—there were plenty of such tasks.

Whether he was kept busy or not, it must have been a fearful time: from his account, Jackson was discovered on the seventh or eighth day of the voyage and would have had to travel in fear and uncertainty for the rest of the trip, which typically would have taken close to twelve days.[2]

Arriving in the harbor of the free state of Massachusetts was a stunning accomplishment for a man fleeing the cotton fields of Sumter County, but getting *off* the *Smyrna* would require quite another kind of escape. And whom could he trust? Captain Scott had already demonstrated mixed feelings about the stowaway: he continued to badger Jackson about whether or not he had been placed aboard as part of some plot to discredit its captain. Could Scott be relied upon to allow Jackson to debark without drawing attention to himself or the *Smyrna*?

To make the situation even more worrisome, Jackson's experience with both the Charleston work gangs who had questioned him and also the *Smyrna*'s Black cook, who had reneged on an offer to hide him, demonstrated that other Black people, as much or more so than white people, were under terrible pressure to turn fugitives in. He could hope that they might look away. But simply looking away wasn't going to be sufficient assistance for a man who needed to get ashore and find sanctuary somewhere, anywhere.

And yet, with none of these problems solved, the *Smyrna* pulled in toward Boston.

Once the *Smyrna* entered Boston Harbor, a small pilot ship pulled up, and a licensed local inspector came aboard. This was all standard procedure. The inspector was there to ascertain the crew's health, the state of the ship, and the nature of its cargo to authorize its official arrival. As the legal authority now responsible for getting the vessel safely docked, the pilot inspector was supposed to report any crimes or concerns he might have about what he saw. Would the inspector be sympathetic to a stowaway? No one could count on that.

This moment of the inspection demands attention: it was this moment that a stowaway should have been reported. And yet, Jackson writes, "the pilot came on board, and I was sent into the forecastle to prevent his seeing me."[3] Hidden in this raised and front or "fore" part of the ship, usually an area on a barque where some sailors would have narrow quarters, Jackson must have trembled in the dark, probably wrapped up in blankets.[4]

Nonetheless, being able to hide there at all was a win. It meant that the captain's wavering notions about turning Jackson in were finally resolved; hiding Jackson in the forecastle couldn't have happened without Captain Scott's direct authorization. He must have decided that hiding Jackson might just work. Perhaps it was his conscience combined with a desire to avoid the hassles of reporting the stowaway (which probably would have included unwelcome paperwork and possibly even forced Captain Scott to hang around Boston to make an appearance as an unwilling formal witness). But, whatever the cause, the entire crew of the *Smyrna*, certainly under the captain's direction, stayed mum about the fugitive hidden in their midst.

What happened next makes sense when we align events as Jackson reports them with a new kind of document to center this chapter. The 1850 United States Census, taken in Boston some three years after Jackson arrived in 1847, provides us with retroactive corroboration and suggests clues for how we can understand how fugitives and their allies could operate. Even more, it suggests how freedom seekers such as Jackson could fashion themselves as free citizens in Massachusetts during the late 1840s.

So, to start, we need to ask who persuaded Captain Scott that Jackson wasn't worth the trouble of turning him in. He might have come to that conclusion himself, but it required more than just him. Every man on that ship knew about Jackson, and none said anything to the pilot.

Was there pressure on the captain to do nothing, pressure applied by the Black sailors? It seems likely. These would have been the same men Jackson had heard sing songs of farewell and relief at the moment they pulled out of the Charleston harbor. These were the free men who would have been, by law, housed in a Charleston jail for the duration of the time the *Smyrna* was docked in South Carolina to keep them from mingling with enslaved people.[5] Black sailors, of course, didn't appreciate this treatment, but stopping in Southern ports was an unavoidable hardship for most Black mariners in North America, and being housed in jail in Charleston for a night was expected, although much loathed, treatment. They would have had no fondness for the Charleston authorities or any Southern law regulating Black bodies.

It is not surprising, therefore, that Jackson writes it was three Black sailors ("Jim Jones, Frank, and Dennis") who finally escorted him off the *Smyrna* under the cover of darkness.[6] Surely these same men also played a part in assuring Captain Scott that if he didn't report Jackson, they would make sure the stowaway got off the ship quietly and without any trouble.

We shouldn't take any persuasion of Captain Scott for granted. It might have been an uphill argument. There had been several notorious conflicts in Boston in the 1840s between authorities and renegade antislavery activists over fugitives being turned over to Massachusetts authorities at the point of arrival. And the captain knew that by hiding Jackson he was running a serious risk. While he wasn't likely to face significant jail time, he would be subject to fines under the established laws, as well as a good deal of paperwork, court appearances, and unpleasant conversations.

Even if Captain Scott came out of the situation relatively unscathed legally, his reputation would be such that he might not be welcome at Southern ports of trade anymore. And, in the best-case scenario, he *still* would have likely had his work disrupted and his time in Boston complicated, and his smooth unloading of cargo and returning to his family in Wiscasset, Maine, would all be put in jeopardy.

One recent and disastrous incident in Boston Harbor from only a few months earlier probably loomed large in his mind. Captain Scott would have known all too well about the case of George, an unfortunate stowaway found aboard a ship called the *Ottoman*, which pulled into Boston Harbor in September 1846. In this incident, which was heavily covered in both local and national newspapers, George was discovered, and the *Ottoman*'s captain was angry but a bit unsure how to next proceed.[7] The captain thus took George, under guard, to Spectacle Island in Boston Harbor to have a "drop of consolation" at a small hotel while he considered what to do next.[8] While the captain was fortifying himself, George escaped from custody. The desperate man stole a small boat and headed for the mainland. Sadly, his escape was quickly noticed, and the now-fortified captain and his men pursued George over the water as he pulled toward the mainland.

Then, after George jumped out of his boat and made it ashore, they chased him across some fields until they finally captured him again. He was then hustled aboard an imminently southbound ship, the *Niagara*, that agreed to carry him back to Southern authorities. Local abolitionists in Boston were alerted to the situation. They quickly sent out a team on a rescue boat, but, in a dreadful mistake, they chased the *Ottoman* instead of the *Niagara*. By the time they realized their error, the *Niagara* was long gone. George was never heard from again.

George's awful fate loomed large in the minds of Bostonians that winter, whatever their feelings about slavery. And distress over states' rights as much as antislavery became linked to his case's media coverage. This incident from September 1846 almost immediately attracted an enormous amount of attention, in part because abolitionists, horrified by their failure to rescue George, held a large, open meeting in the most central and prominent public space in the city, Faneuil Hall—a meeting presided over by former president John Quincy Adams. At this gathering, Black and white Bostonians railed against laws that encouraged such renditions of fugitives from slavery. They vowed to reorganize, regroup, and work even harder to ensure that no person would be abducted from their state. The fiery antislavery activist Wendell Phillips addressed the crowd with words that would have been most welcome to Jackson:

> Law or no law, Constitution or no Constitution, humanity shall be paramount. I would send out a voice from Faneuil Hall that would reach every hovel in South Carolina and say to the slave, "Come here, and find an asylum of freedom here, where no talon of the national eagle shall ever snatch you away."[9]

Captain Scott of the *Smyrna* didn't want another George on his hands. He didn't want to deal with the Boston abolitionists but was also disinclined to go through any drama with the authorities. So he made up his mind. He allowed the Black sailors, Jim Jones, Frank, and Dennis, to quietly make the problem disappear. Years later, Jackson remembered the captain as "a humane man."[10]

What happened next was one of luckiest turns in Jackson's life: under cover of darkness, Jim Jones, Frank, and Dennis smuggled him ashore and delivered him to a wharfside boarding house for Black seamen run by Henry Foreman, a freeborn Black man.[11] Black sailors during this era rarely had

Here, the skiff is being rowed ashore under a full moon. On February 10, 1847, Jackson would have seen a waning crescent moon, and thus when he was rowed ashore by the Black sailors of the *Smyrna*, it would have been even darker than this depiction has it.[12]

many options for places to stay ashore, even when they landed in friendly Northern ports. For the young sailors who were less likely to have wives or children onshore, even in their hometown ports, boarding houses for Black seamen were where they could find a family of fellows. Jackson was to stay on and off with Foreman for the next several years, and it became if not exactly a home, at least a home base for him. The friendships he forged there saved his life more than once.

We can learn a bit about how this all happened, though, thanks to the seemingly straightforward enumeration of the 1850 Census. However, that census was anything but straightforward and demands a close reading here. It is another document that cements Jackson's often slippery story in a broader context.

II

The 1850 Census for Boston is full of surprises. Henry Foreman, the stalwart proprietor of a temperance policy boarding house, was still operating his business on Ann Street three years after Jackson debarked from the *Smyrna* in February 1847. When approached by a census taker in September 1850, Foreman must have had much faith in the government authorities, for he essentially laid out his books for inspection, including some things that might have been best left hidden.

Twenty-six people are listed as living in that Ann Street boarding house, including Foreman's wife, Almira, and their two sons, Robert and William. We can get a hint of their family life by seeing that the eldest son, Robert, was listed as working as a "clerk," and William, age sixteen, has no occupation at all, which suggests the Foreman parents knew enough about a sailor's life to keep their own sons at home.

The building must have been crowded to fit all those people in the narrow, two-story wooden structure. By nineteenth-century standards for density in tenements and boarding houses, though, it wouldn't have been outrageously overpopulated. The cooking and meal preparations were certainly done on-site, and, especially since the boarders were mostly mariners, they would have moved in and out of the house at unpredictable and erratic times as their ship schedules dictated, perhaps sleeping in shifts in their assigned spaces. An outhouse of some sort for the entire house to share was probably in a grim back courtyard or alley space, and noise from raucous streets outside would have kept the house a bit unsettled at all times. Laundry was probably dealt with in the small yard, and sailors' clothing would have been hung out to dry there. A table on the lower level where they took turns eating their meals would have been the site where news and tips could be shared, debts and credit negotiated, schemes hatched, and alliances, even friendships, forged.

We can get a sense of the site thanks to the cluster of names listed and an even more valuable sense of an allied and unified community there thanks to how these names are listed. The page of the 1850 Census that features Foreman's family and the residents of his boarding house marks the very first moment we see Jackson listed under the name he preferred at that time. Or at least it was what Foreman probably reported to the census taker. On this page, we can see "Andrew Jackson, Seaman, Age 24, Black and from a place of birth unknown."[13]

"Andrew Jackson" is a common name, but we can be confident it is him. Jackson lived on and off with Henry Foreman during his time in Massachusetts, but the detail that clinches his corroborative story is found on the following page—for it is here we can see Dennis Young, a sailor twenty years of age.

Was this "Dennis" the same Black sailor Jackson remembered from the *Smyrna*, who, three years earlier, had helped Jackson get off the boat? The

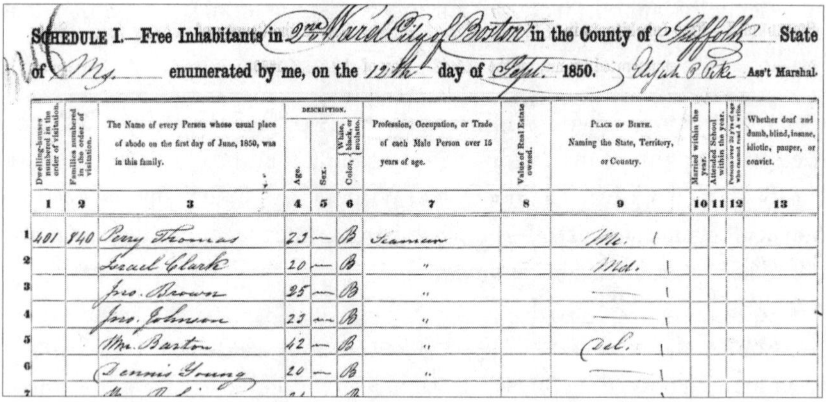

SCHEDULE I.—Free Inhabitants in 2nd Ward City of Boston in the County of Suffolk State of Ms. enumerated by me, on the 12th day of Sept. 1850. Elijah P. Pike Ass't Marshal.

Dwelling-houses numbered in the order of visitation.	Families numbered in the order of visitation.	The Name of every Person whose usual place of abode on the first day of June, 1850, was in this family.	Description: Age.	Sex.	Color, White, black, or mulatto.	Profession, Occupation, or Trade of each Male Person over 15 years of age.	Value of Real Estate owned.	Place of Birth. Naming the State, Territory, or Country.	Married within the year.	Attended School within the year.	Persons over 20 y'rs of age who cannot read & write.	Whether deaf and dumb, blind, insane, idiotic, pauper, or convict.
1	2	3	4	5	6	7	8	9	10	11	12	13
401	840	Perry Thomas	23	—	B	Seaman		Me.				
		Israel Clark	20	—	B	"		Md.				
		Jno. Brown	25	—	B	"		—				
		Jno. Johnson	23	—	B	"		—				
		Wm. Barton	42	—	B	"		Del.				
		Dennis Young	20	—	B	"		—				

Second page of 1850 United States Census listing showing Dennis Young, a Black sailor, residing with Henry Foreman.

name "Dennis" is relatively uncommon, and it seems likely to have been the same sailor. And while it is more of a speculative stretch, there was another sailor listed at the boarding house with the name "Wesley Jones." Could he have been the "Jim Jones" who helped Jackson get ashore off the *Smyrna* back in 1847?

These names cement Jackson's presence in that boarding house more firmly. The names also demonstrate a pattern of long-term allegiances to place and to one another that made up the Black maritime community and culture. In this 1850 Census, as in the early years of his freedom, we see Jackson invoke different versions of his name. Here he is called "Andrew Jackson." Was this the name he had supplied to the boarding house, or was this the name accidentally attributed to him by whoever provided all the residents' information to the census taker? We cannot know. But there Jackson was in 1850, clearly noted in the ledger—an entry full of subterfuge.

After 1850, perhaps to avoid sharing a name with the recently deceased president, Jackson seems to have emphasized the name "John" in most appearances in print, and by the time he had a few years of freedom, he was asserting his full name as "John Andrew Jackson" whenever possible.[14] But the significance here is not merely in his name or presence in the ledger. What is astonishing in this census is the brazen use of his name while he was still a fugitive!

When this census was taken in early September 1850, Jackson had been in Massachusetts for almost three and a half years. He may have been getting comfortable in his relatively safe position in the free state. However, this census marks a transition: circumstances for free Black people and former captives alike were about to change—suddenly and with terrifying consequences.

Jackson and the landlord Henry Foreman, who was an antislavery activist, had witnessed the increasing and well-known incidents of fugitives being forcibly returned to the South (such as the sad situation with George, who had fled and been recaptured in Boston Harbor). Thus Jackson's comfort in using his name freely speaks to the security he and Foreman must have felt in that early fall of 1850. After all, if Jackson was a fugitive, Foreman was harboring one, an action which could bring some trouble. Evidently, though, Foreman thought it wasn't likely anyone would care much. He didn't see Jackson as being as vulnerable as poor George had been, and if Jackson wanted to live publicly and loudly under his own name, who was Foreman to disagree?

For a fugitive to assert his name publicly took courage, but it also needed to be done only where he would feel some degree of safety. Why Jackson felt safe to list his name in the early fall of 1850 arises from a broader sense of his community and situation—a feeling of refuge created by the remarkable place he had initially landed in, the Foreman boarding house and its environs on Ann Street. Any security he felt, however, would soon prove false.

III

Henry Foreman was a free man of color, born in Maryland around 1800 and who had resettled in Boston. While he was never part of the elite class of Black activists, he was certainly known in antislavery circles. Among other things, Foreman would regularly promote his business in *The Liberator*, the influential antislavery newspaper. For many years, Foreman managed to successfully operate his "genteel" house for "respectable colored seamen" run on the "Temperance system," as his advertisements read. His establishment was a two-story wooden structure described as "a tenement" in the papers and conveniently located near the docks but, perhaps less fortuitously, sited at the intersection of Ann and Richmond Streets.

Ann Street was the heart of what was then known as the "Black Sea."[15] This neighborhood was densely filled with dance halls, rum shops, brothels, taverns, and dangerous, dark alleys. Indeed, in 1851, a police officer assigned to the neighborhood estimated that on Ann Street and its immediate environs there were 227 brothels, 26 gambling dens, and 1,500 places where liquor was sold.[16] As a poor neighborhood right near the water, it was one of the first places new immigrants from Ireland would find housing. The huge influx of immigrants from Ireland that arrived during the Irish famine years—a migration that peaked in the late 1840s—meant that the rough and tumble streets in this area of Boston's "North End" would have been filled with Irish accents and strivers and hunters from the Old World hoping to build more successful and settled lives, even when starting amid American squalor.

It smelled, of course. Not surprisingly, the neighborhood was thick with refuse. There was little access to clean water or sunlight. Cholera and other diseases raged. Many policemen were reportedly afraid to venture there. But both despite and precisely because of its reputation, Ann Street was a neighborhood where several Black-owned businesses, such as boarding houses, could operate without too much unwelcome scrutiny. Some Black folks could find employment at such places, where no difficult questions might be asked about their origins, and Black mariners who needed temporary and convenient housing could carve out a place for themselves. Foreman and his wife, Almira, raised their children there. It wasn't entirely secure, but they maintained it as a site of temperance and calm refuge amid the chaos of the streets.

Their security was tested, though. An 1852 police report noted that "the depraved of both sexes and all colors constantly congregated" on Ann Street.[17] This mingling resulted in an uneasy tolerance with some eruptions from time to time. Back in 1843, that tolerance had been tested: a race riot erupted directly in front of Foreman's house, illustrating how day-to-day racist animus shaped the kind of world Jackson had landed into. The riot also taught Foreman about how to protect and defend his space, his Black space, and his community in ways that would later benefit Jackson.

According to witnesses at the 1843 Ann Street riot, white sailors passing along the street demanded that some of the Black boarders at Foreman's place step off the sidewalk to let them pass. The Black sailors refused. Things escalated quickly, and a crowd of white rioters shouting "Down with the negroes" rushed into Foreman's establishment.[19] Returning from church and happening upon this scene, Foreman was himself violently attacked and found his building pilfered, with broken furniture and a shattered window.[20] Perhaps surprisingly, the Boston police, in a review of the incident, agreed that the white sailors had started the violence. The fact that the incident could have been officially concluded with no fault assigned to Foreman and

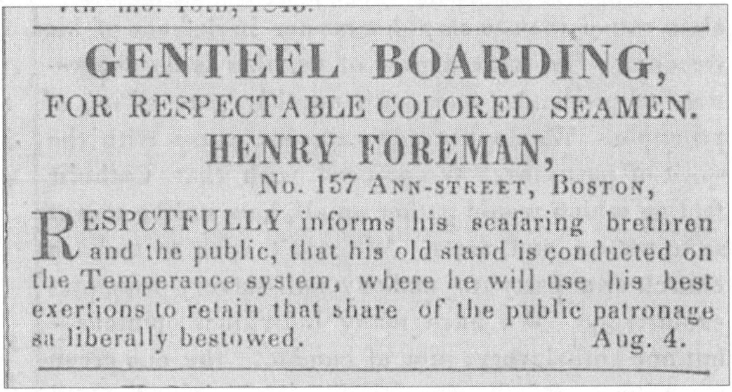

GENTEEL BOARDING,

FOR RESPECTABLE COLORED SEAMEN.

HENRY FOREMAN,

No. 157 Ann-street, Boston,

RESPCTFULLY informs his seafaring brethren and the public, that his old stand is conducted on the Temperance system, where he will use his best exertions to retain that share of the public patronage sa liberally bestowed. Aug. 4.

This advertisement ran in many issues of *The Liberator* between 1843 and 1844. Foreman was not discouraged by the riot of 1843 and repaired his property so that the boarding house could continue for several more years.[18]

Ann Street (photo from 1881, thirty-one years after Jackson lived there). The buildings in the picture had four stories, while Foreman's boarding house had only two. Other buildings at the intersection of North Street (formerly Ann) and Richmond Street today are from the 1850s and are four or five stories high, so Foreman's building must have been dwarfed by larger structures.

his Black boarders speaks to the considerable standing this business on Ann Street must have had in the Black and white communities alike.[21] But it was also a reminder that hatred toward Black people and their right to exist freely was ever present.

Foreman was resilient, and thus his business continued despite the damage. Glass was replaced, furniture acquired. Perhaps iron bars were installed. He and Almira persisted, and their boarding house became an even more important establishment for the Black community; it sustained the well-being of the many Black sailors who needed safe respite whenever their ships were docked nearby. And that safe respite was not just for mariners; Foreman continued to use his central location and network of connections to support the cause of antislavery. In 1845, for instance, he sold tickets to fund-raisers for the New England Freedom Association at his boarding house.[22] By the late 1840s, though, the needs of the movement and the needs of the cause became greater than simply supporting *The Liberator* and genial fund-raising could handle. Foreman was sited precisely where fugitives could either be hidden or be caught. Direct action was going to be part of his story.

The kindness of Foreman and his good connections with Black and white citizens in Boston proved invaluable to Jackson, who needed his help finding work. Because, despite the later obfuscating claim of the 1850 Census,

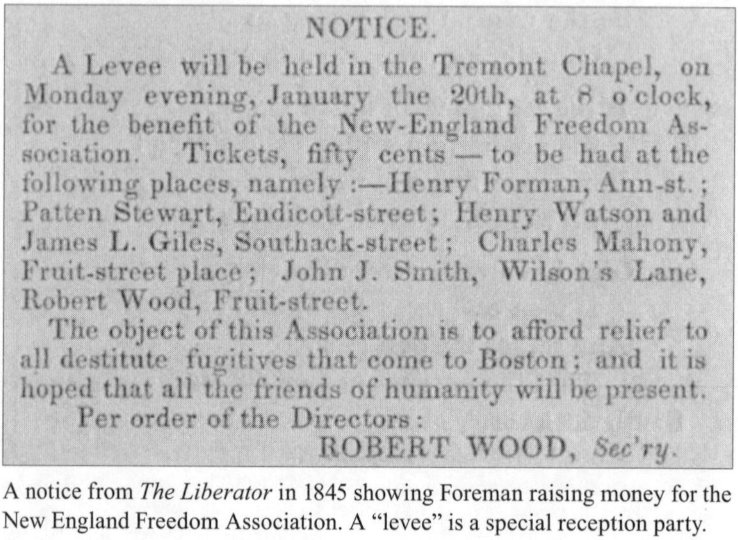

NOTICE.

A Levee will be held in the Tremont Chapel, on Monday evening, January the 20th, at 8 o'clock, for the benefit of the New-England Freedom Association. Tickets, fifty cents — to be had at the following places, namely :—Henry Forman, Ann-st. ; Patten Stewart, Endicott-street ; Henry Watson and James L. Giles, Southack-street ; Charles Mahony, Fruit-street place ; John J. Smith, Wilson's Lane, Robert Wood, Fruit-street.

The object of this Association is to afford relief to all destitute fugitives that come to Boston ; and it is hoped that all the friends of humanity will be present.

Per order of the Directors :

ROBERT WOOD, *Sec'ry.*

A notice from *The Liberator* in 1845 showing Foreman raising money for the New England Freedom Association. A "levee" is a special reception party.

Jackson was no sailor. He would have had no interest in getting aboard ships that might sail south. And yet, Jackson needed a way to make a living.

He had temporary respite; Foreman allowed Jackson to stay for several months, perhaps even a year or more. As Jackson wrote: "I became his [Foreman's] servant and received my board as payment."[23] Jackson was likely helping with the enormous amounts of cooking, cleaning, laundry, and such tasks that would have been necessary for a boarding house. He might, too, have been manning the door. The Foremans now knew the value of keeping the stable presence of a defensive force in the house.

As Jackson learned about Boston, he may have been commissioned to run errands. He could be useful. He could earn his keep. For a time, this situation was sustainable. The Foreman family and their busy household provided stability and probably a friendly warmth. It must have meant a lot to him to see an intact and free Black family able to make decisions about their children and one another with no one else's interference. He could see, too, that they didn't simply keep to themselves. They used their good fortune to help others.

During these months and relying upon the security that the Foreman family provided, Jackson now had time and support to adjust to life in Boston as he figured out how to pass, as best as he could, as a free citizen of Massachusetts.

To function as a free man and avoid detection as a fugitive might sound easy for a man who could now hide out in a community with other men of color, but it would have required skills and knowledge. His clothing would have to change. He would need to learn how to carry himself around white Bostonians, how to navigate the streets, how to alter his speech to reflect local phrases, cadences, and accents, and how to maneuver within myriad unfamiliar cultural cues and practices. He needed help.

Did Jackson join one of the city's Black congregations or church groups? Did he attend any antislavery meetings with Foreman at Boston's African Meeting House, a central community site for Black people and their allies during the Antebellum Period?[24] Did he embrace or engage with the Black community of Boston in any way outside of his sanctuary on Ann Street? Boston was an enormous city, the second-largest port in the United States, and its Black population was close to two thousand during this time.[25] We can presume that, as a bold and energetic young person, he sought out friends and company in his new home. He doesn't say much about his time there, but we know of at least one significant action that happened: someone in Boston, possibly one of the Foremans, helped him compose and post a letter to the English family back in Lynchburg, in the hope of opening negotiations to purchase his family.

This was to prove a terrible mistake.

IV

Louisa and Jinny couldn't have known then that Jackson was free—that he was dreaming of them. But he was. And Jackson was a man of action.

By June 1847, determined to accrue some savings to liberate Louisa and Jinny, Jackson relocated to Salem, Massachusetts. His time there proved to be a calm interlude that allowed him to dream of a new kind of future, perhaps one in which he could prosper and be reunited with his family. Parting from the Foremans must have been difficult, but worth it. It was time, and he was ready. Only twenty miles from the heart of Boston, Salem was about a full day's walk or a short ride by wagon, boat, or train away from his friends on Ann Street. The population there was close to 22,000 people, but within that, overall, there was a substantial Black community of around 400 to welcome him.[26] Salem made sense. He quickly found work in local tanning yards and found friends and allies anew.

Salem, located on the north shore of Massachusetts Bay, had been a vital maritime port since its first settlement in the seventeenth century. It had long been a center of international trade, fishing-related activities, and whaling. Some of Salem's significance as a port and maritime center was waning by the mid-nineteenth century as larger port cities grew up along the North American coast.

Other commercial enterprises, though, began to develop—most notably leather processing and its attendant industries such as bleacheries, glue making, and, not surprisingly, a host of shoe manufacturing businesses in that region. By 1850 there were eighty-three different tanning businesses in the area of Salem known as the "Hollows." These companies based in and near Salem would often process hides from South America or Africa that were brought in on trade ships. These hides would then be processed or "tanned" into various products. The area around Salem, however, became particularly known for delivering the hides to regional shoe manufacturers who could, in an irony that would not have been lost on Jackson, then transform them into cheap and rough shoes often sold in bulk for Southern purchasers to distribute for enslaved workers on plantation labor camps.

Irish immigrants with experience in leather work had started to flock to Salem in the 1840s for such work. However, even with that influx of labor, there were still possibilities for others in the burgeoning businesses. Black workers were not entirely shut out of the labor market in Salem, which was, as in everywhere else in the North, still shaped by race, caste, and class. The opportunities might be lowly, but they were real. Jackson joined this community and found a place to stay and what he understood as fair employment.

"I received a dollar-and-a-half per day, out of which I saved one hundred dollars in the course of a year, which I put in the savings bank," Jackson wrote. He described these as "good wages" and remembered Salem as having finally provided him with "a comfortable home."[27] Considering that entrepreneur Joseph Putnam, who ran one of the most prominent and successful tanneries in Salem, reported that in 1850 he paid his workers an average of $7.50 a week for up to 60 hours of work, Jackson's salary was surprisingly high in comparison at $10.50 a week.[28] Things were turning around. He now had time to build hope and build plans.

No obvious paper trail documents what happened to Jackson during his time in Salem and how he began his advocacy campaign. But clues are there. The *Salem Directory* of 1850 listed a John Jackson simply as a "laborer" who lived along the turnpike, a part of the town known for clustering poor Black families.[29] In his memoir, Jackson reports that he worked in Salem tan yards for "James Brayton, Samuel Pittman, and many others."[30] In later years, Jackson looked to some white citizens of Salem, such as Samuel Higbee and John Gilmer, for endorsements and recommendations, so clearly he earned a local reputation as a good worker and honest broker.[31]

Here in Salem, he could finally control his own time and invest his energies as he saw fit. He was particularly pleased to realize that this tan yard job offered him some time off during waking hours which allowed him to saw wood to supplement his income. Being able to earn his own income on his own terms, no matter the difficulty of the work, meant more to Jackson than just accruing savings. *It was different now.* He wrote:

> I used often to work at sawing wood during the night, and it did not seem such a hardship as when I did the same in South Carolina. Why? Because I felt that I was free, and that I worked because I wished; whilst in South Carolina I worked because my master compelled me.[32]

Jackson summed up his feelings by writing: "This fact is, in my mind, more satisfactory than twenty theories, as to the superiority of free labor over slave labor."[33]

That is not to romanticize Jackson's experiences. He speaks of "turning the splitting machine" at the tan yard, a task that uses a knife to strip the thick hide of a horse off its body. It involved a complicated mechanism and ceiling hoist with heavy blades needing human guides.[34] As one historian of Salem's nineteenth-century tanning industry noted: "There was scarcely a splitter of experience who had not had one or both arms broken." In the early nineteenth century, witnesses reported that it was "not uncommon for workers to get their aprons caught and be pulled into the machine, snapping their spines."[35]

But the dangers were worth it. Saving was hard, but the money was adding up. Jackson wrote that he had managed to accrue $100 during his time in Salem.[36] And it is evident from Jackson's actions that the security of his position in Salem allowed him to launch the next phase of his life: that of working to free Louisa and Jinny, with the help of sympathetic antislavery activists if possible, but on his own if necessary.

While Jackson would have lived and labored among the poorer working population of the city, that doesn't mean he would have been unaware of or entirely disconnected from opportunities to learn about activism and advocacy. Did he attend the Salem Baptist Church, led by the Reverend Cyrus P. Grosvenor, which had been hosting antislavery society meetings since the 1830s?[37] As the most prominent community gathering place for Black people in town, it was a place where it seems likely that Jackson would have learned about new kinds of activism.

Other Black leaders also built up a strong community of political consciousness. Salem was home to some of the most important Black activists of the nineteenth century. Jackson was working too hard with his various jobs, desperately earning every penny he could, to be much involved in the more elite circles of genteel, freeborn people of color. And yet, he was nonetheless part of that broader community in Salem, and it's impossible not to speculate about whether or not he crossed paths with any of them.

One family, in particular, could have been helpful to Jackson if he had known them. Could he have met with Salem's illustrious Remond family of successful Black civic leaders during those years, for example? He must have known about this family, and his potential contact with them does merit consideration, for they were leaders of abolitionist activity in

Salem. Jackson needed to network and find strategic legal assistance for his schemes, so contacting or getting help from the local Black leaders would have made sense.

To understand the Black world of Salem it is useful to differentiate between the elite activist circles and the impoverished Black laborers to see how they likely kept largely separate with a few crucial exceptions.[38] The most prominent Black community members were the Remond family of Salem, headed up by Charles Remond, an immigrant from Curaçao who had become a successful barber and celebrated caterer. He, his wife, and their children advocated for abolition, desegregation, and women's rights. Their children, Charles Lenox and Sarah, both became professional antislavery advocates and lectured throughout Europe during the 1840s and 1850s. Their family certainly set the positive and engaged tone for local abolitionist activities. It seems unlikely that there would have been any casual contact with Jackson since the Remond family didn't attend the primary Black church in Salem and otherwise seem to have kept themselves somewhat apart from the poorer Black community.[39] Nonetheless, their work involved hosting, attending, and organizing social and political events, both because of their professional catering business and because of their activism. Surely Jackson, a man who wasn't known to be shy, would have made it his business to call upon, meet, consult, and make an impression, if possible, upon these Black activist luminaries.

The reason it is important to speculate about a possible connection between Jackson and the Remond family or the antislavery activities of the area during the late 1840s and 1850s is that, during Jackson's time in Salem, his plan to free his family changed. While he had initially planned to raise the money for their freedom by himself, he now began to hope he might be able to find outside help. He wasn't yet literate, so his education in how to effectively advocate for his cause would have come from listening and learning, from conversations, and perhaps from attending public events or church services.

During his time in Salem, we see Jackson invent himself anew. Leveraging his courage and charisma and doubtless gathering his information about how to be heard, Jackson began to plot a way to take a public stance and share his story across the state. And at this moment, money and legal help were what he needed. If Jackson were to raise money and find people to negotiate legal documents on his behalf, he was going to need letters of introduction, letters of connections, and a guide.

V

And so, Jackson reinvented himself. Again. He had been passing as a freeman, but now he knew that wouldn't help him save his family. He needed to fashion himself afresh into a plausibly capable man who could both present himself as a victim needing charity but also carry himself as a man of confidence and integrity—someone accomplished enough to be trusted to use donations well. He would need to hone his storytelling skills in order to launch a campaign for Louisa and Jinny.

Whether from the tan yards or the public meetings of antislavery groups, Jackson found more allies. In Boston and Salem, he could have listened to or learned about men or women who could serve as models for how to create or fashion oneself into a public figure. Several prominent African Americans had made a name for themselves, lecturing and collecting money for the antislavery cause by this time, sometimes speaking from passion and knowledge, such as Charles Lenox and Sarah Remond, but others, such as Frederick Douglass, had come to prominence speaking about their own experiences.

If Jackson had ever met or listened to Douglass, he doesn't say. But for Jackson, a more probable model or mentor he likely encountered would have been Lewis Hayden, who had escaped from slavery, settled in Canada for some years, and then, remarkably, returned by 1849 to the United States to work as a professional lecturer and antislavery activist. Hayden was indisputably one of the most important Black leaders of the Underground Railroad (UGRR) in Boston during this period, and some scholars estimate that one-fourth of all fugitives who passed through Boston may have stopped by Hayden's house.[40] Advised by Foreman and his circle, Jackson would likely have been directed to seek out Hayden or the other members of the Black community centered around the African Meeting House in Boston. From them or from friends in Salem, Jackson would have learned of allies to contact beyond the confines of coastal Massachusetts. Boston and Salem were increasingly full of activists, speechmakers, and competing events. Nonetheless, with good counsel, good friends, and good speaking skills, Jackson might attract sympathetic attention to his situation, and his cause, by sharing his story further afield.

By late 1849 or early 1850, Jackson took leave from his work in the Salem tan yards and, with his savings for travel money, ventured out to western Massachusetts, probably traveling by a combination of foot, train, or wagon as means or opportunities allowed. Did friends from Boston or Salem provide him advice? Funds? Letters of introduction? Some years earlier, Charles Lenox Remond of Salem had lectured out in Worcester and other locations across the state.[41] Perhaps he made some suggestions or connected Jackson with likely hosts. Perhaps, too, by leaving the coastal part of the state, Jackson imagined that he might get noticed. While in Boston and Salem, there were a fair number of formerly enslaved people sharing their stories and seeking donations, and he was thus competing with other fugitives for attention. Moreover, he needed to be clear that he was raising money for a very specific cause—Louisa and Jinny—not a generalized antislavery organization. It is possible he reasoned that by traveling to other parts of the state, he might stand out a bit more and attract patrons. Whatever went into it, he made a bold decision to redirect his life. Simply laboring and trying to save a dollar here and there wasn't going to be enough to save his family. Risking his job and his inadequate but hard-earned savings, he took the gamble and began to travel.

Jackson doesn't speak much of this part of his life in his memoir or later interviews. Fortunately, a paper trail of correspondence written to, for, and (remarkably) *from* him during his months on the road in 1850 indicates his growing stature and sophistication. These letters also tell us about his strategically selected allies from the Black and white communities and how success and failure need to be measured under the circumstances.

The new hurdles Jackson was to face were considerable. Even if he somehow got hold of the money necessary to liberate his family, how would he track down the people who held Louisa and Jinny in captivity? By 1850, all of his information was several years out of date. Were they still even alive? What if they had been sold? Or, even worse, what if they had been sold apart? And if they were found, and negotiations could be opened, how much could one trust bad-faith actors who held a woman and child as hostages?

Being taken seriously among Northern patrons was another challenge. How was Jackson to establish himself as a trustworthy itinerant speaker who could handle donations and manage the banking logistics of transferring significant sums down south? And even if all went well, how could he manage securing arrangements for Louisa and Jinny to be safely transported up north? As a fugitive, he was in no position to go south to pick them up and accompany them north. All these tasks must have seemed almost impossible. As the letters demonstrate, even the most benevolent allies he found, both Black and white, were nervous about his ability to carry out all that would be necessary for these freedom dreams.

Hence, the next stage of Jackson's life was dominated by his desperation to find donations, to make sure the donations were passed along to white patrons who would have the cultural capital to be taken seriously as trustworthy individuals, and to coordinate such donations from many different locales so they could be consolidated to launch a preliminary sally with the enslavers in the South holding the lives and futures of Louisa and Jinny in their hands.

At first, things went well. One of his first strokes of luck was making a friend in Martin Stowell, a white man working as a shoemaker and living outside of Worcester, a populous industrial city forty miles west of Boston and deep in the heart of the state.[42] As a shoemaker, Stowell wasn't part of any sort of white elite activist class. He wasn't a clergyman. And he wasn't the sort of person to redirect Jackson's pleas for individual help to instead discuss raising money for the antislavery cause more generally. Stowell was interested in immediate justice, immediate action, and immediate kindness.

And perhaps that is why he was the man to finally sit down with Jackson and really listen.

It was time, they must have agreed; between small donations and the savings Jackson had accrued from chopping wood in Salem, funds were accumulating. Not quickly, perhaps, but they were building. The amount probably wouldn't be sufficient quite yet—they feared the costs might be enormous—but now someone needed to reach out to the enslavers down south. Find Louisa. Find Jinny. What ransom might their captors demand? And so, in the spring of 1850, acting as a nineteenth-century hostage negotiator, Stowell stepped up.

Stowell wrote a letter for Jackson. The letter evidently inquired about Louisa and Jinny's well-being and asked what price it might take to liberate them. The letter they sent isn't extant but we can guess at its contents from the responses it received.

Jackson and Stowell may have added a few other remarks. Stowell and Jackson probably couldn't have restrained themselves: Stowell was no carefully measured lawyer, and Jackson—well, Jackson was known for speaking his mind. Strategically, the letter should have been a bit of businesslike outreach. Keep it cool. Don't agitate any more than necessary. But despite the stakes, that would have been hard for these two. They were both men of passion. Jackson's fiery emotions had propelled him for much of his life, and Stowell, too, was known for his commitment to his beliefs. In 1854 Stowell was to attack a Boston courthouse that had imprisoned a fugitive, Anthony Burns. In this failed raid, Stowell shot and killed a policeman. It's hard to imagine such a man authoring a letter with Jackson that didn't express some of his or their feelings about what kind of people could separate a family and hold a woman and child in captivity.

Or perhaps they didn't. Even the most measured and diplomatic request for a ransom figure would have been an offense. After all, the letter was a repudiation of all that the slaver culture held dear—on behalf of enslaved people who wanted to be free.

Whatever the tone of the initial missive, it was met with a full-throated reply of disdain and only grudging suggestions of cooperation in redeeming the captives. The answer to Stowell (and Jackson) did, however, verify much of Jackson's account. It became a vital tool for Jackson to share a glimpse of the world he had left with his audiences in the North.

The response on the behalf of Louisa's enslavers was written not directly by her enslavers but instead by one of their neighbors, Henry Haynsworth of Sumter, who inserted himself into the affair as an agent for his neighbor, Igby Wells.[43] Haynsworth was then working as the postmaster for the city of Sumterville (later known as Sumter) and was conveniently in the middle of all these missives. Haynsworth acknowledged that both Louisa and Jinny were alive and well and did suggest a minimum price for their freedom: $800. This letter was so combative, however, that it was difficult to imagine an actual transaction could ever be agreed to or trusted. Indeed, it was so unpleasant that Jackson and Stowell provided a copy of the letter to a local newspaper in Massachusetts to underscore the validity of Jackson's cause and help advertise his upcoming lecture in Northampton, Massachusetts. The letter was found so illustrative of Southern thinking about slavery and horrifying in its own right that it was even eventually reprinted in *The Liberator* as "A Specimen of Southern Rascality and Piety" as a case study in proslavery rhetoric.[44]

According to Haynsworth, a letter had been received "*purporting* certain inquiries of a negro fellow calling himself Andrew Jackson" [emphasis mine]. Despite these rhetorical qualifications implying Jackson was a fraud, Haynsworth grudgingly shared some news of Louisa and Jinny, noting, "Mr. Wells informs me that they are both well and still the property of Mr. Law." With cruel mockery, he wrote: "Poor Andrew Jackson!"[45]

In the letter, Haynsworth wrote to the "said" Jackson in tones of indignation and disdain. While on one hand affirming Jackson's story, he framed his letter to deny him any ounce of credibility. Jackson was not a plausible man, according to Haynsworth's values—not because his story of family separation wasn't true, but because his humanity and character were to be questioned. After all, who *was* this Jackson, as he saw it?

Returning to his theme of discrediting Jackson, Haynsworth sought to persuade Stowell that Jackson was inherently dishonest:

> Recollect you are aiding and abetting a great rascal who was so dishonest as to run away from a kind master and to violate one of the precepts of our great Teacher, which was, "Obey your master in all things, for that is acceptable with God."

Haynsworth ended by arguing about how happy enslaved people were, citing their joyful participation in Sumter County camp revival meetings as evidence:

> I sincerely believe the negroes, as a class of laborers, are the most happy class of beings in the world. And I have often thought so when I have seen them together in the field, talking and cracking their jokes; or, at the corn-shucking, singing their merry songs; or, at the camp-meeting, joining in glorious hallelujahs and praise to a true God, and clapping their hands with very joy, that things were as well with them as they are.

Later, in 1865, when Haynsworth's house was occupied by Union troops who threw out his family and quartered themselves there for a bit, enslaved people fled the Haynsworth labor camp, putting a lie to Haynsworth's convenient delusions about their joy.[46]

Despite the vicious tone of Haynsworth's reply, Jackson's letter to Louisa's enslavers worked: he now knew the price of his family's freedom, and his life story could carry even more credibility, having been inadvertently vouched for by Haynsworth. Seeing that letter reprinted in all of its aggrieved rhetoric in *The Liberator* and other papers helped advance Jackson's aims. At this point, Jackson was now making the rounds of lecture halls in western Massachusetts, testifying to his story and gathering resources and sympathy as best as he could.[47] The Haynsworth letter, with its affronted umbrage and performative cruelty, was perhaps the best possible publicity for Jackson's cause.

By March 1850, Jackson had spoken with some modest success in Worcester, Springfield, and other Massachusetts locales.[48] He passed through Northampton, where prominent experiments in cross-racial alliances and enterprises had taken place in the 1840s. Memories were still fresh of the disbanded abolitionist community of the Northampton Association for Education and Industry, an ambitious project that had run a silk mill and farm with both Black and white participants living and working alongside one another. These revolutionary ideas and exposure to experimental thinking would have been abstract at that moment to a man primarily concerned with immediately liberating his family members—but their radical visions may way have made their mark on him.

Bucking a system, banding together, facing off against racist expectations about how families might live their lives, and creating a community of labor that was beholden to no one: decades later, when surveying the starvation, violence, and abandonment of freedmen in the postbellum South, these ideas and these ideals would return to Jackson. They could be handy.

While Jackson's memoir doesn't tell much about this first foray into a career of solicitation and advocacy, traces remain. Through the letters of others, we can tell he was making friends with people in both Black and white communities. And as part of his informal affidavits of credibility, it appears that he shared the reprinted Haynsworth letter in a newspaper clipping.[49] He was gaining advocates. He was going to need them. Sympathetic nods, encouraging applause, and warm handshakes were not what he was after. He needed money. And help.

Collecting money would have been hard enough, but actually consolidating the money and ensuring it was held in reliable hands would be even more complicated. Having the political, cultural, and financial capital and wherewithal to negotiate for the liberation of people many states away would require knowledgeable brokers. Maybe lawyers.

The complications of Jackson's dealings are worth examining. How, exactly, was he hoping to pull this off? His illiteracy, his lack of sophistication, and his general ignorance about exactly how his family might be found and redeemed were enormous challenges that illustrate how mere money (which he didn't fully have at this point, either) would not be sufficient in and of itself to enable these transactions. Geography, communications, and, of course, working around the craven hostility from enslavers down in the South were all going to be part of the task.

But Jackson had been living in the North for three years, and he must have had a good idea of what he was up against. He knew about the cruelty of enslavers better than anyone. He wasn't going to be deterred. He may not have had sponsors, an agent, or an official patronage group, but he could trust in himself and his determination.

The thought of Louisa and Jinny drove him, again and again, to knock on doors, present himself to strangers, and beg for help.

Jackson found allies. A young white Quaker from Worcester, Lucy Chase, took an early interest in John Andrew Jackson, presumably after hearing him speak, and was to prove a crucial friend. Chase was in her late twenties and perhaps a bit old for the marriage market at that time. Had her parents despaired of her ever finding the right match? Perhaps. But they also supported their smart and steely daughter, who was determined to make a change in this rough world. The best way for a genteel young woman of Worcester to build out her life without a husband in those days was to attend talks, lectures, and meetings to see if there were ways she might impact the world. And indeed, the world was soon to have a great impact on her.

Speakers such as Frederick Douglass, Charles Lenox Remond, William Wells Brown, Sojourner Truth, and Henry "Box" Brown had all come through Worcester for speaking engagements during the 1840s, and the Chase family took a keen interest in such events.[50] Chase must have heard Jackson speak somehow early in that year and tried to attend on additional occasions, making an irritated note in her journal when she missed one of his engagements: "Went to Spruce Street meeting . . . hoping to hear John Jackson, who did not attend the meeting."

It is hard to know precisely where or when Chase and Jackson first met, but this powerful young man made an impression on her. In an act a bit surprising for a young unmarried woman with no particular expertise in banking, legal matters, or cross-state negotiations, albeit with a dedication to abolitionism, she volunteered her services and those of her father, Anthony Benezet Chase, to assist in collecting and consolidating donations.

Chase's involvement with Jackson is known today only because of a couple of extant letters to her from influential figures in the Massachusetts antislavery movement. And it is thanks to her correspondence and archive of her family papers that we can get a sense of how Jackson had begun to move among a tier of activists that were beyond his kindly boarding house friend Henry Foreman.

The Black abolitionist Henry Highland Garnet, one of the most prominent antislavery activists in the nation at that time, must have met Jackson in Massachusetts at about this time. He reached out to Chase to update her about Jackson's affairs. On March 19, 1850, Garnet wrote:

> Madam Chase, A colored Gentleman known by the Name of Jackson called on me this morning, with a letter addressed to him by yourself asking information respecting the Name of the Owners of his Wife & Child in the South.[51]

Garnet updated Lucy Chase with the information about the Law family's whereabouts as supplied to him by Jackson and told her that Jackson suggested the best way to find his family would be to contact a "Mr. Wells" (a member of the family that had sent Louisa and Jinny to Georgia). In his letter, Garnet also shared that Jackson thought a man held captive by the Law family, named Enoch, might have good information about Louisa, writing, "Jackson thinks they can be found by him. Jackson seems to fear they have gone to Florida. Yours, a Friend of the oppressed, H.H.G."

With this request and reference to Enoch as a likely connection to Louisa, we can glimpse the agonized complications formerly enslaved people often had when explaining or justifying the relationship bonds they had constructed under constrained conditions. As mentioned in an earlier chapter, according to Jackson's discussions of courtship, his beloved Louisa had been forcibly married to an older man named Enoch for the convenience of their enslavers. Jackson had maintained his relationship (and marriage) with furtive visits to a woman he recognized as his wife, even if his enslavers did not. As Jackson wrote, "Marriage in the slave States among the slaves is absolutely 'Nil.'"[52]

Sharing these types of stories about relationships with even the most sympathetic of antislavery activists could invite painful moralizing judgments about survival decisions and unnecessarily complicate solicitations for assistance. Garnet would not have been aware of the agonized poignancy of this request.[53]

Garnet had escaped from slavery himself as a child and had family members still in bondage. He would have been one of the best advocates Jackson could have found. More than any white sympathizer Jackson might meet, Garnet could at least have an inkling of the pain and fear that Jackson carried. Nonetheless, Garnet had spent his adulthood in the free states of the North and had never had to face the situations Jackson, Louisa, and even Enoch had known. Keeping that particular story from him was for the best. However, even with his limited information, Garnet came through. In addition to writing letters for Jackson, Garnet almost certainly helped direct Jackson to even more advocates in the areas in and around Worcester, Springfield, and Northampton.[54]

Thanks to this help, Jackson made good progress in collecting funds, but confusion about how to handle these affairs continued. It was a bit of a mess. Transmitting and forwarding money was a tricky business in the mid-nineteenth century, even under the best of circumstances. And these were far from that.

Chase received another letter on Jackson's behalf dated April 1, 1850. This time, it was a communique from the white antislavery leader Reverend Samuel Osgood of Springfield, Massachusetts, who might well have met Jackson through Garnet. Osgood was known for personally harboring fugitives and for helping organize fugitives throughout the city who needed sanctuary. Jackson had made a trustworthy friend in Osgood and likely spent a few days with him, planning his next steps to gather donations. To help, Osgood wrote to Chase with details about how the money might best be collected. He also expressed concern that Jackson didn't really know what he was doing.

> Miss Lucy Chase,
>
> A fugitive slave by the name of John Jackson left with me $58 which he desired me to transmit to Worcester to your father, whose name he said was Anthony, to put the money in the bank, & he said he had caused a letter to be sent to you, giving notice of the fact, & that your father was to transmit it to Mr. Martin Stowel of Leicester. *He is so extremely ignorant that I scarcely know how to act in reference to his money* [emphasis mine]. I saw the kind letter you wrote him, & have concluded to write to you, & request you to inform me whether it will be correct for me to send a check on the Springfield Bank payable either to your order or your father—for the money. I will wait until I hear from you, & then act accordingly. If I send the check as proposed, your order upon it, or your Father's, will be my voucher that it has been paid. I hope the poor fellow will always find as kind friends as he has in you.

By now, Jackson was remarkably knowledgeable about the world and its cruelties, so Osgood's comment about his "ignorance" was both unkind and unhelpful. Nonetheless, Jackson did not yet have a good idea about how to transact interstate purchases of humans. As these letters demonstrate, digging out knowledge about his family's whereabouts, soliciting and holding donations, and then managing money transfers was an elaborate and painstaking series of negotiations. But he was learning more and more, and was increasingly able to leverage all that he learned.

Jackson was passed along through a network of antislavery allies who were assisting him in setting up speaking engagements, directing him to other charitable folks, and starting to organize ways for him to persuasively—and with accountability—collect money for his cause.[55] It appears here that Lucy Chase's father had been persuaded by his daughter to handle the business end of things. By 1850, Anthony Benezet Chase had served as the Worcester County treasurer for twenty years and, therefore, was clearly a reliable authority on fiscal dealings and local banking.[56] Things were surely looking up for Jackson.

By late April 1850, in what is the very first evidence we have of Jackson's direct voice (undoubtedly dictated at this point, for he wasn't literate yet), Jackson commissioned a letter to Lucy Chase, updating her on his progress:

> Dear Madam,
>
> I am still well, and still collecting money to get my wife from slavery. I want to know if you have received an answer from Macon, Georgia, also, and if you have received an answer, write to Doctor Osgood at Springfield. I am going there. And you may feel assured that my wife is in Macon, Georgia. After I go to Springfield, I shall come to Worcester but it will be some time. Mr. Ofley, a minister, has received ten Dollars to pay to your father for me. Just keep still till you see me.[57]
>
> Yours
> John Jackson[58]

Influential allies were well and good, but, as Jackson learned from the Haynsworth letter, he would need an enormous sum of money to purchase and safely transport the members of his family north. That $800 Haynsworth cited was likely only the beginning of the total needed sum, not the final figure. Jackson's appeal for help had to compete with other charitable pleas, and yet, thanks to the power of his pain, he did make an impression upon people who were not in the prominent positions of the Reverends Garnet, Offley, and Osgood.

As the summer went on, a local farmer, Eldridge Mann, sent Lucy Chase and her father $2 to help free Louisa and Jinny, writing, "I here enclose two dollars to you to be appropriated for the above purpose or as he says if they cannot be found he wishes to purchase his parents."[59] This kindly letter from Mann hints that Jackson might have voiced in public some despair about finding, much less freeing, Louisa and Jinny. Perhaps the letter from Haynsworth had made clear the obstacles ahead, or perhaps Jackson had heard other news that hinted Louisa and Jinny were lost to him.[60] Whatever the cause, things appear to have changed around this moment. Jackson's efforts from this point became directed more toward freeing his parents and other family members rather than his wife and child.

By the end of his travels to cities and towns across central and western Massachusetts, Jackson surely felt a mixture of hope and despair. He had hoped that his months of hard travel to find resources to free his family would have paid off by now, but the amounts raised weren't yet sufficient. "Not enough," he must have mourned to himself every time a collection box was passed around. He might have felt that he had failed. But he had learned a lot about himself and his abilities. Earlier that year, Reverend Osgood had characterized him as "extremely ignorant" and unable to advocate for himself, but that was not going to be the case going forward.

Jackson returned to the coast from his cross-state travels with new knowledge about how to agitate for his cause. Transportation was no longer a mystery to him; he had learned a bit about life as a Black man on the road in New England. He had spoken to audiences in public and pleaded with advocates in private. Churches, stages, and lecture halls were now familiar venues. He had learned a bit about how to leverage media, dictate compelling correspondence, and present himself as a plausibly trustworthy and increasingly public figure. These experiences would all put him in good stead for the future, more than he could have known at the time. Most of all, the connections he made with Black and white sympathizers during the spring and summer of 1850 were to prove more vital than he could have anticipated.

The 1850 Census that we examined to illuminate his relationships with the community of Black Bostonians and that had shown Jackson brazenly residing under his own name at Foreman's boarding house was taken during September of that year. That means that, after his spring and summer traveling throughout the state, Jackson returned east that fall and took temporary refuge on Ann Street with his Boston friends for at least a short time.

As before, though, Jackson soon needed better work opportunities than Boston could provide. That fall he returned to Salem to start working at the tan yards again. He knew the situation there and could likely fall pretty quickly back into routines with the friends and community with whom he was now familiar.

Jackson needed to process and reflect upon what he had and had not accomplished. He may have needed some time to digest any news he had heard from the South about Louisa and Jinny. He also now needed to figure out how to raise the rest of the sums necessary to free his parents. Had he tapped out his donors? Had his speaking engagements been disappointing in some way? Could he find a new angle in his presentation to appeal to new audiences? It must have seemed daunting but not impossible. What he needed now was a bit of grace, a bit of time, and a bit of luck.

Surely Jackson still had some optimism: he now had advocates across the state, some with considerable clout. And while he hadn't collected all that he needed, it was a start. He was so buoyed by his successes that spring and early summer in Worcester and Springfield that, while resting in Boston before returning to Salem, he commissioned another letter to the English family asking this time about freeing his parents, Betty and Doctor. Someone from Boston sent it on his behalf during this stretch of time.

Jackson now felt secure in his good relationships with people in Massachusetts. Salem offered him a modest but steady income. Perhaps he had dreamed that within a year or so, he might have both his parents, if not Louisa and Jinny, living in freedom with him in the North. Whatever his dreams were at that point, though, they would soon change dramatically—and not for the better. He had made mistakes that were catching up to him.

VI

Jackson's letter to the English family asking about his parents had somehow revealed his connection with Foreman's boarding house. The English family, most likely the Reverend Thomas Reese English, who was by now running affairs for his now widowed mother Elizabeth English, sent a man named Anderson up to Boston to track him down. Anderson was a man known to Jackson as "my old slave-driver" who had long tormented his family and friends.[61] Jackson knew him as a murderer.

> He was accustomed to being hired to whip negroes, and he used to revel in this (to him) delightful occupation. He would sneak about during the night, for the purpose of catching negroes wandering from their plantations, so that he might have the pleasure of whipping them. I heard since my escape, of my mother's death, and that she died under him. I therefore cannot but conclude that my mistress, who hated her, incited him to whip her in particular, and that, horrible to think of, she must have died under his lash. I believe, also, that my youngest brother, Casey, must have fallen victim to his cruelty; for I have heard of his death also, and that Anderson had given him some severe whippings.[62]

"Had I sufficient space," Jackson wrote, "I could fill a volume with instances of his wickedness and cruelty."[63]

Using the Boston return address provided in the letter, Anderson showed up at Foreman's residence with at least one or two other men, asking for Jackson. Fortunately for Jackson, Anderson was unprepared for his reception on Ann Street. The residents of that particular boarding house had experience with high-handed white men making demands, and they weren't going to acquiesce.

Foreman bluntly denied any knowledge of Jackson. According to Jackson, Anderson replied: "I know better, here is the letter he wrote home, wishing to know what he can buy his father and mother for and I now want to see him." Black sailors staying at Foreman's house, perhaps including some of his old friends such as Jim Jones, Frank, or Dennis, were not pleased by Anderson's inquiries. They said, as Jackson told it: "'Here are the slave hunters, hunting for niggers' and drove them from the house."[64]

While temporarily dissuaded, Anderson and the English family were nonetheless close on Jackson's trail. They were closing in, and the threat was real. After this incident, Foreman immediately wrote to Jackson, warning him to stay safely in Salem and keep far away from Boston.

As instructed, Jackson kept to his work in Salem, sawing wood at night and laboring in the tan yards by day, still thinking he could be safe while accruing the money he would need for his family and perhaps planning another circuit of solicitations or talks that he might attempt. He kept his head down. But national events were soon to take a turn that would render all his labors and all his dreams for naught. In the fall of 1850, the lives of

While this image of a tannery was taken from an 1884 issue of *Harper's Magazine*, the sight of long racks of hides with the smokestacks behind them would have been quite similar to how the tan yards of Salem would have looked in 1850.

fugitives from slavery residing in the North, already lives fraught with difficulty and fear, were about to change for the worse.

People who had escaped enslavement and lived in Massachusetts in 1850 could be recaptured under various laws stemming mostly from the federal Fugitive Slave Act of 1793. But it was a rare situation for formerly enslaved people to be recaptured from a Northern location and officially sent back. Northern officials, for the most part, were loath to prioritize enforcement over issues that didn't affect them directly. Moreover, various "personal liberty" laws were passed in many Northern states to directly counter the 1793 act. These laws, which enraged many white Southerners, allowed jury trials for people accused of having escaped from slavery, and some of these personal liberty laws forbade state authorities to even cooperate with the capture or return of fugitives. Therefore, assuming freedom seekers from the South kept a low profile once they made it to a free state, up through 1850 at least, they had a minimal but real amount of security, particularly if they had some friends or allies in the local white community. This security was, if not entirely legal, at least generally understood and practiced.

The Fugitive Slave Act of 1850, sometimes known as the "Bloodhound Law," now gave enslavers almost unbridled power to recapture people regardless of where they had fled. [65] It made the federal government responsible for finding, returning, and trying fugitives as well as prosecuting anyone who had assisted them. Section 5 even commanded citizens "to aid and assist in the prompt and efficient execution of this law, whenever their services may be required." This law limited protections for suspected runaways (there was no longer the right of a jury trial for people fingered by others as escaped slaves, for example). Section 7 of the law even declared that persons lending shelter, food, or assistance to a fugitive from slavery could be levied a fine of $1,000 and sentenced to six months in prison.[66]

William Wells Brown, the Black author and abolitionist who had also self-emancipated himself, observed that the Compromise of 1850 and particularly the Fugitive Slave Act represented a contest between the South's attempts to "make the institution of slavery national, and the equally powerful growing public sentiment at the North to make freedom universal."[67]

White citizens across the country had the luxury to debate, despair, or even delight in the act's passage.[68] The Black people of Massachusetts, whether free or enslaved, had no time for the indulgences of detached debate. As soon as the law was passed on September 18, 1850, they knew this situation was a game changer. Black people of any legal status had, in effect, fewer legal protections the moment that law went into force. And as for individuals who had liberated themselves, they knew that whatever precarious peace they had found was now threatened. For Jackson, it had one message: *Run.*

Jackson's choice isn't difficult to understand. Some fugitives might have been able to change their names or hope to fly under the radar and stay quietly in their Northern communities. Some had built up businesses and had families with ties to the area. But Jackson's case was different. Not only was he a fugitive, but he had become a prominent one who was living loudly under his own name with directories, census data, and a paper trail of newspaper announcements and letters providing clues to his whereabouts.

Thanks to letters sent on his behalf about Louisa and Jinny and then, later, the letter that asked after Jackson's parents, the English family now knew that he was in Massachusetts. Before this moment, they knew he had white allies in Massachusetts to protect him, as the Haynsworth letter demonstrated. But now, as of mid-September, that situation had utterly changed, and any such protection would be moot. The new power of the Fugitive Slave Act gave the English family effective legal tools to force his arrest and return quickly. It would take only one bribe from a slave hunter or one accidental remark for someone to point him out and have him taken up by the legal system. He wrote:

> Just as I was beginning to be settled at Salem, that most atrocious of all laws, the "Fugitive Slave Law," was passed, and I was compelled to flee in disguise from a comfortable home, a comfortable situation, and good wages. . . .[69]

As soon as the Fugitive Slave Act went into effect, a new era of bondage, resistance, and desperate freedom seeking was launched. Individuals and entire families began to flee. Nobody wanted to pull up ties, lose their savings, break with friends, and again engage in the risky and terrifying notion of fleeing capture and hoping they might make it out of the country's borders. But for many, there wasn't much choice.[70]

And so, Jackson came to understand that the threat wasn't going to blow over. It would have been in October or November when Jackson acted: he gathered his money and belongings and set off to seek freedom again. The danger was his, the challenge was his, and the risk of rendition was, of course, his own horrifying nightmare. This time, however, he knew how to find help. He could have confidence that his luck and cleverness had gotten him this far. Surely, he could talk his way to freedom again.

CHAPTER FIVE

"A GENUINE ARTICLE"—HARRIET BEECHER STOWE'S LETTER TO HER SISTER (1850)

Maine (November 1850–March 1851)

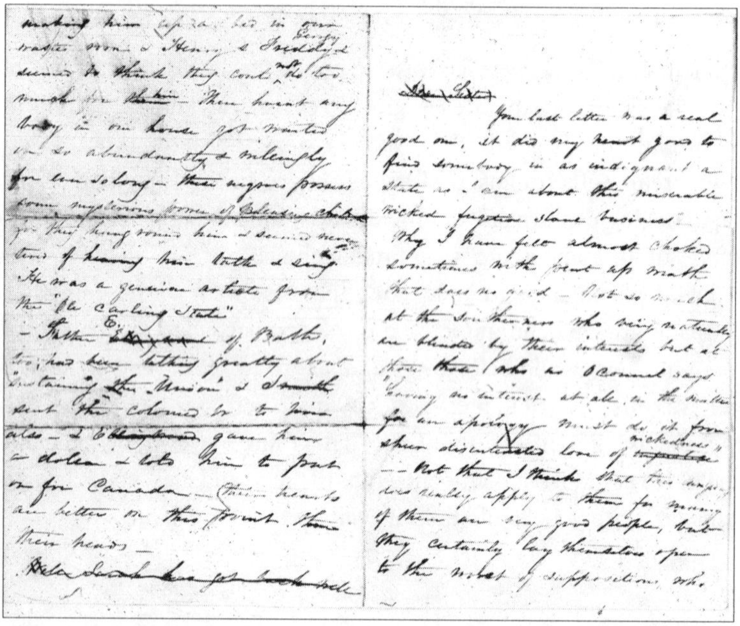

making him up a bed in our wash room & Henry & Freddy & Georgy seemed to think they could not do too much for him — There hasn't any body in our house got waited on so abundantly & willingly for ever so long — these negroes possess some mysterious power of blessing for they hung round him & seemed never tired of hearing him talk & sing. He was a genuine article from the "Old Carling State" — Father E. of Bath, too, had been talking greatly about "sustaining the Union" & I sent the coloured bo to him also — & E. gave him a dollar & told him to push on for Canada — Their hearts are better on this point than their heads —

Your last letter was a real good one, it did my heart good to find somebody in as indignant a state as I am about this miserable wicked fugitive slave business. Why I have felt almost choked sometimes with pent up wrath that does no good — Not so much at the southerners who being naturally are blinded by their interests but at those who as O'Connel says "having no interest at all in the matter for an apology must do it from sheer disinterested love of wickedness" — Not that I think that this [illegible] does really apply to them for many of them are very good people, but they certainly lay themselves open to the worst of suppositions, who

Harriet Beecher Stowe wrote to her older sister Catharine Beecher and told her of a fugitive who had made his way into her town and whom she hid in her home. The scene she sketched out in this letter inspired a similar scene in *Uncle Tom's Cabin* and may have helped instigate her entire book. The man was John Andrew Jackson.

With some savings and a few connections, probably with good advice from activists in Salem, Jackson set out north at the end of 1850. But where? And how? And what was he heading into? Jackson kept his maneuvers at this stage of his flight close to himself. But a letter from Harriet Beecher Stowe unlocks an extraordinary encounter.

I

When Jackson escaped from the English family plantation on Christmas Day back in 1846, he had put the ones near and dear to him at terrible risk. If we have learned anything about the English family, it is that they likely tortured his family members to see if they could get information out of them about his plans. Doctor, Betty, Ephraim, and others remaining in bondage in Lynchburg likely suffered because of his decision to flee. He was not willing to put others at risk again. We shouldn't be surprised that he is a bit cautious in his accounts about the illegal help others gave him.

Information about those first weeks of travel out of Massachusetts in late 1850 is a bit elusive. We must piece together conjectures with context and hints.[1] But the story unfolds when we look at the broader context of his travels and examine who he would have encountered. As always, Jackson made an impression.

Jackson seems to have traveled chiefly by land, likely moving from town to town, partly on his own and possibly with an occasional escort, knowing only in general terms which house to stop in, which communities to head toward, and which person to ask for along the way. Frightening, for sure, but unlike his previous solitary journey across South Carolina and aboard the *Smyrna.*

His discretion in narrating this second stage of freedom journeying had one clear exception. In an act of irresistible and strategic celebrity name-dropping in his 1862 narrative, he wrote:

> I may mention that during my flight from Salem to Canada, I met with a very sincere friend and helper, who gave me a refuge during the night and set me on my way. Her name was Mrs. Beecher Stowe.[2]

With these words, Jackson referenced the most well-known American writer in the world, Harriet Beecher Stowe, who began to publish her blockbuster serialized novel, *Uncle Tom's Cabin*, in 1851. He knew what he was doing. His encounter with Stowe, a meeting that only gets a few scant sentences in his memoir, was nonetheless an encounter that, quite possibly, changed the world.

Jackson affected Stowe. He was, she attested, "a genuine article."[3] When she sat down only a few weeks later with her experience with Jackson fresh in her mind, she started writing *Uncle Tom's Cabin*, a novel that was to help instigate the most consequential social revolution of the modern world: the overthrow of modern slavery.

II

To understand what brought Jackson to this place and this moment, we have to view Jackson's movement up to Brunswick, Portland, and elsewhere in Maine as a story of self-liberation. The danger was always his. The mistakes were his. The courage was his. The success was his. During this stage of his escape, he was assisted by courageous people, both Black and white. But that assistance was never assured and never secure. It was inconstant and always contingent on someone else's moods, funds, or even the weather.

Each step would have been tense. With hindsight, we might be tempted to think of his move through Maine toward Canada as triumphant; it was doubtless filled with some terror. Even with the optimism and tenacity that characterized his way of functioning in the world, he could not have known that he would succeed. After all, every step toward a supposedly more assured freedom also took him further and further from everyone he knew and loved.

Jackson took whatever money he had saved and got out of town as fast as he could. Hitching rides on a wagon or simply hiking on the road would be wiser than a stage or train, even if he had the money for any tickets. Trains, although there were many leading north out of Massachusetts, could and often were inspected by conductors and government agents who could ask uncomfortable questions. There were plenty of rural roads wending their way north out of Salem, and it would have been quieter to endure the frozen and bumpy roads on a wagon when possible and by foot when not than to draw attention with other choices.

As Jackson probably saw it, another escape by ship would have been too risky. Everyone was now on alert for Black people scrambling to get north. Even a sympathetic captain or crew on a vessel heading north might encounter another ship, be boarded by officials, or be inspected upon arrival. He would be foolish to test his luck with another sea voyage. And so he went along the coast, probably directed and occasionally escorted to sympathetic households. While archival traces of his journey hint at or provide small details about his encounters with white people along the way, such meetings weren't enough. He needed free Black people, people who looked like him.

They were far better positioned to hide him. He could pass as one of them. Town by town, then, Jackson headed north. He would have crossed out of Massachusetts and gone briefly through New Hampshire, probably passing a night or two there. Then, he would have entered the state of Maine with its long stretch north to the Canadian border.

Arriving in Maine was an achievement; every mile north was a bit further from Anderson, the overseer sent to track him. Thanks to the Fugitive Slave Act of 1850, though, crossing state borders was now essentially meaningless: there was no formal protection from the reach of federal law. And it was still a long way to Canada, with no standardized route or system for a fugitive to get there. Traveling from Salem just to the border of New Hampshire was over thirty miles. Moving along the New Hampshire coast toward Maine would have been at least another twenty miles. Getting from the Maine border there up to Canada (and the roads would become fewer and rougher the more north he got) would have been close to an additional three hundred miles. Walking the entire way in winter was almost unthinkable.

Trusting fate, he would have to move along as best as he could, altering plans when necessary, all the while soliciting whatever food, money, or lifts he could scrounge. He was ready to listen if he ran into people with more knowledge or better strategies for crossing that border and finding sanctuary. One foot in front of the other. Just accumulate the miles.

III

Maine was home to some of the most ardent antislavery movements and activists. But most people in Maine were not extremists. Jackson needed to be careful about whom he asked for help.

The truth was that Maine was a state dependent upon maritime trade, which meant that loyalties, for white citizens at least, were usually to one's livelihood at the expense of acknowledging the inconvenience of a moral stand against slavery. The state's primary economic engine was deeply invested in not alienating its Southern trading partners. As one antislavery editorial in a Portland, Maine, paper lamented: "It is quite respectable and popular, even in the city of Portland, to be identified with the slave owners—slave pirates and man stealers. It subjects no man to loss of caste or character in Portland, to be found on the side of the oppressor and man thief."[4]

And so, even in 1850, when the Fugitive Slave Act had begun to mobilize activists, it was only a tiny network that operated, sometimes effectively and sometimes not so effectively, to support and otherwise assist people seeking their own emancipation. Some coastal Maine hubs for activists could be found in southern and midstate locales, such as Hallowell, Bath, Topsham, Brunswick, and Portland. Such hubs were usually where a free Black community or at least a few Black residents lived alongside a couple of white families with antislavery sympathies.

When people imagine the Underground Railroad's workings, they often think of a highly covert and organized system. There is some truth to that. Organizers and central conductors did exist in some places. As they became increasingly experienced, many of these Black and white activists developed hiding places and ways to collect and organize the considerable finances necessary to operate these endeavors (supplies, bribes, tickets, and so on). On the other hand, people fleeing on the UGRR rarely experienced it in a predictable or organized manner, particularly in the flurry of months right after the 1850 Fugitive Slave Act passed and the number of people seeking to escape from the Northern states, as well as the Southern states, grew. Plans could be haphazard and unclear.

Uncertainty abounded. Fugitives might be directed from place to place by people who were generally sympathetic but not necessarily clear on what might happen at the next stop: Could they be sure that a person was home and would welcome a strange fugitive showing up at the door? What happened to Jackson was probably fairly typical for this region and at this point. He probably had a list of names in his head that he had been told to ask for when reaching a certain town. One of those people might shelter him for a night or two and help him with transport or directions to the next town. The cold weather of winter in New England wouldn't make travel easy. Jackson would have needed to stay put in some places for days or weeks at a time, ideally with other Black families or communities where he would be less conspicuous. While there, he had to make himself useful and at least try to earn his keep and possibly earn funds to help move forward. He wouldn't want to lose touch with the white activists, though, and would probably need to keep checking in with them until they could coordinate his next steps.

Brunswick, Maine, was and is still a small college town on the coast. By the mid-nineteenth century, it was known as the home of Bowdoin College, a small but prestigious institution that catered to New England's elite and prosperous families. Also at that time, lumber was a significant industry there, mainly for shipbuilding, and Brunswick boasted a small but active port and, notably, a cotton mill—dependent upon bales from the Southern states.

Somehow or another, Jackson had been directed to the home of one of the most well-known antislavery activists in the state, William Smyth. Smyth was a Bowdoin College professor of mathematics and natural philosophy and founder of Maine's first antislavery newspaper, the *Advocate of Freedom*.

Most important for Jackson, Smyth had spent decades agitating against human bondage and was an experienced strategist.[5] His connections and knowledge of the literal and figurative terrain fugitives would need to cross were unmatched. He had helped fugitives before, and his experience and commitment now meant he was a central organizer for the latest desperate influx of freedom seekers.

Despite Smyth's prominence in the movement, antislavery activists were always in the minority, even in small college towns. As his son put it, the Bowdoin College trustees did not feel the abolitionist cause necessarily advanced the interests of the institution; thus, Smyth and others still had to tread carefully in their balance between private activism and scholarly professionalism.

As Smyth's son later recollected:

> Brunswick, like so many other towns in Maine, had many citizens whose interests were involved in the cotton trade. I remember my father's being mobbed in Brunswick with some antislavery speakers. His house was one of the stations of the underground railway. Slaves secreted themselves in vessels coming to Portland, or in other ways reached that city, and friends would send them on to Brunswick. There was a black settlement about four miles further on, and they were helped on to Canada. I remember the wales and scars on the backs of the poor creatures.[6]

By 1850, Smyth was no longer a young firebrand. Now he was a weary middle-aged academic, but he was still ready to help. In addition to several older and grown children, he had five children under the age of thirteen, presumably all living at home with him and his wife, Harriet Porter Coffin Smyth. The Smyth family shared a two-story structure, with an attic, that was divided down the middle; another faculty family occupied the other half. Not surprisingly, he wasn't in a good position to shelter people on his

William Smyth (1797–1868). A committed antislavery activist and founder of Maine's first antislavery newspaper, the *Advocate of Freedom*, Smyth was also a distant relative of Stowe's. He was a professor at Bowdoin College in Brunswick when Stowe moved there.

premises for long. But he could help direct and transport fugitives to temporary resting places or otherwise onward in their journeys. As the longtime editor of his antislavery newspaper, he knew the local and even the national antislavery networks. Most important, he was familiar with the Black families in the area. Those families would have been in a far better place to discreetly shelter a Black man in their homes than he, a white professor living in a shared house adjacent to campus, could ever have been. He knew how to both address immediate needs and set fugitives up for some longer-term strategic planning.

After welcoming Jackson and probably sitting with him to scheme a bit, Smyth likely directed Jackson to walk down the street and knock on the door of his neighbors, the Uphams. Perhaps these neighbors might have food, comfort, money, prayer, or ideas to share. Smyth must have assured Jackson that he would be in no danger by crossing the Upham family threshold. Smyth knew he needed to keep his antislavery activities discreet from the Bowdoin authorities, so sending Jackson to one of his colleagues who lived a tad further away from campus and who didn't share a wall with another family, was probably a wise move. Jackson couldn't have known it then, but the door he was about to knock on was to become immortalized in *Uncle Tom's Cabin*.

IV

To get at the truth of what happened next, we can align our limited information from Jackson with an extraordinary account written by Smyth's distant relative and Brunswick neighbor, Harriet Beecher Stowe.[7]

Stowe was, at that time, a busy mother, keeping house with an infant, an Irish wet nurse, a handful of older children, and a husband who, for much of that year, was often, and annoyingly, absent. Their family had moved to

Harriet Beecher Stowe.

Brunswick only a few months earlier so her husband could start a job at Bowdoin College.

By the fall of 1850, she was facing her first long winter in Maine. She was an occasional magazine writer and had seen some success with her short stories but had not yet written anything that had attracted much national attention. She had been raising a bevy of children, and finding focused time to write had always been a challenge. Brunswick was working out well for her overall, although her house was a bit rickety for the rent they were paying, and the settling-in process without her husband around was irksome. But it would do. And if she could just bring in a bit more money and if her husband would finally just come to Maine permanently, it promised to be a good life.

Harriet Beecher Stowe's husband, Calvin Stowe, had achieved prominence as a theologian and scholar. He had taught at Lane Seminary in Ohio for over eighteen years. However, Calvin Stowe was lured away by an offer of a named professorship at his alma mater, Bowdoin College, a job that would allow his family to return to New England. Born and raised in Connecticut, Harriet was joyful at the notion of returning East and leaving Ohio far behind. Her sixth child, an infant son, had died in an Ohio cholera epidemic in 1849. The idea of a fresh start, somewhere far from that tragedy, must have seemed like a godsend.[8] By early 1850 she was pregnant again and, while still grieving her loss, could begin to raise her eyes to the future.

Inconveniently for everyone, especially his newly aggrieved employers at Bowdoin College, who expected him to begin teaching that fall, Calvin Stowe promised to finish a winter term (late 1850 through early 1851) teaching at the Lane Seminary before taking up his new position at Bowdoin. He had not communicated his situation and commitments very well to any of the concerned parties, and it was a mess.[9]

Thus, Calvin Stowe sent his pregnant wife and children ahead from Ohio to Maine to organize their new household alone. Advanced pregnancy would make travel difficult, so Harriet was in a bit of a race to get to Maine before she was too far along. With several stops to visit relatives along the way, she set out for Maine in April 1850. She was well settled into her Brunswick rental house close to the campus by the beginning of July, when she gave birth to her seventh child, a son, Charles Edward.

While Stowe was nurturing her newborn son, she followed with horror the debates over the evolving Compromise of 1850 and the consequent passage of the Fugitive Slave Act. Thus, only a few weeks after giving birth,

The Titcomb house at 63 Federal Street in Brunswick, Maine (now known as the Stowe House and owned by Bowdoin College), was rented by the Stowe family from 1850–1852. Initially built for a printer's family, it also boarded students, including the poet Henry Wadsworth Longfellow in the 1820s. The white clapboard house was an attractive structure but needed a lot of repairs and upkeep that the landlord was slow to provide. Stowe fretted about needing to publish more to help defray household expenses and cover their rent. In later decades many modifications were made, and it operated as an inn and a college dormitory. It has since been restored and houses faculty offices and public exhibit space. It is currently a National Historic Landmark and a National Underground Railroad Network to Freedom site.

in August 1850 she published a sketch in the *National Era* titled "The Freeman's Dream."[10] In this tale, she imagined a farmer who refused to help a desperate family of fugitives out of fear of violating the new law. Eventually, however, he was to face a more horrific justice. As the story went, his confrontation in the afterlife made it clear that God's judgment of his sins was more consequential than any earthly legal punishment.

Although President Abraham Lincoln famously credited Stowe as "the little lady who started" the Civil War, at least with this early short story, she could not stop the course of events. It's unlikely Lincoln delivered that exact statement, but the fact that it has been seen as a plausible anecdote tells us how impactful Stowe's later work was to become.

The fact that, when the Fugitive Slave Act went into effect, she was already writing fiction about ways to respond to the injustices and cruelties of slavery in a domestic sphere certainly shaped what was to come in her own life. Stowe was concerned not only with the law's effects but also with issues of how to represent, imagine, and enact defiance of it at the very moment of its inception. She didn't know it then, but she was primed for craft and action.

With Calvin Stowe absent from Brunswick, Stowe looked to new friends for community. The neighboring Upham family, in particular, had swiftly become intimate with her and her brood, and it is easy to see why. The families had much in common: Thomas C. Upham was a professor of mental and moral philosophy at Bowdoin College and a reverend. He and his wife, the brainy and bustling Phebe Upham, welcomed the Stowes as kindred spirits. They were both large families led by intellectual and engaged parents. The Stowe family had six children at that time, and the Uphams had themselves adopted six children, so they all quickly understood the challenges of managing such busy households.[11]

The Reverend Thomas C. Upham (1799–1872).

The Uphams were a bit older than Stowe, and she probably looked up to them as models for a stable and prosperous academic household (after all, Calvin Stowe hadn't yet managed to sort out his different job responsibilities, and they had rented a house in Brunswick that was more expensive than they could afford). Life for the Stowes was still a scramble. The Uphams, by contrast, were far more affluent (Phebe Upham had come from money).[12] The Reverend Upham had been teaching at Bowdoin for years and enjoyed both rank and security. Their large and beautiful Federal-style house stood atop a hill near the college and was one of the finest buildings in the town.

Phebe Upham was a writer, too. She was slightly younger than her husband and was known as a bit of a loose cannon. She was generally loyal to her husband's more conservative views on theology and life and not likely to oppose him too openly, but she wasn't easily cowed, either. She was known in town for regularly arguing with the pastor at the First Parish Church over his prohibition against women speaking in church meetings. That same year she also authored a religious tract that told of the inspiring life of Phebe Ann Jacobs, a freed slave. (Various scholars have pointed to this tract as possibly influencing Stowe's later portrayal of pious Uncle Tom.)[13] Phebe Upham and Stowe became fast friends.

While Thomas Upham generally embraced the antislavery cause, he was also a cautious man. He served as the vice president of the American Colonization Society, which promoted the idea that the problem of slavery could be solved by educating enslaved people, freeing them, and sending them to the African continent. Not surprisingly, while he had a distaste for the Fugitive Slave Law, he would not support violating it.[14] He was a law-abiding man.

The intellectually minded Upham family was certainly primed to engage in a passionate debate on these subjects, but Upham himself was known for wanting to avoid conflict. Stowe must have had some understanding of where he was coming from. At this point, she was hardly a radical on the topic. She and many members of her illustrious family of preachers, activists, and authors had long been advocates of cautious antislavery positions. Earlier, her father and various brothers and sisters had advocated conciliatory approaches. For years they had carefully sidestepped more radical arguments for immediate emancipation and full social and civic equality. But that was no longer enough. She and her family, including her brother the Reverend Henry Ward Beecher, were now on a path toward more immediatist notions of antislavery action: people needed to be freed now.

By 1850, Stowe no longer had much patience for types such as Thomas Upham.[15]

As Stowe explained, with some frustration, to her sister in the following letter, Upham's mealymouthed hesitancy on the subject was shaped by his foolish notions of simply sending Black people away:

> He has got his mind filled with an idea of the negroes having been brought into this country in order to acquire civilization & christianity & be sent back to evanglise Africa & that our nation ought to buy them with the public money & send them off—& until that is done he is for bearing everything in silence & stroking and saying "pussy"—so as to allay all prejudice and avoid all agitation![16]

Stowe was, however, able to set aside her frequent irritation at the Reverend Upham to nonetheless enjoy his fundamental kindness and hospitality. This particular evening, though, demonstrated that dinner with the Uphams, as Stowe recounted in the letter to her sister, was ever one for lively debate. And while the domestic sphere might not be where decisions were made, as Stowe understood it, it could be where they were shaped. As she described it, Stowe held her own in a fiery dispute with Thomas Upham over the Fugitive Slave Act:

> He & I had over the tea table the other night that sort of argument which consists in both sides saying over & over just what they said before, for any length of time—but when I asked him flatly if he would obey the law supposing a fugitive came to him, Mrs. Upham laughed & he hemmed & hawed & little Mary Upham broke out "I wouldn't I know."[17]

And then, in a scene to be powerfully and poignantly recast in *Uncle Tom's Cabin*, Reverend Upham, when faced with an actual fugitive at his door, asking for help, was able to overcome his fussy civic scruples. As Stowe explained to her sister:

> Well, the next day there come along a fugitive bound for Canada & Proff Smyth sends him right up to Proff Upham who takes him into his study & hears his story, gives him a dollar & Mrs.

> Upham puts in bountifully in the provision line & then he comes here for lodging—.[18]

At this point, the story of Jackson and Stowe truly unfolds.

The Uphams directed him to the Stowe house, only another block away. As Jackson approached, he would have seen the light in the window against what was surely already a dark sky, for, in Maine, the darkness comes early in December. Stowe complained that it was a cold house, but it must have seemed warm and welcoming to Jackson.

Even if the Uphams had assured him that he would be welcome at their neighbor's home, would he have had the nerve to knock on the front door? As an unknown Black man arriving unexpectedly in the dark, that wouldn't have seemed sensible. He didn't want to startle anyone. He more likely went around to the back door and knocked until one of Stowe's children or possibly the Irish wet nurse opened the door. They would have been surprised, and even if the Upham name was invoked, they probably didn't let him in until Stowe herself came to the door, perhaps carrying her infant, to decide what to do.

As Stowe recounts in her letter, even with her husband away (as well as her teenage twin daughters Eliza and Hattie, who were staying with relatives for much of that year), she opened her door to this unnamed man and welcomed him in from the cold. She hardly had time or energy to take on a new challenge. She had a young baby in the house and three other children underfoot. But she couldn't say no if the Uphams had sent him along. The visit went well, she assured her sister, and she marveled at how lovingly her children (Henry, twelve; Frederick, ten; and Georgiana, seven) interacted with this charismatic man:

> Now our beds were all full & before this law passed I might have tried to send him somewhere else [but] As it was, all hands in the house united in making him up a bed in our waste room & Henry & Freddy & Georgy seemed to think they could not do too much for him—

Stowe continued with some racist bemusement:

> There hasn't [been] any body in our house got waited on so abundantly & willingly for ever so long—these negroes posses

> [sic] some mysterious power of pleasing children for they hung around him & seemed never tired of hearing him talk & sing.[19]

In a closing assessment, Stowe declared, "He was a genuine article from the 'Ole Carliny State.'"

The condescending ways in which Stowe generalized about Black people were consistent with her other writing and views, which were often rife with stereotypes. She seems to have been glad to host him but also glad to have him gone. And yet, her comments about his interactions with her children do persuasively portray an encounter with a man known to be charismatic, charming, and a droll raconteur—traits people who knew Jackson commented upon again and again. He was, in a word, a talker.

The storytelling might have been thrilling. Jackson knew how to work an audience by now. But another aspect of this interaction stands out: the children listened to him sing. Jackson loved music and later was to sing at lectures and public events. In his memoir some years later, he dedicated an entire chapter to sharing lyrics of what he termed slave songs and antislavery songs and unpacking their significance. In this chapter of his, Jackson included lyrics to a handful of songs, including a section on "The Slave Song," which he opens with his version of "Dearest May [sic]":

> Now, freemen, listen to my song, a story I'll relate,
> It happened in the valley of the *old Carolina State*:
> They marched me to the cotton field, at early break of day,
> And worked me there till late sunset, without a cent of pay [emphasis mine].[20]

The lyrics, as Jackson presented them, echoed a story that would have felt familiar. They chronicle the story of a man who fled from the cotton field on a "holiday" and took a boat down a river, keeping an eye on the North Star and thinking "of liberty." This fugitive then abandons the vessel and flees fast overland during the night before encountering a white man who observes, "You are run away." The fugitive talks his way out of this encounter by admitting that he was heading to Canada, where "all men were free."[21] If Jackson remembered the lyrics well enough in 1862 while in England to be able to recite them to his friends there, it seems believable he knew them well enough in 1850 to sing them for Stowe.

This well-known minstrel tune, in broad circulation during the late 1840s and 1850s, was known interchangeably as "Dearest Mae" and "Old Carolina State"—a title obviously taken from its second line.[22] Stowe's reference to "Ole Carliny State" in her letter suggests she thinks her sister would recognize the reference. Perhaps she and Catharine Beecher had attended a concert, antislavery meeting, or fund-raiser together when this song was performed. More important, it appears she was quoting Jackson singing one of his favorite songs.

Jackson doesn't mention the singing, but wrote more simply of the encounter, saying that

> She took me in and fed me, and gave me some clothes and five dollars. She also inspected my back, which is covered with scars which I shall carry with me to the grave.[23]

The $5 was generous; back in Salem, that would have been close to half a week's salary for Jackson. More astounding, though, is this rather shocking detail of a bodily inspection. It is a bit surprising in context: for Stowe, a highly decorous and modest individual with no man in the house, to have viewed Jackson in such a way almost beggars belief. Perhaps the horror of his tale gave her the courage to throw off decorum and ask or agree to view his scarred body.

What could this moment have been like? She would surely have ushered the children out of the space. Jackson would have told her soberly and probably in ways she couldn't have fully comprehended of the whippings he had survived. At this point he was in his late twenties or early thirties at most and had been laboring in the tan yards of Salem and chopping wood in the previous years, so he doubtless cut a formidable and muscular figure. Revealing one's scars upon request was a common, albeit distasteful, practice for Black people put in positions where they needed to use their bodies as evidence of atrocities or to underscore with their flesh the truth of their experiences. But for Jackson to have bared his body to her hints that there was more power to this encounter than Stowe revealed in her rather breezy letter to her sister. They shared an intimate and harrowing moment.

Whether it was Stowe's keen interest, her children's kindness, or her warm home on a cold evening, the encounter certainly stayed with him, too. In his memoir, he sketched out the scene a bit further: "She listened with great interest to my story and sympathized with me when I told her how long I had been parted from my wife Louisa and my daughter Jinny, and perhaps, for ever."[24]

Despite the heartfelt talks and happy times with the eager children waiting on him, the visit was brief. Spending more than a short time in a household full of chatty children might have seemed unwise, and the runaway was directed elsewhere the next day.

What happened then? It would have been dark and cold, but Jackson would have roused himself in the small waste room behind the chimney and offered to help around the house. The waste room was a long narrow closet-like space, likely filled with kitchen trash and perhaps even excess furniture or additional pantry supplies. What with the kitchen (and perhaps even human waste) temporarily stored in this room, it might not have smelled good.

Jackson had seen far worse sleeping arrangements, though. Back in South Carolina, he and other enslaved workers were often denied shoes, which, as he explained, meant that their feet would freeze, swell, and crack. Upon awakening, they sometimes discovered that rats "had actually eaten a part of our feet."[25] Stowe's waste room would have felt luxurious in comparison. The cold in the Brunswick house, particularly in this uninsulated waste room not designed for sleeping, was intense, so the children's blankets and comforts would have been appreciated. The room still exists in the exact layout of the house today. It wraps back from the rear side of the chimney, so it probably benefited from that remaining heat, and while not exactly cozy, it would have been tolerable enough to support a decent night's sleep.

Perhaps that morning he brought up some coal, chopped some firewood, carried out trash and slop basins, or briefly lent a strong arm around this house. Stowe was short on money those days, as Calvin Stowe's salary wasn't sufficient to cover their rent and expenses. She couldn't have offered Jackson steady work or security. The best she could do was to direct him generally toward Bath, a larger seaport community only a few miles away from Brunswick. Smyth had presumably counseled Jackson to head that way not only because there was the possibility of a few sympathetic white patrons to be found there, but, more important, because the area between Bath and Brunswick had a free Black community where he might find more sustained shelter, sanctuary, or guidance.

She had one last thing she could offer, though: Stowe found some better clothes for Jackson to take with him. Since the only males in the house were her preadolescent sons, the male clothes she must have shared would have been her husband's. And so, Jackson set out that morning fed and encouraged. He leaned into the wind and weather with Calvin Stowe's old clothes shielding him from the elements.

It is tempting to speculate about what more Jackson might have told Stowe on the night, but we can never ultimately know much more than the historical record has given us. Perhaps the pivotal nature of the incident lies in its domestic presence. It happened in her home, at her hearth.

Only a few weeks after meeting Jackson, between January and early March 1851, Stowe sat in the Upham family's church pew in the First Parish Church in Brunswick. Did she clutch the arm of her friend Phebe Upham at a sudden moment in the sermons? By her own account, something was revealed to her at that moment. She was overcome by a sudden vision of a Black man being whipped to death and saw in this figure Christ revealed. Seeing slavery now as systematic crucifixion—a system that was, in essence, a rejection of God—demanded action. She began to write scenes of what might have led to this man's suffering in her vision and planned out a novel that would warn of God's impending judgment.

This vision and the book it inspired drew upon a lifetime of impressions, research, knowledge, and experiences. Jackson was a part of that crucible of influences. His visit didn't inspire a particular character—for example, Uncle Tom; it was more powerful than that. Their encounter was a crucially instigating factor in her inspiration to write, to act. She didn't see Jackson at that moment of divine vision; she saw pain. And she realized that the only way abstract injustices could be addressed was to reveal Christ's face on anyone crossing your threshold, to render them real. Jackson had brought the suffering of captivity to her hearth and her heart.

V

Uncle Tom's Cabin became the bestselling American novel of the entire nineteenth century, famously known to have been outsold only by the Bible.[26] Stowe's book helped galvanize the most consequential social revolution in American history, the end of modern slavery The novel exploded onto the world with a force hitherto unimaginable, and Stowe and Jackson became caught up in its wake.

It started as an image. A revelation. But images weren't Stowe's tools. Words were.

Stowe was a newly inspired artist and a mother who desperately needed to supplement family funds to cover their rent. Calvin Stowe had budgeted $75 dollars a month for housing while the Brunswick house was draining them of $125 each month. Now propelled in part by her vision and in part by pragmatic necessity, she sketched out a plan for a novel and sent the packet to *National Era* editor Gamaliel Bailey in early March 1850. It would be longer than anything she had attempted before. That was all right. She had something to say, a great deal, in fact.

Bailey was hooked. The *National Era* signed on. It wasn't much of a gamble; Stowe had published a handful of stories with this antislavery weekly newspaper before. She was a known entity—both a compelling writer and a reliable contributor. Dependability would be the key, Bailey knew, if he were to promise an extended serial novel that was designed to entice subscribers. The *Era*'s circulation wasn't much to boast about—around 17,000 readers at the time.[27] Bailey needed something to get people talking. And paying up. The topic of the Fugitive Slave Act was as current as it could be, and yet little fiction had yet been written on the subject. Stowe's timing was perfect.

And thus, with some excitement, on May 8, 1851, the *National Era* made an announcement: it was about to launch an upcoming serial—one that merited full capitals: UNCLE TOM'S CABIN, OR THE MAN THAT WAS A THING. The editors were optimistic but parsimonious. Stowe was to receive only $300 for her serial novel, not even three months' rent. That was more than she had ever received before, though, so she accepted the offer and starting writing furiously. On June 5 the first installment appeared.

The story opens with a supposedly genial slaveholder in Kentucky deciding to sell people he held captive. The breakup of these Black families launches two parallel plotlines: a gentle and pious older man, Uncle Tom, is sold south away from his wife and children, while a young woman, Eliza, flees before the sale, taking her young son, Harry, with her.

Tom's tale involves him being sold to a white family in New Orleans in which a languid but kindly slave owner, St. Clare, presides over a household of enslaved people who wait upon his querulous invalid wife, his angelic daughter, and his visiting spinster sister from the North, and who, of course, attend to St. Clare's own comforts. Many scenes of this bustling and unhappy household focus especially upon a young, enslaved child named Topsy, who, although providing many comic scenes of relief, is understood to have been raised in abject suffering and neglect.

When that household falls apart, Tom is sold to a plantation run by a cruel Northerner, Simon Legree, who mocks and despises Tom's piousness. After much suffering at the hands of Legree and Legree's enslaved collaborators, Tom helps two women escape. He is whipped to death rather than revealing their whereabouts.

The flight of Eliza from Kentucky means that, as Tom goes deeper south, she heads north. Her escape is quickly discovered and some of Stowe's most thrilling chapters chronicle her pursuit. Most famously, Eliza leaps from ice floe to ice floe across the Ohio River while carrying her child in a wild and desperate attempt to make it across. Even on the other side, the Fugitive Slave Act allows her no respite. The novel follows her taking brief refuge from house to house. She is eventually joined by her self-emancipated husband, George Harris, who has also fled bondage to save his family; they face many dangers before making it to Canada.

While Uncle Tom was the titular character of the book and very much the emotional center, many other characters and scenes took on powerful and even iconic forms in cultural memory. Scenes of the mischievous Topsy, the witty but morally weak St. Clare, and the drawn-out death of Little Eva became commonplace references almost instantly. But one of the most famous and carefully drawn scenes, which Stowe titled "In Which It Appears That a Senator Is But a Man," clearly reveals John Andrew Jackson's influence.

This chapter opens with a conversation between Senator Bird of Ohio and his wife. Their talk quickly turns to the Fugitive Slave Act and their conversation unfolds much as the chat with the Reverend Upham back in Brunswick had gone:

> "Is it true," Mrs. Bird asks, "that they have been passing a law forbidding people to give meat and drink to those poor colored folks that come along? I heard they were talking of some such law, but I didn't think any Christian legislature would pass it!"[28]

Her husband, the senator, dismisses her concerns and belittles her understanding of such issues:

> "But, Mary, just listen to me. Your feelings are all quite right, dear, and interesting, and I love you for them; but, then, dear, we mustn't suffer our feelings to run away with our judgment;

you must consider it's not a matter of private feeling,—there are great public interests involved—."[29]

And then, Eliza and little Harry appear in their kitchen. Eliza is nearly dead from cold and exhaustion. Without much hesitation, Senator Bird abandons his legalistic compunctions. He and his wife open their home and their hearts to the fugitive. He quickly plans how to get Eliza to safety and even offers her clothes that had belonged to his own dead child, a young boy who had passed away only a month earlier. Mrs. Bird observes, "Your heart is better than your head. . . ."[30]

The unmistakable parallels in this scene to the incident when Jackson had knocked on the Uphams' door don't mean that Jackson was the model for fictional Eliza any more than his separation from his own family meant that he was a model for fictional Uncle Tom, who had been similarly separated from his wife. Stowe had taken the basic premise of the beautiful irony of Jackson's visit to Upham and played it out with wit and nuance.

Jackson's appearance on the threshold of the Upham house and then in Stowe's drafty rental had irrevocably changed things for all of them. Upham was now a lawbreaker. Stowe was to become a novelist. And Jackson—well, Jackson was to use this encounter, too. Partly in a transactional way, to be sure, but it also helped galvanize what was to become his own weaponizing of words. First, though, Stowe's novel needed to make a splash. And it would.

It's hard to overstate the novel's widespread success and impact locally and globally. *Uncle Tom's Cabin* was an enormous hit as it gathered more and more readers during its serialization run in the *National Era*. Indeed, the *National Era*'s subscriber base grew from 17,000 to 28,000 across the run of her novel.[31] And yet its success couldn't easily be measured or fully apprehended until it was brought out in book form in 1852. That's when this book began to change publishing history and, arguably, the course of the nineteenth century.

Only five months into the serialization (with many more installments still to come), the publisher John P. Jewett & Co. of Boston announced that it would be publishing a two-volume bound version of the entire novel.

At that point, and to Jewett's delight, it sold 10,000 copies in the United States during its first week and 300,000 copies in its first year. Presses in the United States had to run twenty-four hours a day in order to keep up with the demand. In Great Britain, the novel reportedly sold 1.5 million in a year.[32] Its impact was greater than even the astounding publication figures might suggest, for international copyright law of the period didn't cover the thousands of translations, parodies, unauthorized editions, spin-offs, abridgements, and other iterations of her intellectual labor in an international sphere. Of the millions of copies of her work published around the globe, Stowe received virtually nothing.[33]

Stowe could take comfort in the fact that her novel and her message was reaching millions. It might be enough to change hearts. And would minds follow? That was the plan.

VI

Despite all the detail that Stowe sketched out in the letter to her sister, she does not name the runaway. And while it was undoubtedly Jackson who, in later years, obtained a testimonial letter from Stowe, affirming their knowledge of one another, the evidence for exactly how he inspired her literary creations is a bit less clear cut, as discussions about inspiration and art ever are. How she handled those attributions, acknowledgments, debts, and disavowals helps us understand why Jackson's name wasn't present in the intense discussions over her sources at that time.

The explosive success of *Uncle Tom's Cabin* meant that its author was immediately pulled into the spotlight. Her authority to write on such matters was furiously challenged. Her authority, like that of many women writers of the nineteenth century, kept home in a domestic sphere, was a combination of personal experience and a great deal of mediated knowledge from her family and her readings. Stowe had met other men and women seeking freedom, particularly when she lived in Cincinnati, Ohio, across the river from the slave state of Kentucky. And many of those individuals doubtless influenced her writing and inspired her concerns. A "mosaic" of influence (as the scholar David S. Reynolds has discussed) shaped her novel.[34] Scholars have long speculated about the array of influences that went into the imaginative construction of the iconic Black characters in *Uncle Tom's Cabin,* such as Uncle Tom, Topsy, and others.[35]

Stowe had read widely of the desperate circumstances enslaved people faced, studied how they sought their freedom, and learned about the issues from her father and brothers, all of whom regularly preached, debated, and wrote about slavery, although often from evolving perspectives on topics such as immediate emancipation and colonization. One brother, Charles, had lived for a time in Louisiana, and as Stowe's story progressed, he came to stay with her to share his knowledge of New Orleans to help her create persuasively accurate scenes set in that region. Another brother, the Boston minister Edward Beecher and his wife, Isabella, kept her up to speed on the increasingly fervent conflicts over renditions of fugitives in Boston during this time. There was plenty to discuss.

We know that in 1833, long before Stowe ever met Jackson and wrote *Uncle Tom's Cabin*, she witnessed a slave auction in Kentucky. In Ohio, she once helped a family servant, whom they had mistakenly thought was free for years, escape from her former enslaver's pursuit. In addition to those experiences, she had also read several autobiographical narratives written by formerly enslaved people such as Frederick Douglass, Josiah Henson, Lewis Clarke, William Wells Brown, and others, and was likely familiar with some of the prominent titles of antislavery fiction as well, including Richard Hildreth's hugely successful novel of 1836, *Archy Moore, the White Slave; or, Memoirs of a Fugitive*. There is a long list of the different kinds of shaping influences that may have informed her book.[36]

All these experiences may have seemed paltry to the Southern critics who railed against her ignorance of the South after the publication of *Uncle Tom's Cabin*. Still, these experiences were sufficient for Stowe to create a literary work that would influence the course of American history.

So why does Harriet Beecher Stowe's brief encounter with Jackson in 1850 matter? How was her effort to help this man hide in the "waste room" of her house different from her earlier encounters with African Americans, whether real or fictional, free or enslaved, and whether mediated by the writing of others or experienced immediately in person?

Stowe and Jackson's meeting was different for several reasons: the time and context in which it occurred, how it happened, and the effect it had on her. But there was more. This encounter was different because of the identity of this particular man and the future he went on to make for himself.

Stowe took a fugitive into her home, waited upon him, hid him, and allowed her children to help care for him. She could never again think of slavery as a distant problem when it had arrived at her door in Maine.

By Stowe's admission, Jackson, who spent one night hidden in her back room, strongly influenced her feelings about slavery. Her children had sat and sung with him. Maybe he even held her baby or joked with her older boys. This interaction helped form her belief that domestic sentiment could have a political and personal impact upon the actions of men—that it could help them "feel right," as she phrased it in her "Concluding Remarks" of *Uncle Tom's Cabin*.[37]

If Jackson had taught Stowe anything about slavery, why didn't she mention him again in public? Why was he never cited in her 1853 exposition of facts about the institution of slavery in her annotated bibliography *A Key to Uncle Tom's Cabin*?[38] After all, other specific individuals were mentioned in this work as having helped shape or inform her literary creations. And, since she was intensely defending herself against charges of exaggeration and unreliability in her art, surely Stowe would have added as many real-life accounts of slavery as she could.

One of the first and most apparent explanations for such omission is that it is quite possible she did not know Jackson's name. He may have even not shared it during their furtive visit (this would have been the safest option for him). It wasn't until 1856 that he got back in touch with her, using his name, several years after she had written *A Key*. Moreover, his stay with her had been illegal. To make it even worse, he had visited her home when her husband was away, and thus the entire event would have appeared unseemly according to the mores of Victorian America. Stowe may have been a forceful artist, but she was acutely concerned with gendered notions of modesty. She was, after all, a woman who, as possibly the most famous living writer in the world, toured Europe to promote her work and arranged to sit quietly while her husband did most of the public speaking. It wouldn't have fit her persona to share a story in which she had once illegally hosted a young Black man, had him strip to his shirt so that she might inspect his body, and had him sleep in her house, all while her husband was away.

For his part, Jackson was surprisingly restrained in how he invoked his connection to Stowe.

Jackson may not even have been aware of the novel for the first year or so while it was being published incrementally and then when it appeared in book form. By the time *Uncle Tom's Cabin* was being serialized from June 1851 to April 1852, he was living in Canada and preoccupied with his day-to-day survival. He was illiterate and no longer in close contact with formal antislavery associations and their attendant cultural interests. It's hard to imagine he would have had access to or knowledge of the *National Era* and its explosively successful serial novel quite yet. By the time he became aware that his former Brunswick host was now the author of a renowned novel—the most impactful work of fiction published that century—and that he had figured in its creation in some way, he wisely chose to use her name only with her permission.[39]

The temptation to flaunt the connection must have been powerful. Many others succumbed to such behavior, much to Stowe's irritation. In a letter dated December 9, 1895, she grumbled about upstarts "going about the country representing themselves to be the originals of Uncle Tom, or George Harris, as the case might be," but she doesn't mention Jackson as one of those upstarts.[40]

While it is almost irresistible to speculate about what else Jackson might have told Stowe on the one night he spent under her roof, we can never ultimately know. Did his longing for his wife remind Stowe a bit about her distance from her husband? Did his longing for little Jinny stir Stowe's feelings as she looked on at her young daughter, Georgiana, making a fuss over Jackson?

Again, the importance of the incident seems to be the fact that it happened in her home, around her kitchen. A man fleeing for his life was not an abstraction or an inspiration. He was someone who brought the effects of the Fugitive Slave Act into her very house in Maine. Even her home in the northernmost state could not escape the pain and injustice she now understood as her shared responsibility as an American and as a Christian. Surely, she would have seen Jackson's visit as a sign of divine messaging.

VII

Jackson was undoubtedly the unnamed man who spent one night under the roof of Harriet Beecher Stowe in Brunswick, Maine, and, to center Jackson as the object of focus here, it is only fitting that we recognize his meeting with Stowe as fully and constitutionally mutual. He didn't just inspire Stowe. She inspired him, too. And with that in mind, how might we interpret this meeting's influence on another important nineteenth-century text—not *Uncle Tom's Cabin*, but John Andrew Jackson's memoir written eleven years later? How might his encounter with such an author influence his decision to pursue a career in letters and social change? Was this part of a long journey of self-creation that enabled him to assert that his own words, his witness, might matter? Indeed, it was so.

Like Stowe, Jackson drew upon a variety of sources for his writing. His memoir drew on spirituals and protest songs, Dickensian structure, and the shaping of other slave narratives. He invoked both biblical references and jocular humor. And yet, leaving aside the question of influence, we can still see that just as Stowe doubtless used Jackson in some way as the emotional impetus for launching *Uncle Tom's Cabin*, so, too, did Jackson likely use Stowe as part of consolidating the emotional and intellectual confidence necessary to put his own life story down in words. After all, while it is true that many slave narratives had been published throughout the previous decades, the audacious self-possession it takes to create a memoir should not be underestimated.

Jackson never tells readers how and when he learned to read and write. We can speculate with some confidence, however, that it happened when he was a free adult. Significantly, it almost certainly took a series of experiences with men and women of letters—people who put their activism into permanent textual form—that helped him come to the belief that he could and should write his own story. Notably, he confidently and almost casually claimed his name on the title page of his book: "By John Andrew Jackson." He pointedly refrained from using the by then rote phrase "written by himself" often appended to similar narratives. This meeting with Stowe would have been a foundational one for Jackson. He knew that his own life story was worth telling and that his words might potentially have the power to change at least some part of this world.

Stowe's influence on Jackson isn't conjured out of mere speculation. Jackson's 1862 memoir, *The Experience of a Slave in South Carolina*, was explicitly introduced with his permission as a supplement to Stowe's legacy. As the preface to this memoir stated, Jackson's mission was to discuss the evils that even Stowe had been unable to reveal:

> In aiming to arrest the attention of the reader, ere he proceeds to the unvarnished, but our true tale of John Andrew Jackson, the escaped Carolinian slave, it might be fairly said that "truth was stranger than fiction," and that the experience of slavery produces a full exhibition of all that is vile and devilish in human nature.
>
> Mrs. Stowe, as a virtuous woman, dared only allude to some of the hellish works of slavery—it was too foul to sully her pen; but the time is come when iniquity should no longer be hidden. . . .[41]

From his account, we can see that while Jackson never excessively capitalized upon the fateful past he and Stowe shared, he did move ahead with his life fully aware of the impact of stories, the courage of kindness, and the power of the pen to help him fashion his fate. Their lives and books became intertwined with one another and with the nation.

VIII

So what happened when Jackson left the Stowe house the following day? We know something about Stowe and how she processed what had occurred, both emotionally and artistically. But all we know about Jackson's next step was another key sentence she wrote in this same letter to her sister:

> Father E—of Bath, too, had been talking greatly about "sustaining the Union" & Smith sent the coloured br[other] to him also—& E—gave him a dollar & told him to put on for Canada—their hearts are better on this point than their heads.[42]

Here Stowe references the Reverend Joseph Ellingwood, a man in his late sixties residing in Bath, a town quite close to Brunswick. He had once married the Uphams and was a prominent religious leader in Maine. Although he was not known for radical positions on abolition, now, when faced with the human embodiment of what Northern appeasement and ineffective prayer had allowed to happen, things changed. In a decision similar to Upham's and similar to the chapter about the fictional senator and his wife from *Uncle Tom's Cabin*, Ellingwood overcame his scruples and opened his heart.

Bath, like Brunswick, was a town of contradictions. Although known as a "cotton town" because of the allegiance so many people there had to the maritime cotton trade and working with their white Southern partners, Bath and the areas between the towns of Bath and Brunswick were inhabited by a relatively dense population of Black families—by the standards of Maine, at least.[43]

Ellingwood would have been in the minority in that town in his benevolence to a fugitive. But there would have been enough Black people in that location for Jackson to have a good chance at finding a place to hunker down for a while. This area was second only to Portland in the number of

Black inhabitants in Maine at that time (the combined Bath/Brunswick area featured 220 Black people according to the 1850 Census).[44] These people, primarily employed in ship construction, timber, domestic work, and general maritime trades, were poor for the most part and probably didn't have much to spare in terms of money or food. But they did provide Jackson with options. He could now hide while he figured out who, exactly, would be able to work with him to get him out of there and across the border.

The timeline of events next suggests that Jackson stopped bouncing from town to town for a few months and made his way to Portland (which would have been thirty miles south of Bath, but a significant detour that might have been worth it in terms of security). Portland then was, as now, the largest city in Maine. It would have seemed like a better place to pass the winter than Bath. In this vibrant urban port, there was an even more dense cluster of Black families to hide among and, unlike the "cotton town" of Bath, it was a city where he might find more white patrons to lend money and provide counsel.[45]

It wasn't going to be easy. White citizens of Maine were broadly sympathetic to the cause of unionism between the North and the South at all costs. Most white people in Portland were willing to appease their Southern neighbors and their practices of human bondage to keep going the economic engine that the coastal cotton trade provided. There were plenty of people in Portland who would turn a supposed fugitive over to the authorities. But staying there would allow Jackson to cease the door-to-door begging, which surely was both draining and stressful, at best. Biding his time in Portland would provide him with time to regroup and strategize, save money for an unknown future, and, most of all, figure out whom he might fully trust.

IX

The winter in Maine between 1850 and 1851 was terribly, frightfully cold. Stowe herself wrote lengthy letters complaining about her need for a better furnace in the face of the bitter weather, with biscuits freezing to the counter and water freezing in pails throughout the house they rented in Brunswick: "Everybody says that we have not had so severe a winter for fifteen years. . . . It is intensely cold."[46]

For Stowe, the discomfort in her domestic sphere was no small matter, with an infant and young children at home. The impact of this weather was far more significant, however, for John Andrew Jackson, who by January

1851 was in Portland, Maine, waiting to find a way to Canada.[47] With no rail link yet across the border from Portland to Canada (although one was completed only two years later), and cold weather making a land crossing unwise, Jackson was forced to plan for a water route.[48] He would need to quietly board some ship that would take him out of the country and to a place where he could find shelter, some assistance, and build a life in freedom. And, as before, he would need to secure a sympathetic crew, resources for survival and settlements, a plan for his destination, and a way to account for himself across an international border. After his experiences on the *Smyrna*, he knew this wasn't a given. This was all going to take some time. And money.

Even though Portland was one of the busiest maritime cities in North America, smuggling fugitives aboard ships anchored in its harbor was no simple task. There might be a few captains willing to hide fugitives for no fee, but they usually expected some sort of money to compensate for the dangers of such transport. And, of course, the overwhelming majority of ship captains would want nothing to do with such activities. Worst of all, many people might well prefer to turn fugitives in to the authorities as the law required and perhaps accept a reward for their troubles.

Fortunately, Jackson connected with a handful of influential activists, particularly Samuel C. Fessenden (1784–1869) of Portland, who, working with a substantial and engaged community of Black families in the city, helped Jackson survive. Because much of this was done on the sly, we need to piece things together from retrospective witness reports. It is clear, though, that Jackson must have thanked his lucky stars when he was first introduced to Fessenden. The man had money, connections, and a commitment to the cause and knew the ins and outs of Portland. He was going to help Jackson get to freedom, for sure.

Jackson couldn't have known then that this meeting with Fessenden would open up doors for him for decades. In befriending him, Jackson linked himself to one of the most influential political dynasties of the Northeast. Fessenden served in the Massachusetts State Senate and the Massachusetts House of Representatives before the Missouri Compromise, which enabled Maine to become its own state in 1820, and he had also run for Congress and for governor on the platform of the antislavery Liberty Party. He was advanced in years, perhaps sixty-seven years old, when Jackson met him, but as an elder statesman and still committed activist with a bevy of descendants and ancestors all involved in politics and, soon, the Union cause, Fessenden was about the most valuable white man for a person fleeing slavery to ever encounter in New England. Jackson appreciated Fessenden, and evidently, the feeling was mutual. Of Jackson, Fessenden wrote: "I believe him to be a reliable man for integrity and truth."[49]

What exactly Jackson did while living in Portland under the sponsorship of Fessenden and the protection of the Black community there we cannot

Samuel C. Fessenden (1784–1869), abolitionist, state legislator, lawyer, and supporter of Portland's African American community. In 1848 he ran for governor of Maine on the Liberty Party (an antislavery party) ticket. He assisted Underground Railroad activities in Portland and personally sponsored Jackson as he hid for some weeks there. An ardent Republican and well-networked politician, Fessenden had connections that would prove invaluable to Jackson long after he had escaped from the United States.

exactly know. Still, we can assume it would have been both a cautious and hopeful time. Despite the overall conservative nature of the city's politics and the broader population's inclinations toward leaving the issue of slavery well enough alone, the Black population of Portland would have provided Jackson with advice, supplies, work, and perhaps a sense of community and family for at least a few weeks. According to the 1850 Census, approximately 395 Black people lived in Portland. This means there would have been a significant enough population for him to make friends, get a variety of counsel, learn about temporary and permanent opportunities to make a living, and, most important, blend in as needed.[50]

Portland was an enormously successful port hub for ships from overseas as well as up and down the North American coast. Thus, unsurprisingly, most African American activity in Portland was centered around the shipping industry. Black people held positions as mariners, stewards, sailors, cooks, dock hands, stevedores, and other related trades. The Black population was thus largely clustered near the wharves downtown, where Black families and workers would find community and stability or at least be left to their own devices as much as possible.

The Reverend Amos Noe Freeman was the most prominent Black minister in the city at that time and ran a local school for Black children (still a relatively rare institution in the 1840s and 1850s in New England). Freeman had his hand in leading and facilitating numerous civic leadership and Black mutual aid groups. As the leader of the influential Abyssinian Meeting House, a prominent gathering place for social and political activities, he would have been at the center of all activities involving fugitives in the city. We can be reasonably sure, therefore, that this would have been one of the first places Jackson would have sought out when arriving in Portland. The Abyssinian Meeting House was only a few blocks from the waterfront and accustomed to taking in destitute and desperate souls; Jackson would have found fellowship there.

While it served as a hub of Black life in the city, the Abyssinian Meeting House was only one part of a larger urban community Jackson could lean on.[51] Black-owned barbershops, hack stands, laundries, and secondhand clothing stores in Portland were run by savvy and experienced community leaders who knew well how to hide and counsel fugitives from captivity. Provisioning a person determined to make it north, particularly in the winter months, would require a considerable investment in suitable winter gear. The Black secondhand clothing retailers would have known how to advise

The Reverend Amos Noe Freeman of Portland, Maine (1809–1893). His leadership of the Abyssinian Meeting House in Portland meant that he was at the heart of the Black community. He was known to have harbored fugitives on more than one occasion. Probably well before Jackson even reached the city of Portland, he would have learned through the antislavery networks that the Abyssinian Meeting House could be a source of solace, aid, and strategy while he waited for the right time to smuggle himself across the border to Canada. In later years Freeman moved to New York and sheltered John Brown on his way to the raid at Harpers Ferry.

fugitives about what they might need, even if they couldn't donate everything necessary.

Other resources and probably some camaraderie could be found for Jackson and other self-emancipated men and women in the local Mariner's Church, which sponsored an antislavery bookstore and print shop in its basement. Jackson wasn't yet able to read then, but knowing he was surrounded by a tight community of people willing to educate and advocate for him surely would have been some comfort.[52]

No matter how welcoming the scene, Jackson wouldn't want to be wholly dependent upon those local Black families who had few resources and were often living on the thin edge of survival themselves. And more fugitives were arriving in Portland regularly with ever-increasing demands for help. Jackson certainly couldn't have, in good conscience, put local families or individuals in danger for harboring him for long.

Jackson may have stayed for a bit in housing provided by Fessenden or benefited from his patronage in some manner, but as was steadily the case for Jackson and other freedom seekers, staying too close to white patrons wasn't a sustainable strategy. He would have likely migrated first to the places where he would have been more comfortable: local boarding houses used by Black sailors coming in and out of Portland. Perhaps Foreman or Jackson's friends from Boston would have suggested likely boarding houses for Black men hoping to go unnoticed when stopping by Portland. He might not have been a sailor, but he knew the scene and counted Black mariners as his friends. Those circles would have been familiar to him. He knew how they worked.

It might have been tempting to stay in Portland. Jackson was a long way from the Southern border, and while there were horrible stories out of Boston about remanded individuals forced back into slavery, Portland in early 1851 hadn't seen too much chaos on that front. He had established good connections with prominent white folks and surely would have found some solace and hope among the community of freemen in Portland. While living in Portland, he would have attended church gatherings, antislavery rallies, and civic meetings. Given that he had experience traveling, soliciting, and public speaking in western Massachusetts only a few months earlier, it isn't implausible that he might have testified in church or shared his life story at interracial antislavery coalition meetings. For the garrulous and social Jackson (the man who couldn't resist going out in public to a camp meeting on a black-market horse), staying quiet in Portland wasn't an option.

And while we cannot be sure about Jackson's leisure activities, we can be confident that he would have immediately established himself with some sort of job to pay for his keep and set some money aside. He could chop wood, haul and load cargo, and deal with animals. He knew his way around the tanning industry. And he was personable enough to interview well. Surely those skills could be useful. He was young and strong, with a work ethic and a motivation to survive.

Jackson wouldn't have let himself be lulled into a sense of security, however. He would have known Portland could be only a temporary and uneasy refuge. He might make friends, but, again, he would need to part with them. He could never relax.

Even in Portland, where several of its leading figures were self-proclaimed abolitionists, there was no consensus about the righteousness of the antislavery cause. Local churches in Portland had a history of refusing antislavery societies use of meeting spaces. For many upright white citizens of Maine, abolitionists were simply fringe and cringe. Such citizens might not exactly see themselves as supporters of the institution of slavery, but the abolitionists were too much. To the genteel classes, abolitionist activists were pushy, loud, and meddling with something they probably shouldn't be concerned with. It involved another state, after all. They must have seemed delusional and annoying.

The opposition to the antislavery movement could, even in a Northern state, occasionally be violent: the first of several proslavery riots in Portland happened in 1836, for example, outside Portland's Quaker meeting house when an abolitionist was speaking. A few years later, in 1842, an especially vicious protest occurred. In that case, a crowd that wished to prevent antislavery speakers from lecturing at the Portland Congregational Church became agitated by their failure to prevent the event from occurring. The speaker was beaten viciously over the head and was rescued only because several women who were part of Portland's Anti-Slavery Society managed to pull him away. When, in 1847, William Lloyd Garrison, Frederick Douglass, and Charles Lenox Remond tried to speak, they were similarly met with a riot.[53] By 1850, Portland had some Black and white antislavery activists, but the movement still had a long way yet to go. They still couldn't advertise actually hiding fugitives in their midst.

And yet, ships came and went up the coast, northward into Canada's maritime provinces every day. Vessels were liable to be boarded or questioned carefully upon arrival. Still, when the time felt right, and a reliable ship could be found that knew its way into those international waters, action could be taken. Did a team of interracial activists select a particular ship for hire? Did some members of the Abyssinian Meeting House plumb their connections with friendly mariners? Who was willing to take the risk?

The most kindly of smugglers usually wanted payment, but some captains and crew stepped up to make voyages happen—with or without compensation. Fugitives were sometimes encouraged to leave Maine on steamships in clusters; on at least one occasion, a group from Portland left with twenty individuals.[54] Perhaps they had all been waiting together in Portland, or perhaps they had been picked up in groups from Boston or elsewhere along the way. Plans would have been a bit uncertain once they arrived in Canada; there was no official Anti-Slavery Society welcome wagon in Saint John, New Brunswick. But sympathizers among the citizens there could be found, and whether Jackson traveled in a large or small group, or even on his own, the networks from Portland would have made sure that fugitives in such circumstances would be met by someone friendly. Someone discreet.

With bedding and blankets for the short but cold voyage, they would now leave the nation for an unknown future.

CHAPTER SIX

RACE: UNITED STATES— THE NEW BRUNSWICK CENSUS OF 1851

Saint John, New Brunswick, Canada (1851–1856)

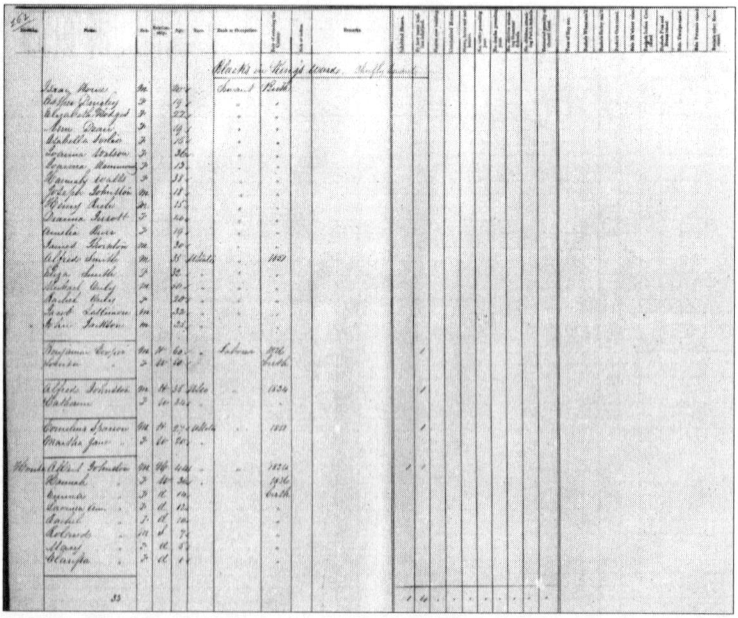

Page from the 1851 Census for Saint John County, Kings and Sydney Wards. Note heading of "Blacks in King's Ward—Chiefly Servants" and John Jackson, age thirty-five, listed as the nineteenth name in the far left column.

Once again, Jackson had to get off a boat. And, as before in Boston, that would have been easier said than done.

Disoriented, excited, and probably a bit fearful, the men and women might have been directed to a temporary place to stay. The Black settlement on the outskirts of town would have been the most likely place for them to find some refuge until they got on their feet, as it were. But the city of Saint John was not exactly a haven for Black refugees, and the Black settlements there were poor, with tiny lots and rocky farmland.

As one might imagine, there was no straightforward process for requesting asylum in a twenty-first-century sense of such things. The boat could easily have been instructed to turn around by a harried Canadian official. After all, the legal status of people like Jackson was still unclear. At this critical moment, Jackson would have to hope for the best.

In some ways, at least, that hope came to be. A new woman came into his life, Julia, but she carried with her troubled memories and a past as complex as his own. New friends in Canada helped him find his feet, but simply standing still was never enough for Jackson. And, with a quiet act of "guerrilla transcription," a clerk records a baffling bit of census data and signals to us what kind of world Jackson had entered and why he might again have to leave.

I

This chapter centers itself around yet another strange census page. By working through clues and the strategic restraint of information, we can see on this odd document how a powerful story of Jackson and the Black experience of Saint John emerges: a tale that grounds him again in place and community.

The 1851 parish census for Saint John, a harbor city in the British colony of New Brunswick, Canada, was carefully done, but it had its failings. The parish census taker was likely a bit overwhelmed because Irish immigrants had been pouring into the city for the past few years in tremendous numbers thanks to the deprivations and conditions of famine in Ireland during the late 1840s and 1850s. Keeping track of the old and new residents, not to mention thousands upon thousands of transient folks of uncertain destinations who were landing at Saint John simply because it was one of the closest stopping points from Ireland to North America, must have been a complicated census challenge.[1]

Hence the decision of the local census taker to deal with the curious status of fugitives fleeing the United States by separating them from the other residents of the area and aligning them instead all on one page and listing them by *race* as "United States" is worth our attention. Whether it was strategic or just a casual solution to a tricky question of ambiguous legal and cultural identity for those freedom seekers, the census takers of Saint John's County had created a unique document.[2] These records, in effect, gave Black fugitives from the United States some archival room, as it were, to elide a tricky and incriminating status.

That decision to simultaneously blur and clarify traditional notions of racial and national origin with this awkward census entry had the result of signaling far more than just *where* Jackson ended up in 1851. It signaled *who* he ended up with and hints also at why he did not stay.

Jackson is no help here. He does not devote much time in his memoir or in his later interviews to discussing his time in Canada. His sojourn there, however, was marked by several critical life events and encounters. From the brief two sentences in his memoir that encompass five years of his life, we cannot learn too much aside from the fact that he assumed his reading audience in 1862 would have little interest in his Canadian experiences. He wrote:

> I . . . finally arrived in safety at St. John's, where I met my present wife, to whom I was married lawfully, and who was also an escaped slave from North Carolina. I stayed there some time, and followed the trade of whitewasher, and at last I embarked for England.[3]

Indeed, Jackson's extreme reticence to supply information about his life in Canada is itself worth examination. Perhaps he felt it wouldn't have been of much interest to his readers. We might also consider the narrative effect of such silence. He was not only occluding what might have been difficult events to share from his personal life (such as his second marriage), but more than mere decorum may be in play. After all, by the time he was writing, he was in a position to know his life in Canada had only been a transitional phase, and he may have assessed it as of little interest to readers only intent on learning about his experiences in bondage in the United States.

And yet, we can learn a few salient facts about his pivotal five years there, which teach us about what this kind of refugee existence might have been like. In addition to his few remarks in his memoir, Jackson also hints about his time in Saint John in a handful of lectures which reporters summarized. Fortunately, a few small records from Saint John suggest a bit about his life there.[4] Because he was a fugitive and had experienced the terror of aggressive pursuit, it should not be surprising that while in Canada he kept a low profile as he tried to build a life for himself.

On the other hand, being Jackson, a low profile was likely hard to sustain.

Since few documents chronicle his years in Canada, we can build on only a handful of facts to cautiously consider what may have led him to choose a life of activism over a life of secure family settlement. When Jackson crossed the border from Maine to Canada in 1851, he was a young man, perhaps despairing of his future and of ever being reunited with his family. He had left behind both humble and influential friends in Massachusetts and Maine. At that moment, when he arrived, he was just another poor, uneducated Black refugee with few resources, few employable skills, and no family to support or sustain him.

And yet, by the time he left Canada in late 1856, he had started a new life. It was in Saint John that he remarried and established a social network. He made friends with fellow freedom seekers from the United States who would become key players in his future life. He developed a handy new skill, professional whitewashing, or what he later termed "rough painting," that served him well in future years abroad.[5] It wouldn't be easy to build a future in Saint John, but it must have looked possible.

When that future wasn't unfolding quite the way he had hoped, Jackson was able to pivot. In Saint John, he developed relationships with antislavery activists, both white and Black, who may have helped him in some way to pay for a passage to England. Even more important than any financial assistance such activists might have provided, though, would have been any help or guidance they may have shared about how to build contacts within the global antislavery network and how to survive, even thrive, when advocating for the antislavery cause once overseas. As he knew, connections were always the most vital currency a man could have.

It was during this time in Canada that Jackson may have begun to learn to read and write. Regardless of any education in terms of literacy, he certainly gained confidence that enabled him to imagine a greater notion of himself and how he might make a difference for himself and others.

Jackson was able to see what a free society might look like—not a fully equitable one, to be sure, but a nation with an economy and social logic that was not fundamentally or overtly predicated upon the torture and bondage of millions of its inhabitants. He was able to see a diverse notion of what it was to be Black. While in Salem or Boston, he had encountered free Black men and women as well as formerly enslaved people, people of mixed race, and people from the Caribbean or around the world; it was in Saint John that he would have truly encountered a Black identity that was entirely separate from the affiliations he had known before. The rich heterogeneity of Black life to be found in this region meant that Black identity could offer nuances that he had not before encountered. Most of all, while in Canada, Jackson gained a family—not to replace the one he had lost, but to build new connections of love.

II

Our last firm trace of Jackson in the United States seems to have been somewhere in the harbor town of Bath, Maine, in late December or perhaps early January 1851 when he visited with the elderly Reverend Joseph Ellingwood, as reported by Stowe. Clues suggest, however, that Jackson stayed in Maine for a few more weeks in early 1851, planning his future. As we speculated in the previous chapter, Jackson's next stop after Bath was likely hiding with

Black people in Portland, Maine, under some sponsorship from Samuel Fessenden, before boarding a steamer with a small group bound for Saint John, New Brunswick, Canada. He had most likely waited through the late winter or early spring of 1851 when more boats were available because the weather was less ferocious.[6] Only a few months later, still in 1851, John Andrew Jackson registered as one of the Black inhabitants of Kings Ward in the city of Saint John and was, according to the parish census, working as a "servant."[7]

And so, where had Jackson landed? This region was a destination that may not always have been welcoming to the generations of Black people who had ended up there, but an overview of its history does suggest some aspects of what Jackson might have experienced as he started to build his new life. This region had a complex history of Black settlement and, by 1851, could boast of several distinct kinds of Black populations. Jackson would need to learn to mingle and move between caste and class in the Black Canadian communities in ways that would have been entirely new to him.

Fortunately, with his swagger, Jackson was as well poised as anyone could be to negotiate such things.

The province of New Brunswick is a little smaller than the state of Maine and is marked dramatically by two Atlantic-facing coasts: one looks north toward the Gulf of Saint Lawrence, and the other looks across some of the world's most powerful tides in the enormous Bay of Fundy that separates New Brunswick from the inner coast of the peninsula of Nova Scotia (which then and now was dominated by the Atlantic-facing city of Halifax). Although Nova Scotia and New Brunswick have been separate provinces since the mid-eighteenth century, they are known (along with Prince Edward Island) more loosely as "The Maritimes."

Farming, fishing, and the European fur trade dominated the activities of the pre–American Revolution French and then British settlements. The climate of Canada meant that the region never developed the agricultural or labor-intensive staples for an export economy that would rely upon the large-scale exploitation of enslaved people such as had developed in the Southern United States.

There were certainly scattered enslaved individuals forced to accompany French or British settlers who explored and settled the region. And their enslaved situation was no less dreadful simply because there were not many people in similar circumstances. But with the new influx of settlers in the late eighteenth century, many of whom demanded and were granted tracts of land by the British government in exchange for their wartime services, denser settlements of European immigrants evolved with occasional people of color in their households and their communities in various states of freedom and dependency.

After the American Revolution and the subsequent exodus of British loyalists from the victorious United States, New Brunswick in general, and the city of Saint John in particular, changed dramatically. Many white Loyalist refugees settled in New Brunswick, perhaps up to 15,000 of them just in the mid-1780s.

Not surprisingly, the white Loyalist refugees brought with them enslaved people to ease the challenges of clearing land and building the rough settlement into what was to be a city.[8] One estimate has it that fleeing slaveholders brought with them an estimated 1,200 enslaved people to the Maritimes region.[9]

More surprising than Loyalists transporting people brought in bondage, though, is that some 3,500 formerly enslaved people were transported at British government expense as liberated and free settlers at the end of the American Revolution as compensation for their services to the British forces.[10]

These arrivals were sometimes termed "Black Loyalists," although these words can be misleading—after all, the phrase implies an allegiance to a political structure that superseded their identity as former slaves.[11] Their fundamental rebellion was against their enslavers, regardless of political affiliations, be they British or American. When, in the aftermath of the War of 1812, even more Black Americans (most of them formerly enslaved) fled in the chaos of war or were deliberately freed by British troops, they joined the earlier mix of Black populations in Saint John. All this complex mixing and different delineations of free and enslaved origins further entangled notions of Canadian civic and political identity for Black residents in Saint John. Truly, their world of Black identity demanded that they create an entirely new way of being. For Black residents, it was a city of self-fashioning.

By 1851, Saint John was populated with descendants of Black Loyalists who had never been enslaved and who had willingly settled in Canada; Black people who had been formally freed by the British and brought to Canada; the fugitive slaves or free men and women of color who had arrived at various points in time; and people of African descent who had forcibly or willingly come from the Caribbean, the West Indies, and Africa itself.[12] It was a confusing mélange! And that list does not even consider all the descendants from these groups that married and intermingled. Saint John was likely both as cohesive and as fraught as any community of such mixed heritage could be.[13] Records suggest that in 1851 approximately 1,058 people within the county of Saint John identified as Black, 505 of them men and 553 women.[14] What this means for Jackson is that it would have been a community big enough to find friends and allies within but small enough so that he could come to know almost everyone else within a short time of arriving.

Enough Black people lived in New Brunswick to create several poor but stable Black settlements—settlements that were, by supremacist design, set on the outskirts of the city of Saint John.[15] With few resources and little assistance, Black families in these marginalized areas gamely persevered to establish churches, schools, and cultural centers.[16] They were forced to look inward. They tried to take care of their own.

Thanks to laws that were part of the 1785 Charter of Saint John, Black men and women of Saint John had long been effectively prevented from fully participating in their city's society. Right before Jackson arrived, however, an 1849 amendment was passed to allow Black residents to become citizens. Thus, while Black people in Saint John had long been excluded from voting, practicing a trade, fishing in the harbor, or even residing within the city's center unless they were servants to white families, the situation was evolving.[17] He had arrived at a hopeful time.

The status of Black communities in places like Saint John was, of course, still marginal at best. Enduring the caste, class, and race prejudice of their neighbors, the Black citizens of Saint John were often faced with no choice but to labor as domestics or work in timber and agricultural labor for others. To make the situation even grimmer, the influx of Irish immigrants, especially intense during the Irish famine years of the 1840s, meant that a generally underprovisioned population (but, by virtue of their whiteness, higher ranked in the societal prejudices of the time) was placed in a position to compete with what little access to jobs and services the Black people of Saint John had enjoyed.

Thus, the local economy was under stress from the recently arrived Irish famine refugees just as American refugees from the Fugitive Slave Act started arriving. Indeed, at the height of the Irish famine in 1847, some 15,000 Irish refugees landed in Saint John.[18] Many of them left soon afterward for more western settlements in Canada or down south into the United

States. Still, many of them stayed, and they vastly outnumbered the small Black population that was already present in the city. This dramatic demographic shift in the city's population and the attendant legal constraints on Black employment would have jointly shaped Jackson's entry and assimilation into Saint John from the moment he stepped ashore. He was entering a city already deep in a refugee crisis and hardly ready to attend to the needs of Black fugitives.

It was some years later, in 1864, that abolitionist Samuel Gridley Howe observed of Black Canadian settlements, "The truth of the matter seems to be that, as long as the colored people form a very small proportion of the population and are dependent, they receive protection and favors; but when they increase, and compete with the laboring class for a living, and especially when they begin to aspire to social equality, they cease to be 'interesting negroes' and become 'niggers.'"[19] While Howe's comment about the casual racist disdain operating in Canada was generalized, it seems to sum up how the white society of Saint John dealt with its Black inhabitants. The abolitionist Henry Highland Garnet, Jackson's friend from his time in central Massachusetts, observed, too, that what he termed "color phobia" was as serious in Canada as in the United States.[20] And Ellen and William Craft, who had also escaped from enslavement and who spent some time in Halifax, Nova Scotia, seeking passage to England, found that in Canada they still had to reckon with the N-word, the prejudices of a Halifax landlady, and the racism of ticket sellers. The Crafts decried the "vulgar prejudice" they found there.[21] Black fugitives entering Canada knew all too well that hatred, racism, and injustice would never be stopped by a mere border.

In all, when the Congress of the United States enacted the Fugitive Slave Act in 1850, the city of Saint John wasn't an ideal place for fugitives or refugees to settle. Far more Black freedom seekers of the first decades of the twentieth century migrated toward Canada West (the area now known as Ontario) or borders near the Great Lakes and the settlements of places such as Chatham, Elgin, or Buxton. Saint John was an uncommon destination for Americans seeking freedom from slavery.

But there were some. Most important for Jackson would have been Robert J. Patterson, who escaped enslavement in Virginia in 1842 and made his way to Saint John by 1852. By 1856, Patterson helped organize an Emancipation Society in Saint John to agitate against slavery. Jackson would have undoubtedly become acquainted with Patterson and his work. While there is not much known about the Saint John Emancipation Society's activities, its existence indicates a rising and assertive politicized community of Black and white inhabitants who were intent upon engaging with and supporting the refugees from slavery as well as the people still in bondage in the Southern states.[22] There was space in the city for agitation. Jackson would have made himself known.

III

Despite the uncertain welcome of Saint John, Jackson found friends and work. Most important of all, he found love again.

On Saturday, November 20, 1852, the *New Brunswick Courier* announced that "John A. Jackson / Miss Julia A. Watson, both of Saint John," were married.[23]

There are few clues as to who Julia A. Watson was. She doesn't appear on the 1850 New Brunswick Census in the way Jackson did. And it isn't clear if she resided alone or with a family in Saint John for any length of time before 1850.[24]

In an interview Jackson gave, probably in his late seventies or early eighties, he noted that he had heard his first wife from South Carolina, Louisa, was dead, and thus, he was free to remarry. Since he recounts it over four decades after meeting Julia, this memory is a bit suspect. In an 1893 interview, Jackson said that back in 1850, he had arranged for a minister to write the English family with inquiries about her and had learned that she had been "married to another slave and a short time afterward died."[25]

In truth, it seems unlikely that Louisa was dead in 1852 when she had been reported alive and well in 1850 by H. Haynsworth, the Southern correspondent who had written about Jackson's negotiations in the incident discussed in chapter 4 of this book.[26] But death can come quickly. She may have died by the time Jackson was settling in Canada. Yet, perhaps, it was something Jackson felt he needed to say for his audience and believe for himself. His life with Louisa and Jinny might have seemed sadly but irrevocably over by the time he arrived in Canada. Now, in Saint John, it was time for him to start anew.

As he may have understood it, it was Julia who might give him new children, a new family. Surely they must have clung to one another and the hopes of a new future together in a cold world far north of all they had known.

Julia's origins may have been something she kept to herself or which she and Jackson shared only strategically.

A few years after their marriage, British papers described Julia as a "Creole,"[27] and the *Western Times*, using the condescending parlance of the time, praised her as "a fine specimen of her race."[28] The *Dundee Courier* ventured that "Mrs. Jackson would be designated by the Americans 'a bright mulatto,' "[29] and Scotland's *Fife Herald* (April 23, 1857) observed of the couple: "He is a stout mulatto, . . . and his wife, a runaway slave also, who was present, seemed to be a decent sort of person, with a shade less of African blood than her husband."[30]

The press was certainly intrigued by her. Perhaps with a hint of salaciousness? It is hard to say. The *Christian News* noted that she was "an interesting looking Creole, for whose capture a reward of 1,000 dollars was offered by her late master."[31]

If Julia intrinsically had a quiet manner or if she was publicly deferent to her husband as Victorian mores concerning public speaking would have it, we cannot know. She certainly accompanied Jackson for many speeches in later years, but, even when she did participate, she confined herself to only a few remarks. Any story about an enslaver offering 1,000 dollars for her has yet to be uncovered.

Julia did, however, occasionally let slip some details about her escape. And those details hint at a harrowing experience.

So, how had Julia first come to Canada? She asserted that she was born in North Carolina. Escapes from the Deep South were, of course, rare in themselves. Those states were a long way from Northern states, much less the Canadian border. And whether she traveled alone or with a group is lost to time, but her journey was unlike Jackson's. For while he had close calls, he still managed to make it north unimpeded. Julia, though, was to tell reporters that she had been recaptured and then liberated. The details of her tale were scanty. What hints emerge, though, offer clues about how she might have made it to freedom in Saint John.

Julia told a British audience that at some point in her escape a group of abolitionists—a group that included some women—had come to her aid. It is hard to know precisely what she said because the account in London's *Saturday Review* quotes an unnamed "Country newspaper" saying, "Mrs. Jackson also gave an account of her escape and her arrival in New York. An attempt was made to kidnap her, but, when being taken to a boat at Sandy Hook, she was rescued by a number of ladies."[32]

The specific incident to which this might refer may be lost to history. But we can piece together some plausible scenarios: "Sandy Hook" here was certainly a reference to Sandy Hook, New Jersey, a peninsula that, because of its prominent sandy outcropping into New York Bay, is one of the most famous navigational landmarks on the eastern seaboard. Often, passengers would be taken from New York City by ferry out into the harbor to Sandy Hook, where boats would then sail them to their destinations. The Sandy Hook lighthouse would have been a harrowing visual marker for any fugitive recaptured in New York and shipped out of the Northern states: it would have been a visual cue to give up hope. Beyond Sandy Hook was the open sea with its gulf stream steering boats south. It might well be a renditioned or kidnapped person's last sight of a free state.

How a group of abolitionists (a group that sometimes included women in their actions) managed to intervene before Julia was taken to Sandy Hook is hard to imagine, but studies of operations of the Underground Railroad in the mid-1850s offer some clues. Julia's rescue predated what little firm evidence we have for how such incidents were handled, but men such as Black abolitionist David Ruggles had been plucking slaves off ships in the New York harbor, often assisted by Black citizens of New York and occasionally funded and accompanied by white allies. Spiriting a fugitive off a ship that had just arrived could, if one was lucky, be a quiet affair. Liberating someone, or a group, off a ship that was about to sail south would be an entirely different undertaking—that project might require violent confrontations with captors.

While the paraphrased historical details of her escape are scanty, a probable scenario is that Julia Jackson had been liberated in a New York rescue mission—a mission led by a team that had the wherewithal to bring along female allies to accompany or comfort women or children who were being held against their will. Activists would have been most likely to intercept the ferry boat to Sandy Hook before the enslaved people would have been transferred onto the more defensible and quickly moving sailing ships. If this were the case, it would then suggest that Julia made it to Canada from New York City with the sponsorship or assistance of an organized group—almost certainly the biracial New York Committee of Vigilance.

This New York Committee of Vigilance was founded in 1835 but was increasingly active in the late 1840s and early 1950s—the years when Julia most likely escaped. During those years, the New York Committee of Vigilance was well networked with sympathetic groups in Syracuse, Albany,

Rochester, Boston, and Philadelphia.[33] While we cannot know the precise manner in which she was helped once she was taken off the boat bound toward Sandy Hook, it is unlikely she fled by train or overland in the manner that Jackson did in his route through New England from house to house. Not only was there no easy rail line from New York to Albany, there certainly was no easy rail route then onward to Saint John before 1851. And as for an overland route, it is almost inconceivable for a lone young Black woman to have negotiated the house-to-house glorified begging that Jackson seems to have endured for months on end to escape. Her route must have been different.

Thus, Julia Jackson's next stage of escape, if it was before 1851, might well have been, in part, on a barge up the Hudson River—a strategy used on several occasions. One account by a New York Committee of Vigilance member of the era, a white man named Charles Ray, gives a sense of how this would have worked: On one occasion, he stated, he helped a group of twenty-eight men and women seeking freedom out of New York, a group that might well have included Julia. Ray frames the incident as a typical, albeit somewhat larger than usual, operation:

> We had on once occasion, a party of twenty-eight persons of all ages. . . . We destined them for Canada. I secured passage for them in a barge, and Mr. Wright and myself spent the day in providing food, and personally saw them off on the barge. I then took the regular passenger boat [at the] foot of Cortland Street and started. Arriving in the morning, I reported to the Committee at Albany, and then returned to Troy and gave Brother Garnet notice, and he had I spent the day in visiting friends of the cause there, to raise money to help the party through to Toronto, Canada, via Oswego.[34]

Suppose this had been the route Julia had taken. In that case, it also suggests a tantalizing clue to how she might later have met Jackson, for the "Brother Garnet" who championed the activities of the New York Committee of Vigilance was the Black abolitionist Henry Highland Garnet, who wrote endorsements on Jackson's behalf in 1850. Nonetheless, such a route would have landed her in Toronto, and it is hard to contemplate why and how she might then leave Toronto for the smaller Black community of Saint

John. Perhaps she and Jackson met in Toronto or in a Black settlement he was visiting.[35] Sadly, Julia Jackson's story remains to be fully uncovered. But one way or another, her route brought her to Canada and to meet with Jackson. In November 1852, they married in Saint John.[36]

That a recently enslaved woman of childbearing age did not have children is worth pointing out, in a consideration of who Julia Jackson was and what her circumstances might have been. On September 1, 1860, the *Gravesend Reporter* noted with racist condescension that "Mrs. Jackson addressed the audience after her husband had concluded. She speaks English very well, somewhat in a peculiar American tone, but had the advantage of being brought up in the house and had been a lady's maid."[37] This assumption that life had been easier when enslaved as a domestic as opposed to out in the fields was mistaken and offensive, of course. But it does provide us with a window for some careful reflections on her situation.

When raising money, Jackson never mentions trying to liberate any of Julia's children, so she probably didn't leave any living children behind in North Carolina—or at least none she could tell Jackson about. We can also speculate that she may well have escaped from North Carolina at a young age, an age too young to have children. There is no indication of when exactly she arrived in Canada. Or, too, perhaps she was physically unable to bear children. Starvation, nutritional depletion, and arduous labor conditions could all play a part in infertility for enslaved women of childbearing age. In the decades to come, she never did have any children with Jackson, or at least no records suggest that she did.[38] But for a woman somewhere between nineteen and thirty-one years of age to be childless and having emancipated herself from a world in which rape was assumed, sexual violations were common, and children were forcibly bred to increase enslavers' stock, we might consider the possibility that Julia had been perhaps in a somewhat protected situation while enslaved in North Carolina.

Perhaps, too, Julia had been enslaved by individuals whose notion of ownership didn't extend to rape. Perhaps she had been a lady's maid for a white woman who had taken her along for a visit to New York—a visit which might have afforded her an opportunity to escape. These are, of course, all loose speculations. Yet while we cannot quite know what the exact circumstances were that allowed Julia not to have had children by this point, the possibility that she might have been in some sort of enslaved situation quite unlike that of Jackson, who labored as a field hand, seems real. This is important to consider, for, in future years, both she and Jackson are listed on a census as able to read and write.[39] Assuming this is true, we might even entertain the possibility that she had learned to read and write as a young person—a remarkably rare but not entirely unprecedented circumstance for an enslaved girl from North Carolina.[40]

But who really was Julia Jackson? She must have been remarkable. She and Jackson remained married for two decades, and any experiences, expertise, or trauma she brought into that marriage helped shape both their destinies. In particular, the question of Julia Jackson's literacy and how she might have learned to read brings us to John Andrew Jackson and how he, in turn, may have learned to read and write. When he first fled to Massachusetts, it was clear he was illiterate, and he had people write letters on his behalf. While in Massachusetts from 1847 to 1850, Jackson had been too busy earning money to have time for schooling. (In Salem, remember, by his own account, he worked at the tannery during the day and sawed wood by night.) But a decade later, he was authoring his own manifesto. Something had changed for him, and evidence suggests Julia's help. Did she teach him? What kind of partnership did they have?

Jackson probably began to learn to read while in Canada. After all, his whitewashing work would presumably have occurred during the daylight hours. While there is no evidence of any Black schools in Saint John at the time that took on adult students, the long dark days of a Canadian winter suggest that there might have been an opportunity for him to begin to learn privately.[41] And there were some schools for Black children where he might have sat in, as his work and circumstances allowed.[42] Perhaps if his wife could read a bit, she might have taught him. In all his memoirs, letters, and lectures, he tells us nothing about how or when he learned to read. But, as we shall see, in later years, the evidence for his acquired literacy is strong, and we can carefully imagine Julia working with him to teach him at least the fundamentals of reading and writing during their early years together in Saint John. Whatever happened ahead, they were to be a team.

One sign we have of the optimism he and Julia must have felt during these early, heady days of his arrival and acculturation to Saint John was that in 1852, Jackson registered to vote under his full name in the city of Saint John.[43] He was ready to be a citizen and a political actor in this new world.

Jackson, along with the other Black men and women listed alongside him in the 1851 Census, would surely have felt freer than they ever had before, perhaps particularly those who, like Jackson, soon registered to vote. And now, with a new wife and a recognized civic identity in his new home, Jackson must have felt grateful for the ability to exert control over his life again.

IV

What was it like to feel free in Saint John? And how would this free life allow the fugitives to carve out their futures? We can get a sense of the options and challenges Jackson would have had by considering the choices made by other fugitives who had landed in Saint John.

One of the best sources to understand the world Jackson and Julia now faced in Canada was a man who was doubtless Jackson's acquaintance and, quite possibly, a friend—the Reverend Thomas H. Jones. He and Jackson had a great deal in common. Jones had escaped slavery by stowing away on a boat leaving North Carolina. He arrived in Canada sometime in late 1850 or early 1851. He soon thereafter wrote a friend to assure him he was now safe in Saint John and gives us a good picture of what Saint John may have meant to the Black refugees there:

> I know it will be a source of pleasure to you to be informed of my safe arrival here on British ground. Quite free from terror, I now feel that my bones are a property bequeathed to me for my own use, and not for the servitude or gratification of the white man, in that gloomy and sultry region, where the hue of the skin has left my race in thraldom and misery for ages.

Jones went on to describe what it meant to have a sense that the government itself, the scaffolding of civic society, for once, might be on his side:

> The atrocity of the hideous system under which I groaned for more than forty years was never so strikingly demonstrated to my mind as it has been by breathing under the auspices and protection of a Government that allows all its children to go abroad in the true liberty of nature, every person free to frequent the altar or the sanctuary to which Conscience would lead him; no

> cause for degradation but vice, and no lever of promotion but virtue and intelligence.

Moreover, Jones, despite not being allocated the full rights of a British citizen, felt that his new compatriots embraced him. He wrote of New Brunswick:

> As to this Province, I have found a home of refuge, full of true, warm, generous Christians, whose hearts, abounding with the love of God, are full of sympathy for the slave. . . . The citizens of St. John have received me in the spirit of brotherhood.[44]

We cannot know if Jackson shared this reaction to the city, but Jones's enthusiasm may have been infectious, if not inspiring. And Jones's life had parallels to Jackson's, which can suggest more context to their overlapping lives in Saint John's small Black community.

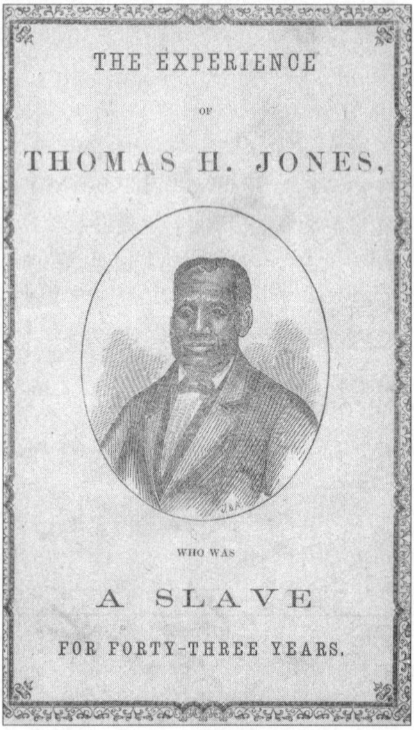

Image of Thomas H. Jones's memoir (1868).

During his handful of years in New Brunswick, Jones set himself up as an itinerant lecturer and preacher around Saint John. He also worked as an agent selling subscriptions to the abolitionist paper *The Liberator*. He intended to gather resources to travel to England but, due to poor funding and poor health, never quite managed the voyage. Even more telling, though, was that once Jones's initial joy at his freedom in Saint John wore off, he made the somewhat surprising decision to return to Massachusetts in 1853. Life in the British Empire had not lived up to its promises, and he felt the risk of return worthwhile.

Jackson and Jones would have crossed paths. How could they not? Perhaps they encouraged each other or, if they viewed one another as competition, they inspired or spurred each other on as rivals for the antislavery collection plates. Jones and Jackson could not have easily avoided one another in this small and tight community of Black residents in the Maritimes.

Jones and Jackson had mutual acquaintances, too, such as the ubiquitous Henry Highland Garnet. There was also an even earlier Salem connection: Thomas Jones, after escaping to the North in the 1840s, had, like Jackson, settled in Salem (a town where the 1850 Census indicated only 412 Black residents). And in 1849–1850, Jones at least occasionally preached at Salem's Wesleyan Church during the same years Jackson was laboring in the tan yards. Thus, while neither Jones nor Jackson mentions one another in any known documents, their parallel lives are telling. Indeed, it seems fair to speculate that Jones might have been part of why Jackson headed from Salem toward Saint John. Was he a friendly face Jackson knew he might meet there?

V

Another man whose name appears on that appended page of the New Brunswick 1851 Census, five lines below Jackson, and similarly categorized

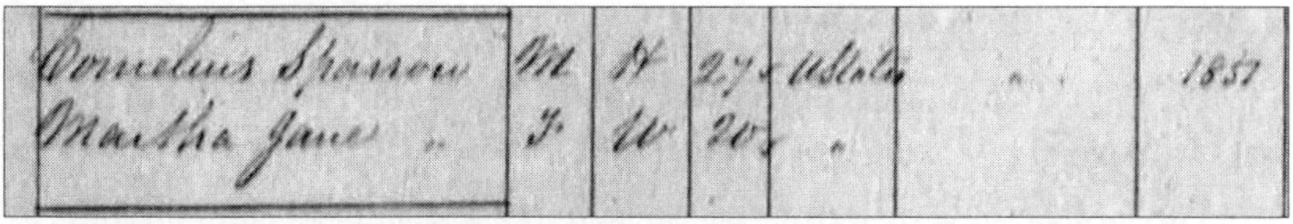

Cornelius Sparrow	M	H	27	U States	"	1851
Martha Jane "	F	W	20	"		

On the same page as Jackson and clustered in a group of eleven names under "Blacks in Saint John—Kings Ward" in the 1851 Census of New Brunswick, Cornelius Sparrow and his wife, Martha Jane Sparrow, are listed as arriving in 1851, and in the "Race" column, they, like Jackson, are listed as "U. States."

as "Race: United States," was twenty-seven-year-old Cornelius Sparrow. He was accompanied by his wife, Martha. Together they were one of the most well-known fugitive couples who had ever eluded captivity from Southern slavers. But it was in Saint John that they became known for other, more conventional, accomplishments.

In addition to showing up on the same page as Jackson in the 1851 Census, Sparrow appears in one of the most remarkable surviving documents of the antislavery movement in the United States: that of the account books of Francis Jackson, the treasurer of the Boston Vigilance Committee. In his records, Francis Jackson noted that on February 26, 1851, a member of the committee was reimbursed for having paid a "passage" for Cornelius Sparrow.[45]

Sparrow's presence in Saint John could not be ignored, for he, within a few years of arriving, became the best-known Black person in the town during the same years that Jackson was also there. Sparrow's singular life story provides tantalizing clues to uncovering Jackson's life in Canada. It offers insight into how savvy and fortunate Black refugees could occasionally work their way into solid and successful community positions in Saint John in ways unimaginable in their earlier lives.

Sparrow never published his life story as Jones and Jackson did. It is a pity, for the paper trail he did leave behind him powerfully demonstrates that the plight of self-emancipated men and women was endangered by the mere threat of the Fugitive Slave Act as much as it ever was by the actual enforcement of it.

Details about Sparrow's early years are uncertain. He may have been enslaved in his early life, but he may also have been a free Black man from Richmond, Virginia. Either way, he relocated to Boston sometime in the late 1840s, accompanied by an enslaved woman. We know this because Sparrow could not simply disappear into New England society; under the new climate of terror and intimidation for Black people in the Northern states created by the Fugitive Slave Act, Sparrow became entwined in an important incident that made his presence and that of his wife very public. This case made agonizingly visible the way in which the newly enacted Fugitive Slave Act enabled and encouraged all sorts of easy kidnapping and blackmail crimes against a vulnerable population.

In November 1850, Sparrow was tracked to Massachusetts and threatened by a Virginia merchant who claimed to own Sparrow's wife, Martha. This merchant demanded that Sparrow pay him $450 to stop pursuing her.[46] It was essentially a blackmail or ransom case cleverly strategized to be more complicated because the merchant also involved Charles Devens, a federal marshal in Massachusetts. The merchant promised Marshal Devens an additional $200 to pressure Sparrow to pay up. It was a cruel but savvy plan.

The threat of invoking the full enforcement of the Fugitive Slave Act was leveraged against Sparrow, who was presented with a choice: either pay up to purchase his wife's freedom and her former enslaver's silence or be fully reported to the authorities and gamble on the impossible odds the Fugitive Slave Act would present.

Loath to be an instrument of this enslaver's scheme and righteously rejecting the considerable financial incentives dangled in front of him, Marshal Devens refused to cooperate with the request. He warned Sparrow and his wife that they were in imminent danger. The couple went into immediate hiding. Within three months, Sparrow, accompanied by his wife, arrived in Canada, aided in part with passage purchased by the Boston Vigilance Committee, likely on one of the many boats plying the Atlantic coast route of Boston, Portland, and Saint John.[47]

Sparrow's story is a happy one. He settled in the city of Saint John and worked around the many constraints of the time to become a successful restaurateur and businessman. Like Jackson, he registered to vote and embraced his new Canadian identity.[48] He became a well-known fixture in the city and the African Canadian community for almost three decades before moving back to the United States to retire in Hartford, Connecticut. During the 1850s, though, he quickly became known as a stalwart citizen and entrepreneur. During those years Sparrow regularly advertised in one of Saint John's leading newspapers, the *Morning News*, announcing that he would be serving fresh oysters and fruit at his dining establishment. An additional notice to his advertisement, however, reveals a tantalizing clue to Jackson's life: Sparrow had a side hustle. He also ran a painting or "White-washing" service. It was a business he could legally purvey within the city, and while it was distinctly seasonal, there must have been a demand. In March 1856, for example, he declared:

> Notice!
> As the first of May is drawing near, persons
> requiring my services to do good White-
> washing will find me at my Oyster Saloon, 13
> Charlotte street, where I shall be happy to receive

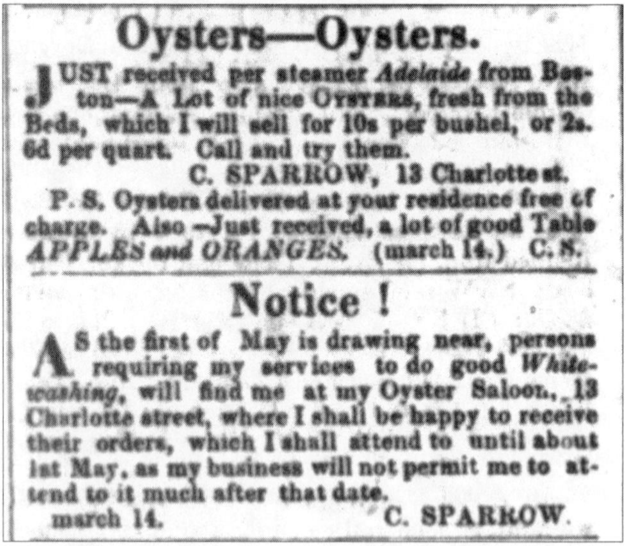

Oysters—Oysters.

JUST received per steamer *Adelaide* from Boston—A Lot of nice OYSTERS, fresh from the Beds, which I will sell for 10s per bushel, or 2s. 6d per quart. Call and try them.

C. SPARROW, 13 Charlotte st.

P. S. Oysters delivered at your residence free of charge. Also—Just received, a lot of good Table *APPLES and ORANGES.* (march 14.) C. S.

Notice !

AS the first of May is drawing near, persons requiring my services to do good *Whitewashing,* will find me at my Oyster Saloon, 13 Charlotte street, where I shall be happy to receive their orders, which I shall attend to until about 1st May, as my business will not permit me to attend to it much after that date.

march 14. C. SPARROW.

A two-part advertisement placed by Cornelius Sparrow in the *Morning News*, March 1856.

> their orders, which I shall attend to until about
> 1st May, as my business, will not permit me to at-
> tend to it much after that date.

This whitewashing business may be key to understanding Jackson's life in Saint John. One of the only things he tells us about his time in Canada was that he worked as a whitewasher and honed his skills enough that, in later years in England, he was able to support himself in the warm months by working as a "rough painter." We can read this advertisement placed by a man he surely knew, and likely knew well by this time, as uniquely telling. Jackson was still in Saint John during the spring and summer of 1856, and it is hard not to conclude that during his years in Saint John, he worked with the rising man of business, Sparrow.[49]

From the story of Sparrow, we can see what was to become a pattern with Jackson. He would have a propensity *to be with people who understood.* Whenever he could, Jackson was drawn to or sought out other survivors of slavery and people who understood the terror of the Fugitive Slave Act. Those people would know, as he did, the terror of pursuit or recapture. He traveled with, lived near, among, or sometimes in the same building and household with other survivors whenever he could. When possible, his

Cornelius Sparrow and his brother in front of their successful establishment in Saint John (probably 1870s but date unknown).

addresses and the people he was close to indicate he would try to immerse himself in communities that would have seen him for who he was: a person carrying a mixture of trauma, guilt, and fury—a mixture that would have been familiar to other survivors of bondage. We cannot know for sure if Cornelius Sparrow hired Jackson or worked with Jackson during their time in Saint John. Nor can we know if Jackson knew Thomas Jones. Nonetheless, given the comfort and solace that drew Jackson to other fugitives for the rest of his life, we cannot doubt that once in Saint John, he found his people.

As considered earlier, Jackson was largely, although not entirely, safe under the culture and practice of British law at that time. Although one could hardly blame him or other recent refugees from bondage for harboring nagging doubts about their complete security, the fact is that no fugitive slaves were renditioned back to the United States from Canada after 1843.[50] He had a legal border to protect him now. Anderson, that overseer and slave catcher who had traced him to Boston, had no reach here. Jackson might not have had a prosperous career as a whitewasher, but he was not in real danger of kidnapping, rendition, or recapture in Canada. Safety could never be absolute, of course, but he was on comparatively solid footing.

On the other hand, Saint John was cold for someone born in South Carolina, and with the notable exception of Cornelius Sparrow, opportunities there for Black people were limited. The weather might be tolerable for people with the means to heat, house, and clothe themselves adequately, but the poverty of most Black people of Saint John meant that their lives would have been brutal, their comforts few, and their prospects dismal. Jackson may have intended to settle there forever, but he may have chafed against the very finite possibilities he felt for himself in Saint John. And now, he had Julia, too, to consider. What kind of life might they build together?

VI

At some moment in Canada, Jackson decided to live a life of activism—to forcefully intervene in the global politics of slavery with nothing more than his witness and testimony. He had dabbled in such a life in Massachusetts, but now he might be able to embrace it completely. He would bare his own body as evidence of slavery's cruelty. He could try to raise money to help the family he had left behind. If not Louisa and Jinny, then at least he might be able to help his many siblings or his elderly parents, who were still living under torture and abuse back on the English family labor camps.

Certainly by this time Jackson had heard of Frederick Douglass, William Wells Brown, or Ellen and William Craft, all people who had, like him, fled slavery and moved through Canada, eventually sailing overseas to advocate for the end of slavery. The work and life of these self-emancipated lecturers were regularly covered in antislavery papers as well as in the press more generally. But learning about celebrity activists circling the globe is one thing, while lining up one's own schemes to do so is quite a different matter. Surely his friends, perhaps Sparrow, who had a direct line to prominent activists in Boston, helped him figure out what to do. And he now had Julia, who agreed to accompany him and provide him with the companionship and support he might need. As a team, they could go places.

But how far? Leaving their lives in Canada, and for Julia, leaving her family, would be difficult. And whatever hardships they had faced in Saint John, these were hardships they knew. But the possibilities for Jackson in Saint John seemed meager in terms of his ambitions. He was ready to vote in Canada, ready to be a citizen, ready to build a better life. But, as he must have understood it, that nation wasn't ready for him. He and Julia would chase a bigger dream for themselves and for the people they had left behind in the Carolinas. To do so, they were ready to cross the ocean.

Encouragement to carry on the overseas work of advocating antislavery is one thing; providing solid financial support is quite another. Tickets to

Liverpool were expensive for refugees working menial jobs for survival. It's hard to imagine any of them saving sufficient funds to travel overseas (much less with a spouse) without some patronage.[51] The most likely route Jackson and Julia would have taken would have been to sail quickly from the city of Saint John around the tip of Nova Scotia to the Atlantic-facing port of Halifax in Nova Scotia. There they might have lingered for a week or two before securing tickets for a British-bound vessel. All this waiting around in Halifax would have also had a cost in terms of food and lodging, so these travelers would have needed money for the trip generally, in addition to basic money for tickets.

Much as the prominent fugitive abolitionists such as Frederick Douglass or William and Ellen Craft discovered, formal or informal sponsorship to even purchase passage was necessary for such an undertaking.[52] Second-class tickets advertised on the Royal Mail steamships that same month leaving Liverpool for Halifax were fifteen guineas, or what was probably close to two months of a salary for a white workingman of the time.[53] Steerage was, of course, a lot cheaper, and on the speedy mail ships, the kinds most frequently used for passengers at this point heading away from North America, there were always berths at that price point.[54] Of course, Jackson and Julia would have had to purchase two tickets, so their joint outlay, even for steerage berths, would have been an enormous sum of money, the product of months of savings if they hadn't received outside help. But whether through their savings or with the help of someone else, they soon held a pair of tickets.

The mystery of Jackson's travel funding may remain, but we can be sure he didn't hop on a ship unprepared. During these years, most trips from Halifax (the most likely departure point) to Liverpool (his known destination) would take between a week to ten days. Julia and Jackson would have packed some provisions, organized their funds, obtained some carpetbags or trunks, and secured their valuables. Most of all, they would have gone over every possible scenario in conversation with one another. What if they didn't meet up with the people they were hoping to find? What if they were forbidden from ascending the gangplank? What if people wouldn't let them eat in public spaces? What might happen if they were expected to share cramped quarters with white travelers? What would happen if they encountered Southerners aboard? They couldn't have known all the answers, but at least they could talk it through, together.

VII

During the spring and summer of 1856, whether alone or under the guidance of friends, Jackson got to work.

Money for travel was going to be a challenge, but even more so, he needed a network of friends to guide him overseas. He knew all too well what it meant to travel as an itinerant speaker from his time in Massachusetts, and he knew that letters of introduction would be key for travel to a strange land.

Jackson contacted people who knew him well. On April 30, 1856, two tradesmen from the tan yards in Salem replied to his request by supplying him with the following note:

> Be it known that we know John Andrew Jackson, a coloured man to be industrious and honest; . . . We further state that we believe said John Andrew Jackson was formerly a slave, and that his word may be relied upon, as we think him a man of integrity and truth.
>
> Samuel Higbee and John Gilmer[55]

Clues about Jackson's past are revealed from these endorsements. In addition to the Higbee and Gilmer letter, Jackson obtained one from another Salem businessman, G.W. Cochrane—a man who owned or directed a small shoe and boot manufactory.[56] And in this letter, Cochrane took a particular interest in the details of Jackson's story back in Boston. He wrote:

> I went with the above John Andrew Jackson and saw Mrs. Foreman, in Richmond Street, Boston, and she fully corroborated his statement in reference to his being a slave; also said her son had been on board the vessel, and seen the spot where the said John Andrew Jackson was cut out. . . .[57]

Thus, we learn that not only did Jackson still have loyal white friends in Massachusetts, but his friends had taken considerable effort to verify his story, knowing all that was on the line.

Successful Salem businessmen and upright white citizens were useful but wouldn't carry Jackson far. He needed people with more national and international clout. Good thing he had two final tricks up his sleeve.

Jackson solicited another critical endorsement from Samuel Fessenden, the lawyer who had helped him hide for several weeks in Portland, Maine. Fessenden's letter was brief: "I have known Mr. John Andrew Jackson more than five years; I believe him to be a reliable man for integrity and truth. His history, which is very thrilling, may be relied on, as he relates it. He is anxious to redeem his father and two children of a sister in slavery. He has a claim on your sympathies."[58] Coming from an influential political family in New England and from a man known as a hero for the antislavery Liberty Party, this letter would have had clout. Fessenden's name might not have been well known in England generally, but among certain circles who followed the American antislavery movement, the name Fessenden would have opened doors. Jackson's arsenal of endorsements was coming along well.

And yet, these letters would not suffice. Jackson needed a "character" from an influential figure known in international antislavery circles. And for that, Jackson, of course, looked to Harriet Beecher Stowe.

Jackson might not have known anything about Stowe when they first met back in 1850, but by 1856 he surely knew that he had had the good fortune to cross paths with the best-known living writer in the world. *Uncle Tom's Cabin* appeared first in serial form between 1851–1852 and, in March 1852, was published to enormous acclaim in two volumes, quickly breaking publication and distribution records worldwide.[59] It was everywhere.

By the spring and early summer of 1856, when Jackson was living with Julia in Saint John and planning for his journey, Stowe no longer lived in Maine. Instead, she lived in Andover, Massachusetts, with her husband, who had settled there for another teaching job. As she was frantically composing her next novel, *Dred*, she couldn't have welcomed such a request from Jackson. But reply she did. And what she penned must have been both heartfelt and heartening, judging by reactions it received. Even though her letter seems lost to time, he did have it with him for long enough to share it with others.[60] That such a reply existed is certain.

It was a golden ticket, and he would cash it in, repeatedly.[61] Missives from clergy that are reproduced in Jackson's memoir remark upon Stowe's endorsement: David Guthrie and William Anderson, two prominent Scottish ministers, jointly wrote that they saw convincing "testimonials produced by Mr. Jackson, given by Mrs. Beecher Stowe," and another pair of Scottish ministers agreed that when they had met him, Jackson had carried with him various testimonials including "a particularly a strong one from Mrs. Beecher Stowe."[62]

With letters of introduction carefully packed, Jackson and Julia were ready. At that time the primary mode of crossing that Atlantic from the Canadian Maritimes would have been one of the state-of-the-art steamships which customarily left from Halifax. The couple could have ferried across the bay and landed at Windsor, Nova Scotia, but then they still would have had almost 40 miles of travel to get to Halifax, a cumbersome option. It seems more likely that they sailed from Saint John all the way to Halifax, where they would then have stayed in or near the city for a bit while they arranged to purchase tickets for one of the Cunard Line steamships. And while Jackson never names the boat they traveled on, all evidence points to it being the *Canada*, a Cunard-owned vessel that could carry eighty-five passengers along with bags of trans-Atlantic mail.[63]

Julia and Jackson would have walked up the *Canada*'s gangplank on Friday, October 10. Surely they would have looked back on the city of Halifax and felt torn. Canada hadn't been what either of them had hoped. Jackson had registered to vote there and clearly, at one time, had planned to stay. Now, they were leaving for an adventure and for a cause. But they were also leaving behind the nation that had taken them in. They were leaving behind friends like Cornelius Sparrow and his family. Julia may have been leaving behind family members who had escaped from North Carolina with her. They were leaving behind any friends they had found among the members of Saint John's Emancipation Society. The white clergy of the city who had married them and served as witnesses of their union in Saint John would no longer be nearby to counsel or intervene when problems arose.

The *Canada* was a sizable twin-engine vessel with a distinct red steam funnel in the center. Jackson and Julia would have looked up to see the solid black band around the top, the hallmark of a Cunard ship. Its paddle wheel in the center was a modern innovation representing a powerful and stabilizing effect, both on their hearts and on the swells, allowing the boat to cross the Atlantic in record time.

Did Julia and Jackson agree to stay in their cabin to avoid offending or interacting with white passengers, as some Black passengers of that era were encouraged to do, officially or unofficially, by authorities? Or did they roam the boat freely and interact with their white sailing companions? Did they practice their lectures or take their meals in public? The diseases that ravaged passengers, particularly those in steerage, such as typhus or cholera, were more common in the crowded immigrant ships heading toward the New World than those traveling away from it. Nonetheless, everyone would have been wary of illnesses. Julia and Jackson surely would have monitored

This image from 1859 shows the *America* breaking through ice in Halifax's harbor. The *America* was one of the Cunard Line's sister ships to the *Canada*, the ship Jackson and Julia traveled on in 1856, and was built along very similar lines.

every symptom or shiver they might have felt during the crossing. Whether they remained huddled in their berths or ventured out on deck, they had time to compare notes and plans.

Jackson never says anything about this crossing, but we can imagine that, whatever happened, they counted the moments until they were safe across the Atlantic. The trip from Halifax was a fast and smooth course that October 1856 and took only ten days.[64]

Jackson had arrived in Canada as a laborer, but he left it now as a lecturer. And, this time, at least, he wasn't traveling alone.

CHAPTER SEVEN

THE EXPERIENCE OF A SLAVE IN SOUTH CAROLINA BY JOHN ANDREW JACKSON (1862)

The British Isles (1856–1862)

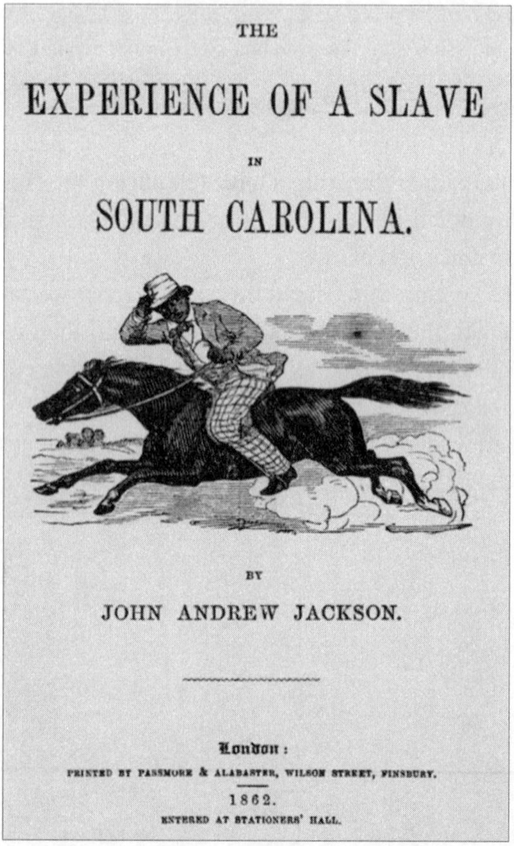

THE

EXPERIENCE OF A SLAVE

IN

SOUTH CAROLINA.

BY

JOHN ANDREW JACKSON.

London:

PRINTED BY PASSMORE & ALABASTER, WILSON STREET, FINSBURY.

1862.

ENTERED AT STATIONERS' HALL.

Title page for *The Experience of a Slave in South Carolina* by John Andrew Jackson (London: Printed by Passmore & Alabaster, Wilson Street, Finsbury, 1862).

Jackson and Julia must have been both thrilled and terrified to arrive in Liverpool. But as we know, just disembarking could itself be a challenge. What steps could they take to find shelter and safety? Where could they find the networks and advice they would need? And how could they be taken seriously, found legitimate by any authorities, and market their stories? They would need to use the Stowe connection effectively but delicately, and that could get tricky. Some of their failures and gradual successes unfold through newspaper articles and coverage of their joint lecturing careers. But a fateful encounter with a celebrity preacher was to alter the course of their lives and allowed Jackson to finally claim his own story and song, in print.[1]

I

The only image of Jackson known today comes from this engraving made in England for the title page of his book in 1862.[2]

Jackson's story had to sell. He needed the money, and he needed the impact. If his testimony would help the cause of his enslaved brethren in the United States, that would be an answered prayer, too. But for any of those things to happen, it had to catch people's attention. Competitors were about. Slave narratives such as his were sold throughout the British Isles and many would be distributed or sold after lectures or church services. Frederick Douglass's narrative was especially well known, but other titles, such as those by William Wells Brown, William and Ellen Craft, Josiah Henson, James Pennington, and Henry Bibb, were broadly read in the British antislavery circles.

If Jackson wanted his narrative to make a splash, he would need a hook, a special angle. He couldn't talk of escaping by mailing himself inside a box—a brilliant stunt that catapulted Henry Box Brown to freedom, fame, and a career on the lecture circuit. And he couldn't boast of a brilliant subterfuge such as was practiced by the Crafts, a couple who had escaped slavery with Ellen posing as a white male invalid attended to by William, her darker-skin husband posing as her enslaved attendant. And Jackson couldn't simply make things up about his past for attention. His credibility and truthfulness were part of the currency of character that he needed to woo the support of sympathetic audiences. So, to stand out from the other Black lecturers and authors roaming Britain, he needed to showcase qualities that would make him memorable.

In his picture for his book, Jackson wears a jacket with a shawl lapel, checked trousers, a hat, a waistcoat or vest, and a cravat. He is atop a speeding horse and holding the reins with one hand and his hat with the other. He is looking behind, presumably for pursuers. The dust is kicked up behind the horse to convey a sense of speed.

Jackson had been a field hand. Checked trousers might have been within his reach, and a hat and coat would have made sense for him to wear at the time of his escape. But a vest and cravat? It is hard to know if the British engraver was working off information Jackson supplied to him some fourteen years after the event or if he was simply imagining the scene with fanciful details. Either way, Jackson's depiction on this page was at least true to how he saw himself: snappy, bold, a horseman, and in-your-face audacious.

Jackson's horse, or his "pony" as he called it, became key to his brand. It had been his ticket out of Sumter County and now it was his unique calling card; few freedom seekers could boast of a horse, and featuring it on his title page would help his volume stand out.

At the moment of his flight, Jackson knew the roads, having once helped drive cattle to market in Charleston. He had a few days during Christmas week when his absence might not be noticed. He had an elderly enslaver who was ill, and the regular surveillance of the slave labor camp was distracted. But all those other factors, helpful though they were, didn't add up to the greatest advantage he needed: confidence. Not simply in his abilities or in providence. What he needed was bravado and an ability to hide by standing out. He needed to be believable, to be plausible.

The dandyish outfit was likely not an accurate reproduction of what Jackson actually wore. But it is accurate, indeed, for how he needed to represent himself at both the time of his flight and afterward. They were how he needed to be seen.

Before we look too closely at Jackson's book, the document that anchors this chapter and, indeed, this entire life study, we must examine what happened when he and Julia first arrived in Liverpool. For it was these initial hopes and burdens that shaped the choices he and Julia were to make. They needed to find their way, make a living, liberate their families, and discover a way to make a difference. They needed to be seen.

II

On October 18, 1856, after a ten-day journey, Jackson and Julia stepped off the *Canada*.[3] They must have been grateful for solid land. After all, even a relatively uneventful and smooth trip by the standards of the experienced crew could be utterly miserable for land-loving passengers. The British novelist William Makepeace Thackeray, who had traveled on the *Canada* a year or two before Jackson did, complained, "I'm weary of guzzling and gorging and bumping in bed all night and being 1/2 sick all day."[4] And Thackeray had presumably enjoyed a higher standard of accommodations and comfort on the *Canada* than Jackson and Julia could have afforded.

Crossing the North Atlantic had challenges for passengers, regardless of their ticket class. It could get terribly cold, of course, but there were other irritations. In 1854 there had been two terrible collisions at sea involving the *Canada* and other boats, and in both cases, several lives were lost.[5] By

1856 when Jackson and Julia boarded, as a safety measure, the *Canada* was now required to use loud screaming steam whistles every few minutes when sailing through fog and ice, which the ship would have encountered a good measure of during a typical October voyage. While supposedly an assuring measure to forestall collisions with other boats, these whistles also meant that passengers, especially those with the least amount of soundproofing in their compartments, would have been kept awake for long periods, ensuring they would have been strung out and exhausted when finally arriving at their destination.[6]

And yet, whether the voyage was peaceful or rough, they made it. Customs officials in Liverpool would have checked over their trunks or parcels but didn't require a passport at that time, so Jackson and Julia could arrive without any difficulties in asserting their ambiguous national status and legal circumstances. Once the hurdle of customs was cleared, they fully arrived in Liverpool, then a teeming city of roughly 400,000 people, known for its opportunities, its tragedies, and its cotton wealth.[7] They would have seen occasional Black faces in Liverpool, for sure, and while the couple may have felt discombobulated or disoriented, they wouldn't have stood out too much as they disembarked.

There were people at the docks ready to greet passengers with ill as well as friendly intentions. Such folks would have homed in on Jackson and Julia's dark faces the minute they looked over the railings as the boat pulled in, probably cold but happy as they saw their destination.

At the wharves of Liverpool, men posed as porters ready to steal luggage, men posed as officials seeking to steal their money for bogus arrival fees, and others were ready to direct them to decrepit or dangerous lodgings simply because proprietors promised commissions. Dinah Hope Browne, for one, a fugitive from Virginia, made her way to England and had all her savings stolen from her during her very first night in England when a cabman drove her to an unsafe lodging house.[8] These kinds of scams on vulnerable newcomers were more common than not. Prostitutes would have plied the streets. Pickpockets of all sorts would have been at the ready the moment a new steamer pulled in. Money-changing cons were common, and Jackson and Julia might have seen charlatans posing as bank representatives eager to take their money. Julia and Jackson, though, weren't born yesterday. Saint John was a tough seaport, too. They pulled their wraps tight, held onto one another, and somehow forged ahead.

Liverpool was a city of some contradictions, with a long history of receiving Black people as slaves, sailors, migrants, refugees, and visitors both from Africa and from the Americas. It had tremendous deprivation and industrial-era poverty. Its municipal wealth in the eighteenth and nineteenth centuries hugely depended on the slave trade directly or indirectly. Even once that practice was officially abolished in England in 1808, local and national commerce still was reliant upon the trade in sugar, cotton, tobacco, and other products that were grown, processed, or manufactured from the forced labor of enslaved people. The cotton mills of Lancashire and elsewhere in central and northern England had an almost insatiable need for the cotton pouring through Liverpool's ports. Hence, not unlike those in Charleston, South Carolina, the thoroughfares of Liverpool were framed by huge warehouse buildings, often built for the express purpose of handling Southern slave-grown cotton. Indeed, well through the nineteenth century, almost half of the imports and exports that went through the port of Liverpool were cotton.[9]

The American preacher and famous antislavery activist, and Stowe's younger brother, the Reverend Henry Ward Beecher, visited Liverpool in the 1840s and had been mobbed by proslavery or, rather, procotton crowds. And Ida Mae Wells, the antilynching activist, was to call out Liverpool's history by noting, "A disturbance of the institution meant a possible depletion of their purses, and so, they were in favor of its continuance."[10] For mid-century visitors hoping for a sympathetic audience on the topic of abolition, Liverpool would prove a tough crowd.

And yet, when Jackson and Julia first laid their eyes on the city in 1856, they would have recognized how the wealth and poverty around them were

Liverpool Town Hall frieze depicting an African woman. Built between 1749 and 1754, this building was constructed by the most prominent slave merchants in England during the eighteenth century.

organized around global exploitation and suffering. They knew this scene. They knew its costs. They would have known to step carefully.

They would have found familiar, for example, how the global slave economy had structured the open urban spaces for cotton market trading and the huge warehouses constructed to move the product. But they might have missed or not fully apprehended the many markers in the city that paid homage to the great wealth grown from the Caribbean or African trade in the eighteenth century, such as the Liverpool warehouses along Goree Street, named after the West African island that facilitated the trade of human beings. On the other hand, they would have easily recognized the head of the African woman on the frieze of Liverpool's enormous Town Hall located in the center of the city as the marker of the human exploitation that had built the wealth of that metropolis.

They certainly would have found familiar the culture of preening Southern self-aggrandizement, evidenced by those who came to secure themselves in a row of buildings on Liverpool's fashionable Abercromby Square starting in the 1840s and 1850s and which came to full bloom when in 1862 a residence there was constructed and conceived of as an unofficial Confederate embassy and perhaps someday a European "White House" for Confederate president Jefferson Davis.[11] The ceiling of the entrance even featured a picture of a palmetto tree, the symbol of South Carolina.

Previous Black lecturers who had fled slavery in the United States via Canada had pioneered this junket through Liverpool. It was almost always the first and most convenient port to arrive at from North America. But few of them sought to linger in Liverpool for long.

Ellen and William Craft, for example, who arrived in Liverpool in 1850, had quickly sought out advice from William Wells Brown, a man who had similarly fled from captivity in the United States and who had constructed a new life as a lecturer and author in the United Kingdom. He, along with various white clergy of the area, evidently met with the Crafts in Liverpool and helped them leave that city. He also assisted them in attending public lectures about antislavery to acclimate them to expectations from British audiences. Most helpfully of all, he arranged events for them to share their tale of escape as they had done in the United States.[12]

Unfortunately, Jackson and Julia didn't have anyone prominent to greet them that we know of. Yet it is hard to imagine that they would have planned their trip without knowing how to connect with supporters. They certainly would have burnished letters from their American allies to quickly find sanctuary in England. It might have taken them a few days to connect with the right people, but they made sure to make it happen.

The pair must have found some immediate shelter in the city for the first few days, perhaps at a rough boarding house catering to Black sailors and Black travelers, perhaps not unlike the one Henry Foreman ran back on Ann Street in Boston. But, since Julia was along, they probably sought out more genteel lodgings if they had the funds. Even the most temperate and tidy sailors' boarding house in Liverpool would have been raucous at best.

William Wells Brown, the self-emancipated Black lecturer who had arrived in Liverpool from the United States six years earlier and in similar circumstances with little cash on hand, had faced a similar dilemma with uncertain choices. Brown had found comfortable lodgings in an establishment called, fittingly, Brown's Temperance Hotel near Clayton Square.[13] And in 1847, the young Frederick Douglass, too, had found welcome there.[14] That hotel had changed hands the year before Jackson arrived, but it still billed itself as a Temperance establishment, and the chances are that it was still one of the places in the city willing to board Black people.[15] We can hope that Jackson and Julia ended up there—if their budgets extended that far.

Did an antislavery activist, Black or white, meet them in Liverpool to hustle them somewhere safe and help them acclimate? It seems possible, for within a few weeks of their arrival in England, Jackson began giving speeches and lectures in public venues, gigs that someone knowing the lay of the land must have helped him arrange. It seems that they found a friend to serve as a liaison of sorts, perhaps someone who had been alerted to their arrival by overseas allies.[16]

Liverpool was a transitional site for these travelers, but they must have found some sort of help. They were quickly able to lay plans, almost certainly thanks to antislavery activists and helpful church organizations. Within a few weeks, Jackson and Julia started appearing in newspapers. They had arrived.

III

Jackson and Julia now embarked on what must have been a difficult but buoyant life on the road and rail. They immediately headed north, visiting a few places in northern England, and then traveling around Scotland. The couple would have seen some hardships during these early months, but newspapers hail their appearances and laud them for their successes.

Between 1856 and 1857 Jackson delivered at least fifteen lectures but probably far, far more than that since so many papers vaguely reference additional earlier or upcoming talks.[17] Little could he have imagined that within a few years, as it was reported, he had lectured in "almost all the Churches in Edinburgh and Glasgow."[18]

How did this itinerant kind of lecture tour work? Jackson appears to have been brandishing his letter from Stowe but relied on introductions from clergy to clergy as most of his talks occur in houses of worship or with ministers on the platform with him. Did he ask friends to write letters and send them on ahead or would he rely upon delivering the letters himself? It would make sense to do it both ways when possible.

The first few times Jackson and Julia needed to travel, they probably got a bit of help and advice about how to purchase tickets or rides. The locations of the lectures suggest they often traveled by train and sometimes carriage along established routes. Still, when money was tight or if conveyances refused to let a Black person travel, as could happen, he and Julia may have tried walking or begging rides as they were able. Even the cheapest train tickets would have allowed them to crisscross the country on the already well-established rail networks of northern England with speed and, if not exactly comfort, then comfort knowing the trip wouldn't be long.

Fifteen years later, when Jackson was on the North Carolina chain gang, digging out rocks for railroad tracks, he would remember those moments when he and Julia had traveled free and fast on the trains in England.

After arriving in a town or city, hopefully during the daylight hours, Jackson would immediately contact any of the local ministers or clergy he could find. He needed them to see if they might vouch for him and help him secure a speaking venue. He would also have asked for their help in finding a suitable place to stay or places to eat that would welcome Black Americans.

Once a local patron or host was identified, other arrangements would still need to be put in place. Speakers such as Jackson would even occasionally use bell ringers to attract a crowd or notify people of the event. Most important, Jackson would have summoned up all his charm to ask his hosts if they would be willing to "chair" the meeting or appear alongside him on stage. Victorian audiences had extensive experience with frauds and con artists and would be wary of unvetted speakers.[19] These audiences would rarely accept the testimony of a Black speaker who came without the imprimatur of a white master of ceremonies, preferably clerical.[20]

Once Jackson had overcome those hurdles and found his chair or master of ceremonies, he would seek out local newspapers to let them know of any talks he had arranged and get their assistance in promoting the event either as a paid advertisement or occasionally as a news item they might promote free of charge. In some cases, he would have sought out print shops to have them print out posters and broadsides announcing his events, which he would plaster around town.[21] He probably would settle into his lodging with Julia and practice a bit or make sure he got a good sleep. Julia would have tried to dust off or prepare their clothes for the big day. They needed to look as respectable as they could for the stage or the pulpit without looking too well clad or amply provisioned. It was a difficult line to walk.

Selling things or having some kind of takeaway that people could leave the church or town hall event with could be an income stream and a bit of promotional branding. In the first few years, Jackson likely didn't have any supplementary items to sell, such as pamphlets or books. He could only tell his story and hope his character and charisma would be enough. Later, when he was a more established performer, he helped produce promotional pamphlets and eventually had copies of his book on hand to tout as well. Presumably, he and perhaps Julia would arrange with the venue, be it a church or a town hall, to set up a table to facilitate these sales and to watch over any money collected, always making sure that money went safely into the hands of his white trustees.

Starting in the fall of 1856, newspapers in places such as Preston, Dumfries, Fife, Aberdeen, and Stirling began to note Jackson's presence. He was heading north to Scotland and learning his new trade, getting better as he went along. A correspondent for the *Preston Guardian* reported on "His 'spirited, eloquent, and very humorous discourse'" when delivering a talk to "collect funds in order to purchase the freedom of some of his family."[22]

Other papers reporting on talks Jackson delivered during these first few months in the British Isles shared a few backhanded compliments, such as that in one Scottish paper which wrote that Jackson "narrated in a desultory yet graphic and interesting way."[23] Another paper commented: "With the drawback of not speaking English very distinctly, he is a really effective speaker, possessing much of the humour characteristic of his brethren."[24]

Damning praise, indeed.

This kind of belittling and racist coverage mixed with sometimes enthused but sometimes halfhearted endorsement of the entertainment value of Jackson's speeches nonetheless demonstrated that he was honing his skills and learning how to work a room.

Jackson learned how to project his voice and make himself seen. Julia surely would have coached him about how his shoulders needed to be held back or how his posture mattered. He would have practiced his hand gestures. He learned when to milk his accent for novelty purposes and when to slow down and enunciate as precisely as he could for his audience unaccustomed to his manner of speech. He tried out when to pause and when to hurry on. He became aware that it was important to finish before audiences were ready to leave or, especially, to make sure a donation plate was passed *before* people started to disperse. He knew when to turn to the audience with an aside to lighten the mood or address specific constituents—the ladies, say, or sometimes even the children who attended. He would have practiced answering questions he knew would come up, such as how the conditions of enslavement in the United States compared with the conditions of laborers in poor urban areas of England or Ireland.

Lecturers are performers, of course, and like any kind of performer, they must create a persona that is a bit separate from their individual self—a challenge especially tricky when one is telling one's own life story! Their bodies, whether they are Black or white, are their tools. For Jackson and other self-emancipated Black lecturers, their bodies needed to serve as stories—as substitutes or in place of a book the audience could read (whether such a book existed). Even once Jackson did write down his story, he was always in

Durham Town Hall was one of the secular venues in northern England where Jackson spoke. In 1858 he lectured here and described slavery as an "unmixed evil."

a bit of a paradox; by standing in front of audiences, he was making himself a commodity not that different from what he had been in Lynchburg. Now, however, he needed to sell himself.[25]

As these early notices show, Jackson and Julia were building momentum and collecting funds. Exactly how that money was handled became a source of concern in later years. But, in these early months of their time in England, it seems that some money was set aside to support their travels, and most likely one of the prominent white ministers he met early on served as a collector and consolidator of monies raised. For the Victorian audience, even the antislavery sympathizers who found Jackson credible and persuasive, simply entrusting him with coins might have seemed a bit risky, given the common racist assumptions about Black people's inabilities to handle their affairs. But when assured the money would be handled by a white caretaker, men and women of all classes and stations began to make contributions. They believed in change, and they tried, in their modest ways, to intervene in injustice and make a difference in the world. Finally, there was something they could do.

IV

So how might Jackson and Julia keep providing consistent opportunities for charitable well-wishers to do good? How to maintain their interest, and open their purses, particularly among competing draws of lecturers, sermons, shows, and other entertainments common to the age? It couldn't be a one-man show. Julia had to carefully step up and step in.

With no family companion, much less a ladies' maid, Julia likely kept quite close to Jackson during all these travels, accompanying him to every errand, every consultation, and every event. As a Black woman traveling in regions with few dark faces like hers, she would have stood out on the streets and might have been in danger of molestation or harassment if she had wandered these unknown towns and cities alone. Sitting in a rented room waiting for Jackson to return would not be a good use of her time, and her energies were better put toward helping charm clergymen or impress their wives and housekeepers with her respectability. Jackson may have established a base in London at some point in the late 1850s to relieve Julia from the pressures of constant travel, but she appears frequently with him nonetheless, attracting some newspaper attention herself. And, as time went on, she appears to have grown in confidence, with more papers acknowledging her participation in lectures in the 1860s than had done so in the 1850s.

Thanks to local practices and limited tolerance for the presence of women in public life, newspapers were discreet in their reports.[26] Britain was even more conservative than the American stages in tolerating women in the public sphere.[27] It isn't surprising that in almost every case, newspapers did not showcase her comments or quote her directly. While they frequently summarized Jackson's speech in detail, the references to the content of Julia's remarks are frustratingly minimal.

A typical notice ran: "His wife a Creole slave also made a brief speech, and stated how she affected her escape."[28] Another noted that Julia "made her escape, and related her history in a very pleasing and unaffected manner."[29] More detail about the tone of her remarks can be glimpsed in a report from 1863, which points out that she and Jackson were undoubtedly experts at public speaking with years of experience behind them. They would know where to pause, where to joke, and where and when to lower their voices or take a beat. Julia would have experience by now in saying certain things, perhaps things Jackson could or would not, but also, she would have known when to pull back from graphic descriptions that might horrify her audiences. Most of all, Julia's absolute confidence in her righteous cause can be seen by how she delivered her position with force and passion. The correspondent reported with both racist assumptions and admiration:

> Mr. Jackson introduced his wife, who is also a runaway slave. She modestly said that she was no lecturer, but she would make a few remarks on slavery. She is a fine specimen of her race and spoke with earnestness in the cause. She did not spare those persons who pretended to be the friends of the slave, and having power, did not use it to abolish slavery; her statements were warmly applauded.[30]

But what exactly did Julia say? We cannot know. This lack of detail can remind us that the archives will always fall short. In this case, acknowledging that she was there and actively engaged in the event isn't all we can learn. We do not need to stop short with the refusals of the reporters to share her words. The vague delicacy used by these journalists may have been a clue that, in their minds, perhaps she should not have been speaking at all, following Victorian mores. After all, there was no room for women to speak in public among the conservative British audiences of that day. But this documentary silence due to the reporters' cryptic references can teach us a great deal about the pressure Julia must have felt to be quiet. And the fact that she went ahead and spoke nonetheless, not sparing hypocrites, tells us volumes about her courage, determination, and conviction that her words mattered.

We can imagine she delivered her commentary with deftness and care to speak her truth, intrigue her audience, and yet not bring upon herself any charges of vulgarity. It must have been a difficult tightrope to walk, as it were. Formerly enslaved men had been lecturing in Britain for decades by this point, but there don't seem to be any records of women in Julia's situation doing so. Indeed, evidence points to the fact that Julia Jackson was possibly the first African American woman to speak in the British Isles about her enslaved experiences.[31] And in this, by standing up as a woman, she claimed a powerful role even more influential than any her husband could make. Julia Jackson was an asset beyond measure to both Jackson and the cause of the antislavery movement in Britain.

The interest shown in her light skin contrasted with the descriptions of Jackson, which often noted that his skin was, as one paper put it, "of exceedingly dark color."[32] Did this help or hurt Jackson's presentations? It is hard to say. But standing up on a stage was a physical act. It was part of what scholars like to think of as "embodied experiences."[33] And it made a terrible kind of sense. Formerly enslaved Black speakers had been nothing but physical bodies for their enslavers, and both the speakers and the audiences knew that their bodies' physical appearance and presence, whether scarred or beautifully preserved, was part of their performance. They were an exotic spectacle no matter how respectable their presentation.

Just as Julia's body was up for scrutiny at all events, so too was Jackson's. Frederick Douglass, who had a great deal of experience on the lecture circuit in the British Isles, reported that his moderately light skin could be a hindrance. He wrote: "It is quite an advantage to be a nigger here. I find I am hardly black enough for a British taste, but by keeping my hair as wooly as possible I make out to pass for at least half a negro at any rate." Douglass's comment may have been tongue-in-cheek, but, in contrast to Douglass, Jackson did not need to fluff out his hair to fulfill racist expectations for what a Black man should look like. Jackson's dark skin, especially in contrast to his wife's fairer complexion, generated interest from the press all on its own. The media's fascination with his skin color may have helped persuade people that he was indeed a "genuine article," particularly when his dark skin was contrasted with features the reporters deemed "intelligent looking" or shared their assessment of his "intelligent countenance" or an "intelligent face."[34] Several journalists assessed him, with their racist condescension, as a "fine specimen of the negro race."[35]

Jackson's body was part of the show, a fact he and Julia would have been painfully aware of. Only one newspaper mentions the scars on his back, and even then it is not clear if he showed them to audiences or had privately revealed them to his hosts or patrons. He likely only referred to them in his talk, with insincere offers to show his back to anyone who challenged his speech. The report notes: "He is an escaped slave, and bears on his back the scars of floggings inflicted many years ago."[36] Either way, it appears that Jackson resisted showing those violations to curious or prurient eyes. While he might wish to please his sponsors or his audiences, he didn't wish to be regularly served up as the "negro exhibit," as one scholar has termed such a display of the markings of slavery.[37] And yet, these lectures were understood to be both highbrow cultural or educational and even spiritual events while also drawing crowds as sensational and lowbrow types of shows, full of violence and sensation. Jackson understood that he and Julia were for display, but they tried to control how they would be seen.

At this time, other speakers were going around Europe and Great Britain who had more organized sponsorship than Jackson did. This meant they often could book bigger venues and secure more prominent endorsements. Jackson thus needed to carve out a market niche that was uniquely his own. Some speakers had props. Henry Box Brown famously used a box on stage to demonstrate how he had escaped by hiding in one.[38] Various speakers, including Frederick Douglass, during his earliest days as a speaker, would pose with shackles and chains on stage.[39] William Wells Brown brought a metal slave collar in his luggage to use on his British-speaking tour.[40] After a decade or so of seeing Black Americans speak against slavery, there is some indication that British audiences were growing a bit weary of antislavery lecturers, and some speakers began to enhance their events even further with panoramas, maps, magic lanterns, and other such visuals.[41]

Jackson had few such assets or tricks, but he worked with what he had; he arranged for a gimlet to be made identical to the one he had escaped with. He would then hold it up on stage and use it to reenact the moments he desperately bored out air holes on the deck of the ship and called out for help, confusing a sailor who thought it was a ghost from above rather than a starving stowaway below (evidently this story was told to great laughs). He leaned hard, too, into the story about escaping on horseback, for it is mentioned in many newspaper reports that would summarize his talks. A typical notice of 1857 observed:

> The negro proceeded, in wonderfully distinct, interesting, and sometimes highly amusing terms, to state how he managed to escape from the plantation in South Carolina on the back of a pony, which, so far as a slave can be held there to possess property, was his own.

The horse escape became a key part of Jackson's performative arsenal. That pony was his ticket.

Between the compelling presence of Julia, his gimlet, his horse story, and his general charisma, Jackson had a formidable arsenal of tools to distinguish himself from the crowd. He did not have the sophistication of Douglass or the erudite manners of some of the more educated Black orators, such as Remond. Nor could he flourish the rich history of publications to back him up, such as William Wells Brown had when he toured the antislavery lecture circuit. He lacked props other lecturers could boast of, such as panorama displays or slave chains. Nor did he even have a uniquely shocking backstory. His claim to fame and claim to donations needed something more.

V

Thus, for his signature move, Jackson would lean into his connection with Stowe. And how that happened was not as you might predict. His endorsement letter from her was mentioned repeatedly by reporters.[42] Clergy would typically introduce Jackson on stage by noting that they had seen the endorsement letter or had spoken with other divines who had. Moreover, since Stowe was touring England in 1856–1857, references to her would have felt fresh and current. There is no reason to think that Jackson and Stowe ever met in England while she was there, but Jackson certainly sought to be identified, if not defined, by their relationship. He knew that to overstep in his claim would undermine the persona of the lively but humble truth teller he had cultivated, and whom audiences and sponsoring clergy wished to see. He could not claim to be intimate with Stowe. But he was ready to assert the truth of his encounter with her as might serve his purposes.

It is notable, however, that Jackson never appears to invoke any suggestion that he was a model for Uncle Tom or any other character or even that he had been involved in any way with the book's conception. It would have been tempting to do so! (And one newspaper does note admiringly that he delivered "the story of his escape in language quite intelligible, but reminding one strongly of Uncle Tom.")[43]

And if anyone else on the stage hinted at those possibilities of his connection to the novel, not just to Stowe, it was not reported in the media coverage. What *was* reported about Jackson and Stowe was far stranger.

While virtually everyone in these audiences for the lectures or the newspapers would have heard of, if not read, *Uncle Tom's Cabin*, the book that Jackson specifically invoked on stage was her second novel, *Dred*.[44]

Dred was published in the fall of 1856 and sold quite well in Britain. It was a more radical novel than *Uncle Tom's Cabin*. Indeed, part of the reason Stowe wrote it was in response to criticism that many of her characters in *Uncle Tom's Cabin* were too passive or framed only as victims. In this novel, she had the titular character, Dred, plot a slave insurrection in the tradition of Nat Turner's notorious 1831 slave uprising in Virginia. The other marked theme of *Dred*, which revolves around two slave-owning families, the Gordons and the Claytons, concerns the Southern legal apparatus used to enforce the system of human bondage and how that system of white supremacist "codes" infiltrated every system of justice in the United States (a theme which was to fascinate Jackson, too, and reappear in his work).

Stowe had frantically worked on *Dred* throughout the summer of 1856, and by the fall she sailed to England to ensure she could be present on British soil in time to secure her copyright there. She had lost proceeds from the tremendous sales of *Uncle Tom's Cabin* in England and Europe because of this British law about authorial presence.) This was her second trip to England, but it, too, also was covered heavily by the press, and her name and the title of her novel, *Dred*, were on everyone's lips. She didn't travel on the same voyage of the *Canada* as Jackson, but they would have arrived in the United Kingdom within a few weeks of one another. There's no evidence Jackson sought her out, but he was clearly aware of *Dred* and, with some inadvertant cross-promotion, ensured his audience was, too.

The first time the connection between Jackson and *Dred* was made, it was by a reporter who wrote that Jackson had "known several slaves who, being men of strong intellect and naturally active, were shot by their masters *sine forma legis*; and his account of slavery in this respect coincided with the description of *Dred* of the cruel treatment to which the Clayton family were subjected, for attempting to raise the slave in the scale of intelligence."[45]

Did Jackson realize *Dred* was a novel? A few months later it appears that Jackson had begun to incorporate the story of Dred, the character, fully into his performative repertoire. The *Christian News* of June 6, 1857, reported that Jackson told a "thrilling tale of a noble slave named Dred." Jackson's story seems to roughly invoke some part of Stowe's novel but mashes up his version of *Dred* with a story in his own life of Old Peter, who was flogged to death under the direction of Elizabeth English.[46] According to the newspa-

This image of the titular character of Harriet Beecher Stowe's 1856 novel, *Dred: A Tale of the Great Dismal Swamp*, is from an illustrated edition of 1896. Here Dred is seen holding a gun and looking anxiously to the side as he walks through thick underbrush.

per, Jackson told of a giant Black man who worked as a slave driver but was demoted down to laboring as a field hand when the master felt the overseer was too confident in himself. Even in the field, though, this "Dred" did work "better than any slave on the plantation. A double task was assigned him, but his gigantic strength and resolution overcame this also." In Jackson's tale, the "master" orders other enslaved men to help seize him, but, "as Dred was beloved by the slaves, they were not overactive in the attempt." In the fight that ensued, the "master" shot and murdered Dred. As the newspaper concluded, "This story was told with great effect, as were several others of a similar nature."[47]

Whether Jackson was accidentally or carefully merging his personal stories with Stowe's stories, the effect was compelling and curious. He was working for the crowd, perhaps hinting at more of a relationship to Stowe than he could openly claim, and perhaps also testifying in some heightened or imaginative way to a truth he had witnessed or knew of from Lynchburg, South Carolina.

Thanks to his Stowe connection, the helpful and compelling contributions of Julia, his skills of showmanship, and the genuine interest of the community of people who steadily showed up to learn from him, Jackson became more and more polished. Money was coming in to help redeem his family. He was raising awareness of the urgency of the antislavery cause. He was making friends. And he was making his way.

VI

Jackson's early events went well. But it was a learning process. And it's worth considering how these episodes made him stronger, better, and ready for what was to come. There were instances of rowdy audiences and paltry collections. Doubtless he and Julia had some early missteps. The weather in some of the northern areas of England and Scotland through which they traveled must have been painful in these months. And while the bulk of newspaper notices were neutral or kind in their assessment of Jackson and Julia's appearances, racist, cruel, and undermining commentary did slip through. One manifestation of this, which would have been very familiar to Jackson, was the genteel but brutal skepticism he faced. Newspapers often represented him as a suspicious figure because of his race, his nationality, his class, and his claims. Was he who he said he was? Or was he merely precariously *plausible*? The *Surrey Comet,* for example, described his talk as "thrilling and *apparently* truthful [italics mine]."[48] Another notice sneered:

> On Monday evening last, a black man, who *calls himself* Mr. Jackson, and *says* [italics mine] he is an escaped slave, . . . gave a somewhat rambling account of his escape, and of slavery in general. He says his object is to raise money to purchase the freedom of some of his relatives. *If this be true* [italics mine], . . . he will be a long time in raising sufficient money; for although the Meeting House (which is a large one) was densely crowded, the collection only amounted to about two pounds.[49]

Fortunately for Jackson, this was a minority report. He wasn't deterred by skeptics. Overall, the endorsement-by-local-clergy technique worked well. He was welcomed, and audiences came. Coins were collected. But to assuage audiences and patrons, Jackson was forced to repeatedly find new ways to authenticate himself according to the standards of the white British populace. It was a challenge he could step up to and sometimes succeed at in the short term, but he knew this game. It was a trap.

Despite his growing successes, Jackson was endlessly plagued by doubters who were intent on undermining his claim to authenticity. If his Stowe letter and endorsements from upright clergy weren't going to silence some challenges, Jackson needed to find yet another kind of white authenticator.

Early in 1858, Jackson was sent by Huddersfield minister Richard Skinner to be interviewed by a different kind of arbiter. He met with Julia Griffiths, who was a white British woman who had worked closely with Frederick Douglass for several years in the United States (some say too closely; rumors about her possible sexual relationship with Douglass were proving distracting to their antislavery activities). She had returned to Britain in 1855 in part to reduce gossip that might undermine all of Douglass's endeavors, but she remained an indefatigable laborer for the antislavery cause, reportedly starting twenty new antislavery societies.[50] Whoever sent Jackson to Griffiths knew that she would be an impressive assessor.

Griffiths interviewed Jackson about the veracity of his claims. Since she had no experience of South Carolina and no way in which to ascertain the truth of his story, the interview suggests that it was her whiteness, her Britishness, her knowledge of the antislavery movement generally, and her association with Frederick Douglass that gave her authority more than any firsthand knowledge of Jackson's experiences. What could she know of hiding in terror? Running for her life? Losing a family? Whatever precisely happened in that dialogue, we cannot know, but she provided Jackson with useful, albeit vague, approval. As the Reverend Skinner wrote of Griffiths: "She examined him very closely and was fully satisfied that his representations of himself are correct. I believe implicit reliance may be placed in his truthfulness and honesty."[51]

Of course, that wasn't the end of it. In the racist world of midcentury Britain, Jackson was never going to be allowed to simply present himself on his own terms without challenge. In October 1857, the Glasgow New Association for the Abolition of Slavery reported that "the certificates of John Andrew Jackson, a fugitive slave, having been examined and considered satisfactory, it was unanimously agreed to vote him two guineas towards the object of his mission."[52] So that, at least, went well.

Other interrogations, however, were not to prove quite as smooth, and the politics of white external authentication for Jackson grew ever more complicated. What contortions or backflips might he have to make in order to prove himself "plausible" to whatever arbitrary criteria might be thrown at him? He would get through many of these challenges, but they would just reappear as the stakes grew ever higher.

In May 1859, a London-based antislavery organization decided not only to interview Jackson but to write back to the "States" for some corroboration or authorization. Who knows to whom they wrote or what they learned? But a month later, the organization put out a statement that acknowledged the entire enterprise of investigating the testimony of formerly enslaved people now in the British Isles was an inappropriate, if not impossible, task. How could they know the truth of these matters? Instead, they placed a notice in the papers admitting that their organization or their partner ones were not the "proper tribunal for investigating and determining cases of this nature." A caveat was added: as they did not wish to "prejudice" Jackson's case just because they declined to endorse him, they ended with a note stating that their organization's secretary, in a private capacity, thought Jackson was (in another word we have seen recur) "genuine."

This kind of halfhearted validation must have been insulting and exasperating to Jackson as he hustled for more audiences and more opportunities. But he would take what he could get.

Around this same time, across the ocean, the English family filed a report to the government known as a "Slave Schedule." This 1860 document, listed the gender and ages of the people Elizabeth English held in bondage. While individual names are lacking on these forms, some information jumps out. Among the forty-four people listed, a Black man of some forty-three years of age and noted as a "fugitive" is listed as part of her claim.[53] Jackson was long gone by then. It had been fourteen years since he had emancipated himself. But he had not been forgotten, and the English family still demanded his return, if possible. Elizabeth English died in 1860 and her property was divided among her heirs. They had known Jackson when they were growing up. They were ready to pursue their rights. In their eyes and the eyes of the laws of the United States at that time, he was still stolen property, their stolen property.

Jackson wasn't in any immediate danger as he lectured across the Atlantic, but he was still legally vulnerable. Could he lean into that? Lecturers were performers, and the central part of his story was always his thrilling escape. Years after he had left England, audiences still recalled his tales of bloodhounds on the search for him. As transcribed by one reporter, who invoked what he imagined as Black dialect, Jackson said:

> My massa not a very rich massa; he only hab one bloodhound. I feed de bloodhound offen. I make good friend wid de bloodhound. An' de mornin' dat I run away, ven I two, t'ree field off, de massa he see me, an' he say to de bloodhound, "See! Do take dat man." De bloodhound stop an' he look at me, an' he look at de massa, an' he not know vat to do, an' so he do noffin'.

Of course, in England, Jackson was far out of reach of actual bloodhounds. But still . . . it must have added a shiver of danger to the story.[54] The audience could stand with him.

VII

Late in 1859, Jackson was brought into the presence of Charles Hadden Spurgeon (1834–1892), an encounter that was to change both their lives. Spurgeon, who was to become known as "The Prince of Preachers," was a charismatic leader in what was known as the "Particular Baptist" tradition. By 1859, he was already a youthful celebrity among religious leaders of all faiths in the United Kingdom as he rapidly rose through the ranks of the Baptist hierarchy. When Jackson met him, he was already leading the largest nonconformist church in England and was based with the New Park Street Chapel. His sermons were printed and sold around the world. Jackson had seen more of the world than Spurgeon. He was older, too, by at least a decade or more. Yet Spurgeon's star was bright, and Jackson must have known that meeting with him was his big shot.

Jackson had undoubtedly been directed to Spurgeon's London church by other London preachers, but exactly how they first met one another is unclear. What is not unclear is that on Thursday evening, December 8, 1859, Jackson attended a midweek prayer service at the New Park Street Chapel.[55] Jackson was not a planned speaker at this prayer service, but he was invited to share his testimony, and for Jackson, that was a moment to shine.

Jackson spoke for over an hour from Spurgeon's pulpit, evidently enthralling the congregation. He knew when to pause for dramatic effect, and his skills were rewarded: the audience repeatedly interrupted him with a "burst of applause," and when he finished, "the excitement was white-hot."[56] Spurgeon reportedly jumped to his feet, announcing that "Slavery . . . may have to be washed out with blood." He argued that Americans might need to learn lessons "at the point of a bayonet—to carve freedom into her with the Bowie knife or send it home to heart with revolvers." If that violent imagery wasn't enough, Spurgeon added: "Better far should it come to this issue, that north and south should be rent asunder, and the states of the union shivered into a thousand fragments, than that slavery should be permitted to continue."[57]

This kind of language about slavery was somewhat new to Spurgeon. He claimed to have always detested the "wickedness" of slavery and would not have any fellowship with a man stealer. Nonetheless, as he explained, since he had preached "in London and not in New York, [he had] . . . seldom made any allusion to slavery in my sermons." This impetuous, explosive, and vivid invective against slavery in the United States following Jackson's testimony was, of course, immediately reported by newspapers. In many ways, for Spurgeon, it was a disastrous move.

Newspapers crossed the Atlantic swiftly, and within a few weeks, Spurgeon was suddenly under attack in the Southern United States. The sales of his sermons began to plummet. Several American publishers started editing out any references to slavery in his sermons, and a great deal of confusion ensued. Had he recanted? Harriet Beecher Stowe's brother in New York, Henry Ward Beecher, who was the best-known American preacher of the nineteenth century, wrote directly to Spurgeon to ask him what the truth was. Spurgeon, to his credit, stood his ground. While he does not appear to have centered American slavery in his public sermons again, he did continue to hold his absolute position that slavery was "a peculiar institution, just as the devil is a peculiar angel, and as hell is a peculiarly hot place. . . ."[58]

Southern slaveholders sputtered in indignation as word of Spurgeon's confirmed views spread across the Atlantic. A spate of book burnings erupted across the American South from Virginia to South Carolina and from Alabama to Florida, and collections of Spurgeon's sermons were cast into the flames. These events were publicized and celebrated, which, since they were designed for showmanship, makes sense. A newspaper in Alabama wrote, "Spurgeon is in danger of an auto-da-fe." It elaborated, "A Gentleman of this city requests us to invite, and we do hereby invite all persons in Montgomery who possess copies of the sermons of the notorious English abolitionist, Spurgeon, to send them to the jail yard to be burned on next Friday, this day week. A subscription is also on foot to buy of our booksellers all copies of said sermons now in their stores, to be burned on the same occasion. Does anybody say nay?"[59]

Spurgeon, now facing threats to his life by American Southerners who threatened to lynch him, and probably also because the United States was now in a full-blown Civil War, he decided to cancel a much-anticipated overseas trip. He never did cross the Atlantic. He certainly never took on Southern enslavers in a public forum again. He was cautious about such matters thereafter. Jackson's testimony had instigated consequences neither of them could have anticipated.

But what of the effect Spurgeon had on Jackson? It must have been wonderful at first. Here was one of the most prominent religious figures in the world taking his life story seriously. Spurgeon welcomed Jackson and Julia into the congregation. Jackson and Julia would proudly announce this formal church affiliation and their church membership at various talks thereafter. Congregants would help them with jobs, with Bible study, and with donations. Because of Spurgeon, doors opened and opportunities beckoned. Donations were collected. As Jackson understood it, Spurgeon and his circle might finally help him liberate his family. None of this was to play out.

Thanks to this prayer meeting at the New Park Street Chapel and the vital patronage allowed by Spurgeon, and especially the fact that Spurgeon was to let Jackson use his name and his networks for some time to secure opportunities and solicit funds, the future looked bright. Spurgeon didn't seem to have publicly mentioned Jackson by name after this event, but Jackson made sure to keep mentioning Spurgeon. As far as Jackson and Julia were concerned, they were inextricably linked with Spurgeon in the public mind until they weren't.

VIII

Fueled by his newfound association with Spurgeon, Jackson's lecture tours became more systematic, and he could now return to some old venues from time to time to connect with friends, if not necessarily to speak at the same places again. He was now familiar with the rhythms of the speaking circuit. He had a good sense of places he and Julia might comfortably stay and now had connections with editors and newspapers nationwide. Nonetheless, the money he might bring in couldn't support him year-round, especially since the bulk of the donations were presumably being set aside for the liberation of his family. Even if the money had been adequate, the travel must have been grueling. They needed a home base.

We have some clues about how they supported themselves when not lecturing. At one point, Jackson attended an event by Washington Duff from Kentucky, a fellow Black lecturer. At that event, Duff stated that he supported himself by lecturing during the winter months and doing "rough painting" during the summer.[60] Since painting and whitewashing had also been Jackson's trade back in Canada, it seems probable that they were working together at least occasionally. Indeed, Jackson painted on and off over the years to supplement his income.[61] His lecturing schedule also appears to support this speculation. While Jackson had some summer lecture engagements over the nine years he was in Britain, the bulk of his speaking engagements, like Duff's, occurred in the winter. Having a stable London address would have made earning a supplementary income much easier. We can see that by 1861, if not before, Jackson and Julia had found a home in London.

When, in April 1861, an official census taker came by Baker Street in the north London neighborhood of Finsbury, he might have been surprised to see a Black couple there.[62] It would have been a spring day, and even this dense neighborhood would have been a bit fresher and cleaner than in previous months. The rest of his building and his block were populated with artisan-class and working-class folks, mostly native Londoners and presumably white. Although, since the 1861 Census did not ask for the race of any inhabitants, we can imagine what the census taker might have seen.

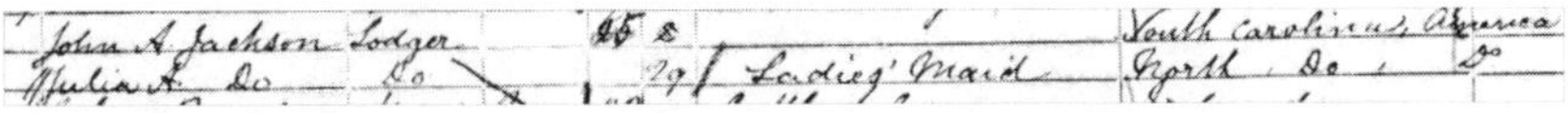
John A Jackson Lodger 45 South Carolina America
Julia A Do Do 29 Ladies' Maid North Do Do

The 1861 British Census featuring Julia and John Andrew Jackson living in the Finsbury neighborhood of London. Their origins in North and South Carolina are registered, but their skin color goes unremarked upon.

After a lifetime of being archived or cataloged by skin color, Jackson and Julia were finally enumerated simply as the people that they were—albeit as curious immigrants hailing from South and North Carolina, respectively. After Jackson's bold census listing as a Black man in Foreman's Boston boarding house and then the inscription in Canada reframing his race as "United States," he had accumulated some quirky kinds of archival presence already. But this census, for better or for worse, erased his color entirely. He was still a Black man. He and Julia would have been seen and identified as such by their neighbors. But something had changed.

It wasn't high-end living. The families on this block were clustered in small flats. But Jackson's closest neighbors included a civil service worker, a governess, a bookseller, various domestic servants, a cattle salesman, and an "agent" of "gold and silver." This isn't surprising since the Clerkenwell/Finsbury neighborhood had, since medieval times, long attracted clock makers, printers, bookbinders, printers, and other artisan trades. This cluster of occupations suggests that it would have been a calm and respectable area at that time, albeit one adjacent to lively commercial activities. It's quite possible that some of the neighbors were themselves Spurgeon acolytes and had helped Jackson and Julia rent and furnish these rooms. Significantly for Jackson and Julia, even if their Baker Street neighbors weren't from their congregation, they must have been tolerant of, if not necessarily warm to, the Black "Ladies Maid" and her Black husband, an occasional painter who often traveled as an itinerant lecturer.

A few days after the census taker visited the Baker Street flat, a mortar shot exploded in the air over the federally held Fort Sumter in the harbor of Charleston, South Carolina. Confederate forces then opened a full attack on the eighty men within. The American Civil War had begun. News traveled to England quickly. When Julia and Jackson heard the news, they must have wondered: If the Confederates won and South Carolina became part of a new country, what would that mean to them? Were they Canadian? British? From the Carolinas, certainly, but *of* the Carolinas? They would have to watch and wait from afar. Fearing. Longing. Praying.

IX

Jackson's new friend, the Reverend Spurgeon, had attracted so many thousands to his sermons that he occasionally needed to preach at overflow music halls and other secular venues. Parishioners recognized his talent and popular appeal and worked hard to collect donations to construct an enormous new edifice for his congregation—a building that opened in 1861 and became known as the Metropolitan Tabernacle, sited in what is known as the Elephant and Castle area today. It was designed to accommodate 6,000 people and was the largest church in London at that time.[63] The Tabernacle was to become both a haven and a horror for Jackson.

Like many twenty-first-century "megachurches," the Metropolitan Tabernacle was more than simply a place for Sunday services. There were prayer services, children's events, finance and organizational sessions, choral singing, and many kinds of charitable endeavors launched from this institution. It was humming with activity on any day of the week. The Tabernacle may have lacked the bowling alleys or gyms that some large churches boast of today, but it similarly worked to construct a community that would attract all sorts of people for all sorts of reasons. It was a place where congre-

C.H. Spurgeon preaching in the Metropolitan Tabernacle.

gants could go for charity, advice, job counseling, education, music, service opportunities, networking, and sometimes just a kind word.

The imposing Metropolitan Tabernacle soon became a home church for Jackson and Julia. Within two or three years after meeting with Spurgeon, the couple decamped from their Finsbury digs to a new home at 17 Hanover Street in Walworth, London, undoubtedly to be closer to the Metropolitan Tabernacle and their Spurgeonite community.[64] They must have still longed for their families left behind in South and North Carolina, but they were now able to build a new world and perhaps, even with the caste and class and race prejudices of Victorian London, a new kind of family.

The most vital connection Jackson made through this community, outside of Spurgeon himself, may have been with Joseph Passmore, a printer and publisher who had for several years specialized in publishing, promoting, and distributing Spurgeon's enormously popular sermons. Passmore had a junior partner, James Alabaster, and together they agreed to publish Jackson's memoir at their press—a decision which could have been made only with the blessing of their mutual patron, Spurgeon. And it was quite convenient, too: the press was close to Jackson and Julia's Baker Street address.

Thanks to Passmore and Alabaster's networks in the book world, we can be sure that Jackson was directed to a local lithographer, probably in the Finsbury neighborhood. This artist must have spoken with Jackson, or at least consulted with people who had spoken with Jackson, for he came up with the image used for the title page of his book, which specifically referenced Jackson's escape astride his horse. It was not a stock image. The artist for Jackson's little 1862 volume also produced an image of a gimlet, similar to the one Jackson had used to make air holes on the *Smyrna.*

Slave narratives had been circulating with great success in England for some twenty-five years by that point.[65] While many of these titles did sell quite well, even when they didn't they had a lot of value. This is in part because it was understood that a Black man lecturing onstage had only an oral claim on experience and authority and still needed a literary license to speak. A book describing his life, even if no one had read or purchased it, added to his always challenged credibility.

And much as it had with the staging of speaking events, this "literary license" had to be granted by a white patron willing to frame the tale.[66] It was around this time that Jackson must have met another ally through Spurgeon's church, a man known by the initials "W.M.S." "W.M.S." wrote a powerful preface for Jackson's book, connecting Jackson's testimony to the history of English support of the slave trade that had created the system of slavery in America. "Before we then heartily condemn the United States," he cautioned, "let us remember that when they would not have slavery, it was forced upon them by the English Government." And as was typical of many such prefaces to narratives written by former slaves, W.M.S. stated that Jackson's tale was positively mild in comparison to the true horrors of global slavery. As he wrote of slavery: "The worse cannot be told."[67]

With this solid preface, a committed press, and a catchy illustration, a bold new endeavor was set into motion. Jackson could now join the ranks of the formally documented. He was to share his witness, display his reason, showcase his humanity, and perhaps find an additional revenue stream. His book, *The Experience of a Slave in South Carolina*, was born.

How exactly Jackson wrote this book when he was probably only somewhat literate at the time is a bit of a mystery. It seems highly like that he received some rudimentary education during his time in Saint John, perhaps from his wife or others in the community there. It is during his years in England, though, that we can see clues that Jackson worked hard to further educate himself and finally put some of his skills to use. A journalist in 1857, for example, observed that Jackson had delivered his lecture with "excellent effect" although he was "*comparatively* illiterate, having been unable to read or write *at the time* of his escape [italics mine]."[68] The implication was, of course, that he was *now* beginning to be able to read and write. By 1862, some five years later, it appears that Jackson had become fluent enough to chronicle his tale for himself, and with "excellent effect." By 1870, only eight years after his book came out, Jackson and Julia were listed on U.S. Census records as able to both read and write. He might have needed help, but there are lots of reasons to think he composed the bulk of his own work.

But how? As we have speculated elsewhere, it seems quite possible Julia was able to read and write. Did Julia help him with his memoir? And might the W.M.S. who wrote a preface for Jackson have similarly assisted with smoothing out errors or fine-tuning the story? Did Passmore or Alabaster use some of their expertise to help edit his drafts? All those possibilities seem reasonable, but the fact remains that Jackson, with the cooperation of his white publisher and his sponsors, doesn't soften or add any note of humility to his title page. The book is his and his alone.

With the assistance of his savvy and experienced publishers Passmore and Alabaster, *The Experience of a Slave in South Carolina* was registered for copyright in 1862.[69]

As happened with many other narratives by self-emancipated people of the era, Jackson laid out his name and claimed his authorship. The title page didn't note that this was "as told to" or attributed to an amanuensis or editors, which was common. Nor did it feature a sentence about how it was "as a statement of fact" either, which was another frequent caveat next to a title. Notably, it didn't even include "as written by himself," which was another common device for these books, most famously used by Frederick Douglass back in 1845 with the first publication of his life story.[70] Jackson was confident enough in his ownership of himself and his story to not need elaboration. This was his story and his experience.

The Experience of a Slave in South Carolina is, in many ways, a memoir that fits into very expected categories for its time. It fits so well into expected formulas for such writing that it suggests Jackson and his editors or friends were aware of the standard shaping of such a testimonial. That Jackson by now knew the formula serves as yet more evidence that he could read by this time. Narratives written or dictated by people who had survived slavery varied over the decades and according to each individual's situation. But certain patterns can be found in the ones published in the antebellum era, and how Jackson followed those patterns in some ways and diverged in others can tell us a bit about how he wanted to present himself to the world.[71]

To start with, the image he commissioned for his title page is an action shot rather than the more dignified portrait that usually accompanies such narratives. This conveys to us quite a bit about his need to be seen as a man of movement, a man of courage, and a man with a vivid personality who was unafraid to be seen. As discussed in the opening of this chapter, his escape was possible in large part because of his bravado and flash. He knew a picture of himself in dandyish checked pants, speeding toward his freedom, could help sell the product—both the book and himself.

Jackson opens with "I was born in South Carolina," with no mention of date. Indeed, the lack of a date underscored the exclusion he felt from the world of documented people born free with the luxuries of recorded status. His book then unfolds the story of how he survived under the torments of the English family. And, even more important, it lingers on the suffering of others that he witnessed. It then, of course, goes on to the remarkable tale of his escape first to Massachusetts, then to Canada, and then to his arrival in England. This all would have been perfectly in line with what audiences expected from such a book.

Narratives of that era were known to depict the lives of enslaved people in a rote and usually chronological way. And while Jackson has some wry asides, the overall life story is rather simply told and only with a bit of rambling here and there. In one such instance, he is about to wrap up a story about how satisfying it had been to finally get paid for his labor once he had a good job in Salem. Still, before letting readers feel too relieved over his momentary happiness, he jumps back in time to digress for a few pages on further abuses he had seen in South Carolina. He was desperate to pay witness to as many injustices as he could, even when they disrupted the text. He then catches himself by noting, "But I am wandering."

Readers can forgive these asides. After all, what's compelling about these digressions is that this kind of unorganized narrative makes a good case for arguing that the newly literate Jackson wrote it himself! Or at least it suggests he constructed most of it. It would have been easy and tempting for a dominant editor or ghostwriter to delete or at least move these digressions to places where they would have made more narrative sense.[72] The fact that they didn't do so suggests that this occasionally disordered story is fully his. The book gives the impression of having been authored by a storyteller who drafted his narrative with an eye for telling details and a rhetorical flair but who lacked sophistication in textual shape and flow. That sounds like Jackson.

As the core source for studying his life, Jackson's short book has been quoted throughout this biography. As we've seen, his often wry authorial voice injects itself amid otherwise harrowing but sadly not remarkable incidents to give them a lift and a life that can jump off the pages. Sometimes he would offer asides: "I belong to South Carolina," he told a questioner. "It was none of their business whom I belonged to; I was trying to belong to myself."[73] He had clever terms: of the English family, he wrote, "I and the pony gave them leg-bail for security."[74] Other times he would make bitter analogies: "The slaveholders live upon their slaves just as the hawk and owl live upon the hen and chickens."[75] And sometimes he would mock with a vengeful tone: "My mistress had two household gods, viz. Her bunch of keys, in which she manifested a peculiar interest, and her brandy bottle, which she consulted with a frequency which was most alarming."[76] His wit, his anger, and his edge come through.

Jackson's dark portrait of human nature, after spending chapter after chapter chronicling cruelties, softens toward the end. He turns toward love, action, and hope through his inclusion of a chapter that contains lyrics from what he calls "slave songs" as well as more rousing antislavery songs. Jackson chose to report from his experience. This was not an ethnographic critique or scholarly analysis. He recalled from his own direct experience not songs of slavery generally but the songs he had himself sung in Robert English's cotton fields.

Formerly enslaved people often appended the words of poems at the beginning or end of their narratives of this era. But sharing song lyrics was less common, and adding musical analysis, such as Jackson's, is almost without precedent. His analysis of the music he had known in South Carolina or the antislavery songs he had come to learn since is some of the very earliest writing by any Black person about the history and culture of American Black music.[77]

In his lectures, Jackson would sometimes sing or try to lead his audiences in song. His inclusion of song lyrics in his book re-creates those moments. He opens this chapter with a piece he calls simply "A Spiritual Hymn" that goes on for fifty-one lines. Indeed, Jackson's narrative could almost work as a songbook for an audience wanting to join in. His songs were an outreached hand to meet his audiences where they were and bring them along. "O Sheperd, wha'thou bin all day," the hymn asks. "You promised my Jesus to mind these lambs."

Jackson doesn't want these lyrics to simply be picked over by white audiences. He doesn't necessarily trust how they might read them. And so, rather remarkably, he unpacks them with his sharp analysis and commentary.[78] He wrote of their practical use, "They sing to keep time while picking cotton in the field under the burning sun." He also takes pains to argue that the structural shaping of the songs reflects an appreciation for storytelling and imagination.[79]

Slave songs were, as Jackson explained, often snatches of hymns overheard and misunderstood but reshaped or reinvigorated in spiritual form. They may have come from "meeting-houses and camp-meetings of white men."[80] He accounts for this phenomenon by remarking that "probably the reason for the number of repeats, is because they [enslaved people] have no books allowed them, and indeed . . . on hearing a single line sung by white people these poor slaves cannot prize it too much, as is shown by their singing it over and over." Jackson's reading of how these songs worked (he notes, for example, that a "hallelujah" grammatically misplaced in the middle of a line is necessary because of the emotive energy behind it) demonstrates how, in the larger story of his life, he sought to weave together the story of all bondsmen, and how their humanity shaped their world.

Jackson also included lyrics to songs that he categorized under the heading of "Antislavery Songs," such as those that might be sung at Emancipation Association meetings. Some of them were specifically the kinds of songs abolitionist groups had been performing around England, and he specifically calls out the Hutchinsons as performers who had popularized some of these songs.[81] He includes lyrics to the rousing tune "The Flight of the Bondman," to the sentimental song "The Bereaved Mother," and to one to specifically encourage activists: "Ye Heralds of Freedom." He also includes the lyrics to a minstrel song often known as "Dearest Mae" but which he retitles as "A Slave Song"—the very song Stowe had quoted after meeting him back in 1850 when she noted he was from "Ole Carliny State"—although by the time he was in England, he had updated the words to echo events in his own life.[82] His version ran:

> They worked me all the day,
> Without a bit of pay
> So I took my flight in the middle of the night
> When the sun was gone away. . . .
> I heard in Canada, all men were free
> And that I was going there in search of liberty.[83]

Jackson's voice comes through in his narrative, even as he wove it into normative formulas. It delivered to this audience. They got their music! They could read an obligatory section about his family. They could shiver to violent scenes of harrowing tragedy; they could breathe easy at the happy ending of his escape. He knew what he was doing. But his tragedies and traumas and his glories and his wins were his alone. *The Experience of a Slave in South Carolina* allowed him an opportunity to call out to all those people he had left behind.

After eight years of professional lecturing around the British Isles, Jackson knew that testimonials were currency. For that reason, he attached to his book several pages worth of testimonials he had collected from 1856 before leaving the United States. Also tipped in were more recent endorsements from various clergy and other upstanding antislavery activists in England testifying to his character.[84]

Most valuable of all, and the testimonial he included first in his collection, was a simple statement from Spurgeon dated April 16, 1860: "I am very happy to say that Mr. Jackson is a member of my Church, and is well worthy of all confidence and regard."[85] Jackson and Spurgeon would not remain allies for much longer. But that letter at that time was everything.

At the conclusion of his core story and before the appendices of lyrics and endorsements, after decrying cruelty and sketching out an untold number of horrors, Jackson ended simply by writing, "I, John Andrew Jackson, once a slave in the United States, had seen and heard all this, therefore I publish it."[86]

How well the book sold is hard to say. One newspaper remarked upon its distribution by writing: "During the lecture a little book, 'The Experience of a Slave in South Carolina by John Andrew Jackson,' met with a deservedly rapid sale."[87] But it is also true that today there are only a small handful of copies held in rare book collections worldwide. It appears it didn't sell too many copies outside England despite the helpful network of Spurgeonites, and, as we shall see, it was never published or formally distributed in the United States.

Regardless of sales figures, whatever they might have been, the volume helped Jackson claim a marketable legitimacy in the eyes of the audience. He could publish his truth on his own terms. His speeches could now be backed up with print. And unlike newspapers, with their unreliable paraphrasing and racist condescension, this time, the print was his.[88]

CHAPTER EIGHT

THE WHITE PREACHER AND THE BLACK SLAVE LECTURER (1865)

England and Scotland (1863–1865)

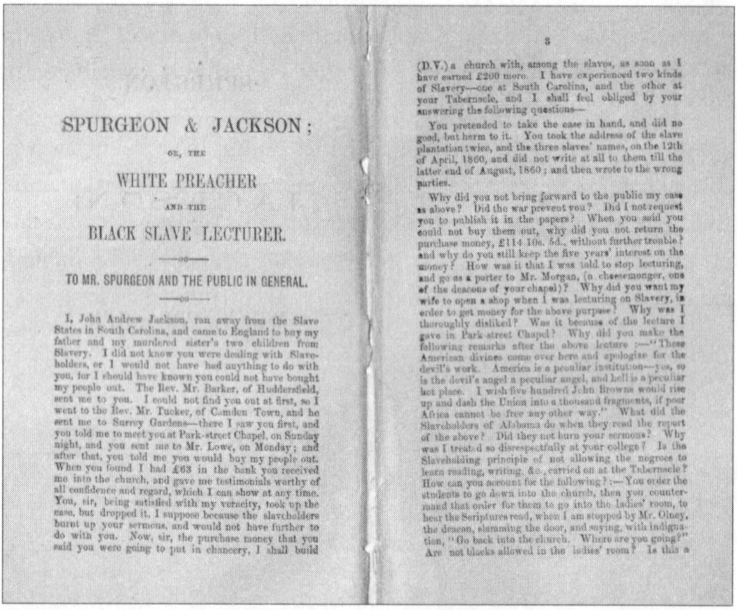

SPURGEON & JACKSON;

OR, THE

WHITE PREACHER

AND THE

BLACK SLAVE LECTURER.

TO MR. SPURGEON AND THE PUBLIC IN GENERAL.

I, John Andrew Jackson, ran away from the Slave States in South Carolina, and came to England to buy my father and my murdered sister's two children from Slavery. I did not know you were dealing with Slaveholders, or I would not have had anything to do with you, for I should have known you could not have bought my people out. The Rev. Mr. Barker, of Huddersfield, sent me to you. I could not find you out at first, so I went to the Rev. Mr. Tucker, of Camden Town, and he sent me to Surrey Gardens—there I saw you first, and you told me to meet you at Park-street Chapel, on Sunday night, and you sent me to Mr. Lowe, on Monday; and after that, you told me you would buy my people out. When you found I had £63 in the bank you received me into the church, and gave me testimonials worthy of all confidence and regard, which I can show at any time. You, sir, being satisfied with my veracity, took up the case, but dropped it, I suppose because the slaveholders burnt up your sermons, and would not have further to do with you. Now, sir, the purchase money that you said you were going to put in chancery, I shall build

3

(D.V.) a church with, among the slaves, as soon as I have earned £200 more. I have experienced two kinds of Slavery—one at South Carolina, and the other at your Tabernacle, and I shall feel obliged by your answering the following questions—

You pretended to take the case in hand, and did no good, but harm to it. You took the address of the slave plantation twice, and the three slaves' names, on the 12th of April, 1860, and did not write at all to them till the latter end of August, 1860; and then wrote to the wrong parties.

Why did you not bring forward to the public my case as above? Did the war prevent you? Did I not request you to publish it in the papers? When you said you could not buy them out, why did you not return the purchase money, £114 10s. 5d., without further trouble? and why do you still keep the five years' interest on the money? How was it that I was told to stop lecturing, and go as a porter to Mr. Morgan, (a cheesemonger, one of the deacons of your chapel)? Why did you want my wife to open a shop when I was lecturing on Slavery, in order to get money for the above purpose? Why was I thoroughly disliked? Was it because of the lecture I gave in Park-street Chapel? Why did you make the following remarks after the above lecture:—"These American divines come over here and apologize for the devil's work. America is a peculiar institution—yes, so is the devil's angel a peculiar angel, and hell is a peculiar hot place. I wish five hundred John Browns would rise up and dash the Union into a thousand fragments, if poor Africa cannot be free any other way." What did the Slaveholders of Alabama do when they read the report of the above? Did they not burn your sermons? Why was I treated so disrespectfully at your college? Is the Slaveholding principle of not allowing the negroes to learn reading, writing, &c., carried on at the Tabernacle? How can you account for the following?:—You order the students to go down into the church, then you countermand that order for them to go into the ladies' room, to hear the Scriptures read, when I am stopped by Mr. Olney, the deacon, slamming the door, and saying, with indignation, "Go back into the church. Where are you going?" Are not blacks allowed in the ladies' room? Is this a

This pamphlet appears to have been self-published. It lays out Jackson's grievances against Spurgeon in the strongest possible language: "I have experienced two kinds of slavery —one at South Carolina and the other at your Tabernacle."

Jackson was now a published author. He and Julia had spoken from pulpits and stages across England and Scotland. But his success was to catch up to him. Jackson's arduously constructed reputation began to fall apart. White sabotage was destroying all that he had built. What had brought him to this point? Newspaper accounts differ, but Jackson started writing again to claim his truth on his terms. When his friends didn't stand with him, and his world began to crumble, what were he and Julia to do?

Jackson penned an enraged account of what had unfolded and laid out his grievances against one of the most powerful men in Europe.[1] In doing so, he also laid out an entirely new and startling path forward.

I

In the spring of 1864, Jackson had lost his patience. He was furious, desperate, and flailing. He was stranded in England, and, as he saw it, his British allies had betrayed him. His most important sponsor, the influential Reverend Charles Haddon Spurgeon of London's Metropolitan Tabernacle, had withdrawn his patronage. But Jackson had encountered betrayal before. With little left to lose and desperate to voice his outrage, he composed his thoughts in a frantic tract titled *Spurgeon and Jackson, or, the White Preacher and the Black Slave Lecturer.*

This tract is challenging to read. The arguments lack a calm editorial hand, which conversely makes it that much more of an authentically self-authored document. For a man who had been functionally illiterate only a few years earlier, the fact that he composed his manifesto of rebellion and grievance against one of the most powerful men of the nineteenth century is extraordinary. But Jackson hadn't spent his life carefully constructing a persona of resilient bravado for nothing. Now was his time to fight back.

What exactly he hoped to accomplish with this pamphlet is a bit hard to say, and it must have cost a fair amount of money to produce, a resource Jackson didn't have in abundance. He had traveled the world hoping to save his family, save himself, and perhaps advance the dream of abolition. He decries the corruption of the church! He rails against the racism of the Spurgeon community! He calls out hypocrisy and greed! Truly, this pamphlet, in all of its frantic fury, is a bit hard to follow, but it demonstrates that he had fully come into his own, ready to take on his adversaries with nothing more than his pen, his wit, and his anger. As he wrote in this open letter to Spurgeon, "I have experienced two kinds of slavery—one at South Carolina and the other at your Tabernacle."[2]

Before we give a close contextual read of this remarkable screed—a document that provides insight into Jackson's motivations, desperation, and confidence in himself as a successful agitator—we need to understand what led to it. How did his hopeful arrival in Britain and the great success he found there all come crashing down?

As we have seen, during his first few years in England, Jackson managed to fashion himself into a polished advocate for himself and the antislavery movement. However, despite his successes, he hadn't quite secured sufficient resources to free his family back in South Carolina. Nor had he found the stability and advancement in the world that he had dreamed of for himself and Julia. In England, he had become an author but was to learn that his words could be wrested away from him. On the other hand, if his white patron had failed him, so be it. He could now fashion himself into his own kind of rebel.

II

With the 1862 publication of *The Experience of a Slave in South Carolina*, a good number of helpful friends in the Spurgeon network, and a new home close to Spurgeon's enormous Metropolitan Tabernacle, Jackson and Julia must have felt things were taking a turn for them. Surely they could accumulate enough money to purchase Jackson's father and the two children of his murdered sister, Bella, soon. And now they had an influential celebrity patron to help facilitate such a complicated transaction. While he and Julia would have followed news from the United States and the Civil War with fearful and hopeful hearts, the fact that the end of the war would surely come soon must have been on their minds every day. Who in their families might live to be free?

There were always challenges on the speaking circuit. Sometimes events didn't receive the turnout expected. One such incident was recorded by the *Western Times* on December 13, 1862: "Very few persons attended, and after waiting some time on the platform, seeing it was a very meagre affair, Mr. Jackson thanked those present and left the room." Other events were attended by hostile audience members, and occasionally, Jackson would have to face scornful attacks from racist Southern sympathizers. One especially vicious account in the *Morning Post* described him as a "whining nigger." It mocked the fact that gullible Baptists would listen to—much less endorse—him. The correspondent suggested Jackson was collecting money under false pretenses, mocked Jackson's singing, and—shockingly—suggested that Jackson should be whipped on-site in the church:

> Mr. Jackson's description would be far more vivid and impressive if he would illustrate it by placing a cowhide in the hand of some able-bodied deacon of the chapel and submitting his able shoulders to flagellation. We should expect that, if the deacon were up to his work, he would ensure Mr. Jackson's singing at least one melody in a feeling style.[3]

Despite its jubilant and performative cruelty, this kind of review seems to have had no significant public effect. Although it would have undoubtedly distressed Julia and Jackson, how could they be surprised? They had both endured bondage in South Carolina. They knew that dehumanizing cruelty was liable to be directed at them at any time. Perhaps they shrugged it off.

Jackson continued to be invited to speak at Baptist venues but also at other venues around the country. Indeed, much like that Haynsworth letter that had been sent in reply to the inquiry about freeing Louisa and little Jinny—being able to boast of this kind of enemy demonstrated to the public what he was up against.

There were signs, now, that Jackson was becoming increasingly comfortable in his public persona. His political engagement was growing. Instead of prayer meetings or informal church gatherings, his events show more and more signs of being organizationally affiliated. He was now beginning to appear at antislavery meetings.[4]

In Chester, Jackson appeared on the stage with the Manchester Union and Emancipation Society. This time he delivered a talk that provided statistics about the number of people estimated to be escaping from enslavement during the war. How could he have been privy to this kind of information? He was now leveraging detailed current events for his own purposes. Since there aren't any specific examples of what he said or what he knew of these statistics, we cannot know how accurate he was or what his source was. Nonetheless, that he was citing statistics suggests he was following newspapers and reading for sources beyond personal testimony to bolster his arguments. His world was now bigger than just himself, and he found it useful to invoke a more worldly perspective when needed. In that meeting, the *Cheshire Observer* noted that Jackson seconded a motion condemning slavery and celebrating the Union cause.[5] Jackson was now recognized as an informed and increasingly sophisticated political actor, a man who could agitate for fundamental social change with new tools.

With this growth came conflict. Jackson's increasing political activism and his deep immersion in the discussion around Britain's supposed neutrality during the Civil War came to the fore when he became embroiled in a strange political debate played out, as always, in the newspapers. In May 1863, he attended a lecture in the town of Bacup delivered by a speaker named "Mr. Lawson" on the topic of the American Civil War. Lawson argued that the South had a moral right, if not a legal right, to secede from the Union in the same way that Jackson (he pointed at him sitting in the audience) had a moral right, but not a legal right, to flee his enslaver.[6] This bad-faith analogy, obscene in its ironic implications, could not have been lost on Jackson. He was surely disgusted and infuriated to hear his suffering disingenuously invoked to support an argument to garner public sympathy for the Confederacy. The newspaper doesn't report on it, but we can well imagine Jackson had a furious retort to share during or after the event.

In addition to the official lectures chronicled by the press, Jackson would speak informally in public venues whenever he could. For years he had been honing a style and approach for those less regulated venues. He must have developed a technique and perhaps had a friend to ensure he could pass the hat for donations without being robbed. Town squares, public greens, urban parks, church courtyards, and sidewalks were all fair game to him. And for the most part, over the years, the public tolerated his informal lectures, but speaking outside was a risky hustle. Because these speeches didn't have the formal protection of organizational sponsors or the protocol expectations of events held in a sacred space, he was especially vulnerable to hecklers. These outdoor talks could attract conflict—usually and doubtlessly shaped by racist assumptions about whose voice belonged in a public forum in the first place. Crowds could let him know that he did not belong.

Once Jackson spoke to a crowd in "the open air" of Lewisham. Things started well, but he was menaced by a drunken onlooker. It began with jeers, but the man decided to take it further—he strode toward the table Jackson was standing on and kicked it out from under him. The table fell to the ground in a dramatic crash, and Jackson fell. Onlookers helped Jackson stand up and held the aggressor while others ran for the police. The police listened to the witnesses in the crowd and arrested the heckler. The case went to the judge, who found the defendant guilty. When the judge asked Jackson if he wished to press for fines, Jackson replied that "the defendant was a poor man like himself, and he would not ask for personal costs. All he wanted was to make an example of him by having the defendant fined."[7]

Of course, Jackson's magnanimity is notable here, but this incident is worth recalling for another aspect. Jackson may have been seeking to ingratiate himself with the judge and the court. The courts had worked for him in this instance, and unlike many other poor Black men in Victorian England, Jackson was gaining some faith that institutions might work for him in the future. The press had usually served him well, and here, when things could have gone very badly, the courts had supported him and saw him as a victim. He must have been feeling optimistic about institutions. Police officers and judges had been on his side. He had seen justice done.

This would not always be the case.

Through late 1863 and early 1864, Jackson and Julia traveled north for a series of lectures in Scotland. He was broadening the scope of his lectures and building on his connections with Spurgeon and other clergy as he went from venue to venue in places such as Edinburgh, Aberdeen, and Dundee. Audiences may have ebbed and flowed a bit, but his reception across Scotland continued to be positive, with one newspaper observing with bemused condescension, "Mr. Jackson, considering that he is a negro, is one of the best speakers of the English language that we have heard for some time, having nearly got over 'de difficulties ob de pronunciation.'"[8]

Let them laugh, Jackson must have thought. They kept coming.

III

Jackson and Julia made their way up to Dundee in the spring of 1864, evidently planning to stay there for a few weeks and making it a base of operations while Jackson would tour churches and other speaking venues in the region. They had been to Scotland before—some of their earliest talks after arriving in Liverpool had been delivered in Scotland—and so, while Dundee itself may have been new territory, they were comfortable with Scottish culture generally and doubtless had friends or acquaintances to connect with there.

As always, Julia and Jackson needed to settle into places that would host them, which for Black travelers was not always a given. Eventually, they secured lodgings on South Tay Street in Dundee, a densely populated area close to the docks on the river Tay but not the wildest end of the street filled with sailors.[9] Instead, their stretch was populated with genteel albeit humble neighbors. A directory of South Tay Street shows a cluster of teachers and clerks living there alongside confectioners, cabinet makers, accountants, and a few milliners and dressmakers. This was not a street populated by the many factory workers who, at that time, made up the overwhelming population of Dundee and who resided in squalid city slums. We can guess, then, that Jackson and Julia tried to differentiate themselves from the city's lower classes. They must have taken care to find a place that would allow them to live within a veneer of genteel respectability while not taking up too much of their money.

Dundee would have reminded them of Saint John back in Canada: it, too, was a tough and northern maritime city with a chilly harbor and an ascending hill up to the busy city center. It, too, had a large population of

Irish immigrants and a focus on international trade. As a city with a longer history than Saint John, though, and a far larger population, it had many factories, mills, churches, chapels, civic buildings, and even castles that Saint John had lacked. If John and Julia had any time to spare, they certainly would have tried to walk around the city to figure out how the medieval streets were now purposed for the industrial revolution of the Victorian age.

The global flow of capital and products that relied upon the slave economy was particularly noticeable in Dundee. Much as Jackson's labor back in Salem had involved processing hides that were then used by the local shoe industry for bulk purchases by Southern labor camps, here were Scottish mills known for spinning cheap fibers from India into coarse, rough cloth which could then be sent to the Southern United States. Quality cotton might be exported *from* South Carolina, but the state also imported unpleasantly rough but durable fabric, sometimes known as "Osnaburg" cloth. Often spun in Scotland and shipped across the Atlantic to either the Caribbean or to the Southern United States, Osnaburg cloth was most often allocated to enslaved workers. Jackson described the clothing he had back on the English plantation as only "rags," which may or may not have been cheap Scottish cloth fit only for people who had no choice. Jacob Stroyer, however, a man enslaved in South Carolina about sixty miles from Lynchburg, remembered that as a child, he had worn shirts made from Scottish cloth; he wrote that his only garment was "an Osnaburg linen shirt, worn by both sexes of the negro children in the summer."[10] In Dundee, Julia and Jackson would have walked by the places that had manufactured the uncomfortable clothes they had surely hated as children in the Southern United States.

Dundee was known then for "Jute, Jam, and Journalism" thanks to its marmalade business, manufacture of jute, and proliferation of punchy journalists. This last claim to fame was to document and shape what happened next.

Many speakers crisscrossed the lecture circuit, opining on any manner of topics and competing fiercely for audiences and donations. Competition between speakers about abolition or antislavery, particularly when their color, national origin, or legal status became part of their marketable novelty or expertise, could be fierce. Sometimes alliances could be forged. But sometimes fractures or disputes could be damaging to all involved. What happened next for Jackson was a terrible unraveling of all he had achieved thus far.

While in Dundee, Jackson became aware of another itinerant Black lecturer, the Reverend Isaac W. Davidson, who was also holding speaking

SLAVERY IN AMERICA.

MR JOHN A. JACKSON, an American Fugitive Slave, will LECTURE in WILLISON FREE CHURCH, Barrack Street, on MONDAY EVENING, at Eight o'clock, and in FREE ST ANDREW'S CHURCH, Meadowside Rev. J. EWING'S), on TUESDAY EVENING, at Eight o'clock.

Jackson's advertisement for his lectures during the spring of 1864 appeared across the same weeks and often in the same Scottish newspapers as advertisements for sermons and public talks by another Black man from the United States, the Reverend Isaac W. Davidson.

THE REV. ISAAC W. DAVISON, of FREE TOWN, Sierra Leone, West Coast of Africa, will (D.V.) PREACH MISSIONARY SERMONS, next SABBATH, the 22d, in CHALMERS' FREE CHURCH, Hunter Street (Mr STIRLING'S), at a Quarter-past Two P.M.; in the REFORMED PRESBYTERIAN CHURCH, Hawkhill (Mr RIDDELL'S), at 6.30, in the Evening. Collections will be made at both in behalf of his Mission.

Advertisement for sermons that the Reverend Isaac W. Davidson delivered in May 1864.

events during this time.[11] Davidson was probably hard to avoid. Not only was he meeting with many of the same clergy that Jackson was, but he was advertising in the same newspapers that Jackson was using. "Did you two know one another?" people would have asked. And "Why should I give to you, when I gave to him only yesterday?" Perhaps people complained that they couldn't distinguish between them. How many Black speakers from the United States might a place like Dundee support?

Davidson, who may have been in Dundee before Jackson arrived, claimed to have been enslaved in Fredericksburg, Virginia, but then had served as a missionary in Sierra Leone. He had temporarily returned to England for health reasons but was now collecting donations to return to his mission work. He had networks and friendly relations with prominent clergy and citizens in the city. The advertisements for Davidson's talks that appeared in Dundee's papers in the spring of 1864 suggest that his lectures and sermons focused more on his mission work than his former bondage. Nonetheless, there is no denying that in a small city like Dundee, Jackson and Davidson were competing for the same core audience. Did they meet? These two men evidently had some sort of undocumented personal encounter, perhaps attending one another's talks and challenging one another.

Whatever had led up to their conflict, Jackson laid out his charges to the public. He found a clearing on High Street in Dundee; he may have stood on a small platform near a construction site. He took a deep breath. His case had to be clear. It had to be punchy. After years onstage, he knew how to gather and excite a crowd. Davidson was "an imposter," he claimed. Jackson then spiraled into a series of charges and accusations witnessed by a large and mostly supportive audience. According to testimony Davidson provided to court shortly thereafter, Jackson slandered him by "falsely, maliciously, and calumniously stating that I was an adulterer and a fornicator, and that I had been out late at night with prostitutes."[12] Moreover, Davidson claimed Jackson had accused him of being a "liar," a "rascal," and then, in a frenzy which does sound a bit like something the passionate but sometimes frantic Jackson would say, called Davidson "a dodger, an old dodger, and is always dodging . . . [also] a coward" who claimed "that I never was a slave as I asserted."[13]

What was at stake here? Professional jealousy? The charge that Davidson was licentious, fraudulent, and corrupt in general might be the kind of charge competing lecturers hurled at one another, but the charge that Davidson had never been enslaved at all seems to have come from somewhere deeper. It was also probably misplaced: Davidson was able to produce impressive testimonials of his character and his origins, including one from W.L. Underwood, who was the United States consul in Glasgow and a native of Fredericksburg, Virginia. Underwood knew the former enslaver of Davidson and vouched for the fact that Davidson was who he said he was.[14]

Jackson was from South Carolina, and Davidson was from Virginia; no matter how different their life experiences, it is astounding that Jackson didn't recognize Davidson as a fellow survivor. Instead, he saw Davidson as a threat—and his attacks on Davidson were to be Jackson's undoing.

Davidson found himself a lawyer and charged Jackson with slander. Jackson would not go down without a fight, and he had seen justice work in his favor before. He found a Scottish lawyer, Archibald Paul, to defend him in court. His lawyer was well situated on Reform Street, close to the courts, where many lawyers, notaries, and people involved in legal affairs all clustered. It's unlikely he would have represented Jackson for free, so Jackson and Julia must have dipped into their savings to pay the necessary fees. They would have been frightened.

A slander case involving two Black men in Dundee caught the attention of local journalists who buzzed around the local court proceedings. The novelty of a Black man suing another Black man in a Scottish court of law could not be resisted, and the media coverage was positively gleeful. Before the court could determine the facts of the charge, it needed to figure out whether the case could be handled at all. As the newspapers reported, discussions quickly devolved into debates over jurisdiction. Lawyer Paul did his best to argue that the conflict did not belong in court. Since neither man was a permanent resident of Dundee, their lawyers and the court authorities debated whether these two men had the standing to bring their cases at all.

The racist undertones of the proceedings were not subtle, as both men were seen as non-Scottish citizens needlessly taking up court time. Headlines characterized the case as "A Black Squabble."[15] The judges and sheriffs quoted in the Dundee papers seem to have found the entire case amusing. Jackson's lawyer tried to characterize the entire affair as a silly argument between two missionaries and quoted a poem he said this situation reminded him of, saying that these two missionaries were trying to eat one another:

I wish I were a cassowary,
In the plains of Timbuctoo
I would eat a missionary
Body, bones, and hymn-book too.[16]

Jackson's lawyer failed to get the case dismissed because of jurisdiction. Still, his attempt to make the entire proceeds seem foolish by playing on the condescending racist attitudes of the white participants may have been calculated to get the charges dismissed.

Nothing was amusing for the two men involved. Jackson was threatened with over £40 in possible damages, a significant sum of money. It might have taken years to save up that much. And if he couldn't pay the fine, he could end up in prison. And for Davidson, the slander was an attack on his livelihood and mission. Neither of them could afford to laugh.

Lawyer Paul, according to the newspaper reports at least, appears to have made a good effort to get Jackson out of trouble. The case was finally dropped upon the urging of Scottish clergy, who vouched for both men and requested Davidson walk away from the conflict.[17] Once the Sheriff's Court dismissed the case, Jackson stood up and asked to have a character certificate letter read aloud to defend his reputation at the case's conclusion, but his lawyer shut that down. The *Dundee Advertiser* reported:

> Mr. Paul said he had received from his client another certificate, but he did not think he should occupy the time of the Court by reading it.
>
> Mr. Jackson—I insist upon its being read.
>
> Mr. Paul (handing him back the paper)—Never mind just now. You have the satisfaction of knowing that you now leave this Court without a stain upon your character. [Laughter][18]

Lawyer Paul's placating comments aside, the damage done was incalculable. In the court proceedings, Jackson's relationship with Spurgeon was challenged. A Scottish supporter of Davidson named J.M. Cunningham took it upon himself to contact Spurgeon back in London to ascertain whether or not he knew Jackson, if he endorsed Jackson, and if he was aware that Jackson was traveling around Scotland collecting money under his name to support a church in South Carolina.[19]

According to the letter Cunningham published in the paper, he had sent Spurgeon a telegram, and "the following reply was received from Mr. Spurgeon's Private Secretary Mr. Blockshaw;—'Mr. Spurgeon knows nothing whatever of Jackson's chapel scheme and has no money in his hand for that purpose.'"[20]

Humiliation. Betrayal. Jackson was now in an impossible position.

It is tricky to understand exactly what happened in the business with Cunningham and Spurgeon's secretary. As Jackson pointed out in a talk he gave shortly afterward, scrambling to defend himself and explain this confusion, Spurgeon had known him back when he was collecting money for his family's freedom. Spurgeon might have misunderstood a query asking about Jackson's new plan. The newspaper summarized:

> He [Jackson] first alluded to the question which had been raised in the recent discussions as to the money alleged by him to have been placed in Mr. Spurgeon's keeping, and said that Mr. Cunningham—whom he styled, with a commendable attempt at a pun, a "cunning one"—might very easily have sent such a message to London as would have brought back a misleading answer.[21]

Jackson's defense notwithstanding (and his clever wordplay demonstrating again his nimble manner of speech), he knew that this case would change his life for the worse. His world as he knew it was now over. Julia's too.

In a final act of corrective defiance, Jackson wrote a letter to the local newspaper in response to another letter writer's submission. Styling himself only as "a citizen," this letter writer suggested that Jackson should return to the United States as there would be job opportunities for him to paint houses there instead of in Scotland and England. The writer appears to have claimed that the Anti-Slavery Association (whether British or American) would be better poised than Jackson to address injustices and needs in the South. Jackson replied to this attack with such power that his letter merits being quoted in full:

> Dundee, June 27, 1864
>
> SIR,—In reference to some remarks by "Citizen," in the Advertiser of to-day, regarding the abundance of labour in America for blacks, I hope you will permit me, through your paper, to say that three years ago, in America, no black man who was ever a slave, could stay and work as a whitewasher, or at any other work; for if they were found out, they would be sent back to slavery under the Fugitive Slave Law. But now, as that law is abolished, I intend to go back next May, if it please God. I am doing what I think is right in lecturing and collecting funds to build a church among the slaves in South Carolina, where I was born. As Mr. Spurgeon has failed, through this war, in buying out of slavery my friends, I will apply the money he has got, and what I can raise, to build a place of worship, and also a school. I cannot help what the "Association" is doing in America. They knew nothing of me when I was running from slavery; but if the slaves are free, I'll go back, and do all the good I can among them. If "Citizen" will call on me, I will show him how my back is cut up; and he will judge whether he would have gone back three years ago, or run the risk of being caught.—I am, &c.,
>
> J.A. Jackson.[22]

There is a lot worthy of analysis in this letter, and it reveals much about Jackon's state of mind: first, the premise that he should return to the United States was insulting, of course, and his offer to bare his scarred back was a powerful rejoinder to the jovial skepticism of the Citizen. His flesh could trump their sneers, as he saw it.

Moreover, Jackson's proclamation that he was already planning a return underscores his presentation as an honest man intent on not overstaying the hospitality of the English people as his intentions toward the American South were true.

Forming a school in South Carolina, though? That was new.

Most remarkable here in this letter may be his comment that "I cannot help what the 'Association' is doing in America. They knew nothing of me when I was running from slavery." The most prominent Black lecturers of the antislavery cause usually did align themselves with official organizations at one point or another. Many of these Black abolitionist lecturers were pragmatic. And when schisms erupted among these predominantly white organizations in Britain, the Black lecturers did their best to move neutrally among them.[23] Jackson had certainly flirted with such relationships by appearing at some "Association"-sponsored events and sessions, as we have seen. But his sharp rejoinder that they had not been there for him when he was enslaved was a stab at the self-satisfied charitable groups he felt had failed him. White do-gooders had no idea what slavery truly was. He had been alone on that road to Charleston.

Additionally, in this letter's polished formality, we also get a hint that someone else might have assisted Jackson in its composition. The claim of authorship here is complete with no mention of help or mediation (such as someone writing on his behalf). "I am, &c., J.A. Jackson," he writes. From what we know of Jackson's pride and his strides toward literacy at this point, we can surmise that he wrote this letter and had its language honed by his wife, his lawyer, or a friend before running it in the paper.

The letter was angry but not intemperate, and it was strategically crafted. Jackson uses carefully diplomatic language about Spurgeon's failure to liberate his family, merely noting that "Mr. Spurgeon has failed . . . in buying out of slavery my friends"—a fact Spurgeon couldn't have contested. But Jackson must have been ready to explode. He knew that Spurgeon's failure to free his family wasn't the issue. It was the public repudiation that was going to haunt Jackson as long as he remained in England.

The overall gist of the letter is that Jackson, furious but calm, still had faith in his ability to persuade the public of who he was and what he stood for. This was his last stand in Dundee.

It was a good effort, but it failed. Jackson delivered a few more talks over the following months, but he knew his career in the British Isles as a public lecturer was over. Newspapers regularly reprinted materials from other cities and regions across the country. Even if the media coverage didn't share the story of Spurgeon's disavowal, Jackson knew that word would spread from church to church. And it wouldn't be confined just to Baptist circles; he would be effectively blackballed from speaking venues wherever he went.

He and Julia hastily returned to London to nurse his wounds for a bit and regroup. He tried to reach out to the Metropolitan Tabernacle to see if he might sort things out with the Spurgeonites but was rebuffed.

For Jackson, that was the last straw. He wasn't a man to back down. In a fury, Jackson took a pen in hand, drafted his grievances, and arranged for a pamphlet to be printed for distribution. As you might suspect, the press of this pamphlet goes unidentified (few people would want to anger Spurgeon), but it was certainly not the Spurgeonite Passmore and Alabaster outfit that had helped Jackson print his book only two years earlier.[24] He was going rogue.

IV

Jackson addressed his pamphlet with some flourish. The title, *Spurgeon and Jackson, or, the White Preacher and the Black Slave Lecturer*, was eye-catching enough, but it was also directed on the next page to, as he put it, "the Public in General."[25]

Jackson's fundamental grievance is that Spurgeon set him up as a liar in Scotland by not vouching for him during his time of need. Jackson theorizes that this happened because Spurgeon took up the cause of slavery only after meeting him. Still, when the book burnings began in the Southern United States, Jackson surmises that Spurgeon got cold feet and regretted having been involved with Jackson. This argument has some logic, for it is true that, whatever his personal feeling on the subject, Spurgeon scarcely ever spoke openly about slavery before Jackson and scarcely ever after the break with him in 1864. Jackson further argues that Spurgeon used money collected on Jackson's behalf to pay off debts incurred by the construction of the Metropolitan Tabernacle.

The pamphlet rages: "When you found I had £63 in the bank you received me into the church and gave me testimonials worthy of all confidence and regard, which I can show at any time." Jackson then goes on to accuse Spurgeon of regretting their involvement. "You, sir, being satisfied with my veracity, took up the case but dropped it, I suppose because the slaveholders burnt up your sermons, and would not have further to do with you."

Jackson then goes into some detail about what he believes occurred with the efforts to purchase his family. Back in Massachusetts, such transactions were fraught with complexity and risk. Now, trying to manage such an affair from Britain, an entirely new level of complication was layered onto the task. It isn't surprising that things had gone tragically awry. As Jackson reveals, however, he believes the attempt at liberating his family had been carried out in a desultory manner and quickly abandoned when minor obstacles arose:

> You pretended to take the case in hand, and did no good, but harm to it. You took the address of the slave plantation twice, and the three slaves' names, on the 12th of April, 1860, and did not write at all to them till the better end of August, 1860; and then wrote the wrong parties.

Jackson goes on to ask why Spurgeon didn't explain to the public that efforts to purchase his relatives had failed, a request that reflects Jackson's now savvy sense of how to leverage the media: "Why did you not bring forward to the public my case? Did the war prevent you? Did I not request you to publish it in the papers?"

Then, getting into the nitty-gritty of the financials, Jackson asks: "When

This image of the Metropolitan Tabernacle dates from the 1890s. When Jackson first met Spurgeon, the Reverend and his congregation were planning a transition from the smaller New Park Street Chapel to this new Metropolitan Tabernacle, which opened in 1861. Sometime after Jackson delivered his talk for Spurgeon at the New Park Street Chapel in late 1859, he started associating himself with the Tabernacle community until he was "cast out," as he understood it, that is. The façade and portico of the building have been preserved through a terrible fire in 1898 and later when it survived bombing damage during World War II. It is now identified as an independent Reformed Baptist church, still proud of its historical association with Spurgeon.

you said you would not buy them out, why did you not return the purchase money, £114 10s 5d, without further trouble?? And why do you still keep the five years' interest on the money?"

Perhaps worst of all, he writes, "It seemed to me as if you had the black-man to collect money to pay off the Tabernacle debt, and not to buy the people out of Slavery; for when your debt was paid off, you wanted me to be off too."

Jackson hurls other complaints at Spurgeon, hoping something will stick: he challenges Spurgeon to "tell how many barrels of ale are in the Tabernacle cellar," and asks, "Is the Slaveholding principle of not allowing negroes to learn reading, writing, &c, carried on at the Tabernacle?" Jackson asserts bitterly that he was denied books that were shared with other congregation members.[26]

While his arguments flew in different directions, his absolute fury is unmistakable: "I have experienced two kinds of slavery—one at South Carolina and the other at your Tabernacle."[27]

And even if his potential audience might not agree with every accusation he levels against one of the world's most prominent and beloved religious figures, Jackson makes sure his audience knows that he, the complainant, is a man of standing. He uses his name with repeated force and clarity. "I, John Andrew Jackson," he writes, was "slandered throughout England and Scotland, and you [Spurgeon] tried your best to shut up my way through London." And he ends by writing, "I belong to the Universal Church above from which you or any Spurgeonite cannot cast anyone out. Signed, John Andrew Jackson."

With this pronouncement, he scorched the earth behind him for sure.

As we saw at the end of his book, written in 1862, Jackson had drafted a final chapter titled "The Negro Songs." At the end of this furious pamphlet, though, Jackson appended an entirely different set of lyrics. He was in no mood to curry favor. Jackson was now a different man. Here, with defiance against false allies and weak advocates, he ends his screed by proclaiming the bold truth of a forward march to freedom. "John Brown's Body lies a mouldering in the grave," he writes. "But his truth goes marching on. Glory Glory Hallelujah."

V

What became of this pamphlet? Was it ever brought to Spurgeon's attention? It's unlikely it ever made it to his desk. Jackson's voice is clear, though, and it remains an astonishing document of Black pain and Black defiance.

We can get a sense of his final struggles from the remaining media coverage Jackson received. He spoke on slavery and freedom but couldn't restrain himself from railing at Spurgeon, much in line with the remarks he printed in his pamphlet. The *Dundee Courier and Argus* noted that in one of his speeches, "Spurgeon came in for a good deal of abuse. . . . He did not hide now that Mr. Spurgeon was no friend of his, and took a good deal of pains to show that he was no friend of the rev. gentleman."[28] The *Courier* then went on to re-create, in execrable dialect, what Jackson had said:

> "Wen I go," said he, "to Mr. Spurgeon to ask him do anything for me, Mr. Spurgeon he scratch him head, an' he says, 'Oh, yes, he do vat he can.' Den I ask him vat he can. He a funny man, Mr. Spurgeon; he try to take de wind out o' me. He say he get me in as porter to a cheesemonger or butter and egg man, a Misser Thomson-Brown-Smit. I see vat he after. Den I say to Mr. Spurgeon, 'Vat dis Massa Thomson-Brown Smit gib me for dat?' Mr. Spurgeon he scratch him head again, an' he say he not know; he spose vun pound a veek! Ven I make two, tree, five pound a veek, preachin; de glorious dospel ob de Lord Jesus. Den Mr. Spurgeon told me to went, an' I goed."[29]

The newspaper played this anecdote for laughs at Jackson's expense, but it does give us a glimpse of what these final months must have been like for Jackson. If this article can be believed, he was now styling himself as a preacher, which hadn't been the case before. But his story about being directed to jobs he thought beneath him is consistent with his tirade in the pamphlet he printed.

Jackson's final lectures appear to have been delivered mostly without formal sponsorship. As he knew well, being a Black man in a public space was risky. And speaking out against Spurgeon, a beloved public figure of vast repute, was not a popular stance. The danger was real. One of Jackson's final speeches was delivered in Hyde Park, London, "near the Crystal Palace," when a white bystander again assaulted him. This time a man tossed handfuls of mud on Jackson's portmanteau suitcase and then "bonneted" Jackson.[30] "Bonneting" meant that Jackson's hat brim was grabbed on two sides, and his hat was aggressively smashed down over his face—an act that might sound tame but was a gross insult. It could also involve breaking a nose or blackening eyes in the process. It would have been frightening.

Did he have friends in the crowd, or was Julia around to help him up or help him out of this situation? Jackson had seen worse, but this was no casual conflict. He was a strong and formidable man; the newspaper account of this incident described him as "powerful." He could have held his own in a fracas.[31] He knew, though, that even in London, a Black man was unlikely to be given the benefit of the doubt if he fought back against a white aggressor. Be steady, he must have told himself. Stay calm.

Jackson, who often experienced this kind of hostile trolling and abuse from his audiences, kept his cool, but the situation was serious enough that the crowds called for the police. The newspapers reported that the drunken man was found guilty and sentenced to a fine or fourteen days' imprisonment (perhaps partly because the man assaulted the police when they arrived). Again, Jackson had been publicly humiliated but had found at least some small satisfaction with the justice system.

His time, though, was running out. He and Julia would have followed the news from the states the best they could. They would have known of the Emancipation Proclamation enacted in occupied territories in the South in January 1863. But would it have freed their families? There was no way to know. They probably had little sense of what was happening on the ground. They knew that war, starvation, chaos, and retaliation could kill people just as easily as overwork, torture, and exploitation under slavery. Many nights, Julia and Jackson would have felt terribly far away from their people.

By the spring of 1865, Julia and Jackson would have known that the war was almost over, and that things back home were changing in ways they could never have imagined. Black Union troops would march along the Black River into Sumter County in early April 1865, exchanging gunfire with Confederates and liberating thousands of enslaved people as they went. These soldiers were part of one of the very last engagements of the Civil War, a campaign known as "Potter's Raid," which sent troops inland into areas of South Carolina.[32] Sumter County and the wealthy properties along the Black River flowing up toward Sumter and Lynchburg were in their sights.

Julia and Jackson would have been stunned but perhaps heartened, too, to learn that Black Union soldiers were raiding plantation labor camps for provisions, burning cotton, occupying Sumter itself, and marching through the very same fields Jackson and his neighbor, the Reverend Irving Lowery, had described back in Lynchburg. The world they had known was upside down.

Henry Haynsworth, the Sumter County postmaster who, back in 1850, had written the mocking reply to Jackson's inquiry about purchasing freedom for his wife and child, had what might be understood as a comeuppance. His house was seized to quarter Union musicians during the occupation of Sumter, an action Jackson would have certainly felt some satisfaction about. And with this occupation, the enslaved fled the property, proving the Haynsworth accounts of their joy in servitude a lie.[33]

The English family would have been hustling to bury their treasures and hide their livestock as these Union soldiers approached, but had Doctor and the rest of the Clavern family rushed out to see these liberators? Did Jackson's younger brothers flee to the quasi-protection of these Union troops and join the thousands of what became known as "contraband" or now-emancipated Black people seeking freedom? The world of Lynchburg was to be entirely reshaped. Jackson and Julia might not have known precisely what was happening, but they knew they had to get back.

In London, Jackson and Julia gathered their savings—whatever was left after their living expenses and funding that pamphlet. They cobbled together funds from his whitewashing work, her salary as a lady's maid, and anything else they had saved over the years. Perhaps Julia sold some dresses, or Jackson parted with painting tools. They were unlikely to have had a bank account, so this may have been a time they unearthed any coins or banknotes hidden under floorboards or in a mattress. They would have guarded their cache with great care, for there was no going back to their comparative affluence and credit from the time when Jackson had patrons and engagements.

Sometime after May 1865, Jackson and Julia purchased two tickets back to the United States. This time, at least, they would have known exactly what to pack and what to leave behind. Traveling was something they had mastered by now. Jackson carefully tucked away his most treasured possessions, including at least one copy of his book.

The return trip would not have been the same kind of hopeful voyage that their first Atlantic crossing had been. Now, though, Jackson and Julia knew they were free and able to assert their identity as Black Americans. Unbowed and resilient, they could return home, find their families, and put the betrayals of the Old World behind them.

CHAPTER NINE

"ONE THOUSAND ACRES"—
A LETTER TO GENERAL HOWARD (1868)

New England and South Carolina (1865–1880)

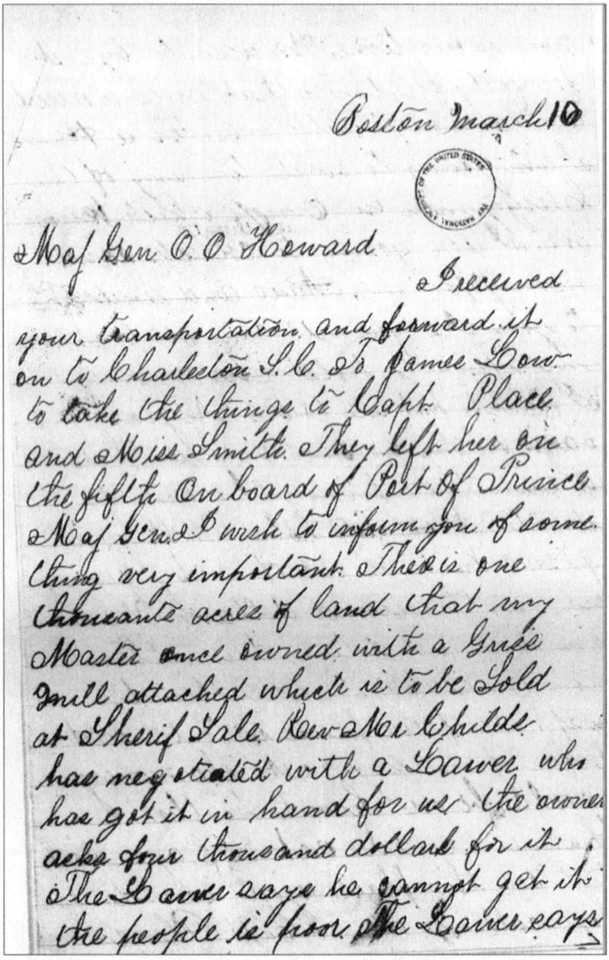

Boston March 10

Maj Gen O O Howard

I received
your transportation and forward it
on to Charleston S.C. To James Low
to take the things to Capt. Place
and Miss Smith. They left her on
the fifth On board of Port of Prince
Maj Gen I wish to inform you of some
thing very important. Thes is one
thousante acres of land that my
Master once owned with a Grist
mill attached which is to be Sold
at Sherif Sale. Rev Mr Childs
has negotiated with a Lawer who
has got it in hand for us the owner
asks four thousand dollars for it.
The Lawer says he cannot get it
the people is poor the Lawer says

Image of letter from John Andrew Jackson to O.O. Howard, March 10, 1868 (from Bowdoin College Library).

Jackson and Julia made it back to the United States. But what kind of world would welcome them? They had to figure out a new way to support themselves and find a place to live, and they desperately wanted to find their families. But what they first found was devastation. Freedom was glorious, of course, but this freedom came without recourse or resources. Jackson wanted to help. He needed to help. So, he did what he did best: he talked, he lectured, he cajoled, and he pleaded. He solicited relief supplies and sent them down to South Carolina, traveling with them himself when he could. He worked his connections. Once in the South, he searched for the friends and family he had lost. It was a long list—Doctor, Ephraim, Louisa, Jinny, and the children of his brothers and sisters.

But the pleading was irritating and wearisome to many of his former patrons, already exhausted from the sacrifice of the Civil War. Newspaper notices chronicle how some venues welcomed him and others warned against him. He and Julia needed support from people who understood that now that slavery was over, the consequences of slavery were incalculable. This led them first to Springfield, Massachusetts, and then down the river to New Haven, Connecticut, where they found sanctuary among a very particular community of survivors.

Settling into a peripatetic life that would take him back and forth between New England and South Carolina was more treacherous than Jackson anticipated. Beatings, jail, and abuse were part of his journeys. He needed safety. So did his family in Lynchburg. And so did Julia, who was often left behind alone, paying what was to be a terrible cost. And thus Jackson concocted an audacious scheme chronicled in a heartbreaking letter. He would buy Robert English's land with the help of the man charged with leading the reconstruction of the nation: General O.O. Howard. Jackson dreamed of building a Black utopia of collective labor and shared safety.

I

A clerk in the Freedmen's Bureau unfolded a letter from John Andrew Jackson addressed to the clerk's boss, General Oliver Otis Howard, who headed the Freedmen's Bureau from 1865 to 1872. The three-page letter was fairly routine. The clerk read, summarized, and registered it for General Howard's review. General Howard was one of the most influential people in the United States at that moment, and everyone wanted something from him; letters asking for help besieged his office. However, one thing wasn't routine: the clerk made a little note about General Howard's answer. John Andrew Jackson had caught the general's attention.

This letter, dated March 10, 1868, is written and signed with Jackson's full name. It is further evidence we have of Jackson's literacy. It is possible, of course, that he would have had someone else write it for him. But the wide loops seem consistent with other letters from 1865 and 1866 and with later signatures—as is the slightly choppy syntax.[1] Whether he wrote it independently or with assistance, he would have known the stakes were high to get it right. He certainly would have drafted it at least once before sending it. You don't want mistakes in a letter begging for help from one of the most powerful men in the United States. You don't get more than one shot at something like this.

Jackson had been working with the Freedmen's Bureau, transporting supplies and donations down to South Carolina; how official or unofficial this work was is unclear.[2] This letter, however, demonstrates that he wrote follow-up notes and updates about his activities. By 1868, he had established a working system with a "Captain Place," the federal representative in the areas near Lynchburg. As Jackson understood, Captain Place would receive and distribute supplies from New England donations. In his letter, Jackson mentions the name of a white schoolteacher he had befriended who was assigned to a freedmen's school near Lynchburg. This teacher, Jane Smith, who may have been just about the only white person Jackson fully trusted in the South, was also set to help receive and distribute whatever General Howard had authorized for Jackson to ship down there. This letter also demonstrates that Jackson had been in touch with his older brother, "Ephraim Claben," who was still alive in South Carolina and ready to help with Jackson's schemes and dreams.

The letter's key point: Jackson had *good news*. One thousand acres of land with a gristmill and rich with timber and room for farming was for sale. The

English family heirs were in disarray, their land was up for grabs, and the fact that some family property was now for sale via the sheriff's office suggests it had been confiscated for back taxes. This tracks. It's hard to imagine that the known-to-be-tight English family would have paid their taxes willingly to the Confederacy much less to federal officials. And now, in 1868, Jackson finally saw an opportunity for revenge.

> Genr'l—I wish to inform you of something very important. There is one thousand acres of land that my Master once owned with a Grist-Mill attached which is to be sold at Sheriff's Sale. Rev. Mr. Childs has negotiated with a Lawyer who has got it in hand for us. The owner asks four thousand (4000) dollars for it. The Lawyer says he cannot get it. The people are poor. The Lawyer says, "Now is our time."

The English mill tract was a fine piece of property, much coveted under normal circumstances. Still, the deprivation of the war years meant that few people, white or Black, had the necessary capital to purchase it. That land sat fallow for many years in legal limbo. As the lawyer noted, this was the time.

(No one then could have known that by the late twentieth century this plot

Lee Correctional Institution, South Carolina's largest maximum-security prison.

of land would be the site of the largest maximum-security prison for men in South Carolina, the Lee Correctional Institution.)

> And thus, since it was the time, Jackson dreamed beyond himself. This was personal, sure, but he didn't want to just site himself on the English family land to feel the righteous if smug satisfaction that might entail. Instead, he laid out a different vision: "We wish to buy it for forty freedmen (that once worked as Slaves on it with me) for a Home."

While buying the English family plantation had been on Jackson's mind for a while, such an enterprise would have been an audacious undertaking. After all, he wasn't proposing buying it for himself—an idea that would have been wild enough in that location and that moment of history. He was, rather, proposing to get hold of a thousand acres and to settle forty Black people there in some sort of communal farming and milling endeavor. He was ready to leverage his connections with clergy back in England, and all he needed was a white guarantor with a big name, if possible. As he saw it, the challenge was to find someone reliable to "hold the money."

Jackson had had problems with white men holding his money before, but General Howard was no Spurgeon, and there simply wasn't any other workaround; no Black man would be trusted to handle donations on the scale he would need.[3] He had been through this before.

The notion of success must have kept him going. Any land held by Black people in the South would now need to be purchased, and even that would be no simple transaction. But it could be done. With luck. With support. With prayer. And perhaps by modeling endeavors after experiments that challenged traditional notions of capital and individualism.

During Jackson's early years in western Massachusetts drumming up donations, he had made his way through the vicinity of Florence and Northampton (likely in the early months of 1850). These travels may have retained a particular hold on his imagination.

Long before the Civil War, that area had been a hotbed of progressive thought and abolitionist sentiment. Jackson surely would have learned about a utopian community that had once been operating there: the Northampton Association of Education and Industry, which had been a kind of modest workers-owned cooperative. The association brought Black and white men and women together to run a mulberry farm and silk factory, among other activities, to counter the slave-produced cotton market.[4] The Northampton Association endeavor had failed after only a few years, but such an audacious scheme would surely have made an impression on Jackson. Capitalism could be leveraged in fresh ways to counter at least some kinds of exploitation. He could fathom how such experiments were possible and that there could potentially be white alliances and patrons to help. It is notable, then, that some fifteen years later, when he proposed taking over his former enslaver's property, he imagined a collective.

Jackson's letter noted that he didn't want just any freed people there; he particularly wanted the ones due reparations in the form of the very land they had once worked: "I want to put all those Negroes back on it who once worked there to earn their living." He might place the Black families into "lots," as he went on to note in his letter, but they nonetheless would be working in a collective and self-managed enterprise of farming and timber. Presumably, they would refurbish and run the abandoned gristmill—a capitalistic endeavor, but one with some sort of communal undergirding,

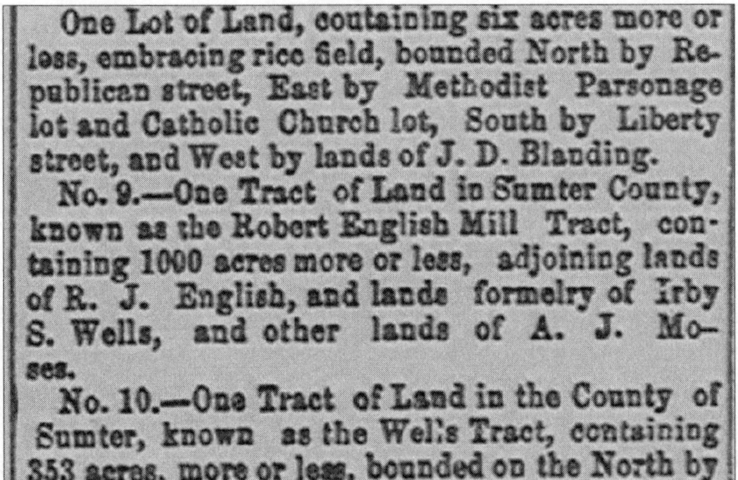
One Lot of Land, containing six acres more or less, embracing rice field, bounded North by Republican street, East by Methodist Parsonage lot and Catholic Church lot, South by Liberty street, and West by lands of J. D. Blanding.

No. 9.—One Tract of Land in Sumter County, known as the Robert English Mill Tract, containing 1000 acres more or less, adjoining lands of R. J. English, and lands formelry of Irby S. Wells, and other lands of A. J. Moses.

No. 10.—One Tract of Land in the County of Sumter, known as the Wells Tract, containing 353 acres, more or less, bounded on the North by

Jackson wasn't able to purchase land in 1866 when it was first mentioned as a goal in the *Springfield Republican*, nor again in 1868 when he wrote to Howard. But it doesn't appear that the land was sold to anyone else very quickly. By 1871 the same English family property was being advertised for sale, possibly because other deals had fallen through and it had been confiscated for taxes due. Jackson might have been forced to give up the dream of reclaiming it for the group of Black families by this point, but he and his friends would surely have been following its eventual sale to other purchasers with some frustration. From the *Sumter Watchman*, February 1, 1871.

designed to provide a self-sufficient and safe world, an alternative kind of future of self-determination.

Land, unsurprisingly, was everything to Black Southerners who, only a few months out of slavery, knew few other ways to survive aside from farm labor. Formerly enslaved people testified relentlessly and consistently that land was the most vital part of a future of freedom. "Night and Day they dream of owning their own land. It is their all in all," stated an 1868 representative to the South Carolina Constitutional Convention. Or, as Tunis Campbell noted at the 1866 Colored Citizen's Convention of Tennessee, "the great cry of our people is to have land."[5]

Fourteen thousand Black families in South Carolina acquired small farms through the South Carolina Land Commission between 1868 and 1871—purchases which required a $10 down payment. Half the land had to be under cultivation within three years, and, notably, taxes had to be paid in full annually in order to retain ownership rights. These land purchases were not understood to be reparations in any way; they were more generally understood as being contracts for the farmers, who were then expected to remain loyal supporters of the Republican Party.

These hopeful days of land acquisition didn't last for long. By 1875, Black farmers across the South owned five million acres of farmland—often poor and infertile land, but land, nonetheless. However, much of this land was lost within a generation due to a combination of reasons involving debt, exploitative usury, the boll weevil, lack of political support or external social structures (such as schools), and, most important for these early years, racist terror.

Landownership for freed people in the South often came with extraordinary danger. But it must have seemed better than the alternative, which at this time was working land under exploitative sharecropping contracts at best. To maximize survival and community, free people came together for collective and communal purchases as soon they had been liberated by the Union Army (or freed themselves by running away to Union lines, a common occurrence). These cooperative agrarian communities didn't tend to last long (with a few notable exceptions), but they could be found across the South.[6] Word of their successes and failures spread quickly, and the Union officers Jackson communicated with would have been familiar with the kind of plan he imagined. They might have been enthused, skeptical, or bemused . . . but wouldn't have been shocked.

As usual, Jackson's gumption and ambition were met with cautious skepticism. And some of his political naïvete shows, too. Was he aware that, by mid-1868, the Freedmen's Bureau was already nearing the end of its heyday, that much of its funding was soon to be cut and many of its programs shut down, and that it was to be entirely disbanded by 1872? Federal troops and any local protections they provided, however modest, would soon be gone.

Federal protection mattered because it was virtually the only bulwark against a wave of terrorism spreading across the South at this time. Founded in 1865 as a vehicle of Southern resistance to Reconstruction generally but most pointedly to promote white supremacy and oppose any rights of the freedmen, the Ku Klux Klan dedicated itself to campaigns to intimidate Black people. Founded in December 1865 in Tennessee, the KKK quickly found a welcoming foothold in South Carolina. In Spartanburg County, for example, over 222 KKK whippings were reported in 1865 alone.[7] Lynchings and house burnings were common. Unreported violence against Black people and even against white people, including Southerners seen as too sympathetic to the freedmen, was rampant. These horrors were evident across the South generally but also locally in Lynchburg.

Waters McIntosh, a Black man born enslaved in Lynchburg, witnessed the reign of the KKK after the Civil War. McIntosh, who remained in Lynchburg after the war and lived there throughout Reconstruction and beyond, would have known Jackson well—if not from their days in bondage on adjacent plantation work camps, then certainly once Jackson started returning with relief supplies and schemes. McIntosh surely had Jackson in mind when he testified about the KKK's activities in his hometown:

> Whenever there was a man of influence, they terrorized him. They were at their height about the time of Grant's election. Many a time my mother and I have watched them pass our door. They wore gowns and some kind of helmet. They would be going to catch same leading Negro and whip him. There was scarcely a night they couldn't take a leading Negro out and whip him if they would catch him alone.[8]

It is hard to imagine how a man such as Jackson—with an extroverted and combative nature, a confidence built upon his worldly experiences and education, and a civic mindedness that would ensure he would always get involved with events—could have avoided the Klan during this era and during his visits back south.

Was Jackson aware that a white teacher had been almost murdered the previous year in the center of Lynchburg, presumably because of his championing of the freedmen?[9] Was he aware that one of his old Lynchburg comrades-in-bondage, a now-emancipated man named Lymus McCloud, had been murdered in Lynchburg in 1867, presumably for having attracted the KKK's attention for attending a political meeting and advocating for freedmen's rights?[10] Did Jackson, writing to General Howard from the safety of Boston, fully apprehend the level of violent backlash against the freedmen and their allies currently brewing in Sumter County? Had his many years in Canada and England given him too much confidence?

Perhaps. But his proposal seemed intriguing and not entirely unfeasible. A Freedmen's Bureau clerk noted: "Gen. Howard will instruct his agent to further this interesting project as much as possible, but he has no authority to donate any money for this purpose."[11]

This is the last we hear of Jackson's scheme: it is another dead-end paper trail. The money and the purchase never came together. He was back in the United States, ready to sink his teeth into making change, making a difference. But he had lost touch with his community. Did he have any idea what was going on?

II

Only two years earlier, Jackson had left England. He and Julia had been there for almost a decade. Before things went south with Spurgeon, had he ever planned to make England his home? It doesn't seem so. Throughout his travels abroad, he steadily proclaimed his intention to free his family or help survivors, which would presumably involve him heading back to the United States to at least facilitate those designs. His time in England was always temporary. Now he'd returned, not as a carpetbagger or part of a liberating army, but as a relic, a long-ago dream.

Would people know him if he stepped back into South Carolina? Would he know himself?

Jackson and Julia must have been overcome with complicated emotions when they saw the coast of North America once more. Were they hopeful? Wary? It was 1865. The war was over. They hadn't returned to the same nation they had once known: they arrived at a collection of states that were now, reluctantly and precariously, united.

Presumably, the couple disembarked in Massachusetts, but it is certainly possible they sailed from Liverpool back to Halifax or Saint John in Canada and then worked their way down the coast on a connecting packet ship. It's possible, too, that they would have disembarked in New York or wherever the cheapest cross-Atlantic ticket they could find might send them to. One way or another, though, we can know they ended up in Massachusetts again. There would be friends there.

Henry Foreman's boarding house in Boston would have been at the top of their list. Julia might have been horrified by the wild scene on Ann Street, but to be welcomed by a Black family of friends would have meant a lot. Sadly for Jackson, though, Henry Foreman had died earlier that year. They had just missed him.[12] But the Foremans' adult children remained in Boston, and seeking out those old friends and former housemates from those wild days on Ann Street would have been important. They had stood by him when bounty hunters were on his trail. He would have wanted to see them again and let them know of all that had happened in the fifteen years since he had left. And maybe, too, they would have had advice for him. News he could use. After all, the war had changed things; so many people had died. He and Julia would need to rebuild his networks and make new friends.

Soon after reuniting with his friends in Boston, Jackson might have made his way to Salem, too, perhaps to reconnect with old circles and get advice and ideas about what to do and how to work. Salem had been good to him, too, and some of his old employers from his days splitting wood and working in the tan yards were still living. The local Black activist community of Salem was still there as well. But there wouldn't have been much time or money for lengthy reunions in Massachusetts.

Jackson and Julia would have been sending letters from London and probably writing them during the crossing as well, getting ready to post them the moment they stepped ashore. Now settled, they needed to know: Who in their families was still alive? How could they reach them? Did Julia still have family in North Carolina? What of any family left behind in Canada? How could they trace people in the aftermath of a devastating war? Where were their people?

By now, Jackson likely had very little money. Correspondence could only do so much. And so, once he arrived in the United States, his first thought would have been to figure out how to fund a trip south to find his family. Train travel was heavily restricted during this period, with tracks destroyed across the South and the government often commandeering and controlling what train travel there was. And sailing south, while faster, still would require ships willing to take on Black passengers able to pay. Getting from Charleston into the state's interior, where he could visit Lynchburg, would be the most difficult part. Without federal auspices, it would be dangerous for him and Julia to take the roads or even a train inland to Lynchburg. He'd seen those dangers back in 1846 when he had first ridden his horse out to Charleston, and he knew returning that way with Julia would require protection.

Jackson did not have much time to fret; he needed to plumb his connections. He probably wrote to everyone he could think of to ask for help, ideas, support, and patronage. He may have knocked on doors in Boston or traveled to Salem to reconnect with friends there. Some may have ignored him. But it seems that Samuel Fessenden or Jackson's other allies from Portland, Maine, came through for him. Someone introduced him to a war hero and rising star in the federal government who would change his life. And Jackson was off and running.

We know this because, within a year of arriving in the United States, Jackson found an affiliation with the Freedmen's Bureau, an organization established by Congress by "An Act to establish a Bureau for the Relief of Freedmen and Refugees." The bureau had what might be understood as a

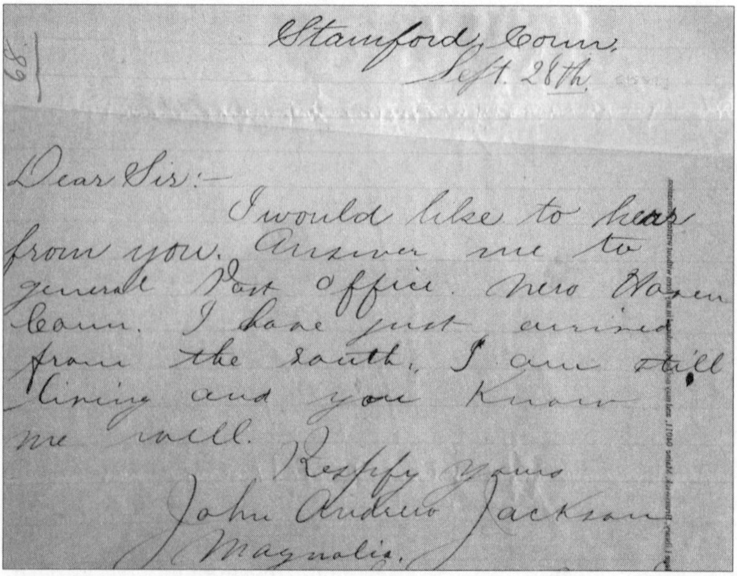

68

Stamford, Conn.
Sept. 28th

Dear Sir:—
I would like to hear from you. Answer me to general Post Office. New Haven Conn. I have just arrived from the south. I am still living and you Know me well.
Respfy yours
John Andrew Jackson
Magnolia.

Jackson's correspondence with Howard between 1865 and 1889 indicates that, at least from Jackson's perspective, they knew one another personally. He reminded Howard, "I am still living and you know me well."

hazy, ambitious, and broad mandate to provide medical services, clothing, food, shelter, and land to both displaced Southerners and newly emancipated Black people. It was also intended to help establish schools, supervise contracts between freed men and women with employers (often former enslavers), and manage confiscated lands. And the connection Jackson had with this organization wasn't a lowly one. The man appointed to run this enormous bureau was a good friend of the Fessenden family, a Bowdoin graduate, an ardent abolitionist, and a Civil War hero: General O.O. Howard.

Did Fessenden recommend Jackson to General Howard and the Freedmen's Bureau's officials? Did he or perhaps other Black or white friends in Maine endorse Jackson's good character and laud his plans for raising up the freedmen in the South? It appears so. And General Howard must have been impressed by Jackson. We can know this because Jackson leveraged General Howard's patronage for years to come, much as he had earlier brandished his endorsements first from Stowe and then from Spurgeon.[13]

He knew invoking fickle white patrons was a gamble. But what in Jackson's life wasn't?

For this era of his career, Jackson had a new white backer he could freely name-check, one who had name recognition in virtually every household in the United States—certainly among everyone in the former Confederacy. Promised safety and employment, presumably from Howard and the Freedmen's Bureau, in the summer or fall of 1865, Jackson and Julia made their way south.

The records of the Freedmen's Bureau do not list Jackson (or Julia) as affiliates in any discoverable way. But Jackson was to claim, in posters and broadsides, that he was "a colored teacher, who has labored for some months under the auspices of the Freedmen's Bureau, in the work of education among the blacks of the South." And the claim seems plausible.

If Jackson labored as a teacher in order to get a ticket south for himself and Julia, the job might have worked for a while, but he shortly returned. Teaching may have just been an excuse to fund travels to see his family and do some reconnaissance work. It was probably just as well that his teaching career didn't continue. His disposition for movement and public engagement was not inclined toward that of living as a schoolmaster. But, importantly, through his formal or informal work with the Freedmen's Bureau, he did manage to get a sense of the postwar scenes in Sumter County, South Carolina. He would have reconnected with his surviving relatives. And he was able to meet some of the teachers who would have the staying power he didn't. One teacher, Jane Smith from Massachusetts, who was assigned to teach in Sumter County, would soon become a key connection. White allies in South Carolina were far otherwise and few between.

Thanks to this early visit back to South Carolina, Jackson also learned which white federal officers there as part of the occupying force might be trusted—information that would prove vital. He could see which railroads had been destroyed and which were functional. He could see where new roads had been built since his escape and learn where the outposts of federal soldiers might be. He could learn which powerful families had collapsed and which were enduring.

Most crucially, though, Jackson could be reunited with those he had left behind.

III

Who was dead? Who was alive? He could easily sort out the fates of the white people, but as for his own family and friends, so many years had passed. Who had been sold away? Who had been tortured to death? Who had starved? He may not have wanted to know all the answers.

Now, in the summer of 1865, Jackson could check on the health of his father, the elderly Doctor; embrace his brother Ephraim and Ephraim's wife, Amelia; and discover the fate of the children of his sister Bella, who was murdered at the hands of the English family. He had been talking about those children through his years in England, hoping to raise money to free them. They would be grown by now if they were living.

Perhaps he met with his little brother William or his younger sisters. He would have tried to reconnect with surviving friends from the Black neighborhoods along the Black River. And he might now be able to ask, carefully since he'd married Julia, about what happened to his first wife Louisa and their daughter, little Jinny. He had heard they were dead, but was it true?

Julia was with him, but she had been enslaved, too. She would understand that their early lives had placed them in terrible circumstances with impossible choices. It might have been upsetting for her, and she likely kept herself as uninvolved as possible, but she would understand that Jackson needed to know. He needed to find out. And did he have a daughter? Where could Jinny be?

Jackson had heard that Louisa and Jinny were dead years back—sometime in 1850, most likely, right before or perhaps shortly after he arrived in

Canada—or at least that is what he claimed at one point.[14] With that knowledge, he was free to marry his second wife, Julia, in Saint John in 1852. But were these facts true, or merely a convenient retelling of his past? Was it something he told himself because he needed to hear it?

Speculating about Louisa and Jinny's survival is worth unpacking because, of course, for Jackson personally, it was everything. But it also models how we need to weave together careful predictions and assumptions on what little information we have.

On one hand, back in 1850, after negotiations for their freedom had broken down and the 1850 Fugitive Slave Act passed, Jackson may have despaired of ever seeing Louisa and Jinny again. He may well have believed they were irretrievably lost to him.

But they were still living in 1850. Not only do we have the letter from the English family neighbor, Haynsworth, asserting that they were "both well," but, more significant, we can know that Louisa and Jinny were alive at least as of June 1851 because they (and Louisa's older "husband" Enoch) were transferred or sold to another Law family member in South Carolina.[15]

Had they survived the last twenty years of bondage? And had they survived the disease, starvation, and violence that took so many Black lives during the Civil War? It seems possible. While Louisa and Jinny had been taken to Macon, Georgia, with the Law family back in 1846, they weren't there very long. The Law family returned to South Carolina by 1850, approximately four years after Jackson's Christmas escape.[16] Louisa and Jinny were deeded to another Law relative in 1851, but the chances that one of them, and possibly both, survived to see emancipation is good.

Moreover, the chances that they had survived and somehow returned or remained in the region were not impossible. While these entwined planter-class white families in Sumter County did occasionally venture away, they often returned and retained their regional connections. As we have seen, the intertwined relationships of white families in this county meant that such families often shared, borrowed, deeded, and willed enslaved people to other white relatives. Louisa and Jinny could still be close by, Jackson must have hoped. Or at least someone might know where they had gone.

It was a long shot, of course. We can imagine his daughter Jinny possibly living to be emancipated and taking her husband's last name after the war. Jackson surely would have sought her out for a reunion if he could. Such an incident is never mentioned in his letters or interviews, but it might have been too delicate to discuss openly. Moreover, Louisa, too, might have survived to remarry and take another last name legally. After all these years, seeing one another with new families might have brought joy. It might have brought sorrow. Perhaps there was fury over his abandonment or anger over his disloyalty.

Or perhaps Louisa and little Jinny had both died under the torments of bondage—starvation, overwork, whippings, assault, disease, despair. No clear census data or other archival paperwork supports any of these notions, but Jackson's ensuing behavior provides us with a clue: he was to return repeatedly to Lynchburg for long stretches over the next four decades without Julia. This suggests that besides his extensive Clavon family members to care for, he may have also had his first family with Louisa to attend to. Surely, he would owe them something. Had Louisa been tortured or interrogated after Jackson's escape back in 1846? If so, and it seems likely, that would be a debt Jackson could never repay.

It may also have been time, finally, for a conversation with some of the English family.

Many of the key players from Jackson's youth had passed: Robert English had died in 1847, only a year after Jackson had escaped. Elizabeth English survived into 1860 but then finally passed away. The Reverend Thomas Reese English, who had placed the runaway advertisement for Jackson, was still in the area, although he was to die in 1869. The Reverend's adult son, Thomas Reese English Jr., was still living nearby. Back in 1860, he had inherited his grandmother's property and thus had, for at least a few years, a legal claim to the body of John Andrew Jackson until emancipation had rendered that particular property claim void.

Even in this postwar era, Jackson would have been wise to keep clear of them. But could he have resisted? Crowing about his triumphant escape and return might have been satisfying. He might not have confronted them, but the news would have traveled fast. He was back. He might not have been riding a horse this time, but he would have found it hard to hide his customary swagger.

Many other grandchildren and descendants of the English family were scattered across Sumter County, especially in the nearby Bishopville area, a bit north of Lynchburg. While the war had lessened their fortunes, they were still a dominant and ubiquitous family spread across the state. Jackson and Julia would need to tread lightly.

What Jackson and Julia saw on the ground in South Carolina must have both shocked and heartened them. There would have been reunions and introductions. There would have been grieving over the many people they had lost. There was hunger and suffering, but in emancipation's early days, there was hope for a better future in freedom. Jackson was always one to seize on hope. He leaves no letters or reports about what happened during this initial trip, but he saw need and knew he could help. He was, after all, a professional fund-raiser. He would have made notes. Within a few months of his arrival in South Carolina, in December, he and Julia packed their bags again to return north.

Their return trip, however, was disastrous.

IV

In an 1865 letter dated Christmas Eve out of Baltimore, Maryland, and addressed to General Howard on rather personal terms, Jackson tried to explain what had gone wrong and to implore General Howard to intervene on his behalf.

During his return from the Carolinas, Jackson had been beaten up, tossed off a train, and thrown in jail overnight. He and Julia would likely have picked up the train near Lynchburg or the nearby area and made it to Wilmington, North Carolina, on the coast, the major stop where they would have needed to switch to a northbound train. Whatever happened evidently occurred right before or at the Wilmington stop.

According to his letter, Jackson had been assaulted not by an ex-Confederate, as one might expect. Instead, he had run afoul of a white Union officer he identified as "Officer Grig." Jackson complained that Grig assaulted him with a sword and had him (and presumably Julia) thrown off a train and put in jail, an event which brought "Great sickness" on her.

Even worse, while in jail, Jackson's money, trunks, and keys were all stolen.

His offense: telling Grig that "their doing the negroes bad in the South."[17]

101 Hill Street Baltimore December 24, 1865

Mr. Howard General

This is the officer Grig you will see his name which was given me by his Colonel who said to me that he would punish him for striking me with his sword and poled [pulled] me in the cars and jank [threw] me out leaving my money and bag He followed and and my Trunk keys and money all was stolen from me while i was in jail Grig put me for nothing Because I told him their doing the negroes bad in the South he made me Lost all that money and my pasage and brought Great sickness on my Wife Yett this very Day I would not have it done for 8 hundred dollars Please see to this mr howard i wasnt savage write please to Conel Gaft Wilmington NC

YOURS TRULY JOHN ANDREW JACKSON

What exactly went down? We can be sure that Jackson's confidence and inability to lay low under any circumstance and in any conversation may have drawn attention to him and Julia. After all, he spent the last decade traveling as a free citizen. He was, moreover, a published author. He had stood on stages and in pulpits across Britain. And he wasn't going to let this incident go unremarked or unresisted. He penned this rather frantic and unpunctuated letter and, as the letter suggests, he also made a separate complaint to Grig's supervisor, the Colonel. Whatever happened to any of these charges is unknown. Probably nothing.

This rough introduction back into the violent racism of the post–Civil War culture of the newly United States couldn't have been wholly shocking. He had been attacked before, both in slavery and in freedom. He knew something about surviving assaults by white men wielding weapons and power. Nonetheless, it seems clear that he underestimated how vocal or assertive a Black man traveling in the Southern states or anywhere in the United States should be only a few months after the end of the Civil War. The Union officers wanted gratitude, not the truth about the suffering Jackson had seen down South. Jackson's closing lines to Howard underscored his humiliation at having his reputation ruined: "I wasnt savage."

Jackson went south again but never with Julia. She hadn't escaped from North Carolina to Canada and then across the ocean to England to return and face terror on Southern trains. He would be on his own with these ventures from here on out. She was done with it.

It was time. He and Julia needed a home base. She had been brought down by a "Great sickness" from the travels south—and perhaps, too, she had had great sorrows. If they had made it to North Carolina, she might well have put in inquiries about her own long-lost family or friends who had remained there, even while she had escaped to Canada more than fifteen years previously. The family news could have been distressing and perhaps pushed her into depression or grief. If she were to ever recover, she would need some stability. They settled on a different plan now. He would find a home for Julia. Clearly, Southern cities were out.

And so, their story turned to Springfield, a lively industrial city in western Massachusetts. It felt safe. It felt right.

Their reasons are not hard to understand: Springfield was familiar to Jackson. He had spent time there before, having visited with the Reverend Samuel Osgood, who had helped him raise money in his attempts to free Louisa and little Jinny way back in 1850. During that visit, Jackson had also met the Black activist Henry Highland Garnet, who had written letters on his behalf. He had known friendship there.

Of course, things had changed. By 1865, Garnet had moved on from Massachusetts, and Osgood had passed away back in 1862. Many of Jackson's old comrades would have been gone.[18] Many Black recruits for the Union forces had been recruited in that city and many hadn't returned. But the Black community in Springfield endured. Moreover, the powerful St. John's Congregational Church in Springfield still served as one of the most powerful and radical sites in New England for Black activism. Its presence in the city meant that Black networking for folks from any denomination had a powerful hub.[19]

Springfield had another quality that may have caught Jackson's attention: this city in western Massachusetts was the hub of the largest daily paper in New England. And Jackson, by now, knew that his success would always be predicated on good neighbors and good press.

Jackson and Julia, therefore, made their home in Springfield. Had she recovered from her illness that had come on during their disastrous joint trip down south? We cannot know, but we can presume that Jackson found somewhere, probably in one of the poorer neighborhoods close to downtown Springfield, to settle her, and he quickly would have sought to find immediate work to support themselves, perhaps factory labor of some sort. But that would have been only temporary. He always had his eyes on bigger things. He needed to work his connections again. His family and friends down in South Carolina were starving.

V

In downtown Springfield, Jackson found his new focus—the headquarters of *The Springfield Republica*n, a prominent newspaper with national reach. The paper had been a strident proponent of antislavery messaging and activism before the Emancipation Proclamation and now, in the post-bellum era was defining itself as the primary organ for the newly established Republican party. Not surprisingly, after the Civil War, the newspaper continued to support the interests of the freedmen. It was housed in an impressive building. Jackson would have entered it many times over the next few years, dropping off announcements, chatting with the staff, and updating them with his whereabouts. Did he go through the front entrance, or did he enter more quietly in the rear? Either way, he would have made himself proudly known.

His obstreperous, persistent presence in their offices might have been charming or irksome. Maybe both. But it turned out to be a good investment of his time. They would remember him, for sure. Down the road, that would save his life.

In 1866 the *Springfield Republican* announced that Jackson was in the vicinity collecting donations for the freemen of South Carolina. Similar announcements were to regularly appear over many years.[20] Indeed, while Jackson can be tracked through dozens of New England newspaper notices in the late 1860s and 1880s, it is his friends at the *Springfield Republican* who followed his news and updates more than at any other paper. Although the peripatetic Jackson didn't live for long in Springfield, they claimed him as one of their own.

Local Springfield businessmen began to take a friendly interest in Jackson's efforts. He was to use such businesses as donation collection points and as places to receive letters. Donations for the freedmen could be received in the office of the Hampden Card Company, noted one such announcement of 1869.[21] He received letters at the Rowers Paper Company at another point. In letters asking for assistance, he could now include signatories of residents of Springfield certifying to his character.[22] His future was uncertain, but his base of support, in Springfield at least, was solid.

But how to solicit donations? Jackson returned to what he did best: persuasion. He was no amateur lecturer anymore. After all, his first speaking engagements had started here in western Massachusetts some fifteen years earlier. After a decade of lecturing in Great Britain, he knew what he was about and thus worked to establish himself in Massachusetts as professionally as possible. Marketing was where he had to start.

One of Jackson's first actions around this time was to print a broadside poster with convenient fill-in-the-blanks to list varying locations and times for his talks. He was still pleased with his book's image of himself astride the horse, so why use anything else? Alas, he no longer had the original engraving—it would have been left behind in London with the Spurgeonite press, Passmore and Alabaster. Now that Spurgeon had blackballed him, there was no hope of ever getting that back. Now back in Massachusetts, the ever-resourceful Jackson commissioned another picture of himself, modeled after the one used on his book; it seems probable he shared his book page with the American engraver who reproduced the jaunty image as closely as he could. Jackson could tip his hat and directly look an American audience in the eye.

The broadside shown here dates from 1866 or 1867 and announces that he was raising funds in Salem to erect a schoolhouse for emancipated men,

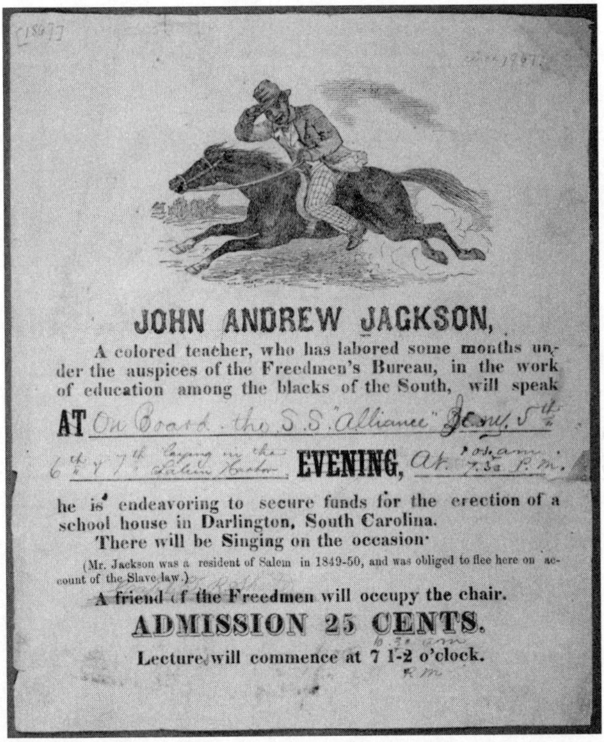
JOHN ANDREW JACKSON,

A colored teacher, who has labored some months under the auspices of the Freedmen's Bureau, in the work of education among the blacks of the South, will speak

AT On Board the S.S. "Alliance" Jany. 5th 6th & 7th Laying in the Salem Harbor EVENING, at 10.30 a.m. 7.30 P.M.

he is endeavoring to secure funds for the erection of a school house in Darlington, South Carolina.

There will be Singing on the occasion.

(Mr. Jackson was a resident of Salem in 1849-50, and was obliged to flee here on account of the Slave law.)

A friend of the Freedmen will occupy the chair.

ADMISSION 25 CENTS.

Lecture will commence at 7 1-2 o'clock.

This broadside held in the collections of the American Antiquarian Society is tentatively dated by its curators as from 1867, although it might more accurately date from 1866 or even 1865. Notice how it is printed with blanks so that it might provide details for various events. Note also that it claims to regularly feature a chair, a strategy Jackson had learned was always wise from his time in England and Scotland. This particular talk was held aboard a ship, the SS *Alliance*, then docked in Salem Harbor. Jackson must have had a good friend, perhaps the captain listed here as the chair, who would allow him to arrange such an event. Darlington, South Carolina, is roughly thirty miles from Lynchburg, South Carolina, where Jackson's family still lived.

women, and children in Darlington, South Carolina, a town about thirty miles from Lynchburg. Darlington had a new field office operating as an administration center for the federal Freedmen's Bureau. It must have seemed like a good location for such a school project. It was close enough to Lynchburg for Jackson to feel personally involved, and, if erected, it would have the proximity to federal officers for protection. Did the school receive funding? Did Jackson channel money back to formal or informal relief efforts? Did he line his own pockets with the proceeds? It's hard to say. But in this period, we see him establishing ways to work with, usually in informal ways, the official organizations delivering relief and overseeing reconstruction efforts in South Carolina.

Newspaper announcements began to accumulate. Dozens of notices such as the following appeared month after month in the late 1860s and 1870s:

- The *Boston Daily Journal*: John Andrew Jackson, a colored man endorsed by Gen. Howard, is now in the city collecting cast-off clothing, &c, for the destitute freedmen of South Carolina. Anything sent to him at Battery wharf will be forwarded and well applied.
- *Boston Daily Evening*: Goods for the Freedmen. We learn that John Andrew Jackson shipped from Boston, by steamer Port au Prince, this day, one plough, two barrels of Indian meal, six cases of merchandise and two kegs of molasses. These goods are destined for the Sumter Bureau Charleston, S.C., in charge of Capt. Place.
- *Boston Daily Advertiser*: Mr. Andrew Jackson, who has been laboring in this vicinity for the freedmen of South Carolina, shipped three boxes of fish (about 2000 pounds) and a barrel of Boston crackers to Maysville yesterday. They were the gift of our merchants.[23]

Jackson's travels back to South Carolina must have been painful; he saw suffering he could do little about. But he kept the relief supplies coming as best as he could. And the suffering he saw began to inspire an audacious scheme, some details of which open this chapter.

By the end of the Civil War, the English family was now in disarray: Robert English had died long before, and the Union forces (including the

Black regiments that had marched through Lynchburg at the very end of the war) had laid waste to many of the houses, fields, and infrastructure that had upheld the wealth of the white ruling class of that area. Many of Robert and Elizabeth English's descendants died or were occupied in professions that led their attention away from land management. The family was trying to sell off land, sell off property. Federal authorities were determined to collect taxes owed. The problem was that there weren't a lot of buyers with fungible capital, as demonstrated by the proliferating land-sale auctions that began to dominate the back pages of Sumter County newspapers.

Jackson smelled blood. And opportunity.

Why not buy up English's property for his own family?

There wasn't much precedence for this notion. While some rare cases of enslaved people individually purchasing their actual enslaver's land exist (Robert Smalls in Beaufort, South Carolina, is one such example), it was more mythical than real.[24] And even when federal officials tried, sometimes halfheartedly, to redistribute confiscated land to the enslaved laborers who had made it profitable, their efforts were short-lived and notoriously unsuccessful. No forty acres and a mule were ever going to be allocated to the freedmen in Lynchburg.

And yet, in June 1866, in the back pages of the *Springfield Republican*, Jackson shared not a dream but an actual plan to purchase English family property and settle his friends and family there, working together in some sort of community "on their own account." The paper reported:

> Mr. John Andrew Jackson, formerly a slave and a fugitive from the South, and lately from Europe, is in this vicinity receiving clothing and supplies to send to the destitute negroes, through the aid society, at No. 76 John Street, New York. He is also trying to raise funds to purchase his old master's plantation so that the former slaves may go to work on it, on their own account. He comes plentifully indorsed [sic] and is apparently worthy of assistance in the causes he represents.[25]

As we saw from the examination of his letter that opened this chapter, Jackson's attempt to purchase the land in 1866 and then again in 1868 failed. But his reputation with the *Springfield Republican* wasn't hurt by this failure. The paper continued to publish positive notices about his activities.

Various local Springfield businessmen and organizations occasionally offered to help hold or store donations.[26]

The city must have started to feel like home. And they needed a safe place. Julia's well-being may have been at stake. Jackson first mentions her health in the letter quoted earlier when she was taken sick partly by her distress over how she and Jackson were ejected from a train in Wilmington, but her health was fragile from this time forward. Jackson had his work ahead; he knew he would have to travel. It appears that Julia would not be traveling with him from now on.

Jackson, as always, had a plan.

VI

Julia needed help. He was going to get it.

Two children in South Carolina, relatives of his, couldn't be cared for back in Lynchburg. Jackson must have met them during his visit down there in 1865 and followed up on their circumstances with family correspondence.

These were desperate times for the emancipated families of South Carolina who were frantic for rations and medical care from the inadequate coffers of the Freedmen's Bureau. Families were starving. Jackson's living siblings needed help with their own children, and orphaned or extraneous nieces or nephews were an additional burden. In conversations with his Clavon family, Jackson got an idea: perhaps these two youngsters, Leah Abraham and Jimmy, could be sent north to live with Julia and Jackson; that would be two fewer mouths for the Lynchburg families to feed.[27] And Julia would get some company.

Leah Abraham was "about" sixteen, according to Jackson, and he reported that Jimmy was six years old.[28] Jackson proposed "to take the girl as my daughter not having any children and being able to support her. . . ." Moreover, the teenager could be a companion for Julia while he traveled. And Jimmy—well, Jimmy could be taken in by a Springfield-area minister who could educate him and perhaps even train him for the church. It seemed like a perfect plan. The only significant challenge, as Jackson saw it, would be getting them out of South Carolina. And yet, there was a rail connection from Lynchburg that could carry the children to Wilmington, North Carolina, and then northward all along the coast.[29] He was optimistic. Everything else should fall into place.

"I want them very much," Jackson wrote.[30]

But transportation was a tremendous obstacle Two youngsters with no education, resources, or sophistication about the world could not travel safely alone, even if Leah was a teenager. Jackson had recently seen what could happen even to two Black adults, affiliated with the Freedmen's Bureau, traveling on a northbound train: that awful incident in Wilmington, North Carolina, when he was assaulted and his possessions stolen. Julia and Jackson knew that getting Leah and Jimmy to Charleston and aboard a boat would prove difficult. The children would need a reliable escort. Julia wasn't going to travel again. It was up to Jackson. And yet, he may have felt that a trip south to pick up the children and escort them himself would be prohibitively expensive and possibly dangerous. He wasn't so easy to forget. There was no way he would risk another run-in with Officer Grig or his cronies.

And so, Jackson leveraged his relationship with General Howard.[31] Even if one could pay for a ticket, official permission to travel on trains was often required during that time because train cars were frequently requisitioned for troops and supplies to support the occupation. Space for any passengers was still scarce in years after the war, and unaccompanied Black children certainly wouldn't be welcome. Moreover, with so many tracks destroyed in the South during the war, train travel immediately after the cessation of hostilities was prioritized for official business. Howard, though, came through for Jackson. He promised to help and provided some authorization or money for travel. Jackson's plan was coming together.

Until something fell apart. The children didn't arrive. It doesn't appear that they had ever left. He complained from Springfield that the original "government transportation" granted by Howard (presumably tickets or authorization for travel) wasn't working.

> General Howard:
>
> Sir:
>
> The government transportation which you sent to me, I forwarded 3 or 4 weeks since but they do not send the children. Will you please yourself forwards a transportation to Capt. Place and Jane Smith, giving them the power to forward the boy and girl to me at once. I want them very much. I have a field for them to work in after school hours.
>
> Yours respectfully John Andrew Jackson
>
> Please inform me if you will do so immediately.[32]

Captain Place was a local federal official in Sumter County, and Jane Smith was the Massachusetts-born white schoolteacher who Jackson knew could be trusted to help with the children. But as weeks passed, Jackson became more frustrated and repeatedly wrote to Howard, begging for the children to be sent. He became defensive, presumably responding to an accusation that he wanted these children for some base or mercenary reason.

"I want them here so that I can give them an education which they cannot get in the South," he explained. In particular, he had a good plan for young Jimmy: a Reverend Cooke was prepared to take him in to study at the prestigious Wesleyan Academy (where Cooke served as headmaster) and train him for the ministry. The Academy was close to Springfield and was known for its progressive inclusiveness. It was a fine plan.

But it was not to be.

In these same letters, Jackson was simultaneously writing Howard about tools and various supplies he was transporting south and his concerns that the supplies were being pilfered, redistributed, misdirected, and just plain stolen along the way. He complained to Howard that the Freedmen's Bureau's representative in Sumter County, Captain Place, was part of the problem. Place, he complained, was commandeering supplies Jackson had collected and allocating their distribution as he saw fit. "Capt. Place has no right to distribute my goods at his disposal as I am not employed by the government and consequently I have my right to dispose of my goods at my pleasure among the needy."[33] He needed to regain control of his project. He wanted those supplies to go to the people he trusted. Jackson's priorities and those of Captain Place were not aligned.

It's hard to know exactly what each transaction was about. Still, the frustration Jackson felt over his inability to sponsor these children, coupled with his inability to control what was happening to supplies he had promised his networks in Sumter County, was now painfully personal.

Ephraim, his older brother who had survived extraordinary brutality at the hands of the English family—the brother who had held the Lynchburg families together once Jackson had left, who had tried to care for Doctor, their elderly father, and who, quite probably, had suffered because of Jackson's flight—was alive in Lynchburg and trying to act as an agent on Jackson's behalf, a role he was not able to fulfill.

In an extraordinary file of the Freedmen's Bureau, a letter from Ephraim to Jackson survives from this period, attached to the formal letter Jackson had written to Howard. This note from Ephraim was dictated, no doubt, but it rings true to the voice of a man in some despair. Jackson found it so troubling that he shared it with Howard, hoping it would persuade him that the situation among the freedmen in Lynchburg was dire.

Ephraim stated, "The goods has not come to hand up to date July 20th. I hope they will soon come as I need these very much at this time. My corn and rice is suffering for rain at this time." He asked Jackson to buy him a horse or mule because "I can't get along without one." He reported on the situation with the children, sadly telling Jackson, "Jimmin and Betsy's daughter cannot go to you because they have no money. I went to see Miss Smith about them and she says she has no way of sending them."

Ephraim reported that Amelia, his wife, was ill and ended with "Hard times and worse coming unless there is a great change with the People both white and Black about to perish."[34]

Jackson continued to try. He gave up on Leah and Jimmy for now. But he would persevere to do what else he could to help. He wrote Howard about the supplies en route, including children's clothes, suspenders for old men, and coffee and tea for the elderly. He had sent two barrels of flour for his family but feared they would be stolen. Jackson wrote: "Ephraim is a poor old man who has received a great deal of hard use and is not able to support himself I fear they are going to keep these goods from these men so not mind what Capt. Place says for he is more of an enemy than a friend to the freedman."[35]

In one last bold attempt to lay the situation out before Howard, even if complaining about the Freedmen's officials might not be well received or believed by the general, Jackson stated plainly: "I think that he has received the goods but he tells me they have not arrived please look this up as I have worked very hard to get these goods together." Jackson added:

> Now to think that those who I intended and who need them very much should be cheated out of them by this rascal seems hard and discouraging for me. I have chosen Ephraim as my agent to see that the goods are distributed right and they feel very huffy towards him for coming so often to see if goods have come.[36]

Ephraim was a man much abused throughout his life—a man on the brink of starvation and desperately trying to take care of his own family. Risking humiliation at best and genuine danger at worst, he was screwing up his courage, making himself known, and making himself a nuisance by repeatedly approaching Captain Place and his officers. As with Lymus McLeod, Black men in Lynchburg were not supposed to call attention to themselves, whether to the former Confederates or the often unsympathetic federal officers. Ephraim was desperate. Riling up the officers and making them "huffy" wouldn't help him any.

Complaining about Captain Place doesn't seem to have helped Jackson, much less Ephraim. Even worse, after this summer of 1868, Jackson appears to have resigned himself to the understanding that anything he wanted to deliver to the freedmen in Sumter County would have to be *despite* the federal officials and not because of them. He wasn't discouraged for long, though. With powerful optimism, he focused on his life in New England for a bit and continued to put plans in place so that he might gather goods and travel back down there himself.

However, Jackson needed to turn his attention, because Julia's health now took a dramatic turn.

On October 19, 1868, his friends at the *Springfield Republican* announced:

> The wife of John Andrew Jackson, the colored solicitor for the freedmen, became partially insane one day last week, and was taken to the Northampton asylum.[37]

Whether this illness was sudden or had been a long time in coming, Jackson was determined to leverage it. By November 24, 1868, he wrote Howard that "my wife has become insane owing to the refusal of Capt Place to permit her niece to be sent to her."[38] What "insane" might have meant at the time is hard to know. Depression? Migraines? Epilepsy? Cancer?

Whatever it was, it must have been terrifying for them both. Jackson wasn't afraid to claim the cause of her illness: loneliness and despair. It was Captain Place's fault. She needed Leah Abraham, her niece who had never been able to arrive. He wrote Howard: "As in my absence she has been left alone, thus being none to stay with her she has finally lost her reason and is at present at Northampton Asylum. . . ."[39]

Founded in 1858, the Northampton Lunatic Asylum was considered a modern and progressive institution designed as a state-of-the-art facility in a bucolic setting.[40] Inmates/patients labored to support their health and the runnings of the institution. While some patients who paid high fees were held in the more luxurious wards and had fewer work expectations, others who paid far less or had nothing to pay were put to more strenuous and challenging daily tasks, dealing with slop jars, laundry, scrubbing, and the like.

We can assume that Julia, as a poor Black woman, was likely living in the worst of the dormitories and was forced to do a great deal of work. For a woman who had escaped slavery in North Carolina to end up in another situation of uncompensated toil might have been a bitter pill to swallow. Still, she might have felt useful and valued within the community. She had been so lonely. Did she find friends there? With few choices, Jackson had found Julia one of the best options available for her care.[41]

VII

With Julia left at the asylum, Jackson returned to his usual peregrinations. His schemes were unstoppable. The needs of the freedmen were unending. He would lecture, and he would collect donations. He would try something new.

The English gristmill land scheme had failed. No matter. There was more land to claim. Once he could sort things out with Julia's health, he would start a "colony" in Cheraw, South Carolina. And now he had a new patron!

On November 25, 1869, the *Springfield Republican* announced:

> John Andrew Jackson . . . has been engaged by W. Sanford, a New York merchant, to settle a large tract of land belonging to him near Cheraw, S. C., about 150 miles from Charleston, with colored people. Mr. Sanford intends that these tenants shall have the use of his land at a nominal rent, and buy it if they become able to do so. Mr. Jackson will begin the colony about January 1. . . .

As had happened before, for some reason, after the announcement the deal fell through.

But perhaps he could still build a school. Maybe a church? On July 20, 1870, the *Springfield Republican* reported that: "It is painful to learn that the 6000 acres of land at Cheraw is ended." Jackson was not defeated and was ready to promote the character he had cultivated. The paper quoted him as saying of himself, "Old John Andrew Jackson is not quite dead yet, you may see him again." The garrulous Jackson must have written his friends at the paper an especially lengthy letter, for they end by saying,

"Mr. Jackson is a forcible writer, it will be seen, and his thoughts are even severely condensed."

Perhaps Jackson couldn't find the necessary local backing, or his patron, Sanford, got cold feet. The situation in Cheraw might have become too dangerous. Or perhaps he realized Julia's situation was such that she needed to get out of the Northampton Asylum but couldn't be safely settled to join him in South Carolina. Whatever happened, by the fall of 1870, Jackson had a new plan: he would return north, spring Julia from the asylum, and start fresh. Again.

VIII

John Andrew Jackson and his wife, Julia A. Jackson, appear in the 1870 Census in New Haven, Connecticut. She was out of the asylum. And they had left Springfield. Their occupations were now listed as "Laborer" and "Keeping House," respectively. Jackson's place of birth is correctly noted as South Carolina and hers as North Carolina, facts consistent with what we have known of them thus far. Their ages are recorded as fifty-one and fifty, which aligns fairly accurately with their census ages earlier recorded in England's 1861 tables. For the first time, they are both listed as able to read and write.[42] Jackson was in South Carolina during the month the New Haven data was collected, so it must have been Julia alone who opened the door to the census taker.

Every census tells a singular kind of story, and this one is no different. And it lets us guess why Jackson felt comfortable leaving his wife, who had only recently been released from the hospital, alone in this new city. This page tells us a great deal about their new environs, despite what initially seems like a paucity of information. Because, as we have seen with earlier census documents, when it comes to people of marginalized race, class, or legal status, our modern ability to understand their worlds is often primarily dependent upon or determined by the people immediately adjacent on the page.[43]

And here, on Winter Street in New Haven, a very particular kind of sanctuary is revealed.

While their precise house address isn't noted, we can track the addresses of several of Jackson's New Haven neighbors. The census recorder would have walked down the block, building by building. Because such folks appear on the same pages as the Jacksons and can be cross-referenced in

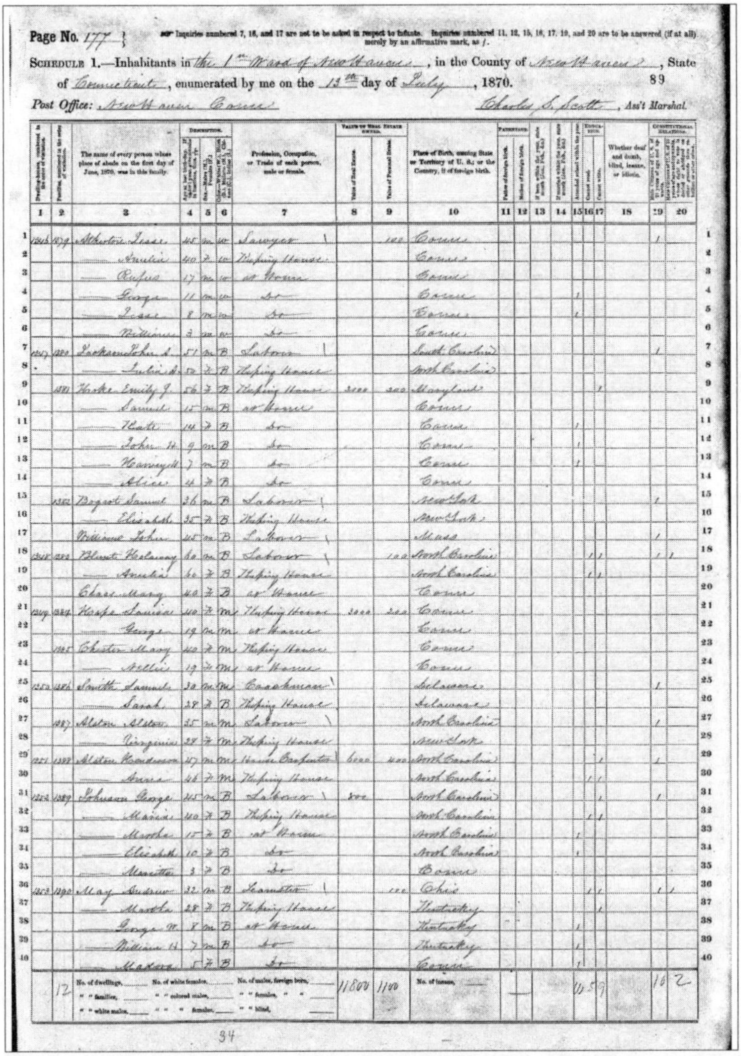

Page No. 177 } Inquiries numbered 7, 16, and 17 are not to be asked in respect to infants. Inquiries numbered 11, 12, 15, 16, 17, 19, and 20 are to be answered (if at all) merely by an affirmative mark, as /.

SCHEDULE 1.—Inhabitants in the 1st Ward of New Haven, in the County of New Haven, State of Connecticut, enumerated by me on the 13th day of July, 1870. 89

Post Office: New Haven Conn — Charles S. Scott, Ass't Marshal.

	1 Dwelling-houses	2 Families	3 Name	4 Age	5 Sex	6 Color	7 Profession, Occupation, or Trade	8 Value of Real Estate	9 Value of Personal Estate	10 Place of Birth	11	12	13	14	15	16	17	18	19	20	
1	1346	1379	Atherton Jesse	45	m	w	Sawyer		100	Conn									1		1
2			— Amelia	40	F	w	Keeping House			Conn											2
3			— Rufus	17	m	w	at Home			Conn											3
4			— George	11	m	w	do			Conn					1						4
5			— Jesse	8	m	w	do			Conn					1						5
6			— William	3	m	w	do			Conn											6
7	1347	1380	Jackson John S.	51	m	B	Laborer			South Carolina									1		7
8			— Julia A.	50	F	B	Keeping House			North Carolina											8
9		1381	Hooke Emily J.	56	F	B	Keeping House	2000	200	Maryland							1				9
10			— Samuel	15	m	B	at Home			Conn											10
11			— Kate	14	F	B	do			Conn					1						11
12			— John H.	9	m	B	do			Conn					1						12
13			— Harry H.	7	m	B	do			Conn					1						13
14			— Alice	4	F	B	do			Conn											14
15		1382	Bogart Samuel	36	m	B	Laborer			New York									1		15
16			— Elizabeth	35	F	B	Keeping House			New York											16
17			Williams John	45	m	B	Laborer			Mass									1		17
18	1348	1383	Blunt Holaway	60	m	B	Laborer		100	North Carolina						1	1		1	1	18
19			— Amelia	60	F	B	Keeping House			North Carolina						1	1				19
20			Chase Mary	40	F	B	at Home			Conn											20
21	1349	1384	Hope Louisa	40	F	M	Keeping House	2000	200	Conn											21
22			— George	19	m	M	at Home			Conn											22
23		1385	Chester Mary	40	F	M	Keeping House			Conn											23
24			— Nellie	19	F	M	at Home			Conn											24
25	1350	1386	Smith Samuel	30	m	M	Coachman			Delaware									1		25
26			— Sarah	28	F	B	Keeping House			Delaware											26
27		1387	Alston Alston	35	m	M	Laborer			North Carolina									1		27
28			— Virginia	28	F	M	Keeping House			New York											28
29	1351	1388	Alston Henderson	47	m	M	House Carpenter	6000	400	North Carolina							1		1		29
30			— Anna	46	F	M	Keeping House			North Carolina						1	1				30
31	1352	1389	Johnson George	45	m	B	Laborer	800		North Carolina							1		1		31
32			— Maria	40	F	B	Keeping House			North Carolina						1	1				32
33			— Martha	15	F	B	at Home			North Carolina					1						33
34			— Elizabeth	10	F	B	do			North Carolina					1						34
35			— Marietta	3	F	B	do			Conn											35
36	1353	1390	May Andrew	32	m	B	Teamster		100	Ohio						1	1		1	1	36
37			— Martha	28	F	B	Keeping House			Kentucky							1				37
38			— George W.	8	m	B	at Home			Kentucky					1						38
39			— William H.	7	m	B	do			Kentucky					1						39
40			— Madora	5	F	B	do			Conn					1						40
		12	No. of dwellings, ___ " " families, ___ " " white males, ___ No. of white females, ___ " " colored males, ___ " " " females, ___ No. of males, foreign born, ___ " " females, " " ___ " " blind, ___					11800	1100	No. of insane, ___					11	5	9		10	2	

34

The Census of 1870 shows Julia and Jackson in New Haven with neighbors on their street who were born in states that had allowed people to be enslaved, suggesting that many of their Connecticut neighbors had also survived bondage in the South. Notice the middle column with the "Place of Birth" listings.

city directories, we can see that almost all these neighbors are Black and are living on Winter Street, a small block between what is now Goffe and Dixwell, in a New Haven neighborhood now known as "lower Dixwell."

So far, all seems straightforward. It was a poor neighborhood then and was still a working-class community in the early twenty-first century, populated largely but not entirely by Black people. It was probably a challenge to collect census data there. On Winter Street, men and women would likely be absent with erratic and extended work shifts; families and boarders likely shared spaces and crowded into smaller rooms than in the fancier houses close to Yale College and its environs. Transient workers would appear and disappear according to factory demands. Working women wouldn't reliably be found at home during the day, and certainly, they didn't have servants to answer their doors. And we can surmise that Black people living in New Haven in 1870 might well have been a bit stressed about engaging with white officials of the government who represented power and authority that could swing in unpredictable ways.

Nonetheless, enough people eventually provided the necessary information for the census collector to paint a portrait of their street and the origins of these neighbors. And, when we look closely, we can see that many of Jackson's Black neighbors on Winter Street, all living in the small wooden houses lining the block, hailed originally from Maryland and Delaware. Other Black family groups on Winter Street were from Kentucky and North Carolina.

This is a cluster of people drawn to one another, many of whom were born in what had been, until recently, slave states. That wasn't a coincidence.

This street wasn't just a gathering spot for Black laborers or working-class people. In 1870 this census page meant one of two things: either this cluster was composed of people who had escaped from slavery, or it was a cluster of people who had been enslaved and very recently immigrated north. These Winter Street folks were not regular members of the long-standing free Black community of New Haven. They were, instead, encircled and protected within that community. New Haven's Winter Street was an epicenter for survivors. Perhaps a fortress.

These Black joiners, jobbers, laborers, and coach makers of Winter Street were strivers and dreamers, people who left the world of bondage in the South behind to make their way to the bustling industrial North, getting jobs at the local mills and factories newly fleshing out the avenues of New Haven.[44] And for Julia and Jackson, we can see that regardless of whatever had drawn them to New Haven generally, they had found among the small wooden houses of Winter Street a home with people who could understand what it had meant to live under the horrors of slavery and its consequent traumas.

Moreover, they were ready to take care of their own: in 1869, Black residents of New Haven formed a colored freedmen's relief group—and we can be sure that Jackson, as soon as he settled Julia in New Haven, would have involved himself in their endeavors, perhaps offering himself up as a local expert to help conduit donations but also to make sure they knew about Julia and could wrap her into their community.[45]

And opportunities there were. This area of New Haven was closely proximate to a canal and, later, the railroad that was laid out along the canal's bed. The New Haven and Northampton Railroad, which could take Jackson back and forth to the towns and friends in Massachusetts he knew well, was only a short walk from Winter Street. The Newell Carriage Company was located nearby and employed many Black people, as did, by 1870, the Winchester Repeating Arms Company.[46] A working-class Black population filled this neighborhood's lower triangle.

The bustling economy of New Haven fueled other social developments that signaled a brighter future for these dreamers. More and more churches that were primarily for Black congregants were established during these years. A possibility for more consistent and equitably funded education seemed near. While there had been a scattering of schools for colored children, primarily for the youngest children, during the antebellum era, there had never been consistent and free school facilities across the city. Thus in 1869, Black residents of New Haven petitioned to end discrimination and segregation in public schools. The New Haven Board of Education recognized their civic history of discrimination had to end and voted that summer to incorporate children of color into the regular school system for the first time.[47]

Julia and Jackson, who were now probably in their fifties, were past the age to start a family themselves. Julia's health was poor. Yet they had been ready to take in teenage Leah and young Jimmy. They might still be able to build out their family and connect with their new community.

For all the promise that this New Haven home suggested, Jackson's situation began to get messier. He was still speaking at churches in New England, especially visiting ones in Connecticut now and building out friendships and patrons from prominent white citizens in these new cities he was getting to know. It wasn't always smooth. There were doubters.

The Middletown, Connecticut, *Constitution* proclaimed, "One John Andrew Jackson, who is collecting funds for a Baptist church and school in South Carolina, is believed to be an imposter."[48]

Jackson might have been distressed by such an accusation, but he couldn't have been too rattled. He'd seen that before.

Now he had a base in Connecticut; he started rotating into Hartford as well, a city only forty miles from New Haven.[49] With its affluence, liberal reputation, and small but well-established Black population, Hartford was an excellent place to hustle for speaking venues and donations.[50] Furthermore, it is tempting to imagine that he might have tried to reconnect with Harriet Beecher Stowe, who by this time had established a house in Hartford. Couldn't he—wouldn't he—have knocked once again on her door? Sent her a card? Reconnecting with such a patron would have been invaluable. She would know he wasn't an imposter.

Yet no records of any such reunion exist. After Jackson's reputation had been so sullied in England, he might have rightfully feared that his enemies from the Spurgeon fiasco would have poisoned her against him. And perhaps, too, he didn't even know she was there. Or he may have tried and been rebuffed. Or maybe he visited her Hartford home during the months when she was in Florida (Calvin and Harriet regularly wintered in Florida between 1867 and 1884). We cannot know. But Jackson was probably too busy to sit with that problem for long.

There were more supplies to collect, more travels to make south, and a stream of updates and letters to send to the local papers to ensure his public was kept current with his activities. In December 1871, he even traveled to Maine to revisit some of his old haunts and reconnect with his friends. The *Portland Daily Press* reported:

> Mr. John Andrew Jackson, a successful teacher connected with the colored schools in South Carolina, will present the claims of his people in the Reception Room of City Hall this Monday evening. Mr. Jackson is desirous of securing means to build a school-house in Darlington, S.C. In 1850 Mr. J. was a resident of Salem and at that time was compelled to flee to Portland on account of the Fugitive slave law, where he was taken care of by the late Gen. Fessenden.[51]

Despite notices such as this that suggest he had plans and activities for the upcoming years (because didn't he always?), Jackson and Julia somewhat disappear from archival view for a stretch between 1872 to 1878. During these years, life may have been especially rough for Julia. She returned to the Northampton Asylum.

Jackson took trips to South Carolina for a good stretch of time once Julia was committed again, perhaps working at the church and school projects in Darlington County that he had long been collecting for. Once down south, he may have realized the wisdom in keeping his head down to avoid trouble and avoid notice. An exuberant Black man with radical dreams and confidence to spare would have to tread very carefully in this post-Reconstruction South, but he had learned some things by now. He was in his midfifties and knew when to keep quiet. Sometimes, at least. While in South Carolina, he laid low. And kept busy.

In 1878, he returned from South Carolina, not back to New Haven, but rather to the city of Springfield once more. This time, however, he returned with a new and much younger companion, the twenty-one-year-old Ella Pooler Jackson from South Carolina.

Had Jackson brought Ella Pooler north with a plan for her to be a caretaker or friend for Julia, just as he had tried to do with his niece, Leah Abraham? Or was a different kind of relationship already underway?

In Springfield, Ella Pooler Jackson gave birth to a daughter, Anna Elizabeth Jackson, in September 1878.[52] The listed father was John Andrew Jackson.

Julia was still alive. Did she know? Was she aware of what had happened: that her husband had left her in the asylum and started a new extralegal family, with a twenty-one-year-old? While records of the Northampton Asylum do not exist that can prove Julia's whereabouts, at some point in the mid- or late 1870s, she probably returned there to live out the rest of her life.

Massachusetts records indicate Julia died in the Northampton Asylum in 1880.[53]

Julia was a casualty of poverty, of medical treatments that could do little to alleviate whatever it was that ailed her, almost certainly of the traumas she had endured, and possibly, too, of a man who was always looking forward, always on the move—a man unable to stay still and to stay true.

Julia had fled slavery in North Carolina. She had thwarted a terrifying attempt at recapture in New York and built a life in the chilly Canadian environs of Saint John, New Brunswick. She took a chance at a new life with another fugitive, an ambitious and impatient dreamer.

Together, Julia and Jackson had traveled the world, and, in defiance of Victorian norms, she had even occasionally taken to the stage to share her witness, to speak her truths. With her demure ways and careful manner, she had been an asset to Jackson and likely tempered his brash impulses. She had stood by Jackson during his trials and betrayals. Their travels south, however, may have broken this woman. From 1868 onward, she never fully recovered. While we can know little about her life in the asylum, at least we know that she died in the North, in a state that had medical facilities for her. We can hope it was among friends.

IX

The chronology of these years is messy because the life of Jackson had taken complicated turns. In those last months of Julia's life, with her alive but ensconced in the Northampton Asylum, Jackson may have felt that his second marriage was effectively over in his heart, if not legally. Perhaps he saw himself as rescuing Ella Pooler from the destitute South and the dismal future it promised for her. Perhaps he was a predatory older man, making promises to a young woman impressed by his worldly ways.

We cannot know if Ella was lured, rescued, or entranced, but leave she did for the promise of life in the North. No marriage certificate (or divorce certificate) for Jackson is extant from this period. Still, he appears to have married young Ella, or at least declared himself married to census takers by 1880, even if Julia was still alive.

After the loss of Louisa and little Jinny, followed by the tragedy of Julia's descent into illness and their childless marriage, Jackson must have been joyful to start a new life afresh with a young and healthy wife who was from his hometown and would have understood at least a little bit about who he was and where he had come from.

The new start and its new joys weren't to last for long.

Baby Anna Elizabeth Jackson appears to have died of cholera or an intestinal illness as a toddler.[54] It must have been horrifying for her parents to witness. Yet Jackson and Ella soldiered on through their grief, and the couple had another daughter almost precisely one year later. In September 1879, they welcomed baby Elizabeth Jackson into their lives.[55]

This time, Jackson and Ella invited Philis McIntosh, up from South Carolina, presumably to stay to help care for Ella and the new baby in Springfield.[56] The 1880 Census, collected in June, shows the four of them all living together on Willow Street. While the records on Philis McIntosh are hazy, she was close in age to Jackson's young wife, and she was probably another Lynchburg relative.[57] Perhaps a Clavon. It would have been good to have someone from South Carolina living with them, able to reminisce and perhaps even laugh or marvel with them about the strange ways of New England. Like Jackson and Ella, McIntosh had survived enslavement in Lynchburg. She knew how to appreciate freedom, but she also knew that with freedom, burdens to care for one another were greater than ever. She could help with Ella. Help with baby Elizabeth.

It would have been most appreciated. Jackson had seen how his travels had left Julia lonely and alone. He had seen the death of his baby the year before. Perhaps he was trying, this time, to do better.

Were his daughters both named after Jackson's dead mother, Betty? We cannot know, and there isn't much information about what might have happened to his second child with Ella, baby Elizabeth. But Ella and Jackson must have prayed for a brighter life for their children than their parents had seen.

This new address on Willow Street wasn't a terrible place to raise a baby. Perhaps it was a step up from the place they had lived where their first baby, Anna Elizabeth, had contracted her cholera. Ella and Jackson's home on Willow Street was a few blocks from the Connecticut River in a working-class neighborhood integrated, however roughly, with recent immigrants from Ireland and Italy alongside Black people. A map of 1875 suggests this pocket of a neighborhood was quieter and a bit less dense than others, but likely less attractive than the more central areas of the city, perhaps because it was near refuse or boggy fallows. Willow Street was only a short walk to the *Springfield Republican* offices on Main Street as well as a reasonable walk to both the train station and easy boat access on the waterfront—all considerations Jackson would have kept in mind.

As with Winter Street in New Haven, Willow Street in Springfield featured several Black neighbors from formerly slave states, and at least three other people on Willow Street listed South Carolina as their birthplace. Whether these people had been fugitives from slavery or whether they had relocated to Springfield in search of jobs and opportunities away from the challenges of the postwar South, it is hard to know. But it looks like Jackson was trying to settle his family into a space where they would be understood. This time, he was wrong.

Jackson's new life was hardly halcyon. He needed money. Julia was still alive in the asylum as of early 1880, but she was nearing death. Ella and baby Elizabeth were at home with Philis McIntosh, and needed support.

Jackson was certainly trying to send help down to his family in Lynchburg, a family which may even have included his first wife, Louisa. And his hope for understanding neighbors was too optimistic.

On July 8, 1880, the *Springfield Republican* reported:

> Alexander Anderson, John Lewis, a special policeman, Griffin Ball and Charles Robinson were arrested on a warrant yesterday for breaking windows in the house of John Andrew Jackson, the colored preacher. Jackson is disliked by his neighbors, who take many opportunities to torment him. The arrest was made last evening with a good deal of tumult in which Jackson got hustled roughly.[58]

What had Jackson done to enrage his neighbors? Why might they "torment" him? His friends and acquaintances, from the elderly Jake McLeod in Lynchburg to Harriet Beecher Stowe and his own enslavers, consistently described him as talkative and occasionally boastful. It is easy to imagine a scenario where his boasting, perhaps of his overseas exploits or his dogged obsession to raise funds for people far flung from Springfield, made him an exasperating neighbor. We cannot know for sure what happened, but this incident marks a curious and perhaps not unexpected event for the fearless and confident Jackson.

The attack must have been terrifying for poor Ella and Philis McIntosh, both living there with a baby less than a year old. Broken glass, shouts in the night. An assault on Jackson. If they couldn't flee, they most certainly would have tried to huddle down, hide, and protect little Elizabeth.

Records suggest that the attacker, "John Lewis" in this newspaper report, was most likely another Black man living only a few houses down on Willow Street from Jackson. John Lewis was only in his twenties and worked as a "private coachman." Griffin Ball, who worked in "a pistol shop," was another young Black man, who lived around the corner from Willow Street.[59] It is hard to identify from the article if Griffin Ball or John Lewis was a special policeman or if the "special policeman" was an entirely separate unnamed person. Regardless, "special policeman" at this time usually referred to a regular citizen who had been given some authority in terms of patrolling or law enforcement. And while it might have been instigated by some sort of provocation of Jackson's, the fact that the police were willing to arrest one of their own on charges presumably brought by Jackson is a testament to the seriousness of the charges, the faith that Jackson had in the legal system serving him justly, and, remarkably, the status Jackson had in the community: he was taken seriously. Despite the neighborly conflict, for the police to arrest other police for harassing a Black man (whom the paper reports as a "colored preacher") is a remarkable event. Jackson's enemies were arrested.

In this instance, the legal system stood up for Jackson. That wouldn't last.

In April 1881, life was getting difficult for Jackson. He announced that he had some personal setbacks and needed donations. According to a letter he sent to his stalwart friends at the *Springfield Republican* while in Connecticut, he was evicted by a landlord and, in the confusion, accidentally packed up his bedclothes and belongings in a box that was somehow mistakenly sent down south, along with three official boxes of donations. Desperate to regain his possessions, he "took the night boat from Hartford to New York" but was "one day too late." Now heading back to Springfield, he would gladly receive "contributions."[60]

With some indignation, Jackson's landlord, A.B. Bush, wrote to the *Springfield Republican* the very next day with his side of the story. As he saw it, Jackson had moved out, "forgetting to leave his keys and the balance of his rent." Bush also stated that Jackson "has written equally false letters before; one to William H. Smith stating that I had put his goods into the street, but . . . Mr. Smith's foreman failed on investigation to find that they had been disturbed."[61]

It might have been a simple landlord dispute. Jackson could easily have fallen behind on rent, and the mix-up with the boxes, while sad, is certainly plausible in the context. Chasing after the box all the way to New York suggests there was more than just bedclothes inside. And Bush's reference to Jackson having written "false letters" before is mystifying but certainly indicates accumulating troubles. What is important here is that the appearance of this conflict in the *Springfield Republican* could have been devastating. Jackson's reputation was now in question. His credibility, an asset he had spent a lifetime cultivating, was under attack.

It was time to get out of New England. In a hurry. Without his usual planning. Without Ella and baby Elizabeth. He fled.

CHAPTER TEN

"HARD LABOR"—COURT MINUTES FROM SURRY COUNTY, NORTH CAROLINA (1881)

North Carolina, Massachusetts, and South Carolina (1881–1900)

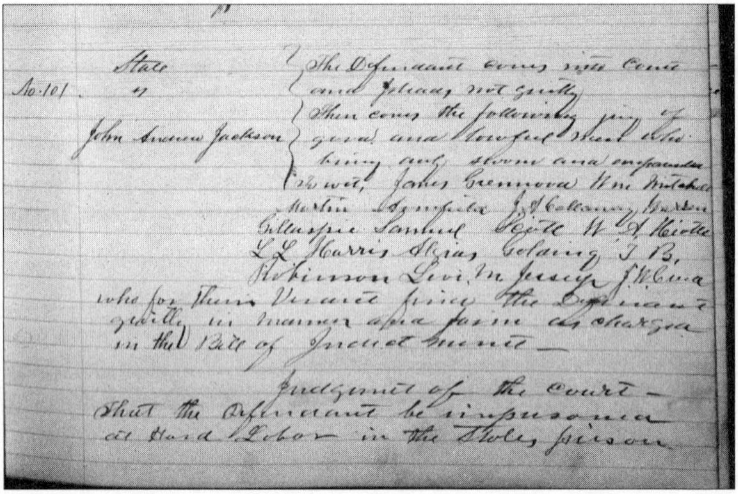

No. 101. State v. John Andrew Jackson

The Defendant comes into Court and pleads not guilty. Then comes the following jury of good and lawful men who being duly sworn and empanelled to wit; James [illegible] Wm Mitchell, Martin [illegible] J. A. [illegible] [illegible] Gillespie, Samuel [illegible] W. A. [illegible], L. L. Harris, [illegible] [illegible] T. B., Robinson, Levi [illegible] J. W. [illegible] who for their verdict find the Defendant guilty in manner and form as charged in the Bill of Indictment—

Judgment of the Court—
That the Defendant be imprisoned at Hard Labor in the State's prison

Minutes from the Supreme Court of Surry County, North Carolina, concerning *State vs. John Andrew Jackson*.

Jackson left his family behind. After a life spent in tireless work to free and care for his family—indeed, his families—it is hard to reckon. This stage of his life is thus difficult to understand in terms of his personal and emotional state. There is no evidence that he ever lived again with Ella, his third wife, and baby Elizabeth. Had they died? Were he and Ella estranged, or had life simply pulled them apart? His hustles, his boasting, and his reckless temper might have been exhausting to be around. Revelations about his multiple and overlapping marriages with Louisa and Julia may have become too painful for Ella to live with. And the traveling? A perpetually absent husband and father might have seemed worse than none at all. Perhaps Ella just washed her hands of him. She was still young. Whatever had unfolded between them, they don't seem to have reunited. From here on out, Jackson would be going it alone.

When we unpack the records that remain of his life at the end of the century, some surprising clues about his activities emerge (receipts, land deed, and, as always, newspaper clippings). But a shocking encounter in North Carolina, chronicled by court records, defied even Jackson's formidable skills at talking his way out of trouble, and presents a terrible tale. Jackson was arrested in a small Southern town and tried on a trumped-up charge. No one was with him to plead for mercy.

It was going to take an audacious act to escape these circumstances and one which would call upon tools he had spent a lifetime honing: courage coupled with bravado, and an unwavering belief in others who could see him and know him for who he truly was. He was, after all, as Jake McLeod had recalled, the man they couldn't catch up with "till it was too late," the man who would always come back to "Ole Carliny."[1]

I

In the official minutes of the Supreme Court of Surry County, North Carolina, in early May 1881, we can see an entry for the *State vs. John Andrew Jackson*. It's brief. He was accused of "obtaining money under false pretenses."[2] Jackson pled not guilty. He must have attempted to speak, to protest, and probably to decry the injustice of it all, but there is no record of anything he may have said.

In what was likely a quick trial, an all-white jury characterized by the court as twelve "good and lawful men" found Jackson "guilty in manner and form as charged in the indictment." The judge sentenced him to five years of "Hard Labor"—capitalized in the document with cruel emphasis. For a Black man probably in his late fifties or older, this was close to a death sentence. One week earlier, he had been on his way from Connecticut back to his friends in Springfield, seeking some contributions to help him buy new bedclothes. His arrest and trial must have been a dizzyingly fast and horrifying turn of events.

A sheriff was conscripted to escort Jackson to the offices of the CF & YVRR (Cape Fear and Yadkin Valley Railroad): he was to serve on a convict work gang. For a man who had spoken at churches and civic halls across the Northeast, who had crisscrossed England and addressed the Reverend Spurgeon's enormous congregation, a man who had met with General Howard—this was a moment of humiliation and frustration. But those emotions would have been subsumed by the more sensible one: abject terror.

Selling or leasing out prisoners for forced labor or essentially renting them out to railroads, mines, factories, road building crews, or construction projects was a practice deeply entrenched in Southern states at this time (and indeed, not unfamiliar to many Northern and western states). But in the rural South, in the decades after the Civil War, millions of poor

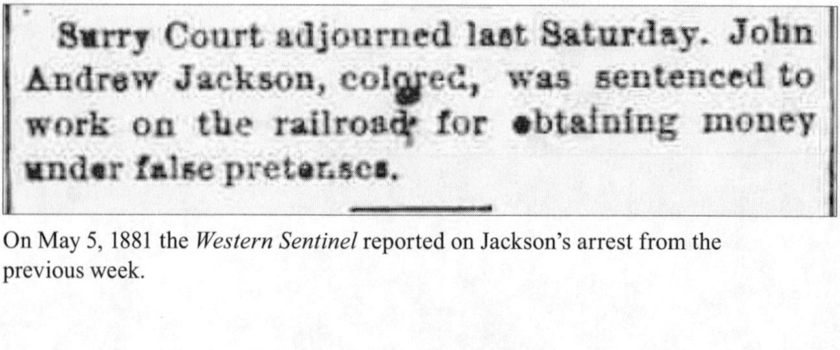
Surry Court adjourned last Saturday. John Andrew Jackson, colored, was sentenced to work on the railroad for obtaining money under false pretenses.

On May 5, 1881 the *Western Sentinel* reported on Jackson's arrest from the previous week.

Black men, often with no land, no steady employment, and little influence, were particularly vulnerable. The convict lease system not only enforced white supremacy but was also designed for quick capital. Like systems that enslaved people, leasing convicts allowed labor costs to be fixed and predictable. Workers couldn't shy away from danger or risk. They could be driven to labor at a pace that wouldn't have been tolerated by anybody who had a choice.[3] This kind of involuntary servitude can best be understood as "Slavery by Another Name," a phrase popularized by journalist and historian Douglas A. Blackmon in his study of convict labor.[4]

The incentive to arrest people arbitrarily, assign them outrageous fines, manufacture fake debts they would be in arrears for, and often even charge them for the cost of their arrests was thus enormous for many local and state governments of the post–Civil War era. Indeed, Southern states, during the decades after the Civil War, rarely used traditional prisons at all. Contracting out prisoners to businesses, farms, agricultural industries, and even other governments was the norm.

How did Jackson find himself in Surry County, North Carolina—and why would he have exposed himself to such risk?

Surry County was directly north of both Winston-Salem, North Carolina, and Charlotte, North Carolina—both major transportation hubs generally north of Sumter County, South Carolina. It seems likely that Jackson was traveling to Lynchburg via North Carolina, possibly alternating between trains and wagons and spending the night in towns when necessary. And once off the train, with no resources or friends, an arrest would have been inevitable.

Jackson was at least fifty-five years of age at this time. He might have been lucky, and the work gang he was assigned to might have had provisions for older, weaker convicts. Sometimes, rarely, there were jobs for men who could read and write. Older men might be given somewhat lighter duties such as carrying water, pushing wheelbarrows, or preparing food for others.[5] But he probably wasn't that lucky. Railroad work was brutal, and the tasks of clearing land, blasting tunnels, constructing bridges, moving rock, and laying track were endless.

Disease was rampant among convict laborers, hygiene was neglected, food was wholly inadequate, whipping and other torture as punishment was generally allowed, and death was common. In 1875, for example, on the Cape Fear and Yadkin Valley Railroad, the very site where Jackson was assigned, 45 out of 182 men sent there had died—a figure just shy of a

25 percent mortality rate. And most of those men would have been younger and more robust than Jackson.

His life in the convict camp, a life in which he was probably chained for at least some of the time and overseen by men with guns, is hard to imagine in some ways, but in other ways, the records and witness testimony make it clear that it was a brutal existence. The Cape Fear and Yadkin Valley Railroad had plans to become a 411-mile carrier by the end of the 1880s.[6] That meant there could be little time for anything other than relentlessly pushing forward to obtain more convict workers to serve their goals. After all, they needed to replace those who had served their sentences, those who were too ill to work, those who fled, and those who died.

During the early 1880s, the Cape Fear and Yadkin Valley Railroad directors were intent on connecting Fayetteville and Greensboro. Jackson almost certainly would have been assigned to that stretch of the project.[7] He would have been assigned to work alongside many illiterate young men convicted for crimes such as vagrancy, trespassing, debt, or even charges of murder, theft, or rape. Having survived slavery on the English family slave labor camp, he would have understood something about their backgrounds and how they might have been caught up by the state in these confusing decades after the Civil War.

Jackson would have also found some surprising comrades with whom he had much in common. Despite the state's interest in using the youngest and healthiest men suited for manual labor, they also used the convict lease system to take anyone understood as an unwelcome or disruptive Black citizen off the streets. This meant that men like Jackson, who didn't sufficiently bend to white expectations for docile behavior, could be targeted for arrest and then assigned to lease labor sentences. As a warden of a Georgia penitentiary remarked in 1875, "Colored preachers, teachers, and politicians" made up a good percentage of his inmates presumably because, according to his logic, they didn't behave as "old 'Cuffee' from the rural districts, who was trained, in antebellum days to gain his bread by the sweat of his brow."[8]

We can hope that Jackson might have made some connections, allies, or even friends during his few hard weeks on the Cape Fear and Yadkin Valley Railroad. Perhaps they told him a bit about the lay of the land. Perhaps not enough.

We can imagine that any attempt by Jackson to complain, protest, or talk his way out of the situation would have been met with cruelty and disdain.

Yet Jackson had another skill he hadn't had to use for a long time: he knew how to flee.

And so, Jackson escaped.

II

When he first fled the English plantation, Jackson knew he could be put to death with impunity, and he could expect nothing from white people along the way other than betrayal. This time, he had reason to believe that, at least occasionally, the law could protect him (although that belief had now been sorely tested). If he could just be in touch with his old friends in the North, someone would be good enough to vouch for him and get him out of this situation. He needed to escape just long enough to get to a post office or find someone to send a telegram on his behalf.

Only a few weeks after he had been transported to the site of the Cape Fear and Yadkin Valley Railroad, the *Granite Post* wrote:

> John Andrew Jackson, who made his escape from the C.F. & Y.V.R.R. a few weeks ago, was recaptured a few days since.[9]

Records indicate escaped convicts from convict camp assignments were an expected, albeit unwelcome, part of the system. Most convict camps kept packs of bloodhounds for just this situation.[10] While statistics suggest 6–9 percent escape rates were not uncommon in different states and over different periods, certain assignments and certain locales produced far higher and, occasionally, astonishingly high rates. Through the late 1870s, North Carolina had an especially appalling record. Historian Matthew Mancini examined statistics from the North Carolina penitentiary reports of 1876. He noted that almost half of the leased convicts that year (including those sent to do railroad construction) had escaped.[11]

And then, just as Jackson's life story appeared to take a turn toward a grim ending, something changed.

In late August 1881, while he was with the convict work gang, Jackson got media attention. One might even say that, in twenty-first-century terms, he went a bit viral. An anodyne notice about Jackson's life ran in over a dozen papers across the nation: Texas. Missouri. Pennsylvania. Maine. And even in the UK.[12] This couldn't have been a coincidence.

> Mr. John A. Jackson, formerly a slave in South Carolina, has been farming in Florence, Mass., during the last season. He escaped from bondage in 1847 by hiding himself on a ship. He afterward lectured through England and since the war has been working on behalf of all freedmen soliciting and forwarding supplies of all kinds to the needy and suffering.[13]

The most likely explanation for Jackson's sudden appearance in so many papers is that a friend at the *Springfield Republican*, perhaps even the stalwart Republican editor-in-chief Samuel Bowles III, received some sort of desperate missive from Jackson posted while he was on the run or posted on his behalf by someone he met. It must be noted, though, that no such letter remains. What we do have are a dozen or so iterations of this anodyne summary of his life, randomly placed in newspaper columns, with no other context, simply asserting his truths.

Did Bowles or someone else at the *Springfield Republican* ask fellow papers to run this notice? Never before had such a notice about Jackson been shared like this. It was a bit of a media splash. The same brief notice, word for word, was repeated in over a dozen papers (likely more yet untraced) across the country within the next two weeks. The information shared was innocuous enough, with no mention of Jackson suffering on a chain gang in North Carolina and whether he had been freed or was still there. But these notices must have triggered something.

Although no extant documents from North Carolina courts indicate Jackson had been released, by late September of that year—only a few weeks after his recapture—Jackson was in Woodstock, Vermont, delivering a poorly attended lecture about the plight of the freedmen. He was still punchy. According to a Vermont newspaper, he called out the town's minister as being a "bad man" for not having helped him publicize his talks.[14] Jackson was back.

Had officials in North Carolina been forced to reluctantly intervene because of some white Northern patrons who wrote on Jackson's behalf? Had Jackson appealed to General Howard (who would have had little sway with local officials by the 1880s as the Freedmen's Bureau had long been disbanded and the federal troops had been largely withdrawn from the South)? Did someone from Massachusetts or Connecticut send a telegram asking the North Carolina state officials to quietly let Jackson go, with an assurance that he would get on a train and never return? Or had Jackson managed to talk his own way out of this? It may have been a combination of all those things. It was hard to keep him down.

III

Jackson was closing in on his sixties by now and his age may have been catching up with him. While it seems like he may have burned through some relationships, his bluster and energy were undiminished. He could still work an audience. He was always working an angle.

Once Jackson's arrest and conviction in North Carolina were effectively behind him, newspapers from the 1880s reported him traveling all over New England, New York's Hudson Valley, and occasionally beyond, still soliciting donations for the freedmen in South Carolina, but occasionally notices reported that he was planning to collect money at his lectures for distribution to the "poor blacks" of Kansas.[15]

Kansas. This was new. Was it true?

The dramatic political disenfranchisement, poverty, suffering, forced convict labor schemes, and general oppression that Black people experienced in Southern states in the 1870s were all what we might understand as "push" factors encouraging people to flee. These factors drove a mass migration of Black Southerners to various locations in the North and the Midwest. Kansas, however, was popularly understood as a particularly welcome destination where these destitute migrants might build a future. These people came to be known as the Kansas Exodusters.[16]

Their poverty meant that many migrants became stranded along the way or arrived in Kansas with nothing to feed or support themselves. For the nation, newly reunited after the Civil War, it was an unprecedented and unwelcome internal refugee problem. Official help was hard to come by, for white Southerners were disinclined to see their cheap labor force disappear. But the need was there and couldn't be denied. Organizations were set up to funnel donations and supplies to the Kansas Exodusters, and such solicitations quickly became well known among affluent Northern communities.

Jackson returned to Canada and delivered a few talks in Saint John about the history of slavery and the plight of the freemen. We can imagine he would have walked the streets there, recollecting his early days with Julia and perhaps trying to track down some of her family to tell them what had happened to her.

In 1877, a massive fire destroyed much of central Saint John.[17] The buildings and streets Jackson had known would have been almost unrecognizable now, only five years later, with new construction interspersed with ruins. But the Black community had survived partly because they had long been pushed to live on the outskirts of the city, which was largely spared the worst of the conflagration. Some friends would have remained. He would have missed Cornelius Sparrow, who had relocated down to Hartford, Connecticut, just a short hop from Springfield. Sparrow had died in Connecticut only two years before Jackson visited Saint John, and his body was returned to Canada for burial in Saint John's Fernhill cemetery.[18] If Jackson had ever connected with him in New England, we cannot know. But now, perhaps, Jackson could go and pay his respects to his old comrade, fellow fugitive, employer, and friend.

IV

By 1885, the *New York Times* reported that Jackson had printed a circular that "comes out strong against the black population marrying into the white race believing 'in two blackbirds walking together, and white doing the same.'"[19] Another report from the *New Haven Register* that year titled "Mr. Johnson's [sic] Errand. He Is Here Collecting and Crying Out Against Miscegenation" also seems to have quoted from the same circular: "I, Andrew Jackson, have great objections against the white and black marrying together, and I will get all the ministers to preach against it north and south."[20]

Jackson may or may not have had a fervent belief in such prohibitions, but opposing interracial marriage was a savvy gesture to audiences who might fear too much interracial solidarity. And if Jackson was going to raise any money from such audiences for his continued solicitations on behalf of a church, a school, and now even a "lecture hall" in Lynchburg that he planned to build, he was wise to entice his crowd with an antimiscegenation angle.[21]

Whatever the cause, his new tactics seemed, at last, to work.

In October 1884, the *Boston Evening Transcript* wrote that Jackson had "shipped to the colored poor of South Carolina" some "twenty-two barrels of fish and several bundles of clothing" and planned to soon "go South himself to visit the scenes of his slavehood days and finish an eventful life."[22]

And so, he did.

Out of all his trips since his initial escape north, this journey may have been his most audacious. After what happened in North Carolina, he knew the real risks of being maliciously impressed into another convict work gang and probably worked to death. But he went anyway. Surely he carried with him letters of patronage and protection. Surely he planned to travel quietly and conduct no solicitations. We can imagine he did his best to travel with allies or friends and to avoid being alone and unprotected. We can assume he avoided any route through North Carolina.

Jackson's friends and family in Lynchburg must have greeted him joyfully, for he undoubtedly arrived with more goods and supplies. Events were to prove he had returned with money. All those donations had added up. Something could happen now.

V

In March 1887, a small plot of land in the heart of Lynchburg changed hands. A prominent lawyer of Sumter, Marion "Major" Moïse, sold it to Jackson. Rather than hold on to the land and the paperwork for himself, Jackson instead arranged for a copy of the deed to be mailed north to Niles and Carr, lawyers in Lynn, Massachusetts, who had almost certainly consolidated the donations and arranged for banks to transfer the necessary purchase funds.[23] At long last, he had reclaimed land for the freed people of Sumter County. And to show it wasn't for his own benefit, it would be safely held in trust up north.

No time to stop, however. No time to celebrate. He jumped back on a train and, within a few weeks, was again in Massachusetts soliciting money for construction.

The next few years show a flurry of speaking gigs, usually with notes about local endorsements and reminders that many should be familiar with him by now. Among other returns, he made his way up to Maine and even revisited the little college town of Brunswick to deliver what must have been an especially resonant talk in the very town where he had met Stowe. And his solicitions seemed roughly consistent with previous endeavors.[24] He has "for a number of years been a collector of aid for a freedmen's schoolhouse and church," wrote the *Boston Journal* in 1891. He has "lectured considerably for the benefit of his people," wrote another. "Hundreds of people in this city probably remember Rev. John Andrew Jackson, the colored preacher," noted the *Boston Transcript*, "who periodically visits Boston for the purpose of collecting money for the church which he desires to build at Magnolia, S.C."[25]

As the reference to him as a "Rev. John Andrew Jackson" as this point suggests, Jackson appears to have been self-styling himself more as an evangelical than in his earlier iterations.[26] Newspapers occasionally identify him as "a colored pupil of the famous Rev. Mr. Spurgeon" during this period. He even published a letter to the readers of the *Boston Transcript*, asking rheotrically that while " . . . the Devil is still yet on earth seeking whom he may Devour, but if god is for us who can be against us.[?]." After all, he continued, "Upon this Rock have I start my church, and the gates of hades shall not prevail against it." Jackson's interest in broadcasting his spiritual sensibility, whether craven or genuine notwithstanding, was evidently effective for soliciting church donations.

The ruse, or perhaps the general presentation of his newly spiritual self, helped. More money came in. While there were undoubtedly some skeptics who continued to challenge his honesty on this point, a good chunk of money was now channeled toward land purchases.[27]

Jackson may never have succeeded in purchasing the large English family holdings, and he certainly never managed to find employment for those forty families he had hoped to help. But the ever-tenacious Jackson never gave up on achieving land ownership for his community. In addition to the initial property he purchased from Moïse, he eventually managed to buy several lots of land located in Lynchburg that almost certainly had, at various points, been owned by English family relatives (since, in its earliest years, the bulk of the tiny town had been owned by such families).

Perhaps it was negligence, confusion, or poverty, coupled with relentless travel, that kept him far from these properties. Still, it appears, not surprisingly, that getting and holding on to land as a poor Black man during the late nineteenth century was challenging. It's a muddled history, but it must have felt muddled and confusing to Jackson and his family in Lynchburg living through it, too.

In 1893, an aggrieved sheriff confiscated two lots of Lynchburg land owned by Jackson. Sumter's *Watchman and Southron* then announced in August 1894 that the county was selling Jackson's land for taxes due. After this advertisement ran, in 1885, the original owner, Moïse, repurchased the land and then seems to have turned around and sold it back to Jackson. Jackson then signed over one or two of the lots, which had buildings on them, to a lawyer up in Massachusetts.

This chain of events is marked by an erratic document trail of conveyances and deeds of the period; in some cases, the records are only partly legible, but since we can place Jackson in Chicago, New Haven, Rochester, and Springfield, among other cities, between 1884 and 1895, we can cautiously conjure up some possibilities for why and how these transactions occurred. Jackson was obviously out of his depth when it came to handling such affairs, and as a Black man in Sumter, he wouldn't have been given much trust from the locals there to handle his transactions even if he wanted to. While he evidently had friends, both Black and white, in both South Carolina and the North, all trying to help him, the pressure to see him fail, which was doubtless the general sentiment from many of his white neighbors, may have meant that a failure was inevitable.

All wasn't well with his Black neighbors either. In 1889 the *Watchman and Southron* newspaper of Sumter reported that a damage suit brought against Jackson by Larry Sadberry, another Black man from Lynchburg, had been resolved with a verdict for the defendant.[28] What this dispute was about isn't clear. In this case, whatever it was, Jackson had again found the law to take his side. On the other hand, it also indicates that Jackson, now a man in at least his midsixties, had a penchant for trouble and conflict that was not going away. And perhaps by now, his string of broken promises and failed schemes had soured his relationship with his community.

VI

In the summer of 1893, Jackson gave a long interview to a reporter for the *Union and Advertiser*, of Rochester, New York, while en route to Chicago "to interest the rich colored men of that place in behalf of a site for an orphan's home and school for destitute colored children." This interview is one of the more remarkable ones of his later life, for we can see how he is, for the first time, explicitly directing his solicitations to affluent Black people, but also because he is, again, scheming for another huge purchase: forty-seven acres in Lynchburg with various structures on it and selling for $4,000.

The story of Jackson's life as he presented it to this reporter was largely consistent with his 1862 memoir, with only a few minor details that seem inconsistent with what we know of his actions—details which might well be the result of the reporter's confusion or of Jackson simply misremembering details. He told this reporter about life on Robert English's slave labor camp and the hunger they experienced there. He spoke of the whippings he had received. He lingered sadly on how his love for his first wife, Louisa, so enraged Robert English, leading English not only to have Jackson whipped and tortured ("My flesh even now has a quivering feeling when I think of those horrible times") but to forcibly marry Louisa off to another. With some poignancy, Jackson ended his interview by saying:

> I came back to this country after the war. I'm getting old and feeble and I only want to live until I get the money for the Home, and then I will go down to Ole Carliny and there is where I want to die, down in my old cabin home.[29]

Jackson had probably first encountered the phrase *Ole Carliny*—from "Dearest Mae" or "Old Carolina State," that minstrel song which had recurred so many times in his life—in Massachusetts soon after he had arrived there in 1847. He may have heard it at antislavery meetings, concerts, or at the table of a Black sailors' boarding house.

During those early years in Massachusetts, Louisa and little Jinny were still down in "Ole Carliny," and the lyrics of that song would have burrowed their way deep in his heart even as he had himself left Carolina behind. Stowe recognized that he was ever one to adopt whatever was handy to render himself plausible to an audience, such as the lyrics of an aptly fitting popular tune. She had, after all, dubbed him the genuine article from "Ole Carliny State" back when he had hidden with her. And we can be sure that when he later sang on the stages of England, trying to end his lectures with a rousing sing-along, that same tune would have featured prominently.

Later in England, when drafting *The Experience of a Slave in South Carolina*, Jackson had rewritten those lyrics, changing them from the original, sadder version that often ended with the death of Dearest Mae and had the singer dolefully returning to his enslaver after visiting Mae's deathbed. In Jackson's version, the song was no longer about Mae. Now, it was his. Even more important, he fully owned the song's story by placing his own circumstances into the words. In most of the popular iterations from the antebellum era, the singer tells that after leaving his master, "I glides along wid my heart so light and free, / To de cottage ob my lubly Mae I'd long'd so much to see."[30] In Jackson's version, the final line of that verse was altered to more standardized language and to a bolder goal for the singer: "I had my eye on the bright north star, and thought of liberty." Instead of reuniting with his lover, Jackson's singer would, instead, seek the world.

The liberty Jackson found was not in the Northern states, not in Canada, and not in England. It was the liberty to return on his own terms.

And, so, he did.

VII

The last trace we have of Jackson is on Christmas Eve 1898, when, with an X, he signed a final land deed in Sumter County. He was literate. Did he sign with an X to not discomfit the white witnesses with his skills? He knew how to be considerate in that way.

The deed registry recorded the transfer of Lynchburg property to Wesley Abraham of Lynchburg. Jackson took only $2 for the lot, which had some building upon it; the site was 55 feet on one end and 210 feet on the other, bounded by the railroad that ran through the center of Lynchburg, and was adjacent to the land of Jacob J. McLeod, the neighbor who was to be interviewed by the federal WPA (Works Progress Administration) about Jackson in 1937.

Abraham, a Black man in his thirties, must have had his reasons for this exchange with Jackson, who was now close to seventy-five years old. Abraham was married with a baby and must have been pleased to settle somewhere new. I like to think that Jackson was letting Abraham take over the land in exchange, perhaps, for taking care of him. Jackson had no wife or child anymore. And Abraham might have been a grandchild, child, or younger brother of Leah Abraham, the sixteen-year-old girl Jackson had fought so hard to bring up from South Carolina to keep Julia company.[31] Jackson hadn't been able to give her the brighter future up north she had deserved. Leah Abraham never received the New England education he had dreamed of for her and little Jimmy. But perhaps with this land exchange in 1898, Jackson was providing her descendant, Wesley Abraham, with that future.

It was another kind of Christmas escape.

Or perhaps it was just a payment for a debt incurred.

The lot was small, in a miserable, noisy location, alongside the railroad. But it was land. It remained in Black hands.[32] It was now Wesley Abraham's. At least one of Jackson's dreams had, in some way, come true.

Today, there is no orphans' home in Lynchburg. No institution for the elderly was ever founded by Jackson. No Black cooperative farm was organized, and none of the local churches seem to have originated at the instigation of Jackson.

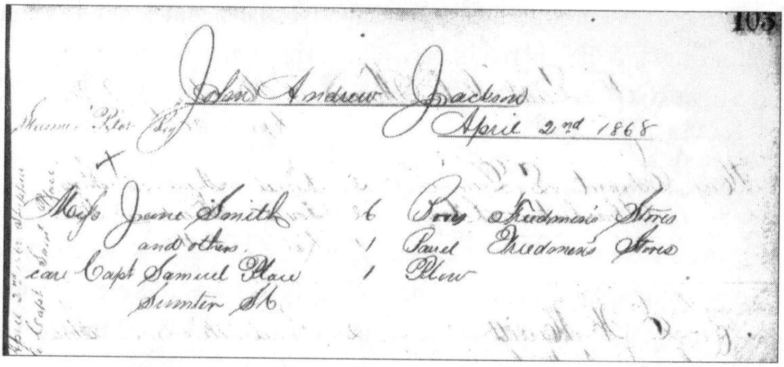
105

John Andrew Jackson
April 2nd 1868

Miss Jane Smith
and others
care Capt Samuel Place
Sumter SC

1 Plow

This April 1868 receipt from the Freedmen's Bureau represents only a tiny fraction of all the supplies Jackson collected over decades.

But we have a receipt.

This receipt shows barrels delivered to Sumter and signed over to Jane Smith and Captain Place—barrels and boxes of "stores" for the freedmen. And a plow.

It's true that those relief supplies, no matter how welcome they must have been, weren't the legacy he had dreamed of. Those Boston crackers, the plows, the clothes, the blankets, the suspenders, the shoes, the flour—all helped some of his neighbors survive, no doubt. The supplies let them know they weren't forgotten. They provided an extra night of warmth. Staved off starvation for a few weeks, perhaps. Enabled men to clothe themselves with dignity. Allowed a few farmers to plant some additional rows of crops.

Decades later, when Jake McLeod remembered him, probably from the 1890s, Jackson might not have been so civic-minded. "Come back wid barrels en boxes of old second hand clothes en accumulated right smart here," McLeod remembered. So perhaps Jackson was pilfering or profiting from goods that had been donated. It's not unlikely. He had always been a bit of a hustler, a survivor.

But his legacy wasn't the material aid he may or may not have provided. His legacy was letting people like his young neighbor Jake McLeod know that people came back. That people cared. That they weren't forgotten. That people could truly get away, and the white folks wouldn't be able to "catch up" or catch on until it was "too late."[33]

VIII

On that cold night of 1850, Harriet Beecher Stowe had heard Jackson's story and inspected his scars. The story and the scars didn't lead to her vision a few weeks later. It wasn't a story that moved her to start writing Uncle Tom's Cabin. *Jackson's influence on her was, rather, from how he interacted with her and her children. His kind and friendly exchanges with her family allowed them all to see one another as people—he was, as she put it, "the genuine article." That phrase had some condescending weight. Who was she to assess his truth? But it does imply that he had succeeded in breaking through some of her racism, some of her skepticism, some of her guard. She saw him for, at least, a little a bit of who he was. And started writing.*

His presence, his physical presence in her home, at her hearth, meant that antislavery wasn't an abstract activist principle. Their nations were each other's. Their careers and futures were entwined more than they could know.

Stowe's novel went through innumerable editions. Movies, plays, songs, games, posters. Aspirations and false consciousness. Violence and peace. Dreams and insults, epithets and cruelties. All were part of that novel's legacy. All were part of that encounter's legacy. Perhaps the Civil War itself was, too.

But a parallel, shadowed career was launched that night. Jackson, a man raised to be a machine for profit, had seen that he might weaponize his own humanity. He might change things by writing his own book and sharing his own story. He learned to read and write and immediately turned those skills to proclaiming his truth and the truth of the people he had left behind.

And there were so many others on the page, so many left behind.

Despite Jackson's fierce and dogged proclamations of his manhood, his rights, and his curated heroics, he did not travel alone. He had Julia, of course. But Louisa and even Ella were with him, too. Jim Jones, Frank, and Dennis—the Black sailors who had smuggled him ashore to Boston—had not been forgotten. Doctor, his father, was in Scotland with him as part of his speeches and prayers. As were those two children of his murdered sister, Bella. And so, too, were Cornelius Sparrow and Thomas H. Jones, his fellow fugitives from Saint John. Henry and Almira Foreman were with him always. The Black community in Bath and Portland had his back as he had theirs. His brother Ephraim was always by his side. And the fellow survivors of bondage, his neighbors from Winter Street in New Haven, were with him, too.

Jackson may be buried in Lynchburg, probably close to his dear brother Ephraim. But burials in the rural South were often haphazard and scrambled affairs for poor Black people, with swampy gullies flooding modest plots that were often sited deep in the woods. Headstones for other Clavon family descendants are there, though, laid out with love in some of the formal local cemeteries that have survived. Jackson may be there, with them, in an unmarked grave.

ACKNOWLEDGMENTS

THE ORIGIN OF THIS BOOK STARTED, AS MANY OF THE BEST ACADEMIC QUEStions do, in a classroom. With students pitching in, I collected and edited a series of little-known memoirs by South Carolinians who had survived enslavement. That collection, *"I Belong to South Carolina:" South Carolina Slave Narratives* (University of South Carolina Press, 2010) was assembled with the help of a cluster of talented and serious-minded students: Robyn E. Adams, Maximilien Blanton, Laura V. Bridges, E. Langston Culler, Cooper Leigh Hill, Deanna L. Panetta, and Kelly E. Riddle. One of these students first called out the passage where John Andrew Jackson, with wry brio, proclaimed, "I belong to South Carolina," to disconcert and mislead an interrogator, as powerfully apt. These words became the title of that book and lingered with me for many years, instigating this project, *A Plausible Man.*

Questions about Jackson nagged at me; I wondered why his story, so precise and meticulous in its telling, wasn't better known. I also wondered what had happened with his references to his encounter with Harriet Beecher Stowe. Initially, I figured he was just name-dropping and doubtless exaggerating his connection to her. It wasn't until I dug into Stowe's letter about the fugitive she hosted in Maine that the astonishing story came together. As far as I know, it is the only story of the Underground Railroad with personal corroboration from both the "conductor" and the "passenger" ever known—and that was apart from the story's connection to the iconic best-selling novel of the entire nineteenth century, *Uncle Tom's Cabin.* As a result of this discovery, the Stowe house site is now recognized on the National Park Service's Network to Freedom listings.

Eager to share the discovery quickly, I wrote up an account of the events for *Commonplace: The Journal of Early American Life.* The Associated Press soon picked up the story (thanks to Clemson media liaisons), and suddenly, opportunities to talk more and figure out more about Jackson appeared. It could be, I realized, a book—not about Stowe and not about their encounter, but instead a story about a fugitive who built a long life of complicated activism, one little known to the world. With this tale, I could deliberately model the process and new methods of archival engagement, approaches that could open up the kind of life story hitherto confined to the gutters of census documents or the margins of white people's paperwork.

Ten years ago, Marc Favreau of The New Press contacted me to learn about my project. That was a lucky day. His good cheer, clear guidance, and clever saves helped me see this project through. Senior managing editor Maury Botton. along with other staff/partners at The New Press (Cathy Dexter, Don Kennison, Emily Mahon) and the Bookbright Media team, did a sensational job assembling this thoughtfully designed volume. The errors within are mine, not theirs.

Initially, my agent, Karen Gantz, was supposed to simply give me advice and pass me along to someone else. Instead, she offered to represent me. I deeply appreciate her skill at then finding *A Plausible Man* the exact home it needed at The New Press.

Clemson University remained a steady investor, supporting this project from when it was a hazy initial idea to its production stages and has granted me awards, research assistance, and subsidies to push this project to completion via its Humanities Hub, the Dean's research council awards, university research grants, sabbaticals, research leaves, conference funding, and the opportunity to work with tremendous English staff and colleagues. My chairs, deans, and provosts have always helped sustain this work; I do not take that for granted. Thank you to Kay Crocker, Chris Wilson, and Karen Parker for their patience and technical help. Since this book has stretched out over twelve years, it's tricky to list all of the Clemson University colleagues who have helped me along the way. They are legion! Still, special thanks are to Elizabeth Rivlin, who suggested the book title, and Mike LeMahieu, who inspired my application to Yale. Rhondda Robinson Thomas has lifted up my scholarship and encouraged me beyond anything I deserve. Special appreciation also to Will Stockton, Lee Morrissey, Gabriel Hankins, Keith Morris, Aga Skrodzka, and Jonathan Field, all of whom have helped me promote, share, brainstorm or create this research at various points along my path.

Outside of my beloved English department, I found assistance from stalwart historians. The late Roger Grant fielded multiple queries from me about railroads in South Carolina and was particularly generous in sharing speculations about what life on the Cape Fear and Yadkin Valley railroad convict work gang might have been like. James Burns and O. Vernon Burton encouraged me to do historical work while bringing interdisciplinary concerns about storytelling to the fore. Paul Anderson helped me think through some issues about Reconstruction-era politics and the proper nomenclature for addressing General O. O. Howard. Lee B. Wilson talked through various legal history scenarios concerning some of Jackson's conflicts, and Jonathan Hepworth, in the early stages of the project, helped imagine Jackson's flight by mapping out his escape with me.

Two writing groups have vastly improved various chapters here, saving me from embarrassment and errors. Thanks are due to to the African American Life Writing Collective (Gregg Hecimovich, Barbara McCaskill, Jennifer Putzi, and Mollie Barnes) for their love and insights. Their models of scholarship and commentary embodied the best of collaborative energies. Gregg, in particular, offered me exquisite scholarly models for storytelling with his work on Hannah Bonds, and I am grateful for his generosity.

Undertaking a biography, something academics are not usually trained in, much less encouraged to do, was frightening. I was fortunate to have found two brilliant women, Mary Chapman and Julia Mickenberg, to help me along this journey in life writing. It's been a privilege to share both progress and setbacks and, alongside one another, to learn about truly listening to our subjects—even when those historical subjects are slippery, surly, or uncooperative ghosts. The camaraderie of these two has helped me grow as a scholar, a writer, and, I hope, as a friend.

Major external funding that supported this work came from Yale University's Gilder Lehrman Center for the Study of Slavery, Resistance, and Abolition under the generous and luminous leadership of David W. Blight. The fellows and staff there (in particular, Sophie White, Genevieve LeBaron, Isabel Kalous, Tom Thurston, Melissa McGrath, and David Spatz) sustained and inspired the early stages of my research.

I was astonishingly fortunate to be invited to work at Harvard's Hutchins Center for African and African American Research, led by the inimitable Henry Louis Gates Jr. His encouragement opened many doors for me, and I shall be forever grateful. At Harvard, I was granted access to the most magnificent research collections I could have ever imagined and a semester of quiet focus to push the book to completion. The fellows there (too many to list, honestly) and staff members Abby Wolf and Krishna Lewis wowed me with their creativity and kindness.

Invitations to speak forced me to learn about new ways to tell Jackson's story as I went along. I am grateful to Cynthia Stretch, Emily Todd, Tess Chakkalakal, Kimberley Johnson, Paul Erickson, Greg Marquis, Julia Eichelberger, Simon Lewis, Scott Peeples, and many others for arranging for different iterations of this work in progress to be shared with audiences at institutions such as the New Brunswick Black History Society in Saint John; Harriet Beecher Stowe Center in Hartford; the Central-Clemson Library; Southern Connecticut State University; Yale University's Gilder Lehrman Center for the Study of Slavery, Resistance and Abolition; Harvard University's Hutchins Center for African and African American Research; Warren Chapel United Methodist Church of Lynchburg; Westfield State University; the University of Texas at El Paso; Barnard College; the American Antiquarian Society; the College of Charleston; the South Carolina African American Heritage Commission; Bowdoin College; and several other sites for hosting me and allowing me an opportunity to learn from audience members. I'll long remember the students at Southern Connecticut State University who, after my talk, escorted me to a couple of reconfigured streets in New Haven to imagine Jackson's work and life there. I'll also forever cherish the audience members and students at Westfield State who sent a bevy of friendly follow-up messages after my talk, volunteering to help search out information about Black life in Springfield and its environs.

Librarians and archival staff have taught me along the way. Professionals at a host of institutions dug up materials and fielded queries from me across years and across continents. In particular, I need to signal my profound gratitude to Clemson University Libraries (particularly Camille Cooper and Anne Grant, Gordon Cochrane and Jennifer Groff), the American Antiquarian Society, the South Caroliniana Library at the University of South Carolina, the Sumter County Genealogical Society, the Charleston County Public Library, the New-York Historical Society, the Boston Athenaeum, the South Carolina Historical Society's main reading room in the Addlestone Library at the College of Charleston, the South Carolina room and the Charleston Archive at the Charleston County Public Library main branch, the Stephen A. Schwarzman Building of the New York Public Library (I cannot recall the name of the librarian there who arranged for me to work in his private office to see the Jackson Spurgeon pamphlet, but I do recall his kindness), the Lyman and Merrie Wood Museum of Springfield History and the Springfield History Library and Archives (especially Cliff McCarthy), the Special Collections at the Mack Library of Bob Jones University, the South Carolina Department of Archives and History, the George J. Mitchell Department of Special Collections and Archives at Bowdoin College Library (especially Roberta Schwartz), the Phillips Library with the Peabody Essex Museum (especially Meaghan Wright, who helped me identify *The Smyrna*), the New Haven Museum, the Salem Public Library, the Beinecke Rare Book and Manuscript Library at Yale University, the Houghton Library at Harvard University, the State Archives of North Carolina (especially Lauren McCoy), the Nova Scotia Archives in Halifax, the Central Library in Dundee, the Dundee City Archives, the New Brunswick Museum Archives, and probably a few I'm not even remembering.

Other supporters and scholars who have helped move this project forward with their expertise and letters of endorsement include Ezra Greenspan, Katharine Kane, and William T. Andrews. Hannah-Rose Murray's scholarship on the British lecture circuit and individual counsel on various topics were invaluable. I appreciate, too, Anna Mae Duane for taking a look at Henry Highland Garnet's writing on my behalf. Timothy D. Walker helped me puzzle through details about Jackson's arrival in Boston. A costume designer with some expertise in the clothing of enslaved people, Kendra L. Johnson, analyzed the Jackson images with me and helped me properly assess his cravat and button situation. Steve Strimer, at the David Ruggles Center for History and Education in Northampton, was full of inspired energy in discussing Jackson's possible experience in Florence. Howard Anderson reviewed an early court record with me on more than one occasion. Daniel Kirk-Davidoff tried to help me hunt down historical weather information. David Killingray at the University College London had wonderful suggestions about understanding the culture of Black lecturing in the 1850s and '60s. Wildlife biologist and fire expert Johnny Stowe toured me around Sumter and Lee Counties to show me overgrown and flooded graveyards. Professor Alan Rice of the University of Central Lancashire in Preston, England, also hosted me during a research trip. Lovely folks with the Warren Chapel at the United Methodist Church welcomed me to their community. Musicians and scholars Kendall Kennison and Mark Burford weighed in on my analysis of "Dearest Mae"; it was particularly heartening to hear Marc point out how Jackson's musical analysis may be important for early studies of Black music. The production company Nutopia was interested at one point in creating a film or documentary that might concern Jackson in some way, and although that project never came to be, along the way, they hired genealogist Toni Carrier to create a family tree or timeline for Jackson, which was an unexpected boon to my investigations. Clemson students Collin Eichhorn, Spencer York, and Kristin Buhrow assisted with transcriptions and investigations. Chelsea McKelvey labored long and hard, helping with my footnotes and fact-checking details on this project, and I valued her meticulous work every step of the way.

Midway through *A Plausible Man*, I was brought in touch with Florida State Professor Emeritus Eric C. Walker, a descendant of the English family who not only provided judicious academic commentary and counsel on many chapters but also brought to his readings a welcome sensitivity to the complexity of fraught American legacies—both his and everyone's. Robert Cooper Manning Jr. also reached out to me back in 2014, and as a distant descendant of the Law family and others mentioned in my research, he kindly corrected many of my misunderstandings about Sumter geography and the local entwined family trees of the area.

Jackson escaped on his own, but his story, ultimately, was one of his family and for his family. I thank the Clavon descendants who have helped me along the way. In 2018, I stood before you and promised Jackson's story would be told. Here it finally is. He lived for you.

As for my own family, you are everything.

NOTES

Introduction

1. Jackson's life and relationship to Stowe is the central question of the title, of course, and in chapter 5 of this book, I chronicle that fateful encounter and its implications not just for Stowe and her legacy but also for Jackson. While he certainly spoke about Stowe in later years and carried a reference letter that served him well, he didn't trumpet his connection as a model for her characters or try to promote himself as the "real Uncle Tom." This is markedly in contrast to Josiah Henson, another survivor of bondage who escaped and settled in Canada. His memoir had been read by Stowe at some point, who noted that Henson's life was certainly a parallel to her character of Uncle Tom. Whatever Henson's relationship to Stowe may have been, it does not contradict the astounding story of how Jackson came into her life a few weeks before she started writing her book and how, while Henson or others may have inspired particular characters in her novel, the fugitive whom she brought into her house and home certainly helped instigate the creative power that unleashed the novel as a whole. See note 40 in chapter 5 for further notes about this matter.

2. It took several years, but I connected with Jackson's descendants from the Clavon family and met with many of them at a wonderful family reunion in 2017. Many family members were enthusiastic about this project to bring to light the contributions of their courageous ancestor.

3. Jackson refers to his father both as "Dr. Clavern" as well as "Old Doctor Clavern" and recounts white enslavers addressing his father as "Old Doc. Clave." John Andrew Jackson, *The Experience of a Slave in South Carolina*, in *I Belong to South Carolina: South Carolina Slave Narratives*, ed. Susanna Ashton (Columbia, SC: University of South Carolina Press, 2010), 89 and 109. Jackson's father's name is also referenced in the will of the Robert English as "Doctor" and, even more interestingly, as "Doctor Clavin" in the voting registration list of Sumter County. For the purposes of consistency, I shall refer to him as "Doctor" or "Doctor Clavern." Many descendants of Doctor spell their name as "Clavon" and so while there are many variations across generations I refer generally to the Clavon family when referring to Jackson's relatives in the nineteenth century and also his descendants today. "Robert English, Deceased, Will," South Carolina Will Books and Estates Index and File Book, 1800–1963, Sumter, Sumter County, South Carolina;

Secretary of State, Abstract of Voter Registrations Reported to the Military Government, 1868, Sumter County Lynchburg Elect. Prect., page 309.

4. Toni Carrier, private research report for author, 2016. Carrier, a genealogist, completed an independent research report on the John Andrew Jackson family tree for a documentary film company, Nutopia, which was shared with me by permission of the author.

5. While I have never been able to definitively establish a connection between longtime U.S. congressman Jim Clyburn from South Carolina and Doctor Clavon/Clavern's descendants, it seems almost certain that there is a familial connection, as the congressman hails from that precise region of Sumter County and variations on that name are endemic to the area. But until there can be a clear connection, of course, it is just speculation.

6. "Ranaway from the Plantation of Robert English," *Sumter Banner*, March 27, 1847.

7. For thoughtful work on the ways in which fabrication and lying played out in the life experiences and representation of African American people during the antebellum era, see Ann Fabian, *The Unvarnished Truth: Personal Narratives in Nineteenth-Century America* (Berkeley: University of California Press, 2000); Lara Langer Cohen, *The Fabrication of American Literature: Fraudulence and Antebellum Print Culture* (Philadelphia: University of Pennsylvania Press, 2012); Martha J. Cutter, "'As White as Most White Women': Racial Passing in Advertisements for Runaway Slaves and the Origins of a Multivalent Term," *American Studies* 54, no. 4 (2016): 73–97.

8. To be clear, I am referring here to the ways in which Uncle Tom became known as a cultural trope, not necessarily the actual Uncle Tom character in the novel who is a more complex, courageous, and even heroic figure than is often understood.

9. Marisa J. Fuentes, *Dispossessed Lives: Enslaved Women, Violence, and the Archive.* Early American Studies. (Philadelphia: University of Pennsylvania Press, 2016). Marisa Fuentes explores this matter with compassion and cautions against always relying upon more sources to appear as not only will that expectation likely be dashed, but, more important, it reinscribes the essential violent power of our archival traditions (page 6 of *Dispossessed Lives*).

10. I am inspired here by Annette Gordon-Reed's courage and confidence in using her informed intuition when writing the story of Sally Hemings's life. See Annette Gordon-Reed, *The Hemingses of Monticello: An American Family* (New York: W.W. Norton, 2008).

Prelude

1. For a thorough understanding of the power dynamics between the interviewers and their administrators back in Washington, see Lynda M. Hill, "Ex-Slave Narratives: The WPA Federal Writers' Project Reappraised," *Oral History* 26, no. 1 (1998): 64–72. See also Gerald James Pierson, *The Nature of Resistance in South Carolina's Works Progress Administration Ex-Slave Narratives* (Irvine: Universal Publishers, 2002), 27–42.

2. "Grady H. Davis," *U.S. National Homes for Disabled Volunteer Soldiers, 1866–1938*, Ancestry.com.

3. This, and all quotations from the interview that follow, are from Jake McLeod. Jake McLeod, interview by Federal Writers' Project: Slave Narrative Project, vol. 14, Library of Congress, www.loc.gov/item/mesn143.

4. Sumter County, South Carolina, *Deed Registry Book LLL*: 498, John Andrew Jackson and Wesley Abraham, State of South Carolina, December 24, 1898.

Chapter 1

1. James English Cousar, *Quaker Turned Presbyterian: The Spiritual Pilgrimage of Robert ("Robin") English* (Savannah, GA: Independent Presbyterian Church, 1956).

2. Cassie Nichols, *Historical Sketches of Sumter County: Its Birth and Growth* (Sumter, SC: Sumter County Historical Commission, 1975), 408–410.

3. David J. McCord, ed., *The Statutes at Large of South Carolina*, vol. 7 (Columbia, SC: A.S. Johnston, 1840), 389–390. According to Act 15, theft of a slave was a felony without benefit of clergy, which meant at that time that if convicted you would be whipped, branded or "suffer death as a felon."

4. *Tyre McCoy vs Robert English, MS Judgment Book B*, roll 615 (Clerk of Court, Sumter, SC., 1821); "Robert Manton English," *Miscellaneous Estate Records, 1784–1960*, Sumter, Sumter County, South Carolina, Ancestry.com, 1. We know this both from the 1821 court record of the conflict and from Robert English's will, where his name is listed as "Doctor."

5. "Index of the 1868 Voter Registrations, Sumter County, South Carolina, Lynchburg," *African Americans in the South Carolina Room*, updated 2008, emilyevaughn.com/1868voterregSumLynchburg.

6. Daina Ramey Berry, *The Price for Their Pound of Flesh: The Value of the Enslaved, from Womb to Grave, in the Building of a Nation* (Boston: Beacon Press, 2017), 6. According to Berry, while enslaved people tended to keep acutely close tabs on their monetary exchange value, they were also aware of and held fiercest to their own sense of self-worth. Her term "soul value" refers to "an intangible marker that defied monetization yet spoke to the spirit and soul" of who he was as a human being. Soul value "represented the self-worth of enslaved people."

7. "Index of the 1868 Voter Registrations, Sumter County, South Carolina, Lynchburg," *African Americans in the South Carolina Room*.

8. Nichols, 408–409. Also see Jackson, 95.

9. For an overview of the Black River and its environs, see "Black Scenic River Management Plan," *South Carolina Department of Natural Resources*, November 2020, www.dnr.sc.gov/water/river/pdf/blackriverplan_final.

10. Cousar, 116. Elizabeth Wilson was a distant relative of Robert English, and the web of local family relationships is difficult to unpack. As English's biographer put it: "Few

men have ever been able to create as many new and complex relationships as Robert did by his marriage . . . he became at once the stepson-in-law of his brother and Edward, already his brother, became his new stepfather-in-law!"

11. Jackson, 95. According to Jackson, English "married a lady who had a few slaves."

12. Stephanie E. Jones-Rogers, *They Were Her Property: White Women as Slave Owners in the American South* (New Haven: Yale University Press, 2019), 2–3.

13. "Robt English," *1840 United States Census*, Sumter, Sumter County, South Carolina, roll 515, 46, Ancestry.com.

14. Nichols, 409.

15. Lee County Chamber of Commerce, *Lee County, South Carolina: Past and Present*, vol. 2 (Bishopville, SC: Lee County Chamber of Commerce, 1992), 29. This mill, which was to play a significant role in Jackson's later imagination, was sited on a bend of the Black River, and today, the English Mill Pond and the English Mill Road are immediately adjacent to the Lee Correctional Institution in Bishopville, SC, a level-three maximum-security prison.

16. For an overview of how the explosive expansion of the short-staple cotton industry profoundly altered the entire U.S. economy, see Sven Beckert, *Empire of Cotton: A Global History* (New York: Vintage Books, 2014) and Walter Johnson, *River of Dark Dreams: Slavery and Empire in the Cotton Kingdom* (Cambridge, MA: Harvard University Press, 2013).

17. MS Old Equity roll 355, office of Clerk of Court, Sumter County, Sumter, SC.

18. Originally, the area was referred to as Murphrey's Crossing, then as Willow Grove, English Crossroads, and Magnolia at various points. It is also important to note that with the advent of the railroad in 1854, the town center was redefined as about half a mile away from the original crossroads, which thus became "South Lynchburg." Borders of the adjacent communities of Mayesville, Elliott, and Bishopville all similarly shifted. Many of the people referenced in this book are variously identified as being in Lynchburg or Mayesville, or even Bishopville at various points in time, though their physical locations might not have changed. For the purposes of this book, the name "Lynchburg" will be used for most references to this town.

19. Nichols, 129–130. The English family mansion house location on the intersection of Highway 527 and County Road 43-59 is actually the exact site of what is now the Sumter County/Lee County dividing boundary.

20. "Lynchburg, South Carolina Population 2021," *World Population Review*, updated 2021, worldpopulationreview.com/us-cities/lynchburg-sc-population.

21. U.S. Census Bureau. 1870 Census: Volume 1. The Statistics of the Population of the United States. Populations of Civil Divisions Less Than Counties, Sumter, SC, www2.census.gov/library/publications/decennial/1870/population.

22. For a heartfelt and lively series of vignettes about life in Lynchburg during the mid-twentieth century from an African American perspective, see the memoir by Hubert Green, who grew up there. Hubert Green, *Magnolia, Magnolia, Where Are You?* (Victoria,

BC: Trafford Publishing, 2003). See also Bruce C. Ford, *A Tree Fell . . . and Its Roots Survived: A Genealogy and Historical Commentary of the Claiborne, Clayborn, Clavon and Claven Families of North Carolina, South Carolina, Virginia, Michigan and More* (self-published, 2011).

23. Lewis L. Gould. *The Most Exclusive Club: A History of the Modern United States Senate* (New York: Basic Books, 2005), 140.

24. Ira Katznelson, *When Affirmative Action Was White: An Untold History of Racial Inequality in Twentieth-Century America* (New York: Norton, 2005), 60–61.

25. For a rich biography of John Leighton Wilson that includes much reflection on the Black River community of Lynchburg and the environs of that era, see Erskine Clarke, *By the Rivers of Water: A Nineteenth-Century Atlantic Odyssey* (New York: Basic Books, 2013).

26. Jackson, 90.

27. Ibid., 99 and 101.

28. Jones-Rogers, 79. Jones-Rogers argues that slave-owning women who decided to abuse, maim, or even kill their slaves were doing so in part to demonstrate their own power and to use evocations of terror to exact submission from other enslaved people.

29. Jackson, 91. Whether despite his cruelty or perhaps because of it, James Wilson English was much esteemed in the community and elected to the South Carolina House of Representatives for two years and then went on for a term in the South Carolina State Senate as well. See Leroy Collier, *Thomas English: Descendents and Some of Their Kin* (self-published, 1986), 54. "James W. English," South Carolina, U.S. Wills and Probate Records, 1670–1980, Miscellaneous Estate Records, 1784–1960, South Carolina, County Court, Sumter County, Ancestry.com. Miraculously, perhaps, Willis appears to have survived the abuse, for he was listed in James Wilson English's will in 1841. Still, Jackson carried Willis's testimony forward in time to make sure it couldn't be erased.

30. *South Carolina Historical Markers: A Guidebook* (S.C. Department of Archives & History, 2019), 350; David Taylor, "Rev. Thomas Reese English, 1806–1869," *Waymarking*, updated 2021, www.waymarking.com/waymarks/.

31. Jackson, 93.

32. Ibid., 93.

33. For a brief overview of the history of cotton, see the well-illustrated little volume by the South Carolina Cotton Museum, *The History of Cotton* (Bishopville, SC: Donning Company Publishers, 2005). For a more thorough and magisterial analysis, see Edward E. Baptist, *The Half Has Never Been Told: Slavery and the Making of American Capitalism* (New York: Basic Books, 2014).

34. Jackson, 95.

35. Ibid.

36. See chapter 3 for a fuller account of this incident and the significance of this particular census record of 1850.

37. "Andrew Jackson," 1850 United States Census, Boston, Ward 2, Suffolk County, Massachusetts, roll 334, 173a, Ancestry.com.

38. "Ranaway from the Plantation of Robert English," *Sumter Banner* (Sumter, SC), March 27, 1847.

39. A man using that name who was quite possibly him shows up in city directories in Springfield, MA, New Haven, CT, and Hartford, CT, at various points during the 1880s through the early 1890s. See chapters 9 and 10 of this book, which track these peripatetic times. Also see: "John Andrew Jackson," *Springfield Republican*, February 9, 1880; "John Andrew Jackson," *Springfield Republican*, March 15, 1880; "John A. Jackson," *1880 United States Census*, Springfield, Hampden County, Massachusetts, roll 536, 166D, Ancestry.com.

40. All of these names are prevalent today in the Black community and to a lesser degree in the white community in that region of South Carolina. See the family history published by Bruce C. Ford, *A Tree Fell . . . and Its Roots Survived*, about how the Black descendants from Doctor Clavern survived and dispersed throughout the United States. Some of his minor details about nineteenth-century genealogy differ from conclusions within my own research on Jackson's life (particularly regarding Ephraim and Amelia Clavon, Jackson's brother and sister-in-law), but the overwhelming narrative of survival and triumph chronicled in Ford's family story is a testament to the strength and determination of generations of this family.

41. Jeffrey Allen Howard, "Andrew Jackson Birthplace," *NCPedia*, updated 2006, www.ncpedia.org/andrew-jackson-birthplace. In 1824 Andrew Jackson (the future president) wrote in a letter that he was born in South Carolina but at the time of his birth the borders between the two states were not entirely clear and he may have been born in North Carolina.

42. "Robert Manton English," *Miscellaneous Estate Records, 1784–1960*, 1.

43. Jackson, 96.

44. "Robert Manton English."

45. Perhaps because of the common name "Elizabeth Jackson," I have not been able to trace what may have become of her in Massachusetts after her birth. It is certainly possible she survived to adulthood.

46. Indeed, there is a street in Lynchburg town known as "Clavon Street."

47. Jackson, 95.

48. Andrew Jackson to Major Gen. Howard, August 4, 1868, Freedmen's Bureau Digital Collection, National Museum of African American History and Culture, Smithsonian Institution.

49. Jackson, 90.

50. Jackson's brother William might have died or been sold by 1848 when Robert English's will was written, for while the will identifies Betty, Doctor, and Ephram (or Ephraim) clearly, there is no mention of an enslaved person with the name of William or Will or any obvious derivative.

51. Andrew Jackson to Major Gen. Howard, Springfield, MA, August 4, 1868.

52. The descendants of Ephraim are lovingly traced and chronicled by Bruce Ford in his book *A Tree Fell . . . and Its Roots Survived.* As of the time of this book's publication, I have not yet located a grave for John Andrew Jackson, but if I were to guess, he is likely buried in Lynchburg close to Ephraim, perhaps in unmarked or overgrown graves.

53. During most of the nineteenth century the area of Sumter County between Lynches River and Black River would have been part of what was known as "Sumter County." In 1897 Lee County was created and much of that land was assigned to this new municipality. The new county was quickly dissolved for logistical and legal reasons but was reestablished firmly in 1900 again as Lee County. The areas Jackson would have been most familiar with (Lynchburg, Elliott, Mayesville, and Bishopville) were in Sumter County at that time, but since 1900 are in a region known as Lee County.

54. I am indebted to the work of historian Anthony E. Kaye, who introduced me to the notion of a slave neighborhood in Anthony E. Kaye, *Joining Places. Slave Neighborhoods in the Old South* (Chapel Hill: University of North Carolina Press, 2007).

55. Jackson specifically uses her full name as Jenny Wilson, and Robert English had purchased her from a neighbor named Wilson.

56. Robert English's estate refers to Jenny and Adam as a pair in his inventory, which accompanied his will. "Robert Manton English," *Miscellaneous Estate Records*, 1784–1960, 1; "Robert English, Deceased, Will," South Carolina Will Books and Estates Index and File Book, 1800–1963, Sumter, Sumter County, South Carolina, Ancestry.com.

57. Tera W. Hunter, *Bound in Wedlock: Slave and Free Black Marriage in the Nineteenth Century* (Cambridge: Harvard University Press, 2017), 32–33. See Hunter on the topic of forced marriages and how such coercion was rarely recognized by enslaved people as creating actual marriages. Later in his narrative Jackson mentions that his older brother Ephraim was also forced to marry against his will. See Jackson, 109.

58. Jackson, 102.

59. Tyler D. Parry, *Jumping the Broom: The Surprising Multicultural Origins of a Black Wedding Ritual* (Chapel Hill: University of North Carolina Press, 2020), 37–67. It is notable here that Jackson makes no mention of "jumping the broomstick," a frequent ceremonial or ritual act performed by African Americans in the antebellum era to recognize the bonding of marriage. See Parry's *Jumping the Broom* for a thorough analysis of how widespread this practice could be and yet also how the lack of such practice or lack of reference to it did not in any way render these relationships less real in the eye of the Black people involved.

60. Hunter, 323, n22. Historian Tera Hunter's work on slave marriages in *Bound in Wedlock* indicates that ceremonies, whether jumping the broomstick or religious ceremonies held individually or sanctioned by enslavers, were not consistently important for how enslaved people chose to view their own marriages as legitimate.

61. In 1893, when Jackson was in his late sixties or early seventies, he told an interviewer in Chicago that Louisa and a baby boy had died and were freed from slavery in that way. It isn't clear if this is just a mistake on the interviewer's part or if Jackson also

had a son. It seems like an odd mistake for even an elderly man to have made, so it is possible there was a baby boy as well as Jinny, but that story is still unclear. "The Story of John Andrew Jackson," *Union and Advertiser*, August 9, 1893.

62. Jackson, 102.

63. "Ranaway from the Plantation of Robert English," *Sumter Banner* (Sumter, SC), March 27, 1847. Evidence that the Law family temporarily moved to Georgia can also be found in this runaway advertisement later placed by Thomas Reese English, which notes that Jackson is supposed to be heading to Georgia to see or rescue his wife.

64. "Jared Laws," *1850 United States Federal Census*, Sumter, Sumter County, South Carolina, roll 850, 417a, Ancestry.com. The is referering to Jared R. McKelvin Law but the name was misspelled with an "S."

65. Jared Law to Thomas Wells, Deed of Trust, Sumter County, South Carolina, June 7, 1851.

66. The Law family returned to Sumter County some years later since they show up in the census of 1860. But whether they still have Louisa and little Jinny with them is unclear. The Laws moved to Texas shortly thereafter and, while it is likely they took their enslaved people along with the rest of their household with that move, the paper trail for Louisa and Jinny gets lost.

Chapter 2

1. I.E. Lowery, *Life on the Old Plantation in Ante-Bellum Days, or a Story Based on the Facts by the Reverend I.E. Lowery (1911)*, in *I Belong to South Carolina.*

2. Jackson, 103.

3. Ibid., 104.

4. Ibid., 102.

5. Ibid.

6. Nichols, 51.

7. See Bruce D. Dickson, *And They All Sang Hallelujah: Plain-Folk Camp Meeting Religion, 1800–1845* (Knoxville: University of Tennessee Press, 1974), 96–122. Dickson provides an analysis of the kinds of hymns and songs shared at these events. Although he doesn't discuss the audience of enslaved people who were regularly in attendance, the role of music for all aspects of these meetings was a defining feature of their appeal.

8. Erskine Clarke, *By the Rivers of Water: A Nineteenth-Century Atlantic Odyssey* (New York: Basic Books, 2013), 43.

9. George Howe, *History of the Presbyterian Church in South Carolina*, vol. 2 (Columbia: W. J. Duffie, 1883), 284–285.

10. See "Salem-Black River Presbyterian (Mayesville, S.C.)," Digital Collections: University of South Carolina Libraries, digital.library.sc.edu/collections/inventory-of-s-c-church-archives. For more on Goodwill Presbyterian Church, see "Goodwill

Presbyterian Church," Historical Marker Project, historicalmarkerproject.com/markers/HMJ66_goodwill-presbyterian-church.

11. Minuette Floyd, Terry K. Hunter, and Tom Stanley, *A Place to Worship: African American Camp Meetings in the Carolinas* (Columbia: University of South Carolina Press, 2018), 18.

12. In addition to Dickson's *And They All Sang Hallelujah*, for more on camp meetings, see John B. Boles, *The Great Revival: Beginnings of the Bible Belt* (Lexington: University Press of Kentucky, 1972); Ellen Jane Lorenz, *Glory, Hallelujah!: The Story of the Campmeeting Spiritual* (Nashville: Abingdon Press, 1980); J. Lawrence Brasher, "Camp Meeting Movement" in *Encyclopedia of Appalachia*, eds. Rudy Abramson and Jean Haskell (2006), 1974, 1317.

13. For a description of these popular and long-standing camp meetings held in that region, see Anne King Gregorie, *History of Sumter County, South Carolina* (Sumter, SC: Library Board of Sumter Count, 1954), 223–224.

14. Lowery, 220.

15. According to Lowery, "Before the war, the relation that existed between the master and his slaves was, in most cases, one of tenderness and affection. There was a mutual attachment between them, which has commanded the admiration of the world" (174). He also refers to his childhood home as located on that "wonderful old plantation" (183).

16. This incident is told through the persona of "Jimmie," which is the name he adopts for himself in some parts of his memoir. Lowery, 216–217.

17. For a discussion of conjuring, voodoo, sorcery, and a conjure man (who was very likely Jackson's father, Doctor Clavon), see Lowery, 206–207.

18. Gregorie, 224–225.

19. Jackson, 103.

20. Ibid., 104.

21. For an overview of the ways in which Maroon activities or different kinds of fugitivity were understood in the New World and how those perspectives and practices manifested in South Carolina, see the introduction to *Maroon Communities in South Carolina: A Documentary Record*, ed. Timothy James Lockley, (Columbia: University of South Carolina Press, 2009), ix–xxi.

22. Jackson, 104.

23. Ibid., 104. According to Stephanie E. Jones-Rogers, women who owned people often outsourced punishment to others; this was done not only because of the physical nature of it, but also because it was the way in which "women cleansed themselves of the dark taint that subsequently stained the men who carried out their orders." Stephanie E. Jones-Rogers, *They Were Her Property*, 69.

24. Jackson, 104.

25. Nichols, 9.

26. Jackson, 104.

27. "You are loosed from your moorings, and are free; I am fast in my chains, and am a slave! You move merrily before the gentle gale, and I sadly before the bloody whip! You are freedom's swift-winged angels, that fly round the world; I am confined in bands of iron! O that I were free! O, that I were on one of your gallant decks, and under your protecting wing! Alas! betwixt me and you, the turbid waters roll. Go on, go on. O that I could also go! Could I but swim! If I could fly! O, why was I born a man, of whom to make a brute! The glad ship is gone; she hides in the dim distance. I am left in the hottest hell of unending slavery." From Frederick Douglass, *Narrative of the Life of Frederick Douglass, An American Slave* (Boston: Anti-Slavery Office, 1849), 64.

28. Jackson, 104.

29. Amie Lumpkin, interview by Federal Writers' Project: Slave Narrative Project, vol. 14, Library of Congress, www.loc.gov/item/mesn143/.

30. For information about the life of James Matthews, see Susanna Ashton, "Re-Collecting Jim," *Commonplace: The Journal of Early American Life* 15, no. 1 (2014), commonplace.online/article/re-collecting-jim. For his narrative, see "Recollections of Slavery by a Runaway Slave," in *I Belong to South Carolina*, 49–82. Please note that in my collection, because it was published before I discovered Matthews's real identity, the memoir is published anonymously. In his memoir, Matthews tells of taking shelter at a boarding house for Black sailors in Boston, quite likely the same one run by Henry Foreman that was to become central to Jackson's experiences a decade later.

31. Lowery, 199.

32. *Narrative of the Life of Frederick Douglass*, Norton Critical Edition, eds. William Andrews and William S. McFeely (New York, Norton, 1997), 51. Christmas was also known as a sorrowful time for people fearing sales of transactions that might break up their communities and which often were implemented on January first.

33. Jackson, 104. By "fandango" he means their amusements, or their happy times of celebration.

Chapter 3

1. "Ranaway from the Plantation of Robert English," *Sumter Banner* (Sumter, SC), vol. 1, March 24, 1847, 3.

2. Ibid.

3. "Slave Schedules," 1860 United States Census, Sumter, Sumter County, South Carolina, M653, 49, Ancestry.com. See also chapter 7, note 53.

4. This advertisement for Jackson in the *Sumter Banner* appears to have run for only two weeks (March 24, 1847, and March 31, 1847). The advertisement I reference in comparison was for a man named Jacob, appearing first in the *Sumter Banner* on December 9, 1846. This advertisement then ran again directly above the "$50 Reward" advertisement for Jackson in the March 27, 1847, issue of the *Sumter Banner.* This demonstrates that Jacob had been gone for a long time and his enslavers were willing to raise the reward. In contrast, the advertisement for Jackson did not run for long, which suggests that the

English family may have gotten a clue that he was further afield than a mere local advertisement would assist. As far I can tell, the advertisement was not repeated after March 1847 and the reward was never raised.

5. Some of this chapter was originally conceived and drafted in an article I co-authored with Jonathan Hepworth. Susanna Ashton and Jonathan D. Hepworth, "Reclaiming a Fugitive Landscape," *The Appendix* 1, no. 4 (2013).

6. Jackson, 104.

7. Jackson estimated this distance to be 150 miles, but it was likely closer to 120 miles. Although, with difficult terrain and nineteenth-century roads, it likely felt far longer. See Ibid., 104.

8. Ibid.

9. Ibid.

10. The most likely candidate would be J. Nelson, who in 1825 held roadside property along Jackson's route. However, since there were several Nelson properties all located nearby, it is also likely that G. Nelson could be a relative of J. Nelson, and that G. Nelson might be the J.J. Nelson listed in the federal 1850 Census as living in that area of Sumter County. See the clipped version of the Sumter District map from 1825 in the Mills Atlas. See Mills Atlas, Sumter District, 1825, www.carolina.com/SC/Maps/Mills_Atlas_Sumter_District_1825; "J.J. Nelson," 1850 United States Census, Sumter, Sumter County, South Carolina, roll 859, 326a, Ancestry.com.

11. Jackson, 104.

12. Jackson, 105.

13. Maps and records suggest that Jackson stopped at a property owned by H. Schipman (not Shipman, as Jackson spells it) in St. Stephen's Parish, South Carolina. Schipman was an immigrant from Germany listed in the 1850 Census as enslaving fifty-three men, women, and children, so it is easy to imagine there were enough people around for Jackson to feel he could take refuge there. "H.B. Schipman," 1850 U.S. Federal Census—Slave Schedules, St. Stephen's Parish, Charleston, South Carolina, M432, Ancestry.com.

14. Jackson, 105.

15. Ibid.

16. Ibid.

17. To understand this kind of urban culture of fugitivity in Southern cities especially, see Viola Franziska Müller, *Escape to the City: Fugitive Slaves in the Antebellum Urban South*, 1st ed. (Chapel Hill: University of North Carolina Press, 2022). While she does reference Jackson's experiences in Charleston, she mistakenly names him as John Andrew Johnson. Nonetheless, this study does indeed emphasize a powerful perspective to understand different iterations of the slavery-to-freedom trope of the Underground Railroad, particularly for Black Americans in Southern cities.

18. Jackson, 105.

19. Greene, Hutchins, and Hutchins estimate that, while statistics are a bit unclear, in 1849–1850 some 23 percent of enslaved people in Charleston were hired out and thus should have had badges on their person. That means roughly that a quarter of the enslaved Black population was registered as "living out" in some way, a term meaning they were sent out to earn wages that would be shared with the owner and that they had to provide at least some of their own food, clothing, or living expenses. See Harlan Greene, Harry S. Hutchins Jr., and Brian E. Hutchins, *Slave Badges and the Slave-Hire System in Charleston, South Carolina, 1783–1865* (Jefferson, NC: McFarland & Company, 2004), 129. For more context see Bernard Powers, *Black Charlestonians: A Social History, 1822–1885* (Fayetteville: University of Arkansas Press, 1994), 9–35; Jackson, 105.

20. Greene et al., 8.

21. Harlan Greene, "Slave Badges," in *South Carolina Encyclopedia* (University of South Carolina, 2020), www.scencyclopedia.org.

22. While it is true that a slave unable to produce a badge was liable to be put in the workhouse or otherwise detained, Jackson is mistaken on his point about the inscription, which makes sense because he did not himself ever have a badge. The name and address of the enslaver would not have been imprinted or inscribed on the badges. See Greene et al., 4.

23. Jackson, 105.

24. Men such as James Matthews and William Grimes both escaped from Southern cities by boats (Matthews from Charleston and Grimes from Savannah) and both wrote about their experiences. See Matthews in the chapter titled "Recollection of Slavery by a Runaway Slave" (1838), which was at that point of publication understood as an anonymous narrative in my edited collection, *I Belong to South Carolina.* James Matthews, "Recollection of Slavery by a Runaway Slave (1838)," in *I Belong to South Carolina*, ed. Susanna Ashton (Columbia, SC: University of South Carolina Press, 2010), 49–82. For Grimes, see William Grimes, *Life of William Grimes, the Runaway Slave*, ed. William L. Andrews and Regina E. Mason (Oxford: Oxford University Press, 2008). For additional work on James Matthews and his South Carolina escape, see Susanna Ashton, "Re-Collecting Jim," *Commonplace* 15, no. 1 (2014), commonplace.online/article/re-collecting-jim.

25. Timothy Walker, "Sailing to Freedom: Maritime Dimensions of the Underground Railroad," in *Sailing to Freedom: Maritime Dimensions of the Underground Railroad*, ed. Timothy Walker, 14–35 (Amherst: University of Massachusetts Press, 2021), 19.

26. Walker notes that in Florida, for example, an 1854 Act was passed to "Prevent the Abduction and Escape from Slaves from this State," which created an officer of inspection and fumigation charged with locating enslaved people attempting to escape aboard northbound vessels. Ibid., 19–20.

27. Jackson, 105. For the day of the week see the summary of Jackson's lecture where he states he left on a Wednesday in the *Cambridge Chronicle and Journal*. "Lecture on Slavery." February 26, 1859, sec. Column 1. British Library Newspapers.

28. Jackson, 105–106.

29. Jackson, 106.

30. A stevedore is someone who unloads or loads ships.

31. Jackson.

32. Ibid., 106.

33. Ibid. In his memoir Jackson recalled that the cloak he purchased in Charleston was a ladies' cloak, not a man's. This may have been what caught the attention of the Black stevedore he was speaking with. Jackson, 105.

34. Captain George Scott (1819–1878) would have been about twenty-eight years of age at this point and only a few years older than Jackson.

35. He cites seven days and seven nights in his interview in 1893 *Union and Advertiser.* "The Story of John Andrew Jackson." August 9, 1893.

36. Jackson, 107.

37. Ibid.

38. Ibid. Later, when Jackson published his memoir, he included some endorsements, one of which was from G.W. Cochrane who testified: "Be it known to whom it may concern, that I went with the above John Andrew Jackson and saw Mrs. Foreman, in Richmond Street, Boston, and she fully corroborated his statement in reference to his being a slave; also said her son had been on board the vessel, and seen the spot where the said John Andrew Jackson was cut out, according to his statement. . . ." Jackson, 125. Cochrane was a white man involved in the business of shoe and leather distribution and likely knew Jackson through his employers in Salem. See *The Boston Directory* (Boston: Sampson & Murdock Company, 1855), 68.

39. In England Jackson spoke about his escape and described the captain as a "humane" man despite his waffling about how to deal with Jackson. See *Fife Herald*, April 23, 1857, 3.

40. Ibid.

Chapter 4

1. See "Almanac for Boston Area, MA, February 10, 1847," *National Weather Service*, www.weather.gov.

2. According to the *Boston Daily Atlas* of February 11, the *Smyrna* arrived from Charleston on the evening of Thursday, February 10. It seems almost certainly to have been the boat Jackson was on. Confusingly, the *Boston Courier* of February 11 suggests the *Smyrna* may have sailed directly from Savannah, Georgia, on that same date, but that seems to be an error. Alternatively, it is possible the *Smyrna*'s itinerary changed along the way, and they stopped in Charleston for a few days to load cotton. Another candidate for the boat Jackson was on might be the *General Green*, which also arrived on February 10, from Charleston. Still, the *Smyrna* is far more likely as it specifically arrived in the evening and, according to Jackson, didn't stop to interact or "speak" with other boats along the way, which the *General Green* did, according to the *Boston Courier*. For the conflicting report on the *Smyrna*, see "Marine Journal," *Boston Courier*, February 11,

1847, 3. For the definition of a "bark" or "barque," see William Falconer, *Dictionary of the Marine* (London, 1784). Historian Timothy Walker helped me pore through the marine announcements of the *Boston Daily Atlas*, and I am grateful for his suggestions about the *Smyrna*. Reference Librarian Meaghan Wright of the Phillips Museum at the Peabody Essex Museum in Salem also helped me work through these possibilities. Jackson mentions having been hidden for seven days and seven nights on the boat in an interview he gave in 1893 to the *Union and Advertiser* ("The Story of John Andrew Jackson." August 9, 1893).

3. Jackson, 107.

4. For information about barques, see "The 15 Different Types of Sailing Ships," www.deepsailing.com/blog/types-of-sailing-ships.

5. For a good analysis of the various laws that impacted free Black seamen in significant Southern ports (such as Charleston), see W. Jeffrey Bolster, *Black Jacks: African American Seamen in the Age of Sail* (Cambridge, MA: Harvard University Press, 2009), 203–209. Southern states enacted various laws for their ports that required free Black seamen to stay on board their ships or in jails, essentially holding these free individuals captive (often on their own ships) whenever the boat arrived in a particular city. The resulting intimidation and harassment that Black seamen faced in these situations meant that they usually dreaded such destinations but rarely had a choice because almost any vessel would sooner or later stop at such a port.

6. Jackson, 107.

7. "Safe Harbor: George," Boston African American National Historic Site, National Park Service, www.nps.gov/media/video/view; Wilbur Henry Siebert, *The Underground Railroad from Slavery to Freedom* (New York: Macmillan, 1898), 40.

8. See Siebert, 40–41; "Capt. Hannum to the Slaveholders!!" *The Emancipator* (New York, NY), October 7, 1846.

9. Siebert, 41.

10. "A Runaway Slave," *Fife Herald* (Cupar, UK), April 23, 1857, 3.

11. In his memoir, Jackson spells the name as "Forman." In an advertisement for the boarding house placed in *The Liberator* from time to time during 1842, 1843, and 1844, an advertisement which Foreman would have himself placed and is more authoritative than Jackson's memory, spells the name "Foreman." Jackson, 107. Foreman is listed as a boarding house proprietor in *The Boston Directory* (George Adams: Boston, 1849), 136.

12. "Moon Calendar for 1847 Year," www.predicalendar.com/moon/calendar/1847.

13. "Andrew Jackson," 1850 United States Census, Boston Ward 2, Suffolk County, Massachusetts, roll 334, 173a, Ancestry.com.

14. Many journalists in both the United States and in England would abbreviate his name as John A. Jackson or J.A. Jackson for the next several decades. Undoubtedly the most significant moment of claiming his own name would be with the publication of his memoir in 1862 under the name of John Andrew Jackson.

15. Barbara Meil Hobson, *Uneasy Virtue: The Politics of Prostitution and the American Reform Tradition* (Chicago: University of Chicago Press, 1990), 41. This area has seen a lot of backfill into the harbor, so the intersection in the twenty-first century is farther from the waterfront today than it would have been in 1849. Currently, it is the heart of the Italian American "North End" of Boston, and the intersection is a lively area filled with patisseries and upscale Italian restaurants. Notably, in his memoir, Jackson describes the corner site as on Richmond Street rather than Ann Street, perhaps attempting to make it sound a bit more respectable than it was. It is also possible that this intersection was a bit calmer than further down the street. Nonetheless, Ann Street was so notorious at the time Jackson would have arrived that its name was changed to "North" Street only four years later in an attempt perhaps to shake off its bad reputation. No one was fooled, and by all reports, the name change had little effect. See Jackson, 107. For info about the name change, see *A Record of the Streets, Alleys, Places, Etc., in the City of Boston* (City of Boston: Printing Department, 1910), 339.

16. As quoted by Hobson, 41. See also Perry R. Duis, *The Saloon: Public Drinking in Chicago and Boston 1880–1920* (Urbana: University of Illinois Press, 1983), 235–236.

17. Quoted in Hobson, 41.

18. "Genteel Boarding for Respectable Colored Seamen, Henry Foreman," *The Liberator*, September 2, 1842. *The Liberator* reprinted this advertisement on November 4, 1842, December 30, 1842, and August 4, 1843.

19. "The Riot," *Boston Evening Transcript* (Boston, MA), August 28, 1843.

20. Ibid. See also "Police Court," *Boston Daily Atlas*, December 31, 1832. See also "Disgraceful Riot in Ann St.," Primary Research, primaryresearch.org/qdisgraceful-riot-in-ann-stq.

21. Ibid.

22. "Notice," *The Liberator* (Boston, MA), January 17, 1845.

23. Jackson, 107.

24. Jackson might have met with like-minded Black abolitionists at the New England Freedom Association, for which Foreman had helped raise money. Donald M. Jacobs, *Courage and Conscience: Black & White Abolitionists in Boston* (Bloomington, IN: Published for the Boston Athenaeum by Indiana University Press, 1993), 144.

25. The 1850 United States Census shows 2,038 "free people of color" living in Boston. See "Massachusetts," 1850 United States Census, www.census.gov/library/publications/1853/dec/1850a, 52.

26. According to the census, 324 free people of color were reported living there in 1850, although at least one historian persuasively puts the population figure as closer to 425. See "Massachusetts," 1850 United States Census, www.census.gov/library/publications/1853/dec/1850a., 52. For the higher figure, Michael Sokolow calculated the census data but included also city directories and such for a higher and likely more accurate number. See Michael Sokolow, "New Guinea at One End, and a Alms-House at the Other. The

Decline of Black Salem, 1850–1920," *New England Quarterly* 17, no. 2 (June 1998): 207, note 7.

27. Jackson, 111.

28. "The Industrial and Social Development of Boston St.Pdf," n.d., 13. For an overview of the growth of the leather industry in Salem and its adjacent town, Peabody, see Charles Stuart Osgood and Henry Morrill Batchelde, *Historical Sketch of Salem, 1626–1879.* Essex Institute, 1879, 228–229.

29. The Salem Directory: *Containing the City Record, Banks, Insurance Companies, Churches and Societies, Names and Business of Citizens, An Almanac for 1850, with a Variety of Miscellaneous Matter*, George Adams (Salem: Henry Whipple, Publisher, 1850).

30. Ibid., 107.

31. Ibid., 125.

32. Ibid., 107.

33. Ibid., 107–108.

34. Ibid., 110. A description of what work on the splitting machine might have entailed can be found in "A Pair of Shoes," *Harper's New Monthly Magazine*, January 1885, 276.

35. Dan Campbell, *The Industrial and Social Development of Boston Street, Salem* (CETA Team Project: Historic Salem, Inc., 1978), 11. Also, for a good understanding of the dangers of the tan yards, see Thomas Carroll, *The History of the Leather Industry in Salem and Danvers, Mass., U.S.A.*, undated pamphlet.

36. Jackson, 110.

37. "Collection: Anti-Slavery Society of Salem and Vicinity Records, 1834–1840, 1886, Phillips Library Finding Aids," pem.as.atlas-sys.com/repositories/2/resources.

38. Sokolow, 204–228. See pages 205–207 for population analysis.

39. Sokolow, 37.

40. Robert L. Hall, "Massachusetts Abolitionists Document the Slave Experience," in Jacobs, 93. Also, see the article by Robby on Hayden, page 599. And finally, for the full figures, see Francis Jackson, *Account Book of Francis Jackson, treasurer, the Vigilance Committee of Boston*, Library of Bostonian Society, Old State House (Boston: *Magazine of History* 31: 220).

41. For a discussion of some of the work Remond did in Worcester and especially his encounters with Frederick Douglass see Gregory P. Lampe, *Frederick Douglass: Freedom's Voice, 1818–1845* (East Lansing: Michigan State University Press, 2012), 98.

42. Martin Stowell worked as a shoemaker in Warren, Massachusetts, at least as of 1846, but took an active role in helping protect and liberate people from slavery. Stowell shot and killed a police officer when trying to rescue Anthony Burns from being sent back into slavery in 1854. James E Potter, "A Nebraska Cavalryman in Dixie: The Letters of Martin Stowell," *Nebraska History* 74 (1993): 22–31, history.nebraska.gov.

43. While H. Haynsworth was a lawyer, one of his relatives, a Dr. Haynsworth, is remembered, somewhat neutrally, by Jackson in his 1862 memoir when he recalls that James English (one of Robert English's sons) took ill and called for a "Dr. Hainsworth" who told him he would die "in a few days." Jackson, 92. So we know the English family, as well as the Wells/Law families, were entwined in various ways with the neighboring Haynsworths. Thus it makes sense that he writes as an authorized agent for either Elizabeth English, the Wells/Law families, or for all of them.

44. H. Haynsworth, "Refuge of Oppression," *The Liberator* (Boston, MA), July 12, 1850.

45. Ibid.

46. Allan D. Thigpen, *The Illustrated Recollections of Potter's Raid, April 5–21, 1865*, rev. ed. (Sumter, SC: A.D. Thigpen, 1998), 369.

47. Lucy Chase, *Diary*, March 14, 1850, Chase Family Papers, American Antiquarian Society.

48. Lucy Chase mentions going to hear him speak somewhere and there is a mention here about his talk in Northhampton.

49. The undated newspaper clipping, later reproduced in *The Liberator*, can be found with Lucy Chase's papers in the Chase Family Papers, 1787–1915, Box 4, American Antiquarian Society, Worcester, Massachusetts.

50. Thomas L. Doughton and B. Eugene McCarthy, *From Bondage to Belonging: The Worcester Slave Narratives* (Amherst, Baltimore, MD.: University of Massachusetts Press, Project MUSE, 2007), xxvii.

51. H.H.G. to Madam Chase, March 29, 1850, Chase Family Papers, American Antiquarian Society.

52. Jackson, 108.

53. See the discussion in chapter 1 about how Louisa was forced to marry Enoch. Jackson may not have mentioned this history because it could have complicated or undermined his own claim as Louisa's rightful husband. Of course, Garnet would likely have been sympathetic since he, too, had escaped from slavery. But most of the time it was difficult to publicly discuss heartbreaking decisions about marriages, and Jackson may not have wished to complicate discussions about his wife. It's difficult to know exactly why Jackson feared they had gone to Florida, but he was evidently mistaken, as demonstrated by the letter he was soon to receive from South Carolina.

54. Garnet appears never to have been in touch with Jackson again, but Jackson may well have remembered and been inspired by Garnet's decision to move to England during that summer of 1849. For studies of Garnet see Joel Schor, *Henry Highland Garnet: A Voice of Black Radicalism in the Nineteenth Century* (Westport, CT: Greenwood Press, 1977) and Martin B. Pasternak, *Rise Now and Fly to Arms: The Life of Henry Highland Garnet* (New York: Garland Publishers, 1995). For a more specialized insight into Garnet's formative experiences and education see Anna Mae Duane, *Educated for Freedom: The*

Incredible Story of Two Fugitive Schoolboys Who Grew Up to Change a Nation (New York: New York University Press, 2020).

55. Lucy Chase, *Diary*, March 14, 1850, Chase Family Papers, American Antiquarian Society.

56. Anthony Benezet Chase (1791–1879) was named after Anthony Benezet (1713–1784), the prominent Quaker abolitionist. "Worcester Historical Museum Archives. 2013 FIA 05. Chase Family Papers and Collection.," n.d.; "Anthony Benezet, Abolitionist Writers in Relation to Olaudah Equiano," Santa Clara University Digital Exhibits, dh.scu.edu /exhibits/exhibits/show/abolitionist-writers-in-relati/anthony-benezet.

57. The "Mr. Ofley" mentioned by Jackson was the Reverend G.W. Offley, a Black man born into slavery whose free father had purchased his freedom. Offley later published the story of his own life in 1859. While he spent much of his life in Hartford, Connecticut, he worked in Worcester for a period of time in the late 1840s and 1850s helping establish the A.M.E. Zion Church there. Christy Webb, "G.W. Offley (Greensbury Washington), b. 1808," *Documenting the American South*, docsouth.unc.edu/neh/offley; *From Bondage to Belonging: The Worcester Slave Narratives*, ed. B. Eugene McCarthy and Thomas L. Doughton (Amherst, MA: University of Massachusetts Press, 2007), 160–164.

58. John Jackson to Madam Chase., 23 or 28 April 1850, Chase Family Papers, American Antiquarian Society.

59. Eldridge Mann to Mr. Chase, 20 July 1850, Chase Family Papers, American Antiquarian Society.

60. In 1893 he remarked in a newspaper interview that a letter from Louisa's enslavers indicated she had remarried someone and then died, leaving him free to remarry: "I learned she had been married to another slave and a short time afterward died." It's hard to know what he had known or thought at that time, but he evidently believed Louisa was lost to him forever and he was free to remarry in Canada around 1850–1851. "The story of John Andrew Jackson," *Union and Advertiser*, August 9, 1893. See chapter 6 of this book for a lengthier consideration of Louisa's circumstances and Jackson's remarriage.

61. Robert English died on December 31, 1847 (a year and a week after Jackson had liberated himself). Jackson was thus in the eyes of the law now legally the property of Robert English's widow, Elizabeth English. See Robert English's gravestone here: Robert English gravestone, Mayesville, Sumter County, South Carolina, Find a Grave, www .findagrave.com/memorial/60442004/robert-english. For discussions of Anderson, see Jackson, 109–110. Anderson may have been David D. Anderson (1797–1873), a white man who was born and died in Lynchburg. Year: 1850; Census Place: Sumter, Sumter, South Carolina; roll M432_859; 310A; image 8.

62. Jackson, 110.

63. Ibid.

64. Ibid.

65. J.D. Thomas, "The Manstealing Law Explained," Accessible Archives, www .accessible-archives.com/2017/02/manstealing-law-explained. The act was constructed

as part of the Compromise of 1850 that sought to avoid war between the South and the North with several decisions, including allowing California to enter as a free state. Its most notorious part, though, was the section about fugitives.

66. "The Fugitive Slave Law [Hartford, Ct.?: s.n. 1850-?]," Library of Congress, www.loc.gov/resource/rbpe.33700200/?st=text.

67. William Wells Brown, *The Rising Son, or, the Antecedents and Advancement of the Colored Race* (A. G. Brown & Company, 1882), 329.

68. "How to Oppose the Fugitive Slave Law," *Independent*, October 24, 1850, 174.

69. Jackson, 84.

70. Sinha, Manisha. *The Slave's Cause: A History of Abolition* (New Haven: Yale University Press, 2016), 502.

Chapter 5

1. One possibility about Jackson's travels is that he might have gone up to Maine as early as October and stayed in the small town of Hallowell for a while. It's possible he was counted in the 1850 Boston Census at the boarding house taken on September 12 and then perhaps also listed on the 1850 Census for Hallowell, Maine, on October 4. A Black man named "Andrew Jackson" shows up in the 1850 Census for Hallowell as listed with "unknown state of origin" and an occupation listed as "sailor." Hallowell was a fairly welcoming place for people seeking their freedom from slavery. For instance, a Joseph Lovejoy who lived there edited an antislavery newspaper, and at that very same time in 1850 another runaway, James Matthews from South Carolina, resided at the "City Poor Farm" for the town. The farm tended to have only from ten to twenty people staying there at any given time, which demonstrates the small-town cluster of people in need. Black transients or fugitives could have stayed in the "City Poor Farm" as a temporary boarding or charitable refuge site. If the man mentioned in the 1850 Census for Maine was James Andrew Jackson from South Carolina, which is hard to say because his name is so common, he decided the Hallowell Poor Farm wasn't a place for permanent protection and made his way to Brunswick and Bath by December of that year. For information on Hallowell and its 1850 Census, James Matthews, and the Lovejoy family, see Susanna Ashton, "Re-Collecting Jim," *Commonplace,* http://commonplace.online; also, *U.S., Selected Federal Census Non-Population Schedules, 1850–1880*, Ancestry.com.

2. Jackson, 111.

3. HBS to "Dear Sister" [Catharine Beecher], n.d. (1850 or 1851), Beecher Family Papers, Sterling Memorial Library, Yale University.

4. *The Pleasure Boat* (1846), vol. 1, no. 33, 3.

5. "Smyth, William," *The National Cyclopedia of American Biography*, vol. 10 (New York: James T. White & Company, 1909), 474.

6. As quoted in Gerald Talbot and H.H. Price, *Maine's Visible Black History* (Gardiner, ME: Tilbury House, 2006), 257.

7. In doing work at the Stowe House in Hartford, in 2015, I established the following facts which demonstrate Smyth was related to Harriet Beecher Stowe in two entirely different ways:

1. Harriet Beecher Stowe's brother Charles was married to the sister of Smyth's wife's (Harriet Porter Smyth) and
2. the mother of Smyth's wife (Harriet Porter Smyth's mother), Mary Porter, was sister to the second wife of Lyman Beecher (Harriet Beecher Stowe's father).

Thus: 1. Smyth was Harriet Beecher Stowe's sister-in-law's sister's husband. And 2. Smyth's mother-in-law's sister was Harriet Beecher Stowe's stepmother.

Understanding these somewhat fraught family connections helps explain why Smyth helped advocate for Calvin Stowe's hiring at Bowdoin College and also why Smyth was assigned to pick up the Stowe family in the nearby town of Bath when they arrived by boat from Boston. This connection also suggests that Smyth may have urged Jackson to visit both the Uphams and the Stowes. William Smyth and his wife, Harriet Porter Coffin Smyth, had children ranging in age from two to twenty-one at the time Stowe moved to Brunswick, so they doubtless had advice and comaraderie for her family.

8. Samuel Charles Stowe (1848–1849) was often called "Charles" or "Charley." After he died, Stowe gave birth to another son in 1850 named "Charles Edward." He would have been a baby of about six months old at the time of her encounter with Jackson. See the Harriet Beecher Stowe Center family tree: www.harrietbeecherstowecenter.org/harriet-beecher-stowe/family.

9. Calvin Stowe had also signaled, to his wife's great frustration, that he was willing to accept a position at Andover Theological Seminary during this time as well (a position he took up after teaching some summer terms at Bowdoin to finish his obligations there). Significantly, though, for the purposes of Stowe and Jackson's encounter, Calvin Stowe was generally away and teaching at Lane for the winter term which lasted between November 1850 and March 1851. See Hedrick, 207–208.

10. Harriet Beecher Stowe, "The Freeman's Dream: A Parable," *National Era*, August 1, 1850, 1.

11. See Frank Upham, *Upham Genealogy: The Descendants of John Upham* (Albany, NY: Joel Munsell's Sons, Publishers, 1892), 306–307. In December 1850 the Stowe family had six children because their son Samuel Charles Stowe had died from cholera in 1849 at the age of eighteen months,

12. Phebe Lord Upham's wealth is referenced in the introduction to her writing about "Happy Phebe." https://courses.bowdoin.edu/there-is-a-woman-in-every-color-2021/labor-force/narrative-of-phebe-ann-jacobs-or-happy-phebe.

13. "Phebe" is the correct spelling here for both the woman married to Thomas Upham as well as the "Happy Phebe" profiled in the tract. For more regarding this character being a partial inspiration for the devout character of Uncle Tom, see Theodore R. Hovet, "Mrs. Thomas C. Upham's 'Happy Phebe': A Feminine Source of Uncle Tom," *American Literature* 51, no. 2 (1979), 267–270. In *A Key to Uncle Tom's Cabin*, Stowe mentions that she had read Phebe Upham's tract on "Happy" Phebe. Harriet Beecher Stowe, *A Key*

to Uncle Tom's Cabin: Presenting the Original Facts and Documents upon Which the Story Is Founded (Boston, Cleveland, OH: J.P. Jewett, 1853), 40–41.

14. Alpheus S. Packard, *Address on the Life and Character of Thomas C. Upham* (Brunswick, ME: Joseph Griffin, 1873), 19.

15. David Reynolds provides an analysis of the evolution of antislavery thought for the Beecher family and Stowe in particular. David S. Reynolds, *Mightier Than the Sword: Uncle Tom's Cabin and the Battle for America* (New York: Norton, 2011), 89–97. Stowe's views on the aims of the American Colonialization Society are complicated, and she had several Black characters in *Uncle Tom's Cabin* sail to Africa at the end of the novel.

16. HBS to "Dear Sister" [Catharine Beecher], n.d. (1850 or 1851), Beecher Family Papers, Sterling Memorial Library, Yale University (MS 71).

17. Ibid.

18. Ibid.

19. Ibid.

20. Jackson, 122. "Dearest Mae" was a popular version of a minstrel song generally attributed to James Power and Francis Lynch and dating from 1847. Notably, this version features an opening line with the N-word rather than the word "freemen," which is how Jackson preferred to share it. Jackson wasn't likely to have heard this song when he was enslaved in South Carolina, but he might have learned it at an antislavery rally or meeting in Massachusetts during his years there. While there are many versions and attributions of this song, one particular version of note was the arrangement of Lynch and Power's tune by the popular Black musician Harry Burleigh in the early twentieth century. See Francis Lynch and James Power. Arranged by L.V.H. Crosby. *Dearest Mae, Celebrated Ethiopian Song*, ed. Harry Thacker Burleigh (New York, G. Schirmer, 1910). I am grateful to scholars Kendall Kennison and Mark Jon Burford for bringing the work of Harry Burleigh to my attention in this instance.

21. Jackson, 122.

22. James Power, Francis Lynch, L.V.H. Crosby, "Dearest Mae," Digital Commons @ Connecticut College, digitalcommons.conncoll.edu/sheetmusic. It is notable that there were many versions of the lyrics of this tune in circulation, but Jackson's version is the only one that ends with a trip to Canada, to freedom. Most versions end with the singer returning to his enslaver, after having visited his wife. This strongly suggests that Jackson, probably while in England, rewrote the lyrics to suit his circumstances.

23. Jackson, 111.

24. Ibid.

25. Ibid., 108.

26. For details about the astounding success of this novel, see Claire Parfait, *The Publishing History of Uncle Tom's Cabin, 1852–2002* (Farnham Surrey, UK: Ashgate Publishing, 2007).

27. "Uncle Tom's Cabin and the Matter of Influence," AP U.S. History Study Guide from the Gilder Lehrman Institute of American History, November 28, 2011, www.gilderlehrman.org.

28. Stowe, *The Annotated Uncle Tom's Cabin*, 1st ed. (New York: Norton, 2007), 87.

29. Ibid., 88.

30. Ibid., 96

31. "Uncle Tom's Cabin and the Matter of Influence."

32. "Stowe's Global Impact," Harriet Beecher Stowe Center, www.harrietbeecherstowecenter.org. See also Charles Dudley Warner who, in "The Story of Uncle Tom's Cabin," published in the *Atlantic Monthly*, asserted that "eight presses running day and night were barely able to keep pace with the demand for it." Charles Dudley Warner "The Story of *Uncle Tom's Cabin*," *Atlantic Monthly* (78) 467, 311–321.

33. Hollis Robbins introduction to *Uncle Tom's Cabin* annotated edition edited with Henry Louis Gates, xlvi.

34. Reynolds, 89.

35. See ibid., 87–116.

36. Ibid., 104.

37. Stowe, *The Annotated Uncle Tom's Cabin*, 468.

38. Stowe, *A Key to Uncle Tom's Cabin*, 65–66.

39. It wasn't until several years after her book was published that Jackson reached out to connect with her and benefit from his association with her, or at least there is no evidence or suggestion he connected with her much before late 1855 or 1856, at which point he was assembling testimonials to support his overseas travels. Thus, even by 1856 when he shared a letter from Stowe with British clergy, he never paraded or promoted himself as a model for Uncle Tom, although, as mentioned in chapter 7, he did occasionally hint that he might have some associations with her character of Dred, in Stowe's novel of that name.

40. While Stowe explicitly cites the remarkable life stories of both Henson and Clarke as influences on her fiction, she never publicly mentions Jackson as a model. See Susan Cooke Soderberg's excellent biography of Henson, which speculates about whether Stowe might have met Henson. There is much confusion over the history of Henson and Stowe. Her youngest son, Charles Stowe, who hadn't yet been born at the time, wrote an anecdotal biography of his mother and asserted that Henson and his mother had met in January 1850 in Boston. And Henson himself asserted that he had met her in Andover in 1849. Other evidence makes it clear that Stowe wasn't in Boston in January 1850 (she visited her brother Edward there later, in May), and she wasn't living in Andover until 1852, so Henson's claim also seems retroactively convenient. Stowe herself never mentions a meeting with Henson before writing her book. Nonetheless, my position is that even if she had met Henson and read his memoir before beginning *Uncle Tom's Cabin*, it would not have lessened Jackson's impact on her work. It seems most likely, when aligning these varying dates and claims, that she and Jackson met in December 1850,

and a few weeks later she was inspired to begin her novel. Later, perhaps midway in her writing, as she was seeking further details and ideas, it seems that she may have read the Henson memoir and found it helpful—hence, she cited it in *A Key to Uncle Tom's Cabin*, although there are many works she cites in *A Key*, which scholars agree she read only after the novel had been published. Nonetheless, she observed that many different influences shaped the depiction of her character Uncle Tom, and, importantly, remarked that his character was consistent with what she knew about other individuals in the world, not that they had necessarily led her to the creation of her particular character. "The character of Uncle Tom," she wrote, "has been objected to as improbable; and yet the writer has received more confirmations of that character, and from a great variety of sources, than of any other in the book" (page 38 of *A Key*), and then after listing many such "confirmations," she added: "A last instance *parallel* [my emphasis] with that of Uncle Tom is to be found in the published memoirs of the venerable Josiah Henson . . . now pastor of the missionary settlement at Dawn, in Canada." (She then went on to recount the salient facts of his memoir that had made an impression upon her on page 43 of *A Key*.) See Harriet Beecher Stowe, *The Key to Uncle Tom's Cabin*. Of note is her careful use of the word "parallel," which suggests she saw her novel's own creation as separate from the particulars of Henson's life. In later years, she did write a friendly preface to an 1876 edition of Henson's memoir, titled "Uncle Tom's Story of His Life," *An Autobiography of the Rev. Josiah Henson (Mrs. Harriet Beecher Stowe's "Uncle Tom") from 1789 to 1876*, ed. John Lobb (London: Christian Age, 1876). Her brief preface praises Henson's life story but doesn't mention any connection to her own writing. Ultimately, she may have just thrown up her hands when it came to separating herself from this popular notion and decided it didn't do anyone any harm to have that claim circulating out there, even if it wasn't how she herself would characterize her creative process. Jackson, on the other hand, used his connections with Stowe and her endorsements to further his career, but he never proclaimed himself as a model for her characters or her novel. In short, Henson may or may not have been a model for the specific character of Uncle Tom, but Jackson's encounter with Stowe helped launch and inspire the novel as a whole. Helpful here is also the work by Hannah-Rose Murray, "'My Name Is Not Tom': Josiah Henson, *Uncle Tom's Cabin*, and Adaptive Resistance after the Civil War 1876–1877," in *Advocates of Freedom: African American Transatlantic Abolitionism in the British Isles* (Cambridge: Cambridge University Press, 2020), 255–291.

41. "Preface" authored by W.M.S. (*I Belong to South Carolina*). I have failed to confidently identify this individual, who was likely a member of Spurgeon's circle. He doesn't appear to have known Jackson well, as the introduction refers to Jackson only in general albeit supportive terms. W.M.S. spends most of his preface arguing that England as a nation is largely responsible for the establishment of slavery in the United States and must therefore work to abolish it.

42. HBS to "Dear Sister" [Catharine Beecher], n.d. [1850 or 1851], Beecher Family Papers, Sterling Memorial Library.

43. Talbot and Price, 263.

44. Ibid., 58–60.

45. Ibid., 263.

46. Hedrick, 199.

47. It is possible that Jackson stayed in Portland for a few weeks and then made his way to Brunswick and Bath, but evidence and the time frame between the passage of the act and his arrival in Brunswick suggests that he more likely traveled to Brunswick and Bath initially and then returned to Portland to wait to join a larger group of enslaved people who could collectively be taken via steamer to Saint John, perhaps in slightly less brutal weather. This is suggested both by his endorsement from Fessenden, who states Jackson was with him for several weeks, and in information about Fessenden and others in Portland who, after 1850, would try to consolidate groups together for travel.

48. "Railroads," *Maine: An Encyclopedia*, maineanencyclopedia.com/railroads.

49. Jackson, 125.

50. Randolph Stakeman, "The Black Population of Maine, 1764–1900," *New England Journal of Black Studies* 8 (1989): 17–35, 30.

51. "The Pastors of Siloam," Siloam Presbyterian, www.siloam-brooklyn.org/the-pastors-of-siloam.

52. James R. Murray, "Mariner's Church," Historical Marker Database, www.hmdb.org.

53. Charles Lenox Remond was from Salem, and it is possible his family would have cautioned Jackson or others heading north that they should be wary of Maine and not get too comfortable there. James R. Murray, "Friends (Quaker) Meeting House," Historical Marker Database, www.hmdb.org.

54. Siebert, 219.

Chapter 6

1. 1851 Census of New Brunswick, Saint John, Saint John County, New Brunswick, 62a, Automated Genealogy. See also Scott W. See, "'An Unprecedented Influx': Nativism and Irish Famine Immigration to Canada," in *Fleeing the Famine: North America and Irish Refugees, 1845–1851*, ed. Margaret M. Mulrooney (Westport, CT: Praeger, 2003), 59–78.

2. This could also be usefully understood as an instance of what scholar Simone Browne identifies as "dark sousveillance"—or as a kind of reading praxis that, intentionally or not, pushes back against surveillance that identifies and registers through the sight of darkness or race. See Simone Browne, *On the Surveillance of Blackness* (Durham, NC: Duke University Press, 2015). Of course, the heading on the census page indicates that these eleven people are Black. Moreover, the many Black people who resided in Saint John and were not fugitives of 1850–1851 are listed in the 1851 Census elsewhere noted as "States" under the "Race" category, but those more settled citizens also usually have a clear marker in a "remarks" column that identifies them as Black which is not present on the page listing the eleven fugitives in question. It is true that the column in the census also identifies other people by national origin—with many people listed as "Irish," or

as "Native" (meaning, in this case, born in Canada—which is of course another racial occlusion of the indigenous population), for example. Nonetheless, that it occurs on this addended page for fugitives gives it an extra degree of complication.

3. John Andrew Jackson, *The Experience of a Slave in South Carolina*, in *I Belong to South Carolina: South Carolina Slave Narratives*, ed. Susanna Ashton (Columbia, SC: University of South Carolina Press, 2010), 111.

4. In 1877 a huge fire in Saint John destroyed many buildings, records, and documents related to the city's history, so much of that history has been lost. "The Great Fire," website.nbm-mnb.ca/CAIN/english/sj_fire.

5. For a sense of how he initially partnered with other Black lecturers, see the report of a joint lecture he delivered in "Slavery," *Cambridge Independent Press*, January 28, 1865, 7.

6. Historian Wilbur Siebert writes that the Grand Trunk Railway running between Portland, Maine, and Saint John often turned a blind eye to fugitives hiding in baggage, freight cars, or among livestock. It would also sometimes give discounted or free tickets to those in need. The line wasn't opened until 1852; therefore, unless Jackson trekked overland, it is hard to imagine Jackson in early 1851 taking any route other than a steamer ship across the international border at this time. Siebert, 80–81. See also Daniel G. Hill, *The Freedom-seekers: Blacks in Early Canada* (Toronto: Book Society of Canada, 1981), 33.

7. The 1851 Census of New Brunswick was actually taken in most areas of New Brunswick in January 1852 and retroactively asked people if they had been living in the area or arrived during the previous year. Thus, this 1851 Census is occasionally referred to as the 1852 Census. For the purposes of this study, I refer to it as the 1851 Census. Referencing back to the runaway advertisement Thomas Reese English placed in 1847 allows us to triangulate another bit of knowledge: in that advertisement, he suggested that Jackson's age was "about thirty," which means Jackson would have been born close to 1817. So it is quite possible that the Canadian census taker was not far off the mark in listing Jackson's age as thirty-five. Indeed, it hews close to what we can know about Jackson's origins. However, in later years Jackson listed his birth year as 1825 to census takers, so his age is always a bit uncertain. The name listed on this 1851 Census is also unlike formulations he used at other points in his life but doesn't seem wildly off base. The clerk might have just ignored the middle name. Or Jackson might not have given it to him. As we know, Jackson deployed different variations of his names as they suited him during his life. We have seen him use Andrew Jackson, John Jackson, and John Andrew Jackson in various scenarios. Additionally, in this document, he is listed as a "servant," which could mean almost anything at that time and doesn't preclude Jackson from later describing himself as having been a painter during his Saint John sojourn.

8. J.W. Lawrence, *Foot-prints: or, Incidents in Early History of New Brunswick* (Saint John, N.B.: J. & A. McMillan, 1883), 58.

9. James W. St. G. Walker, "African Canadians: Migration," *Encyclopedia of Canada's Peoples*, ed. Paul Robert Magocsi (Toronto: University of Toronto Press, 1999), 142.

10. For a summary of the fraught position of enslaved people at the end of the revolution, see Jill Lepore, "Goodbye, Columbus: When America Won Its Independence, What Became of the Slaves Who Fled for Theirs?" *New Yorker*, May 8, 2006. See also Hill, 10–12.

11. As scholar Barry Cahill compellingly argues, the formerly enslaved people arriving during this time were understood as a subcategory of "Blacks," not "Loyalists." See Barry Cahill, "The Black Loyalist Myth in Atlantic Canada," *Acadiensis* 29, no. 1 (1999): 76–87, www.jstor.org/stable.

12. See Harvey Amani Whitfield, *Blacks on the Border: The Black Refugees in British North America, 1815–1860* (Burlington: University of Vermont Press, 2006). Valuable insights may also be found in Robin W. Winks's now somewhat dated but encyclopedic analysis of the different waves of African Canadian identity. Robin W. Winks, *The Blacks in Canada: A History*, 2nd ed. (Montreal & Kingston: McGill-Queen's University Press, 1997).

13. Whitfield, 9–24.

14. For a list of the wards in Saint John County that have no surviving census data see "1851 Census of New Brunswick Index," Automated Genealogy, www.automatedgenealogy.com. For a thoughtful consideration of the problem of undercounting, see Richard M. Reid, *African Canadians in Union Blue: Enlisting for the Cause in the Civil War* (Vancouver: University of British Columbia Press, 2014), 16–18.

15. "Black Loyalists and Land Grants in New Brunswick," Black Loyalists in New Brunswick, preserve.lib.unb.ca/wayback/20141205153643/http://atlanticportal.hil.unb.ca/acva/blackloyalists/en/context/grants.

16. "Black History in Canada," *The Canadian Encyclopedia*, www.thecanadianencyclopedia.ca/en/collection/black-history-in-canada.

17. See Rachel Bryant, "Research Notes: Thomas Carleton, Charter of the City of Saint John (1785)," *Rachel Bryant: Research Notes and Avenues*, March 5, 2020, rachelbryant.ca/2020/03/05/research-notes-thomas-carleton-charter-of-the-city-of-saint-john-1785; "An Act in Further Amendment of the Charter of the City of Saint John," British North American Legislative Database, 1758–1867, bnald.lib.unb.ca/legislation/act-further-amendment-charter-city-saint-john-passed-14th-april-1849.

18. Scott W. See, "'An Unprecedented Influx,'" 61.

19. Samuel Gridley Howe, *The Refugees from Slavery in Canada West: Report to the Freedmen's Inquiry Commission by S. G. Howe* (Boston: Wright & Potter Printers, 1864), 40.

20. As quoted by Winks, 148.

21. *Running a Thousand Miles for Freedom: The Escape of William and Ellen Craft from Slavery.*

22. See information about Robert Patterson's Emancipation Society in Greg Marquis, *In Armageddon's Shadow: The Civil War and Canada's Maritime Provinces* (Montreal:

McGill-Queen's University Press, 1998), 69. See also William Arthur Spray, "Patterson, Robert J," *Dictionary of Canadian Biography*, vol. 11, www.biographi.ca/en/bio.

23. "By the Same, Same Day," *New Brunswick Courier*, vol. 14, November 20, 1852.

24. What little information there is about Julia, aside from this marriage notice, can be garnered from British census data and various newspaper sources, all of which happened well after she and Jackson had left Canada. In his own 1862 memoir, Jackson only notes that it was in Canada a decade earlier that he met Julia and that they were married "lawfully," a comment that might seem like a rebuke to his earlier marriage but was likely designed to assuage any racist concerns the white reading public might have for a supposed Black propensity for casual or unlawful familial family attachments. Julia Jackson's age is a bit unclear because conflicting census records of later decades indicate she was born sometime between 1820 and 1832. Of course, census records err, and people misreport their ages for many reasons. I speculate that she was roughly the same age as Jackson or perhaps a few years younger when they met. Hence, she was most likely twenty-four to thirty-four years of age, while he was probably somewhere between thirty and thirty-five at their meeting.

25. "The Story of John Andrew Jackson," *Union and Advertiser*, August 9, 1893.

26. This information comes from "A Slaveholder's Letter," an undated clipping from an unidentified newspaper. It can be approximately dated to 1850 and it is most likely from a Northampton, MA, newspaper. "A Slaveholder's Letter," *Northern Visions of Race, Region & Reform: In the Press and Letters of Freedmen and Freedmen's Teachers in the Civil War Era*, American Antiquarian Society, www.americanantiquarian.org/Freedmen/Manuscripts/slaveholdersletter.

27. For examples of "Creole" to describe Julia Ann Jackson, see "Jackson Speaks at Cavendish Chapel," *Kentist Gazette*, August 21, 1860, 5, and "Slavery in America," *Islington Gazette*, November 5, 1859, 2.

28. "Slavery," *Western Times*, January 30, 1863, 5.

29. "Black Lectures," *Dundee Courier*, June 15, 1864, 2.

30. "A Runaway Slave," *Fife Herald*, April 23, 1857, 3.

31. "Lecture on Slavery," *Christian News*, June 6, 1857.

32. An October 1861 publication of the *Saturday Review* notes an unnamed "country newspaper" that covered Jackson's lecture. "A Country Newspaper," *Saturday Review*, October 26, 1861, 7.

33. For the operations of the New York Committee of Vigilance, see Eric Foner, *The Gateway to Freedom: A Hidden History of the Underground Railroad* (New York: W.W. Norton, 2015).

34. Charles Ray, as quoted by Sydney Howard Gay; see Don Parson and Tom Calarco, *Secret Lives of the Underground Railroad in New York City: Sydney Howard Gay, Louis Napoleon and the Record of Fugitives* (Jefferson, NC: McFarland and Company, 2015), 172.

35. In one of Jackson's final interviews, a reporter writes that Jackson claimed to have escaped from Boston to Toronto, which belies most other facts we know about his circumstances and activities in New Brunswick. Of course, it is also possible he briefly tried to settle in Toronto and met Julia before returning to Saint John. For this interview, see "The Story of John Andrew Jackson," *Union and Advertiser*, August 9, 1893.

36. "By the Same, Same Day," *New Brunswick Courier*, vol. 14, November 20, 1852.

37. "Mrs. Jackson," *Gravesend Reporter*, September 1, 1860, 4.

38. Jones-Rogers, 23.

39. "Julia A Jackson," 1870 United States Federal Census, New Haven Ward 1, New Haven, Connecticut, roll M593_109, 89A, Ancestry.com.

40. For example, Harriet Jacobs recounts learning to read. See "Harriet A. Jacobs (Harriet Ann), 1813–1897," *Documenting the American South*, docsouth.unc.edu/fpn/jacobs/bio.html. See, too, the life story of the first African American novelist, Hannah Bonds, who was from North Carolina. See Gregg A. Hecimovich, *The Life and Times of Hannah Crafts: The True Story of The Bondwoman's Narrative* (New York: Ecco, 2023).

41. In 1842 the African School of Halifax, the sister city to Saint John, located in Nova Scotia, claimed that "a great majority of the students were adults." It seems plausible to imagine a similar situation may have existed in Saint John in the 1850s although the historical record is scant. "Petition of the Reverend Robert Willis, D.D., Rector of St. Paul's church on behalf of the Coloured People of Halifax," *Looking Back, Moving Forward: Documenting the Heritage of African Nova Scotians*, Nova Scotia Archives, RG 1, vol. 296, no. 48, archives.novascotia.ca/african-heritage/archives.

42. "Black Loyalists in New Brunswick | Discover Saint John," www.discoversaintjohn.com/black-loyalists-new-brunswick.Cookie Policy

43. *A Register of Voters, for the Purposes of the Elections of Mayor, Aldermen, Councillors, and Constables, of the City of Saint John* (Saint John, N.B.: Henry Chubb & Co., 1859). Jackson's entry is on page 51.

44. Thomas H. Jones, *The Experience of Rev. Thomas H. Jones*, in *From Bondage to Belonging: The Worcester Slave Narratives*, eds. Eugene B. McCarthy, Thomas L. Doughton, and John Stauffer (Amherst: University of Massachusetts Press, 2007), 120–159.

45. There is a John Jackson also listed as receiving assistance from the Boston Vigilance Committee for escape. That name is listed under the 1857 heading, which would not fit with the timeline for John Andrew Jackson as we know it. Moreover, John Andrew Jackson didn't depart from Boston, but departed from Salem, it is more likely the Jackson listed as receiving assistance from the Boston Vigilance Committee in 1857 was an entirely different freedom seeker.

46. R.J.M. Blackett, *The Captive's Quest for Freedom: Fugitive Slaves, the 1850 Fugitive Slave Law, and the Politics of Slavery*. Slaveries Since Emancipation (New York: Cambridge University Press, 2018), 71, doi.org/10.1017/9781108275439.

47. Records from February 7, 1851, indicate that a man named Charles Mahony received $5 in reimbursement for passage fee to Sparrow. Francis Jackson, *Account Book of Francis*

Jackson, Vigilance Committee of Boston Papers, primary research, primaryresearch.org/account-book-of-francis-jackson.

48. *A Register of Voters, for the Purposes of the Elections of Mayor, Aldermen, Councillors, and Constables, of the City of Saint John*, 51.

49. See "Slavery," *Cambridge Independent Press*, January 28, 1865, 7. Jackson reports working at painting during the summer months, and he may have done so under the employment of Sparrow. Sparrow came to be a leading figure in the city through the 1870s. He lost his property, possibly two buildings, in the great Saint John fire of 1877, and then appears thereafter to have moved back down to the United States. He shows up in the Hartford, CT, census in 1880, and, what with Jackson traveling up and down between New Haven, CT, and Springfield, MA, during this time, and regularly passing through Hartford, we can imagine that he and Jackson met again. "Cornelius Sparrow," 1880 United States Federal Census, Hartford, Connecticut, roll 97, 74A, Ancestry.com.

I surveyed hundreds of pages of advertisements in Saint John's *Morning News* between 1850–1856 and rarely saw anything like an advertisement for painting placed by other individuals or businesses. Thus, while there were likely other painters in Saint John, Sparrow's whitewashing business was a prominent one.

50. Winks, 174.

51. Prices for cross-Atlantic ship passage tickets varied tremendously, but advertised prices from Halifax to Liverpool in 1849 suggest that tickets could range from six to twenty guineas. A guinea would have equaled about one pound and one shilling in British currency at that time. See "Ship Passage Fares and Railway Fares," The Ships List, www.theshipslist.com/ships/fares/costofpassage.

52. Barbara McCaskill, *Love, Liberation, and Escaping Slavery: William and Ellen Craft in Cultural Memory* (Athens, GA: University of Georgia Press, 2015), 52–53; David W. Blight, *Frederick Douglass: Prophet of Freedom* (New York: Simon & Schuster, 2018), 140–141.

53. "Cost of Passage—Ship Fares," www.theshipslist.com/ships/fares/costofpassage.

54. For information about Douglass's problems on his trip and the official Cunard apology, see Stephen R. Fox, *The Ocean Railway: Isambard Kingdom Brunel, Samuel Cunard and the Revolutionary World of the Great Atlantic Steamships* (London: Harper Perennial, 2004), 200. For information about the number of steerage tickets available on a Cunard steamer see page 172.

55. This letter from Higbee and Gilmer is reproduced at the end of Jackson's book, 125.

56. Ibid.

57. Cochrane, as quoted in Jackson, 125.

58. Fessenden as quoted by Jackson, 125.

59. Reynolds, 128.

60. In the archival collections of Stowe's papers, there is no record of any exchange between Jackson and Stowe in 1856 prior to the letter. However, the volume of correspondence she kept up vastly outnumbers the number of letters that exist for her, so there

is really no way to assess the exchange aside from the testimony of the clergy who saw her replies. Since the mention of her letter is included in endorsements reproduced at the end of Jackson's memoir, but the actual letter isn't reproduced, it appears that sometime between 1856 and 1862 it was mislaid.

61. "Lecture on Slavery," *Fife Herald*, February 5, 1857. This article notes that "Mr. Jackson had testimonials from Mrs. Stowe, the Lord Provost of Edinburgh, Mr. Duncan Maclaren, and others." The letter from the Lord Provost and Mr. Duncan Maclaren would have been obtained after he visited Scotland, but the Stowe letter would doubtless have been obtained before leaving Canada.

62. Both letters are quoted in Jackson, 124.

63. Jackson reportedly arrived in Liverpool on October 18, 1856, according to a report he gave to the *Stirling Observer* on April 16, 1857. The *Canada* left Halifax on the eighth of October and arrived on Saturday evening the eighteenth according to "America," *Liverpool Mercury*, October 20, 1856, 2. This means the ship called the *America* carried this report of the *Canada*'s arrival. See also the *Stirling Observer*, "An American Fugitive Slave." April 16, 1857.

64. *Liverpool Mercury*, October 20, 1856.

Chapter 7

1. The book lists the year of 1862 on it and the copyright claim is also registered in 1862. It probably came out toward the end of that year since the book does have a note at the very end that suggests it was published after the September 22 preliminary declaration of the Emancipation Proclamation (that would take effect on January 1 of the following year). The note read: "I am happy to say, that since writing the foregoing, President Lincoln has issued his proclamation, that 'On January 1st 1863, all slaves within any State or part of a State, the people whereof shall then be in rebellion against the Federal Government, shall be then, thenceforward, and for ever *free*'—J.A.J." John Andrew Jackson, *The Experience of a Slave in South Carolina* (London: Passmore & Alabaster, 1862), 126.

2. This key image was for his book, published in England in 1862. The image was also re-created for use in one of his pamphlets. When Jackson returned to the United States in 1865, he had a broadside designed that shared a very similar image. See John Andrew Jackson, *John Andrew Jackson, a colored teacher*, 1865, broadside poster, Salem, MA. This broadside suggests Jackson had a copy of the British book in his possession or at least a copy of one of his pamphlets and asked a Massachusetts artist to reproduce the title page image as carefully as possible.

3. "America," *Liverpool Mercury*, October 20, 1856.

4. William Makepeace Thackeray, quoted in Stephen R. Fox, *The Ocean Railway: Isambard Kingdom Brunel, Samuel Cunard and the Revolutionary World of the Great Atlantic Steamships* (London: Harper Perennial, 2004), 220. Remarkably, in 1853, Harriet Beecher Stowe had also traveled across the Atlantic on the *Canada*. See Hedrick, 233.

5. "Canada, Cunard Line." Norway Heritage, accessed May 4, 2022, www.norwayheritage.com.

6. For information about steam whistles on the 1850s Cunard steamer ships, see Fox, 223.

7. The 1851 British Census reported 375,955 people living in Liverpool and the 1861 Census reported 443,938 inhabitants, therefore it seems reasonable to estimate that in 1856 there would have been about 400,000 citizens. *Census of England and Wales for the Year 1861: Population Tables,* London, vol. 1, 1862, archive.org/details. See "An American Fugitive Slave," *Stirling Observer*, April 16, 1857, 3.

8. "John Hawkins Simpson. Horrors of the Virginian Slave Trade and of the Slave-Rearing Plantations. The True Story of Dinah, an Escaped Virginian Slave, Now in London, on Whose Body Are Eleven Scars Left by Tortures Which Were Inflicted by Her Master, Her Own Father. Together with Extracts from the Laws of Virginia, Showing That Against These Barbarities the Law Gives Not the Smallest Protection to the Slave, But the Reverse," docsouth.unc.edu/neh/simpson/simpson, page 58.

9. "Cotton Exchange," Liverpool Records Office, National Museums Liverpool, www.liverpoolmuseums.org.uk/city-built-cotton.

10. "Ida B. Wells Abroad. The Nemesis of Southern Lynchers Again in England," *Inter Ocean* (Chicago, IL) 02, April 1894, 12.

11. "Embassy of the Confederacy: 19 Abercromby Square," Liverpool's Abercromby Square and the Confederacy During the U.S. Civil War, Lowcountry Digital History Initiative, ldhi.library.cofc.edu/exhibits/show/liverpools-abercromby-square/abercromby-southern-club/embassy-confederacy.

12. McCaskill, 55–56.

13. Ezra Greenspan, *William Wells Brown: An African American Life* (New York: Norton, 2014), 207.

14. The Gilder Lehrman Center for the Study of Slavery, Resistance, and Abolition. "Letter to the Editor of the London Times (April 3, 1847)," glc.yale.edu/letter-editor-london-times-april-3-1847.

15. "Laurences Temperance Hotel, Clayton Square," Liverpool History Society, August 24, 2010, liverpoolhistorysocietyquestions.wordpress.com.

16. In 1865 Jackson mentions a Reverend Mr. Barker of Huddersfield who introduced him to Reverend Charles H. Spurgeon in London. Since Huddersfield isn't that far from Liverpool (approximately sixty miles), it is possible Barker might have been one of Jackson's early British friends if not someone who necessarily met with him in Liverpool.

17. In 1856, the *Dumfries and Galloway Standard Advertiser*, for example, reported on one of Jackson's earliest talks and then added a note that "the lecturer would give another address in the Independent Chapel tomorrow evening." I haven't included that kind of event in my list because I am not sure if these talks actually happened. However, since many of his talks likely were not covered by papers, and many advertisements for his talks are probably still unknown, I suspect we could, with some confidence, double

the number from fifteen to thirty or so talks he likely delivered during just this first year. "Lecture by a Runaway Slave," *Dumfries and Galloway Standard Advertiser*, December 3, 1856.

18. Jackson, 125.

19. Jeffrey Green has an excellent chapter on how various Black charlatans were successful and unsuccessful in running their grifts in the British Isles. Unfortunately, frauds tainted the entire class of Black lecturers and, when coupled with general racist beliefs about the inherent duplicitous nature of Black people, the lecturers who did speak from their own lived experience suffered from mistrust, attacks, and genuine danger from crowd violence. See Jeffrey Green, *Black Americans in Victorian Britain* (Barnsley: Pen & Sword, 2018), 57–72.

20. Established white philanthropic circles were not vague about the standards they expected Black people to acquiesce to. The *Temperance Chronicle* in 1852, for example, advised that "persons representing themselves as fugitive slaves" should "be required to produce introductory certificates from well-known friends of the anti-slavery cause, and all collections made on their behalf should be forwarded to some person in Great Britain or Ireland who is willing to act as a trustee. . . ." That wasn't enough, though; the article continued that the role of the trustee "would be in part to make sure no more than the exact necessary sum was solicited" (who might establish that number is unsaid, but it wasn't likely the Black speaker in this bit of advice). The quote from the *Temperance Chronicle* is in Green, 59.

21. See "A person of the name of Jackson," *Nottinghamshire Guardian*, December 9, 1858, 5, which notes that his bills are being plastered around town.

22. *Preston Guardian*, November 1, 1856.

23. "Lecture by a Runaway Slave," *Dumfries and Galloway Standard Advertiser*, December 3, 1856.

24. "Lecture on Slavery," *Ashton and Stalybridge Reporter*, April 24, 1858.

25. For a rich study of how author lecture tours in the Victorian era created paradoxes for their speakers, see all of Amanda Adams's book *Performing Authorship in the Nineteenth-Century Transatlantic Lecture Tour*, but especially pp. 10–11.

26. Audrey Fisch has a helpful discussion concerning Sarah Remond from Salem, Massachusetts, who came to England in 1859 to speak against slavery. Fisch asserts that the presence of a woman on a public stage was itself a novelty gimmick, which even when coded as genteel could undermine as much as amplify the woman's message; Fisch's analysis informs my reading of Julia Jackson here. See Audrey Fisch, *American Slaves in Victorian England: Abolitionist Politics in Popular Literature and Culture* (Cambridge: Cambridge University Press, 2000), 83–90.

27. Ibid., 53.

28. "On Tuesday Evening," *Kentish Gazette*, August 21, 1860, 5.

29. "Slavery," *Reading Mercury*, March 23, 1861, 4.

30. "Slavery," *Western Times*, January 30, 1863, 5.

31. In Murray's comprehensive study of Black American lecturers in the British Isles, *Advocates of Freedom: African American Transatlantic Abolitionism in the British Isles*, she claims, persuasively, that Julia Jackson was "possibly the first African American woman to speak publicly on a British stage about her experiences as an enslaved individual, which radically alters our perception of Black female transatlantic activism." See Murray, 25.

32. "Bonneting a Black Man," *Illustrated Times*, May 13, 1865, 303.

33. See Adams, 2–13, and Murray, 13.

34. HBS to "Dear Sister" [Catharine Beecher], n.d. (1850 or 1851), Beecher Family Papers, Sterling Memorial Library, Yale University.

35. "Slavery in America," *Islington Gazette*, November 5, 1859, 2.

36. "Black Lectures," *Dundee Courier and Argus*, June 15, 1864.

37. Houston A. Baker Jr., *Workings of the Spirit: The Poetics of Afro-American Women's Writing* (Chicago: University of Chicago Press, 1991), 13.

38. See Jeffrey Ruggles, *The Unboxing of Henry Brown* (Richmond: Library of Virginia, 2003).

39. Murray, 84. Douglass didn't continue to do this, perhaps because he found it undignified. See Murray, *Frederick Douglass in Britain and Ireland, 1845–1895* (Edinburgh, Scotland: Edinburgh University Press, 2021), 12, doi.org/10.1515/9781474460422.

40. Greenspan, 207.

41. Teresa Goddu, *Selling Antislavery: Abolition and Mass Media in Antebellum America* (Philadelphia: University of Pennsylvania Press, 2020). A magic latern was a nineteenth century image projector, and panoramas used by lecturers were often enormous scrolls of pictures to be unrolled slowly or even to encircle an audience.

42. A letter from Stowe is mentioned in: "Lecture on Slavery," *Fife Herald*, February 5, 1857; "An American Fugitive Slave," *Stirling Observer*, April 16, 1857, 3; a testimonial from May 7, 1857, quoted in Jackson, *The Experience of a Slave* (1862), 45; a testimonial from May 18, 1857, quoted in Jackson, *The Experience of a Slave* (1862), 46; "American Slavery," *Paisley Herald*, June 13, 1857, 8; "A Fugitive Slave," *Leicestershire Mercury*, November 6, 1868, 6; "Slavery," *Leicestershire Mercury*, November 27, 1858, 8.

43. "A Runaway Slave," *Fife Herald*, April 23, 1857, 3.

44. Richard Huzzey's book, *Freedom Burning*, insightfully parses how a nation so consumed by *Uncle Tom's Cabin* could be so unclear about its response to the American Civil War, in chapter 2, titled "Uncle Tom's Britain." See Richard Huzzey, *Freedom Burning: Anti-Slavery and Empire in Victorian Britain* (Ithaca: Cornell University Press, 2012), 21–39. See also Fisch in her chapter "Exhibiting Uncle Tom in some shape or other: the commercialization and reception of *Uncle Tom's Cabin* in England," in her book, *American Slaves in Victorian England*, 11–32.

45. "Lecture on Slavery," *Fife Herald*, February 5, 1857.

46. Jackson, *The Experience of a Slave* (1862), 97–99.

47. "Lecture on Slavery," *Cambridge Chronicle and University Journal*, February 26, 1859, 5.

48. "The Slave's Flight," *Surrey Comet*, April 28, 1860.

49. "Lecture," *Cambridge Chronicle and University Journal*, February 12, 1859.

50. Sarah Meer, "Public and Personal Letters: Julia Griffiths and Frederick Douglass' Papers," *Slavery & Abolition* 33, no. 2 (2012): 251–264. Her reference to twenty antislavery societies is on page 253.

51. Jackson, *The Experience of a Slave* (1862), 124–125.

52. Ibid., 46.

53. "Slave Schedules for Elizabeth English," 1860 United States Census, Sumter County, SC, August 6, 1860, M653, 49, Ancestry.com. One Black man of forty-three years of age is listed as a "fugitive from the State" according to Elizabeth English's schedule.

Elizabeth English certainly died in March 1860 (as her gravestone makes clear), and her estate was being sorted out for the next few months. While the slave schedule has the month and date of August 1860 listed at the top, it seems probable that her son, Thomas Reese English, who was executor of her will, provided the information for this final assessment. Since he had been the person to place the original runaway advertisement for Jackson, he, out of any member of the family, would have been the most likely to still be keeping track of Jackson and noting his absence on behalf of his mother's estate, even fourteen years after the escape. It is notable, too, that the census similarly (and confusingly) reports her alive in August 1860, suggesting that a lot of the data from Sumter County that year might well have been collected a few months before it was actually filed. See https://www.findagrave.com/memorial/60442005/elizabeth-english (memorial page for Elizabeth Wilson English, 13 Jun 1779–20 Mar 1860, Find a Grave Memorial ID 60442005, citing Salem Black River Cemetery, Mayesville, Sumter County, South Carolina, USA); "Slave Schedules for Elizabeth English," 1860 United States Census, Sumter County, SC, August 6, 1860, M653, page 49, Ancestry.com; 1860 United States Census, Sumter, Sumter County, South Carolina, roll M653_1227; page: 113, Ancestry.com.

54. In *Performing Authorship in the Nineteenth-Century*, Adams explains how Frederick Douglass repeatedly invoked bloodhounds on his lecture tour to remind the public of the risk and also what she imagines as the "dramatic opportunity" of standing up in front of an audience to speak when one is a fugitive. I have borrowed this notion to see how it plays out with Jackson. Adams, 26.

55. See J.C. Carlile, *C.H. Spurgeon: An Interpretative Biography* (London: Religious Tract Society and Kingsgate Press, 1934), 159–160, for a version of this encounter with Jackson. Also see G. Holden Pike, *The Life and Work of Charles Haddon Spurgeon*, vol. 11 (London: Cassell & Co., 1892), 323–325.

56. The "burst of applause" is from an article in the *Christian Cabinet*, December 14, 1849.

57. Ibid.

58. "Spurgeon's Sermons—a Bonfire," *Nashville Patriot*, March 15, 1860; see also Pike, 330–334.

59. For a solid summary of the events surrounding the burning of Spurgeon's sermons, see "The Reason Why America Burned Spurgeon's Sermons and Sought to Kill Him," The Spurgeon Center, September 22, 2016, www.spurgeon.org/resource-library/blog-entries.

60. Washington Duff seems to have traveled with two other fugitives from Canada: Jesse Howell and a man named Jackson, probably in 1852 or so. Evidence suggests it was a Benjamin Jackson that Duff traveled with (not John Andrew Jackson), although overlapping dates and events suggest that John Andrew Jackson and Washington Duff came to know one another once in England. See "Slavery" in the *Cambridge Independent Press*, January 28, 1865, 7, See *"American Slavery,"* Borough of Marylebone Mercury, *1865(?)*, for an article that mentions both Benjamin Jackson and John Andrew Jackson—with John Andrew Jackson in the audience of Duff's talk and noting that he (J.A. Jackson) would deliver a talk in another venue about slavery in South Carolina.

61. According to a letter published in 1864, Jackson acknowledges that he has been working as a whitewasher to support himself. "Slavery in America," *Dundee Courier and Argus*, June 28, 1864.

62. England Census, www.ancestry.com/search/collections.

63. Arts, Princeton University, September 7, 2016, graphicarts.princeton.edu.

64. "A Fugitive Slave Assaulted," *South London Chronicle*, October 10, 1863.

65. R.J.M. Blackett writes that slave narratives "sold faster than they could be printed." He also argues that, as customary at the time, these narratives were read aloud, borrowed, shared, and circulated in ways beyond mere initial sales might suggest. R.J.M. Blackett, *Building an Antislavery Wall: Black Americans in the Atlantic Abolitionist Movement: 1830–1860* (Baton Rouge: Louisiana State University Press, 1983), 25–26.

66. "Preface" by W.M.S. in Jackson, pages 87 and 88.

67. "American Slavery," *Paisley Herald*, June 13, 1857, 8.

68. Ibid.

69. The registration of *The Experience of a Slave in South Carolina* appears in a National Archives reference text, *Index to Registers: 1842–1864,* 98.

70. Frederick Douglass, *Narrative of the Life of Frederick Douglass, an American Slave* (Dublin: Webb and Chapter, 1845).

71. Back in 1985, scholar James Olney analyzed the structure of the nineteenth-century slave narrative and identified several characteristics that can be found in most published slave narratives of the nineteenth century. Some of these characteristics include: the title page integrating the claim as an integral part of the title, a handful of testimonials, a poetic epigraph, an opening with a place rather than a date of birth, and a sketchy account of parentage, among other characteristics. I touch on several of these characteristics here in my discussion of Jackson, who does hew closely to these patterns. For full information from the authoritative work of Olney on this matter, see James Olney, "'I was born': Slave

Narratives, Their Status as Autobiography and as Literature" in *The Slave's Narrative,* eds. Charles T. Davis and Henry Louis Gates Jr., 2nd ed. (Oxford: Oxford University Press, 1995), 152–153.

72. Jackson, *The Experience of a Slave* (1862), 109.

73. Ibid., 106.

74. Ibid., 118.

75. Ibid., 113.

76. Ibid., 101.

77. The closing chapter of Jackson's memoir, titled "Slave Songs," responds to the interest of his British audiences in Black music. Expectations they held about how Black people were intrinsically musical certainly arose from racial stereotypes, which was something he could capitalize on. While white enslavers had long demanded enslaved people perform for them, that didn't mean that the music or dancing enslaved people did for themselves wasn't nonetheless filled with meaning on their terms. The resistant power of these songs was something Jackson recognized as worth sharing, but he felt a need to add elucidating commentary. There wasn't much precedent for this. In 1848, William Wells Brown, the formidable fugitive author and lecturer, published an antislavery songbook, *The Anti-Slavery Harp.* Still, it was just that: a simple songbook without commentary or analysis. Earlier publications by white men such as George Clark (who published an antislavery song collection titled *The Liberty Minstrel*) also shared antislavery and slave songs without close readings, as Jackson does. William Wells Brown's *The Anti-Slavery Harp* features several songs precisely replicated in Jackson's book, such as "Flight of the Bondman" and "The Bereaved Mother." Jackson, his publishers, or his friends likely had a copy of the Brown songbook on hand. Some of these songs in Jackson's book also appeared in the 1844 *Liberty Minstrel,* a songbook that includes the music and lyrics. Lyrics to many of these songs were broadly circulated in all sorts of informal ways at this time, so it is hard to say exactly what Jackson's source was. Nonetheless, neither of these well-known collections circulating in the United States and England at that time interpreted and parsed the lyrics as Jackson does, which makes his final chapter unique. See William Wells Brown, *The Anti-Slavery Harp* (Boston: Bela Marsh, 1848); George Clark, *The Liberty Minstrel* (New York: Leavitt & Alden, 1844); Nancy L. Graham, *They Bear Acquaintance: African American Spirituals and the Camp Meetings* (Bern: Peter Lang, 2016); Nikki Giovanni, *On My Journey Now: Looking at African-American History Through the Spirituals* (Cambridge: Candlewick Press, 2007).

78. For an imaginative approach to the breadth of the development and legacy of the music of enslaved people, see Shane White, *The Sounds of Slavery: Discovering African American History through Songs, Sermons, and Speech* (Boston: Beacon Press, 2005).

79. Jackson, *The Experience of a Slave* (1862), 117.

80. Ibid., 115.

81. Jackson specifically mentions that the Hutchinson singers had sung "Flight of the Bondman," a song dedicated to William Wells Brown, a prominent self-emancipated man who had become a lecturer, activist, and author quite well known by the mid–

nineteenth century. Author to his own bestselling life story, *Narrative of William W. Brown, a Fugitive Slave, Written by Himself*, Brown had escaped from bondage in 1834. Probably second only in prominence to Frederick Douglass in terms of being a Black American abolitionist author, Brown lived in England between 1849 and 1854. Thus, he was well known in antislavery circles in Britain and Europe. The best study of Brown is the inestimable biography written by Ezra Greenspan, *William Wells Brown: An African American Life*. Jackson, *The Experience of a Slave* (1862), 119.

82. See chapter 5 of this book for a discussion of "Dearest Mae." Stowe likely knew that song before Jackson hid with her but there is also a hint in her phrasing suggesting that he may have sung or performed it for her children during his stay. Of course, her use of it in her letter also indicates she assumed her sister, Catharine Beecher, would also have been familiar with the tune.

83. Jackson, *The Experience of a Slave* (1862), 122.

84. As noted in chapter 6, it appears that Jackson had lost the Stowe letter by this moment of publication in 1862. Otherwise, surely he would have included it. Another possibility is that perhaps her letter had had some sort of request that he not use it publicly but only use it only as a private character reference.

85. "Slavery," *Western Times*, January 30, 1863.

86. Jackson, *The Experience of a Slave* (1862), 123.

87. As of 2022, WorldCat, the global database for catalog collections, indicates only eight copies held at various institutions, with seven of those in the United States and one in Cambridge, England. It is possible others are out there in private hands or in libraries that haven't cataloged it or shared their catalogs with WorldCat, but it's clear there aren't many extant volumes around and there likely were not that many in the first place.

88. In the introduction to their book, Lara Langer Cohen and Jordan Stein describe how print is a particular technology, but print culture was a broader concept of all sorts of practices that African Americans could explore, exploit, and experience. Jackson, of course, wanted control of both the technology and the culture. See Cohen and Stein, "Introduction," in *Early African American Print Culture* (Philadelphia: University of Pennsylvania Press, 2012), 1–16.

Chapter 8

1. John Andrew Jackson and William Goodell, *Spurgeon and Jackson, or, The white preacher and the black slave lecturer* [England?]: [publisher not identified], 1865?].

2. "Spurgeon and Jackson, or, the White Preacher and the Black Slave Lecturer," pamphlet, in *Bibliotheca Americana: A Dictionary of Books Relating to America*, ed. Joseph Sabin, located at the New York Public Library, New York, NY.

3. This is from an article quoted by the *Morning Post*, October 7, 1861.

4. In the town of Saltaire, for instance, Jackson attended what was simply called an "Anti-Slavery Meeting." There he got caught up in their group's governance and resolutions. For example, he went on the record as supporting one of their motions to protest "aid

rendered to the slave power," both in the form of government loans and in the "building of war vessels" for the Confederacy. "Saltaire: Anti-Slavery Meeting," *Bradford Observer*, March 26, 1863.

5. "Meeting on the American War," *Cheshire Observer*, April 25, 1863.

6. "To the Editor," *Bury Times*, May 30, 1863.

7. "A Fugitive Slave Assaulted," *South London Chronicle*, October 10, 1863.

8. "Lectures on Slavery," *Dundee Advertiser*, May 27, 1864.

9. *The Post Office Dundee Directory Including Lochee and Broughty Ferry for 1864–65; Comprising Among Other Information Public Offices and Postal Directory, General Directory, Street Directory, Trades and Professions Directory* (Dundee: James P. Matthew & Co., Meadowside, 1864), 269–270.

10. Jacob Stroyer, *My Life in the South*, in *I Belong to South Carolina: South Carolina Slave Narratives*, ed. Ashton, 135. Of his clothing while enslaved, Jackson recalls "Our clothes were rags, and we were all half naked" in his *The Experience of a Slave in South Carolina* (1862), 22.

11. In one newspaper account there is a reference to him as "Davison," but the majority of newspaper articles, including those about court proceedings, spell his name as "Davidson." "The Rev. Isaac W. Davison," *People's Journal*, May 28, 1864.

12. "A Black Squabble," *Glasgow Saturday Post*, quoted from *Dundee Courier*, June 25, 1864.

13. Ibid.

14. Was Davidson an impostor? Could he have been feigning that he had been a slave in Fredericksburg, Virginia, and could Jackson have sussed this out? In the court case, Davidson provided positive testimonials from Jas. Smith, the U.S. consul in Dundee, who also shared a good account from W.L. Underwood, the U.S. consul at Glasgow who was a native of Fredericksburg, Virginia, and aquainted with the former enslaver of Davidson. Evidence suggests that Jackson was either mistaken in accusing Davidson of not have survived slavery or Jackson was intentionally challenging that claim for reasons of his own. It also seems conceivable that Davidson had been emancipated as part of the American Colonization Society's efforts to send Black missionaries abroad and thus Jackson felt that Davidson's experience in slavery and emancipation was so unlike his own that it didn't amount to "slavery" as he knew it. That, however, is just speculation. See the full report in the *Dundee Advertiser*, "Tuesday, June 28—Before Sheriff Ogilvy. The Coloured Preachers—Davidson v. Jackson," July 1, 1864.

15. "A Black Squabble," *Glasgow Saturday Post*, quoted from *Dundee Courier*, June 25, 1864.

16. This may be a reference to a nonsense poem often attributed to Tennyson but really of unknown origin. The poem's original publication is "Timbuctoo," *Punch*, February 22, 1868. For information and theories on authorship of this poem, see Marco Graziosi, "Cassowary vs. Missionary," *Edward Lear and Nonsense Literature*, nonsenselit.com/2009/08/22/cassowary-vs-missionary. The *Dundee Courier* evidently found this entire situation

so entertaining that in January 1867, two years after Jackson had returned to the United States, it published a recap of the incident in "A Negro Preacher Story-Telling," which was then reprinted in the *Liverpool Mercury*, the *Leeds Times*, and the *Shields Gazette and Daily Telegraph* among other papers.

17. In "Letters to the Editor," *Dundee Courier and Argus*, June 30, 1864. Gilfillan asserts that Jackson and Davidson are separate people.

18. "Mr. J.A. Jackson's Meeting," *Dundee Advertiser*, June 21, 1864.

19. Ibid.

20. "To the Editor," *Dundee Advertiser*, June 17, 1864.

21. "Mr. J.A. Jackson's Meeting," *Dundee Advertiser*, June 21, 1864.

22. "Slavery in America," *Dundee Courier and Argus*, June 28, 1864.

23. Richard Blackett, quoted in Green, 139.

24. Jackson had used a different printer for a flyer he had made up, probably at this time after his relationship with Spurgeon had deteriorated. It was quite likely this printer in Southampton who helped him create the flyer helped him produce the pamphlet against Spurgeon. The flyer featured an image of Jackson on a horse, similar but not identical to the more detailed one used for his 1862 memoir. He likely showed another artist a copy of his book to see the image and commissioned him create a similar one. After all, he could hardly have any more of his books printed up by Passmore and Alabaster, Spurgeon's press. And they would have certainly held the plates. Jackson's flyer was a modest four pages and was not a narrative of his life. It included only a few personalized caption sentences on the front summarizing his experiences and instead spent most of its space with excerpts from a lengthy listing of Southern slave laws from a book called *The Slave Code* (1853), originally assembled by American abolitionist William Goddell. Notably, Goddell was an American author who hadn't been on British soil when his book was published, so he didn't hold any copyright—if a listing of such laws might have been deemed worthy or even eligible for copyright. This text was effectively free to pilfer (although it is hard to imagine Goddell would have much minded). Henry Watson, Sojourner Truth, Henry Box Brown, and William Wells Brown all similarly reprinted extracts of American slave codes and incorporated them into appendices for their narratives. It was common to frame one's own life story of enslaved experience with a compendium of the dehumanizing laws that could provide proper context for apprehending that life story. It wasn't dissimilar from what Stowe had done after publishing *Uncle Tom's Cabin* and following it up with a companion book for her novel titled *A Key to Uncle Tom's Cabin*. See Goddell, 79. The key point here, though, is that Jackson had made connections with another printer.

25. "Spurgeon and Jackson."

26. "History of the Tabernacle," Metropolitan Tabernacle, metropolitantabernacle.org/history.

27. "Spurgeon and Jackson."

28. This particular article was actually from 1867, long after Jackson had returned to the United States. "A Negro-Preacher Story-Telling," *Dundee Courier and Argus*, January 28, 1867.

29. Ibid.

30. "Spurgeon and Jackson, or the White Preacher and the Black Slave Lecturer," *Cambridge Chronicle and University Journal*, May 27, 1865. (Note that this title is the same as that of Jackson's pamphlet, which the Cambridge article references, but the pamphlet itself was not published within the *Cambridge Chronicle and University Journal.*) "Assault on a Negro Preacher," *Dundee Advertise*r, May 12, 1865.

31. Jackson is described as "a powerful man, of exceedingly dark color" in "Assault on a Negro Preacher," *Dundee Advertiser*, May 12, 1865.

32. Leonne M. Hudson, "The Role of the 54th Massachusetts Regiment in Potter's Raid," *Historical Journal of Massachusetts* 29, no. 2 (2002). See also Allan D. Thigpen, *The Illustrated Recollections of Potter's Raid, April 5–21, 1865*, rev. ed. (Sumter, SC: A.D. Thigpen, 1998).

33. Thigpen, 369.

Chapter 9

1. Letters with similar handwriting written by Jackson that are dated June 25, 1867, and August 9, 1867, can be found in this same collection, as well as letters in the Bowdoin College collection that present similar signatures.

2. The best rundown of how the Freedman's Bureau worked in South Carolina is by Martin Abbott. In this study, while he chronicles the official ways the bureau functioned, he also demonstrates how the bureau's somewhat less organized mission became to coordinate missionaries, volunteer groups, and other less official partners or hangers-on. Martin Abbott, *The Freedmen's Bureau in South Carolina, 1865–1872* (Chapel Hill: University of North Carolina Press, 1967).

3. Another nickname for Howard, both admiring and derisive, was the "Christian General." See William S. McFeely, *Yankee Stepfather: General O.O. Howard and the Freedmen* (New York: Norton, 1970), 15.

4. A thorough overview of this audacious enterprise can be found in Christopher Clark, *The Radical Challenge of the Northampton Association* (Ithaca: Cornell University Press, 1995). Although he first would have gone through the Florence and Northampton area in 1849–1850, Jackson evidently returned to Florence for some period in 1880 and did farming there, so his ties were long-standing. See "Mr. John Andrew Jackson," *Buffalo Daily Courier* (Buffalo, NY), August 31, 1881, which notes that Jackson "has been farming in Florence, Mass., during the last season."

5. Tunis Campbell as quoted by Elizabeth Rauh Bethel in *Promiseland: A Century of Life in a Negro Community* (Philadelphia: Temple University Press, 1981), 7. Tunis Campbell was a significant political figure in Black activism in Georgia. See Russell

Duncan, "Tunis Campbell," *New Georgia Encyclopedia*, www.georgiaencyclopedia.org/articles/arts-culture/tunis-campbell-1812-1891.

6. Elizabeth Rauh Bethel, *Promiseland, a Century of Life in a Negro Community.* (Philadelphia: Temple University Press, 1981).

7. See J.C.A. Stagg, "The Problem of Klan Violence: The South Carolina Up-Country, 1868–1871," *Journal of American Studies* 8, no. 3 (1974): 303–318, doi.org/10.1017/S0021875800015905.

8. Waters McIntosh was born in Lynchburg, and although he was much younger than Jackson, his recollections about life in the immediate aftermath of the Civil War and how the KKK terrorized Black people for generations are consistent with other observations about how the KKK operated there and how, in particular, the KKK menaced Black men of any prominence. McIntosh was interviewed in the 1930s when living in Arkansas, so while his reminiscences are about the South Carolina of his youth, his narrative is classified among those of people interviewed in Arkansas. His narrative can be read in full here: Waters McIntosh, "Born in Slavery: Slave Narratives from the Federal Writers' Project, 1936–1938: Arkansas Narratives," vol. II, part 5, gutenburg.org/files.

9. Jane Briggs Smith to William Fuller Fiske, 5 July 1867, American Antiquarian Society.

10. "Outrage at Lynchburg," *Charleston Advocate* (Charleston, SC), May 11, 1867.

11. This is noted in the same volume including Jackson's letter: John Andrew Jackson to Major General O.O. Howard, 10 March 1868, Freedmen's Bureau Digital Collection, National Museum of African American History and Culture, Smithsonian Institution.

12. Henry Foreman's wife, Almira Foreman, died in 1857; Henry Foreman died in January 1865. "Almira Foreman," Massachusetts, U.S., Town and Vital Records, 1620–1988, Ancestry.com, www.ancestrylibrary.com.

13. John Andrew Jackson to Major Gen. Howard, 4 September 1881, Oliver Otis Howard Papers, George J. Mitchell Department of Special Collections and Archives, Bowdoin College Library, Brunswick, Maine.

14. *Union and Advertiser* interview from 1893.

15. H. Haynsworth, "Refuge from Oppression," *Liberator* (Boston, MA), July 12, 1850. As discussed in chapter 1, whether or not Enoch and Louisa considered themselves married cannot be known since they were forced to marry by their enslavers. See also Sumter County, South Carolina, Deed Registry Book: Jared Law to Thomas Wells, June 7, 1851 (146).

16. "Jared Laws," 1850 United States Census, Sumter, Sumter County, South Carolina, roll 850, 417a, Ancestry.com.

17. John Andrew Jackson to Major General Howard, 24 December 1865, Freedmen's Bureau Digital Collection, National Museum of African American History and Culture, Smithsonian Institution.

18. Worcester, MA, the home of the Chase family, was about fifty miles away but was connected easily by rail. Lucy Chase (1822–1909) wouldn't have been in Worcester at

this time because she and her sister volunteered to work first in "contraband" camps for enslaved people who had been emancipated by or had emancipated themselves with the arrival of Union armies during the war. The sisters then went on to serve as teachers of the freed people in Virginia. Lucia Z. Knoles, "Lucy and Sarah Chase as Freedmen's Teachers," American Antiquarian Society, www.americanantiquarian.org/Freedmen/Intros/chaseduring.

19. Long known as a nexus for abolitionist activity and Underground Railroad work, St. John Congregational Church is also known for having been a church where abolitionist radical John Brown had worshipped.

20. "Mr. John Andrew Jackson," *Springfield Republican* (Springfield, MA), June 6, 1866.

21. "Gifts of clothing," *Springfield Republican* (Springfield, MA), May 11, 1869.

22. A list of signatures of Springfield supporters was included in a letter he wrote to O.O. Howard on August 4, 1868. The Rowers Paper Company was also referenced in that same letter.

23. *Boston Daily Evening*, Friday, March 6, 1868, 3.

24. Few Black people of that era had the resources or the security to transact such business that would attract the ire of returning Confederates and their embittered families. One notable exception is the property purchased by Robert Smalls. "The Robert Smalls House," National Park Service, www.nps.gov/places/the-robert-smalls-house.

25. The National Freedmen's Relief Association, located at 76 John Street in New York, was active in collecting supplies for distribution in South Carolina. "The National Freedman's Relief Association," *New York Times*, May 14, 1865.

26. Back in 1856, Jackson had started raising money to liberate his father and the two children of his sister (according to Samuel Fessenden, who noted this fact in 1856 and was later quoted in Jackson's memoir in an endorsement letter at the end). Throughout the 1850s, newspapers in England regularly mentioned that Jackson was raising money to liberate his father (Doctor Clavern) and the two children of his murdered sister (presumably Bella's children). These do not seem to be the same two children he is later trying to help in 1868. Indeed, Bella's children would certainly be adults by 1868. Now he seems to have turned his attention to other children needing help. His brother Ephraim identifies the older girl, Leah, in a letter in which he notes that "Jimmin and Betsy's daughter cannot go to you. . . ."

27. I have not had success in finding the precise identity of these children in the South Carolina census or other archival records. They are obviously some kind of relative to Jackson and Ephraim, although their description of them is a bit inconsistent. Leah is described as "Jimmin and Betsy's daughter" at one point, and it is noted that young Jimmy was a child of mixed race whose father had been his mother's enslaver. Jackson refers to Leah as Julia's "niece" in his letter. John Andrew Jackson to Howard on November 24, 1868. I speculate that Leah is probably Jackson's niece and the daughter of a younger sister, Betsy, and that young Jimmy may be a half brother to Leah, having been fathered by rape by Betsy's enslaver.

28. In a letter from 1868, Jackson noted that Jimmy was a "Mulatto" and "his father was his master." According to Jackson, Jimmy's mother had eight children and could not support them. John Andrew Jackson to O.O. Howard, 10 August 1868, Freedmen's Bureau Digital Collection, National Museum of African American History and Culture, Smithsonian Institution.

29. James T. Lloyd, "Lloyd's American Railroad Map," New York, 1861, Library of Congress, www.loc.gov.

30. John Andrew Jackson to O.O. Howard, 15 July 1868, Freedmen's Bureau Digital Collection, National Museum of African American History and Culture, Smithsonian Institution.

31. Jackson's relationship with Howard seems to have been well known at this point; the *Springfield Republican* wrote, "He has the confidence of General Howard and others at Washington" on February 27, 1867. The *Springfield Republican* was a prominent enough paper that it is unlikely it would have been duped on this point. Jackson knew that bragging about a patron who might not be pleased was a dangerous gambit, and it is unlikely he would have misrepresented his relationship with Howard to the *Springfield Republican*, which, as the leading Republican newspaper in the United States, would have had easy opportunity to sniff out anything misleading about the situation.

32. John Andrew Jackson to O.O. Howard, 25 July 1868, Freedmen's Bureau Digital Collection, National Museum of African American History and Culture, Smithsonian Institution.

33. John Andrew Jackson to O.O. Howard, 4 August 1868, Freedmen's Bureau Digital Collection, National Museum of African American History and Culture, Smithsonian Institution.

34. Quoted in "We Have Heard," *Springfield Republican* (Springfield, MA), July 20, 1870, 8.

35. Andrew Jackson to O.O Howard, 4 August 1868, Freedmen's Bureau Digital Collection, National Museum of African American History and Culture, Smithsonian Institution.

36. Ibid.

37. "The Wife of John Andrew Jackson," *Springfield Republican* (Springfield, MA), October 19, 1868.

38. John Andrew Jackson to O. O. Howard, 24 November 1868, Oliver Otis Howard Papers, George J. Mitchell Department of Special Collections and Archives, Bowdoin College Library, Brunswick, Maine.

39. Ibid.

40. "Northampton State Hospital," Northampton State Hospital, June 21, 2020, northamptonstatehospital.org.

41. David B. Dill, "Pliny Earle's State Hospital at Northampton: Moral Treatment or Peonage?" *Historical Journal of Massachusetts* 20, no. 2 (1992): 143–159.

42. The British 1861 Census that had located them in London didn't ask about literacy. In this 1870 Census, nothing is checked for them in the columns labeled "Cannot Read" and "Cannot Write," although such columns are checked off for other people on the page. "John A. Jackson," 1870 United States Census, New Haven Ward 1, New Haven, Connecticut, roll M593_109, 89a, Ancestry.com.

43. A great introduction to reading census data and understanding how the questions unasked are often as valuable as the questions asked is addressed in *Democracy's Data* by Dan Bouk. While his study focuses on the census of 1940, many of the principles of questioning and interpreting data, particularly regarding race and population clusters, are also helpful when looking at nineteenth-century information. His Introduction and chapter 5, "Silences and White Supremacy," are handy overviews of how creative insights may be drawn from seemingly staid census information. Dan Bouk, *Democracy's Data: The Hidden Stories in the U.S. Census and How to Read Them* (New York: Farrar, Straus and Giroux, 2022).

44. The New Haven 1870 Census shows that, among others, Holloway Blunt and his wife both were Black residents of Winter Street and were born in North Carolina. George and Maria Johnson and their three children were also Black; all were born in North Carolina and reported living on Winter Street in the 1870 Census. Similarly, Samuel and Sarah Smith were Black residents of Winter Street and note they migrated from Delaware, another slave state, although one that did not secede from the Union. "John A. Jackson," 1861 England Census, folio 89, 25, GSU roll 542589, Ancestry.com, www.ancestrylibrary .com; "John A. Jackson," 1870 United States Census, New Haven Ward 1, New Haven, Connecticut, roll M593_109, 89a, Ancestry.com.

45. There is a mention of setting up a freeman's relief group in Robert Austin Warner, *New Haven Negroes, a Social History* (New Haven: Yale University Press, 1940), 149.

46. Elizabeth Mills Brown, "The Winchester Triangle," in *New Haven: A Guide to Architecture and Urban Design* (New Haven: Yale University Press, 1976), 168–169.

47. Rollin G. Osterweis, *Three Centuries of New Haven 1638–1939* (New Haven: Yale University Press, 1953), 343. This cites the *New Haven Register*, July 1, 1869.

48. "One John Andrew Jackson," *Constitution* (Middletown, CT), June 5, 1872, 2.

49. The *Hartford Courant* reports visits in the area in March and November 1870. "John Andrew Jackson," *Hartford Courant* (Hartford, CT), March 19, 1870; "Andrew Jackson," *Hartford Daily Courant* (Hartford, CT), November 19, 1870.

50. Fiona Vernal, "How Hartford's North End Became an African American Community," *Connecticut Explored*, 2022, www.ctexplored.org.

51. "Mr. John Andrew Jackson," *Portland Daily Press* (Portland, ME), December 11, 1871.

52. In the Massachusetts birth record of 1878, John Andrew Jackson and Ella Pooler Jackson are listed as the parents and Jackson's occupation is listed as "Laborer." "Anna Elizabeth Jackson," Massachusetts, United States, Birth Records, 1840–1915, Ancestry .com, www.ancestrylibrary.com/imageviewer/collections.

53. There is no extant evidence of a divorce between Julia and John Andrew Jackson. It seems mostly likely he despaired of her regaining her health and remarried a young girl he had met in South Carolina during one of his visits there.

54. Her death record states that she had "cholera infantum," a common term for any intestinal illness and not necessarily from cholera per se. "Anna E. Jackson," Death record, Massachusetts, United States, Town and Vital Records, 1620–1988, Ancestry .com, www.ancestrylibrary.com.

55. Elizabeth Jackson was born on September 24, 1879. "Elizabeth Jackson," Massachusetts, United States, Birth Records, 1840–1915, Ancestry.com, www.ancestrylibrary .com.

56. It seems likely that Philis McIntosh was a relative of Ella's or Jackson's or at least a friend of Ella's, but there's no specific documentation making this entirely clear one way or the other. The 1880 Census taken in the same month also shows Philis McIntosh living in Lynchburg with her husband. My guess is that these are listing the same individual, and she was visiting up north in Springfield for only a few months to help out Ella and baby Elizabeth. Hence it seems likely that when a census worker in Lynchburg asked who lived at that South Carolina address, her immediate family members probably listed her as a resident with them, assuming her time up in Massachusetts was only temporary.

57. McIntosh was a common surname among many of the intermarried Black families of Lynchburg during the late nineteenth century.

58. "Alexander Anderson," *Springfield Republican* (Springfield, MA), July 8, 1880.

59. "Griffin Ball," 1880 United States Census, Springfield, Hampden, Massachusetts, roll 536, 163B, Ancestry.com, www.ancestrylibrary.com; "John H. Lewis," 1880 United States Census, Springfield, Hampden, Massachusetts, roll 536, 166c, Ancestry.com, www .ancestrylibrary.com.

60. "John Andrew Jackson Writes from Bridgeport, Ct.," *Springfield Republican* (Springfield, MA), April 29, 1881.

61. "A.B. Bush Writes," *Springfield Republican* (Springfield, MA), April 30, 1881.

Chapter 10

1. Jake McLeod. Jake McLeod, interview by Federal Writers' Project: Slave Narrative Project, vol. 14, Library of Congress, www.loc.gov/item/mesn143. First reference is to the McLeod interview and from the *Union and Advertiser* (Rochester, NY), reproduced in John Blassingham, *Slave Testimony: Two Centuries of Letters, Speeches, Interviews, and Autobiographies* (Baton Rouge: Louisiana State University Press, 1977), 513.

2. "Surry Court Adjourned," *Western Sentinel* (Winston-Salem, NC), May 5, 1881; *State vs. John Andrew Jackson*, April 1881, Minutes of the Superior Court, Jackson County, North Carolina, State Archives of North Carolina.

3. Edward L. Ayers, *Vengeance and Justice: Crime and Punishment in the 19th Century American South* (New York: Oxford University Press, 1984), 195.

4. Douglas A. Blackmon, *Slavery by Another Name: The Re-Enslavement of Black People in America from the Civil War to World War* (New York: Doubleday, 2008).

5. Eminent historian and expert on railroad history Roger Grant wrote me a long letter about what Jackson might have experienced while working on the CF&YVRR. H. Roger Grant, "CF&YV Railway," message to author, August 24, 2021. See Alexander C. Lichtenstein, *Twice the Work of Free Labor: The Political Economy of Convict Labor in the New South* (London: Verso, 1996), 52.

6. Roger Grant, "CF&YV Railway," message to author, August 24, 2021.

7. Ibid.

8. Quoted in Ayers, 210.

9. Quoted in "John Andrew Jackson," *Danbury Report* (Danbury, NC), August 18, 1881.

10. Lichtenstein, 108–109.

11. Mancini writes, "Besides death, the other constant of the leasing camps was escape. Records show that literally thousands of escaped convicts must have inhabited the late-nineteenth-century Southern landscape." He lists statistics such as one from Georgia reporting a mean annual attrition rate over a forty-year period for convicts as nearly 6 percent in this period of time. He also charts numbers from Texas and Arkansas showing even higher rates of escape. Mancini, 68.

12. The article appears in newspapers published in New York, Pennsylvania, Iowa, Missouri, Texas, Kansas, Wisconsin, and the United Kingdom: *Buffalo Daily Courier* (Buffalo, NY), August 31, 1881; *Pittsburgh Post-Gazette* (Pittsburgh, PA), September 2, 1881; *Burlington Daily Hawk-Eye* (Burlington, IA), September 2, 1881; *St. Louis Globe-Democrat* (St. Louis, MO), September 3, 1881; *Dallas Daily Herald* (Dallas, TX), September 4, 1881; *Glens Falls Daily Times* (Glens Falls, NY), September 5, 1881; *Sioux City Journal* (Sioux City, IA), September 7, 1881; *Emporia Ledger* (Emporia, KS), September 8, 1881; *Birmingham Daily Post* (Birmingham, UK), September 14, 1881; *Anglo-American Times* (London, UK), September 16, 1881; *Stevens Point Journal* (Stevens Point, WI), September 17, 1881; *American Settler* (London, UK), September 24, 1881.

13. This notice first appears not in the *Springfield Republican,* as far as I can tell, but instead in the *Buffalo Daily Courier* on August 31, 1881. The reference to his time spent in Florence, Massachusetts, in the previous "season" suggests that Jackson (perhaps after the attack on his house in Springfield in July 1880) may have moved out to Florence briefly with or without Ella and the baby. He had spent time in Florence before the war and may have had friends there. By 1882, the *Fitchburg Daily Sentinel* announced an upcoming lecture of his and identified him as "of Florence, Northampton, and well known in the western part of the State." "John Andrew Jackson," *Fitchburg Daily Sentinel* (Fitchburg, MA), September 8, 1882.

14. "John Andrew Jackson," *Spirit of the Age* (Woodstock, VT), September 28, 1881.

15. "John Andrew Jackson," *Fitchburg Daily Sentinel* (Fitchburg, MA), September 11, 1882.

16. Damani Davis, "Exodus to Kansas," *Prologue Magazine*, 40, no. 2 (2008), www.archives.gov/publications/prologue/2008/summer/exodus.

17. "The Great Fire of Saint John, New Brunswick, 1877," New Brunswick Museum, New Brunswick, Canada, website.nbm-mnb.ca/CAIN/english/sj_fire.

18. It's tempting to imagine they would have met up at some point in Hartford or elsewhere in New England, but there are no extant records to support this notion. David L. Underhill, "Cornelius Sparrow," FindaGrave, www.findagrave.com/memorial/187121136/cornelius-sparrow.

19. "A Colored Evangelist's Plea," *New York Times*, June 13, 1885.

20. "He Is Here Collecting," *New Haven Register* (New Haven, CT), July 11, 1885.

21. Lynchburg is now occasionally referred to as "Magnolia" in both newspapers and historical records during this era, but the name didn't really catch on. The town evolved back into being known as "Lynchburg" more consistently by the turn of the twentieth century. For the sake of clarity and consistency, I have kept the name "Lynchburg" constant in this study.

22. *Boston Transcript*, October 21, 1884, 8.

23. Sumter County, South Carolina, Deed book Z, 538. Marion Moïse to John Andrew Jackson, March 23, 1887.

24. *The Times Record* (Brunswick, Maine), August 31, 1892, 4.

25. "Letter to the Editor," *Boston Evening Transcript* (Boston, MA), April 16, 1888; "John Andrew Jackson," *Springfield Republican* (Springfield, MA), July 25, 1890; "John Andrew Jackson," *Boston Journal* (Boston, MA), November 11, 1891.

26. "John Andrew Jackson," *New York Freeman* (New York, NY), July 18, 1885.

27. On July 11, 1885, the *New Haven Register* compared Jackson as "thoroughly honest as Brother Gardner of the Lime Kiln Club." This comment signaled a reference to a series of stories well known in the popular press of the era satirizing and mocking Black organizations. This kind of notice, although not predominant in his wider media coverage, effectively undermined Jackson's reputation. "He Is Here Collecting," *New Haven Register* (New Haven, CT), July 11, 1885. See also M. Quad, *Brother Gardner's Lime-Kiln Club* (Chicago: Belford, 1882).

28. *The Watchman and Southron*, 1889. Larry Sadberry appears to have been a generation younger than Jackson, married and living in Lynchburg as of the 1900 Census. "Larry Sadberry," 1900 United States Census, Lynchburg, Sumter County, South Carolina, 1900; 10, FHL microfilm 1241543. Ancestry.com.

29. From the *Union and Advertiser* (Rochester, NY), reproduced in Blassingham, 511–513. Some of the facts in the interview may have been the result of a misunderstanding from the reporter because they seem inconsistent with other records. He mentions a "baby boy" (page 513) who died after Jackson had fled South Carolina and he also is quoted as asserting that in his escape in 1850 he traveled north from Boston to Toronto (page 513), which is possible but doesn't seem likely in light of what can be known about his presence in Maine and Saint John.

30. Max Spiegel, "Lyr Add: Dearest Mae (Minstrel)," mudcat.org/thread.cfm?threadid=152100.

31. Unfortunately, census and local records do not make it clear how or if Wesley Abraham would have been related to Leah Abraham. She may have died or changed her name upon marriage. And while he shows up in the 1880 U.S. Census as having been born in 1860, it isn't clear who his parents were. But in such a small town as Lynchburg, it seems like a solid speculation to think they were from the same family. "Wesley Abraham," 1880 United States Census, Lynchburg, Sumter, South Carolina, roll 1241, 77D, Ancestry.com, www.ancestrylibrary.com. Abraham shows up in the 1900 Census with a wife and three-year-old daughter but no indication of Jackson living with them.

32. In the census of 1910, at least, Abraham is still listed as owning the property.

33. Jake McLeod, interview by Federal Writers' Project.

IMAGE SOURCES

xii Taken by Peter Laurence

xviii Library of Congress

xxii Clerk of Court records held by Register of Deeds Office, Sumter County Courthouse, Sumter, South Carolina

5 From James English Cousar, *Quaker Turned Presbyterian: The Spiritual Pilgrimage of Robert ("Robin") English* (Savannah, GA: The Independent Presbyterian Church, 1956)

16 Taken by Susanna Ashton

26 Title page from Irving E. Lowery's *Life on the Old Plantation in Ante-Bellum Days; or, A Story Based on Facts* (Columbia, SC: The State Co. Printers, 1911)

32 Digital Collections: University of South Carolina Libraries

33 Library of Congress

35 Frontispiece photograph of Irving E. Lowery from *Life on the Old Plantation in Ante-Bellum Days; or, A Story Based on Facts* (Columbia, SC: The State Co. Printers, 1911)

44 Library of Congress

47 United States Census (Slave Schedule), 1860 National Archives and Records Administration

53 North Wind Picture Archives/Alamy Stock Photo

55 Courtesy of The Charleston Museum, Charleston, South Carolina

60 Documenting the American South, University Library, The University of North Carolina at Chapel Hill

62 National Archives and Records Administration

68 National Parks Service

70 National Archives and Records Administration

73 Library of Congress

73 Wikipedia

74 Library of Congress

93 Harpers.org

96 Special Collections, Yale University

103 Wikipedia

104 Wikipedia

106 Courtesy Bowdoin College, copyright Michele Stapleton

107 Pejepscot History Center

126 Collections of the Maine Historical Society

128 The Abyssinian Meeting House, Portland, Maine

132 Board of Registration and Statistics, Public Archives, Ontario

148 Documenting the American South, Libraries of the University of North Carolina, Chapel Hill

149 Board of Registration and Statistics, Public Archives, Ontario

152 New Brunswick Museum Archives and Research Library

153 Heritage Resources, Saint John

159 Courtesy of the Maritime Museum of the Atlantic, Halifax, Nova Scotia, a part of the Nova Scotia Museum

160 Documenting the American South, Libraries of the University of North Carolina, Chapel Hill

165 Marc Zakian 2/Alamy Stock Photo

170 Wikipedia

177 Internet Archive

185 The National Archives (UK)

186 Private Collection © Look and Learn/Bridgeman Images

194 Beinecke Rare Book and Manuscript Library, Yale University

202 Library of Congress

202 Library of Congress

209 British History Online

214 George J. Mitchell Special Collections and Archives, Bowdoin College

217 Logan Cyrus/Getty Images

219 Historical Newspapers of South Carolina University of South Carolina Libraries

224 George J. Mitchell Special Collections and Archives, Bowdoin College

233 The American Antiquarian Society

243 National Archives and Records Administration

252 Surry County Minutes of the Superior Court, North Carolina Department of Natural and Cultural Resources. Division of Archives and Records

254 *The Western Sentinel* May 5, 1881, from Digital NC: North Carolina Newspapers

266 Library of Congress

INDEX

NOTE: PAGE NUMBERS IN *ITALICS* REFER TO IMAGES AND CAPTIONS.

Abbott, Martin, 314n2
abolitionists. *See* antislavery movement
Abraham, Leah, 236–39, 240, 265, 316n26, 316n27, 322n31
Abraham, Wesley, 265, 322n31
Abyssinian Meeting House (Portland, Maine), 127, *128*, 130
Adams, Amanda, 308n54
Adams, John Quincy, 67
Advocate of Freedom (antislavery newspaper), 102, *103*
African Meeting House (Boston), 75, 80
Alabaster, James, 187, 188–89, 233, 313n24
America (Cunard Line steamship), *159*, 304n63
American Colonization Society, 108–9, 312n14
American Revolution, 6, 137–39
Anderson, Alexander, 250
Anderson, William, 157
Andover Theological Seminary (Massachusetts), 294n9
Ann Street race riot in Boston (1843), 72–74
antilynching bills of 1935, 10
Anti-Slavery Association, 206–7
The Anti-Slavery Harp (Brown), 310n77
antislavery lecture circuit, 78–80, 154–59, 166–93, 195–213
  British Isles, 162, 166–93, 195–213
  the Crafts, 140, 154, 155, 162, 166
  Davidson, 201–5
  Douglass, 80, 86, 130, 154, 155, 167, 173, 174, 175, 308n54
  Duff, 184, 309n60
  Dundee, Scotland, 200–208
  Durham Town Hall in northern England, *170*
  frauds and charlatans, 168, 306n19
  Henry "Box" Brown, 86, 162, 174, 313n24
  informal speaking at public outdoor venues, 199
  Liverpool, England, 166–67
  Remond, 79, 80, 81, 86, 130, 175, 298n53
  scrutiny of Black lecturers' physical bodies, 170–71, 173–74
  use of props on stage, 174–75
  white hosts and white authentication of speakers, 168–69, 179–80, 187–88, 306n20
  William Wells Brown, 86, 119, 154, 162, 166–67, 174, 175, 310n77, 310–11n81
  women speakers, 79, 80, 171–74, 306n26
  See also Jackson, John Andrew: and the antislavery lecture circuit

antislavery movement
Boston, 67, 71–76, 150–51
British Isles, 162, 179–84, 186–87, 192–93, 198–208, 312n4
Brunswick, Maine, 101–10, 113–14
Chase family, 86–87, 88–90, 315–16n18
Dundee, Scotland, 200–208
Jackson's allies among Black antislavery activists, 14, 71–76, 78–88, 136, 140–41, 144, 147–54, 158, 223, 231
Jackson's allies among white antislavery activists, 82–91, 125–29, 136, 156–57, 224–25
Maine, 100–131
New York abolitionists and Julia Jackson's escape, 142–44
Portland, Maine, 101, 125–31
Remond family, 78–79, 80, 81
Saint John, New Brunswick, 136, 140–41, 147–54, 158
Salem, 76–81, 91–92, 223
Stowe and, 105–21
Upham family, 103–4, 107–10, 114, 117, 123
western Massachusetts, 82–90
antislavery newspapers
Advocate of Freedom, 102, *103*
The Liberator, 71, *73*, 74, 83, 84, 149, 288n11
National Era, 106, 115, 117, 120
Springfield Republican, 231–32
Anti-Slavery Society (Portland, Maine), 130
Archy Moore, or the White Slave; or, Memoirs of a Fugitive (Hildreth), 119

Bailey, Gamaliel, 115
Ball, Griffin, 250
Bath, Maine, 101, 123–24, 136–37
free Black community, 113, 123–24, 267
Jackson's passage through, 136–37, 298n47
Beecher, Catharine, *96*, 109–11, 112, 118, 123
Beecher, Edward, 119
Beecher, Henry Ward, 108, 165, 182–83
Beecher, Isabella, 119
Beecher, Lyman, 294n7
Berry, Daina Ramey, 4, 277n6
Bethune, Mary McLeod, 11
Bibb, Henry, 162
Blackett, R. J. M., 309n65
"Black Loyalists," 138–39
Blackmon, Douglas A., 255
Black Mountain College (Asheville, North Carolina), 10
Black seamen
Charleston, *53*, 57–58, 59, 64–66, 288n5
and Foreman's Ann Street boarding house in Boston, 14, *62*, 67–76, *70*, *73*, 90–92, 223, 288n11
Liverpool, 165, 167
Portland, Maine, 127, 129
and the *Smyrna*, 59–61, 65–68, 69–70
"bonneting," 211–12
Boston, Massachusetts, 62–76
Ann Street neighborhood, 68–76, *73*, 223, 289n15
Ann Street race riot (1843), 72–74
antislavery movement, 67, 71–76, 150–51
census of 1850 and Jackson's name, 14, *62*, 65, 68–71, 90–91, 293n1
Faneuil Hall, 67
Foreman's Ann Street boarding house, 14, *62*, 67–76, *70*, *73*, 90–92, 223, 288n11
free Black community, 14, 41, 71–76, 289n25
Irish immigrants, 72
Jackson and Julia's return to, 223

Jackson's arrival as stowaway, 61, 63–68, *68*, 287–88n2
Boston Daily Advertiser, 234
Boston Daily Evening, 234
Boston Daily Journal, 234
Boston Evening Transcript, 260, 261–62
Boston Journal, 261
Boston Vigilance Committee, 150–51, 302n45
Bouk, Dan, 318n43
Bowdoin College (Brunswick, Maine), 101–8
  Calvin Stowe at, 105–8, 294n7, 294n9
  Smyth at, 102–4, 294n7
  Upham at, 107–10
Bowles, Samuel, III, 258
Brayton, James, 77
British Baptist Evangelicals, x, 181–82. *See also* Spurgeon, Charles Haddon
Brown, Henry "Box," 86, 162, 174, 313n24
Brown, John, *128*, 316n19
Brown, William Wells, 86, 94, 154, 162, 166, 175
  and antislavery songs, 310n77, 310–11n81
  and Liverpool lecture circuit, 166, 167, 174
  slave narrative, 119, 162, 310–11n81, 313n24
  Stowe's reading of, 119
Browne, Dinah Hope, 164
Browne, Simone, 298n2
Brown's Temperance Hotel (Liverpool, England), 167
Brunswick, Maine, 101–17, 261, 298n47
  antislavery activists, 101–10, 113–14
  Bowdoin College, 101–8
  free Black community, 101, 103, 113
  Stowe family and household, ix, 104–14, *106*, 124
  Stowe House (63 Federal Street), *106*, 110–14
  Upham family, 103–4, 107–10, 114, 117, 123
  See also Jackson and Stowe's encounter in Brunswick, Maine (1850)
Buffalo Daily Courier, 320n13
Burleigh, Harry, 295n20
Burns, Anthony, 83, 290n42
Bush, A. B., 251

Campbell, Tunis, 220, 314n5
camp revival meetings, 28–36, *33*, 84
  dangers for Black attendees, 30, 33
  Jackson's appearance on a pony, 28–34, 36, 40
  Lowery's memoir of, 29, 34–36
  role of music and fellowship, 30–31, 282n7
Canada (Cunard Line steamship), 158–59, *159*, 163–64, 176, 304n63
Cape Fear and Yadkin Valley Railroad, 254–57
census data. *See* New Brunswick census of 1851; U.S. Census
Charleston, South Carolina, 53–58
  Black stevedores on the cotton wharf (1870s), *53*
  free Black seamen and dock workers, *53*, 57–58, 59, 64–66, 288n5
  free people of color, 53, 65–66
  fugitive slaves and urban culture of fugitivity, 53, 285n17
  Jackson joining a Black dock workers' gang, 53–56, 64
  Jackson's Christmas escape to, 40, 41–43, 46–52, 98
  Jackson's escape as stowaway on a Boston-bound ship, 54, 56–61, 63–68, 287n2, 287n38
  slave badges and the slave-hire system, 53–56, *55*, 286n19

Chase, Anthony Benezet, 86, 89
Chase, Lucy, 86–87, 88–90, 315–16n18
Cheraw, South Carolina, 241–42
Cheshire Observer, 198
Christian News, 142, 177
Christmas holiday
  Douglass on, 42–43
  for enslaved people, 42–43, 50–51, 284n32
  Jackson's Christmas escape (1846), 40, 41–43, 46–52, 98
Civil War, 84, 183, 197, 198–99
  Black Union troops and "Potter's Raid," 212
  end of, 197, 212–13
  Jackson on, 198–99
  start of, 185
  See also post–Civil War era
Clark, George, 310n77
Clarke, Lewis, 119
Clavern, Betty (Jackson's mother), 5, 7, 16–18, 31, 90, 91–95, 249
Clavern, Doctor ("Doc") (Jackson's father), xi–xiii, 3–5, 7, 13, 17, 31, 36, 226, 267, 275n3
  descendants, xi–xiii, 4–5, 275n3, 280n40
  emancipation, 5
  and English-McCoy altercation over attempted slave theft, xi, *xxii*, 3–4
  Jackson's efforts to free, 90, 91–95, 197, 316n26
Clavon, Amelia, 226, 239
Clavon, Bella (Jackson's sister), 11–12, 18, 19, 197, 226, 267, 316n26
Clavon, Dock, *xii*, xii–xiii
Clavon, Ephraim (Jackson's brother), 4, 13, 18–19, 20, 216, 226, 238–40, 267
  descendants of, 281n52
  and Jackson's efforts send relief supplies to South Carolina, 19, 238–40
  and Jackson's efforts to bring Leah and Jimmy to Massachusetts, 238–39, 316n26, 316n27
Clavon, William (Jackson's brother), 18, 19, 226, 280n50
Clavon family of South Carolina (descendants), xi–xiii, 5, 15–16, 268, 275n2, 275n3, 276n5, 280n40
Clavon Street, Lynchburg, South Carolina, *16*
Clyburn, Jim, 276n5
Cochrane, G. W., 156, 287n38
Cohen, Lara Langer, 311n88
Colored Citizen's Convention of Tennessee (1866), 220
Compromise of 1850, 94, 105–6, 292–93n65. *See also* Fugitive Slave Act of 1850
Constitution (Middletown, Connecticut), 245
convict lease system, x, 254–57
  escapes from work gangs, 257, 320n11
  Jackson sentenced to work gang, x, 254–57
cotton industry
  England, 165–66
  English family and, 6–7, 8, 13, 24–25, 37
  maritime Maine, 102, 123–24
  "Osnaburg" cloth and enslaved workers, 201
  Scotland, 201
  short-staple cotton growing, 6–7
  slavery and, 6–7, 8, 9–10, 13, 24–25, 37, 59, 102, 123–24, 165–66, 201
  South Carolina cotton growing, 6–7, 8, 10
Cousar, John English, Jr., 8
Craft, Ellen, 140, 154, 155, 162, 166
Craft, William, 140, 154, 155, 162, 166
Cunningham, J. M., 205

"dark sousveillance," 298n2
Darlington, South Carolina, *233*, 233–34, 246

Davidson, Rev. Isaac W., 201–5
advertisement, *202*
Jackson's accusations against, 202–5, 312n14
slander case against Jackson, 203–5
Davis, H. Grady, xix
Davis, Jefferson, 166
"Dearest Mae" (minstrel tune), 111–12, 192, 264, 295n20, 295n22, 311n82
Devens, Charles, 151
Dickson, Bruce D., 282n7
"Doc." *See* Clavern, Doctor ("Doc") (Jackson's father)
Douglass, Frederick
as antislavery speaker, 80, 86, 130, 154, 155, 167, 173, 174, 175, 308n54
on the Christmas holiday for enslaved people, 42–43
and Julia Griffiths, 179–80
name, 14
slave narrative, 41, 162, 189, 284n27
Stowe and, 119
Dred: A Tale of the Great Dismal Swamp (Stowe), 157, 176–78, *177*, 296n39
Jackson's on-stage discussions of, 176–78
publication in England, 176–78
Duff, Washington, 184, 309n60
Dundee, Scotland, 200–208
antislavery lecture circuit, 200–208
city atmosphere, 200–201
and global slave economy, 201
itinerant Black lecturer Davidson, 201–5
Jackson and Julia's lodgings on South Tay Street, 200
Jackson's accusations against Davidson, 202–5, 312n14
Jackson's advertisements in Scottish newspapers, *202*
Jackson's letter to a local newspaper announcing his plan to return to the States, 206–7
Dundee Advertiser, 204–5
Dundee Courier, 142
Dundee Courier and Argus, 211
Durham Town Hall (northern England), *170*

Ellingwood, Rev. Joseph, 123–24, 136
Emancipation Association, 192
Emancipation Proclamation, 212, 304n1
England
and the American Civil War, 198–99
antislavery movement in the British Isles, 162, 179–84, 186–87, 192–93, 198–208, 312n4
British interests in Black music, 310n77
cotton trade and global slave economy, 165–66
popularity of slave narratives in, 162, 187, 193, 309n65
slave trade abolished in, 41, 165
Stowe's 1856–57 speaking tour, 175–78
See also Liverpool, England; London, England
English, Eli McFadden ("Mack"), 13, 18
English, Elizabeth Wilson, 7, 12, 91, 277–78n10, 292n61
death, 181, 228, 308n53
and Jackson's first escape and return, 36–40
Jackson's second escape and the runaway slave advertisement, 46–49
Slave Schedule of 1860, 46–47, *47*, 180–81, 308n53
violence and cruelty to enslaved people, 12, 17–18, 36–37, 91–92, 177
English, James Wilson, 12, 279n29, 291n43
English, Martha. *See* McFaddin, Martha English
English, Robert, xxi, 2–9, 12–13, 16–25, 277–78n10

English, Robert (*continued*)
altercation with Tyre McCoy over attempted slave theft, *xxii*, 2–4, 8
cotton crops, 6–7, 8, 13
crossroads store, 6, 8
death, 228, 234–35, 292n61
declining health, 29, 46
enslaved people, 2–9, 16–25, 37, 43, 263–64
Mansion House, *5*, 19–20, 23
saw mill, 8, 278n15
violence and unpleasant temperament, 2–3, 8, 9, 17
See also English family
English, Thomas Reese, 12–13, 46–49, 228
response to Jackson's letter asking to free his parents, 91–92
runaway slave advertisement for Jackson, 14, *44*, 46–49, 299n7, 308n53
and the Slave Schedule of 1860, 308n53
English, Thomas Reese, Jr., 228
"English Crossroads," 9, 278n18. *See also* Lynchburg, South Carolina
English family, 2–25
attempt to recapture Jackson, 91–92, 95
cotton crops, 6–7, 8, 13, 24–25, 37
crossroads store, 6–7
cruelty to enslaved people, 11–13, 16–19, 23–24, 37, 91–92, 177, 263–64
and the end of the Civil War, 213, 217–38, *219*, 228–29, 234–36
enslaved people, 2–9, 11–25, 31, 35–37, 45–49, *47*, 91–92, 177, 180–81, 263–64
and Jackson's 1846 Christmas escape, 40, 41–43, 46–52, 98
Jackson's scheme to buy plantation, x, 216–22, 234–36, 241
"Mansion House" property, *5*, 19–20, 23
response to Jackson's letter asking to free his parents, 91–92, 94–95
runaway slave advertisement for Jackson, xiv–xv, 14, *44*, 45–49, 284n4, 299n7, 308n53
escapes from enslavement, xx, 36–43, 44–61, 63–68
Boston abolitionists' opposition to rendition laws, 67
Charleston fugitives and urban culture of fugitivity in Southern cities, 53, 285n17
communities of "maroons," 38–39
former slaves' stories of, xx, 41–42, 49–50
"grand marronage" (full escape), 38–39
Jackson as stowaway aboard a Boston-bound ship, 54, 56–61, 63–68, 287n2, 287n38
Jackson's Christmas 1846 escape to Charleston, 40, 41–43, 46–52, 98
Jackson's escapes in South Carolina, x, xv, xx–xxi, 14, 36–43, 44–61, 63–68, 98
Jackson's first escape and return, 36–40
Jackson's gimlet used to bore air holes as stowaway, 56, 59–60, *60*, 64, 174–75, 187
Julia Jackson's escape and rescue, 142–46, 247
and "personal liberty" laws passed in the Northern states, 93–94
"petit marronage" (small escape), 38–39
runaway slave advertisements, xiv–xv, 14, *44*, 45–49, 284n4, 299n7, 308n53
stowaways on boats/ships, 54, 56–61, 63–68, 99, 125, 130–31, 137, 143–44,

147, 286n24, 286n26, 287n2, 287n38
See also Fugitive Slave Act of 1850
The Experience of a Slave in South Carolina (Jackson's 1862 memoir), x, 4, 14–15, 121–23, *160*, 160–63, 187–93
authorship and authorial voice, 14–15, 188–89, 190
closing chapter on "Slave Songs" and "Antislavery Songs," 191–92, 310n77
extant copies today, 193, 311n87
how the Stowe encounter influenced, 121–23
narrative digressions and his unfolding story, 189–91
preface by "W.M.S.," 122, 187–88, 297n41
publication date, 304n1
published by Passmore and Alabaster, 187, 188–89, 233, 313n24
sales and distribution in England, 193
song lyrics, 191–92, 264, 310n77
sources and inspiration, 121–22
testimonials in, 192–93
title page and Jackson's image, *160*, 162–63, 187, 189, 233, 304n2

Faneuil Hall (Boston), 67
Federal Writers' Project's slave narratives project (1936–1938), xviii–xxi, 265
Fessenden, Samuel C., 125–29, *126*, 137, 156–57, 224–25, 298n47, 316n26
Fife Herald (Scotland), 142
First Parish Church (Brunswick, Maine), 108, 114
Fisch, Audrey, 306n26
Florence, Massachusetts, 218, 258, 314n4, 320n13
Ford, Bruce C., 280n40, 281n52
Foreman, Almira, 69, 72, 74, 267
Foreman, Henry, 14, 67–76, 92, 267
Ann Street boarding house for Black seamen in Boston, 14, *62*, 67–76, *70*, *73*, 90–92, 223, 288n11
antislavery movement, 14, 71, 74
death, 223
Freedmen's Bureau, xxi, 216–22, 224–26, 236–40
Captain Place in Sumter County, 216, 237–40, 266
creation, 224–25
and Jackson's efforts to send relief supplies to South Carolina, xxi, 234, 238–40, *266*
Jackson's relationship with General Howard, *214*, 216–22, *224*, 225, 229–30, 237–40, 258, 317n31
Jackson's work for, 216, 225–26
South Carolina, 216, 225–26, 234, 236–40, 266, 314n2
Freeman, Rev. Amos Noe, 127, *128*
"The Freeman's Dream: A Parable" (Stowe), 106
Fuentes, Marisa J., 276n9
Fugitive Slave Act of 1793, 93
Fugitive Slave Act of 1850, 14, 63, 93–95, 100–102, 105–9, 116, 139–41, 150–51, 206, 227, 292–93n65
and Black refugees to Canada, 139–41, 150–51, 153
Jackson fleeing Massachusetts, 94–95, 98–100, 293n1
Jackson's passage through Maine toward Canada, 99–131, 136–37, 293n1, 299n6
in Maine, 100–102, 105–14
Section 5 commanding citizens to assist in the execution of, 94
Section 7 sentencing those who assist fugitives, 94
Stowe's reactions to passage of, 105–21
fugitive slaves. *See* escapes from enslavement; runaway slave advertisements

Garnet, Henry Highland, 86–88, 149, 231, 291n53, 291n54
on Black Canadian settlements and "color phobia" in Canada, 140
escape from slavery, 87–88, 291n53
and Julia Jackson's possible escape route to Canada, 144
Garrison, William Lloyd, 130
Gilmer, John, 77, 156
Glasgow New Association for the Abolition of Slavery, 180
Goddell, William, 313n24
Goodwill Presbyterian Church (Mayesville, South Carolina), *32*
Grand Trunk Railway, 299n6
Gravesend Reporter, 145
Great Depression, xviii–xxi, 265
Green, Jeffrey, 306n19
Griffiths, Julia, 179–80
Grimes, William, 286n24
Grosvenor, Rev. Cyrus P., 78
Guthrie, David, 157

Halifax, Nova Scotia, Canada
African School, 302n41
Jackson and Julia's passage to Liverpool from, 155, 158–59, 163–64, 303n51, 304n63
racism in, 140
Hallowell, Maine, 101, 293n1
Hampden Card Company (Springfield, Massachusetts), 232
Harper's Magazine, 93
Harper's Weekly, 33
Hartford, Connecticut, 151, 246, 260
Hayden, Lewis, 80
Haynsworth, Henry, 83–84, 212–13, 291n43
reply to Stowell letter on behalf of Louisa and Jinny's enslavers, 83–84, 89–90, 95, 141, 227
Henson, Josiah, 119, 162, 275n1, 296–97n40
Higbee, Samuel, 77, 156
Hildreth, Richard, 119
Howard, Gen. O. O., 216–22, 225, 229–30, 237–40, 258
Jackson's relationship and correspondence with, *214*, 216–22, *224*, 225, 229–30, 237–40, 258, 317n31
and Jackson's scheme to buy the English family's plantation, *214*, 216–22, 234–36
Howe, Samuel Gridley, 140
Howell, Jesse, 309n60
Hunter, Tera, 281n60
Hutchinson singers, 192, 310–11n81

Irish immigrants
Boston's Ann Street neighborhood, 72
Dundee, Scotland, 200–201
Saint John, New Brunswick, 134, 139–40
Salem, Massachusetts leather workers, 77

Jackson, Andrew (president), 15, 70, 280n41
Jackson, Anna Elizabeth (Jackson and Ella's first daughter), 18, 247, 248, 249, 319n54
Jackson, Benjamin, 309n60
Jackson, Elizabeth (Jackson and Ella's second daughter), 18, 248–50, 253, 319n55
Jackson, Ella Pooler (third wife), 247, 248–50, 253, 267, 319n53, 319n56
Jackson, Francis, 150
Jackson, John Andrew
allies among Black antislavery activists, 14, 71–76, 78–88, 136, 140–41, 144, 147–54, 158, 223, 231
allies among white antislavery activists, 82–91, 125–29, 136, 156–57, 224–25

arrest in North Carolina and sentenced to convict work gang, x, *254*, 254–58
arrival in Boston after escape, 61, 63–68, *68*, 287–88n2
article about Jackson's life (1881), 257–58, 320n12, 320n13
assault and robbery on trip north from the Carolinas, 229–30, 237
assault on his house in Springfield, 250–51
avoiding detection as a fugitive in Boston, 75–76
in Bath, Maine, 136–37, 298n47
in Brunswick, Maine, 101–17, 261, 298n47
camp revival meeting appearance on a pony, 28–34, 36, 40
collecting donations and relief supplies for freemen in South Carolina, xxi, 232–36, *233*, 238–40, 260–63, 265–66, *266*
daughter Anna Elizabeth, 18, 247, 248, 249, 319n54
daughter Elizabeth, 18, 248–50, 253, 319n55
death and unknown burial site, xv, 267–68, 281n52
in Dundee, Scotland, 200–208
efforts to liberate his family, 76–95, 154, 169, 197, 208–10, 226–28, 316n26
efforts to liberate Louisa and Jinny, 76–91, 226–28
efforts to transport Leah and Jimmy to Massachusetts, 236–39, 316n26, 316n27, 317n28
the English family's attempt to recapture, 91–92, 95
on the English family's cruelty, 11–13, 16–19, 23–24, 37, 91–92, 263–64
the English family's runaway slave advertisement, xiv–xv, 14, *44*, 45–49, 284n4, 299n7, 308n53
escape from convict work gang, 257–58
escapes from slavery, x, xv, xx–xxi, 14, 36–43, 44–61, 63–68, 98
experiences as enslaved person, 11–13, 16–25, 28–43, 44–50, 91–92, 122, 190, 263–64
fleeing Springfield without family, 251, 253
at Foreman's Ann Street boarding house in Boston, 14, 67–76, 90–92, 223
gaining experience as a speaker, 84–85, 90, 91, 129
home in London's Finsbury neighborhood, 184–85, *185*, 187
home in New Haven's Winter Street community, 242–47
on interracial marriage, 260
interview with Rochester reporter (1893), 263–64, 321n29
letter to the English family asking to free his parents, 91–92, 94–95
literacy, 122, 136, 146, 188, 207, 216, 242, 265, 318n42
in Liverpool, 164–67, 304n63
marriage to Ella, 247, 248–50, 253, 319n53
marriage to Julia, 141–47, 227, 247–48, 267, 301n24, 319n53
marriage to Louisa, 20–25, 87, 264, 281–82n61, 292n60
name (self-naming), 13–16, 70–71, 288n14
names in the historical record, 14, 15, 69–70, 299n7
passage through Maine to Canada in late 1850, 99–131, 136–37, 293n1, 298n47, 299n6
in Portland, Maine, 124–31, 137, 298n47

Jackson, John Andrew (*continued*)
relationship with General Howard of the Freedmen's Bureau, *214*, 216–22, *224*, 225, 229–30, 237–40, 258, 317n31
relationship with Spurgeon, 181–87, 193, 196–97, 205–11
return to South Carolina, 213, 223–29
return to the United States, x, xx–xxi, 206–7, 213, 215, 216–51
in Saint John, New Brunswick, 131, 132–54
in Salem, Massachusetts, 76–81, 91–92
scheme to buy the English family land for a Black communal farm, x, *214*, 216–22, 234–36, 241
scheme to start a "colony" in Cheraw, South Carolina, 241–42
self-fashioned identity, x, xiv–xvi, 13–16, 79–80, 135–36
song lyrics, 111, 191–92, 210, 264, 295n22, 310n77
in Springfield, Massachusetts, 231–42, 247, 248–51
in western Massachusetts, 80–90
work as a Charleston dock worker, 53–56, 64
work as whitewasher, 135, 136, 146, 151–53, 184, 206, 213, 303n49, 309n61
work for the Freedmen's Bureau, 216, 225–26
work in Salem's tan yards, 76–78, 91
See also *The Experience of a Slave in South Carolina* (Jackson's 1862 memoir); Jackson, John Andrew: and the antislavery lecture circuit; Jackson and Stowe's encounter in Brunswick, Maine (1850)
Jackson, John Andrew: and the antislavery lecture circuit, x, 154–59, 162, 166–93, 195–213, 222, 305n17
accusations against Davidson, 202–5, 312n14
arrival in Liverpool, 164–67, 304n63
association with Spurgeon, 181–87, 193, 196–97, 205–11
attendance at British antislavery meetings, 198–99, 207, 312n4
audiences' scrutiny of his physical body, 170–71, 173–74
in the British Isles, x, 162, 166–93, 195–213, 222, 305n17
Davidson's slander case, 203–5
departure from Halifax and journey to Liverpool, 155, 158–59, 163–64, 303n51, 304n63
discussing Stowe's *Dred* on stage, 176–78
in Dundee, Scotland, 200–208
final lectures, 211–12
funding and letters of endorsements, 154–57, 168, 303–4n60, 304n61
gimlet stage prop, 174–75
home in London's Finsbury neighborhood, 184–85, *185*, 187
informal speaking at public outdoor venues, 199
Julia's roles, 169–70, 171–75, 247–48
Liverpool lecturers' circuit, 166–67
money earned, 169, 171, 184
newspaper coverage, 169, 171–74, 178–79, 197–98, 211
pamphlet airing grievances against Spurgeon, *194*, 194–96, 208–11, 313n24
plan to return the States, 206–7, 213
publishing his memoir, 160–63, 187–93
racist, hostile, and violent critics and audiences, 197–98, 199, 211–12
return to traveling and lecturing/speaking in the U.S. (1880s), 258–63

self-promotion, 162, 168–71, *202*
Spurgeon's withdrawn patronage, 196–97, 205–11
Stowe's testimonial letter, 157, 168, 175, 275n1, 303–4n60, 304n61, 311n84
travels through northern England and Scotland, 167–84, 195, 197–208
white hosts and white external authentication, 168–69, 179–80, 187–88, 306n20
Jackson, Julia A. (second wife), 133, 141–47, 222–31, 240–41, 242–48, 301n24
age, 301n24
antislavery speaking by, 171–73, 247–48
arrival in Liverpool, 164–67
British press on her race and origins, 142
childlessness, 145–46
death, 247–48
departure from Halifax and journey to Liverpool, 155, 158–59, 163–64, 303n51, 304n63
escape from slavery in North Carolina, 142–46, 247
health, 236, 240–41, 242, 245, 246–47
home in London's Finsbury neighborhood, 184–85, *185*, 187
home in New Haven's Winter Street community, 242–47
home in Springfield, Massachusetts, 231, 236–42
hospitalization at Northampton Lunatic Asylum, 240–41, 242, 246–48
and Jackson's lecture circuit in the British Isles, 154–55, 158–59, 167–84, 195, 197–208
literacy, 146, 188, 242, 318n42
marriage to Jackson, 141–47, 227, 247–48, 267, 301n24, 319n53
return to South Carolina with Jackson, 213, 222–29
Jackson and Stowe's encounter in Brunswick, Maine (1850), ix, *96*, 98–99, 104, 110–24, 175–78, 246, 264, 266–67, 275n1, 296–97n40
influence on Jackson's memoir, 121–23
inspiration for *Uncle Tom's Cabin*, ix, 98–99, 104, 110–23, 176, 267, 275n1, 296–97n40
Jackson singing "Dearest Mae" with Stowe's children, 111–12, 192, 264, 295n20, 295n22, 311n82
Jackson's later invocation of the meeting, 120–21, 175–78, 275n1, 296n39, 296–97n40
Jackson's rest in Stowe's waste room, 113, 119
possible later encounter in Hartford, 246
possible reasons Stowe never mentioned Jackson, 120
Stowe offering her husband's clothes for Jackson, 113–14
Stowe's inspection of Jackson's scarred back, ix, 112, 266–67
Stowe's letter to Catharine Beecher concerning the visit, *96*, 109–11, 118, 123
and Stowe's testimonial letter, 157, 168, 175, 275n1, 303–4n60, 304n61, 311n84
Jacobs, Phebe Ann, 108
James, Rev. Robert Wilson, 31
Jimmy (child of Jackson's Clavon relatives), 236–39, 316n27, 317n28
Jinny (Jackson and Louisa's daughter), x, 22–24, 29, 40, 76–91, 113, 121, 226–28, 282n66
Jackson's efforts to liberate, 76–91, 226–28

possible survival, 226–28
John P. Jewett & Co., 117–18
Jones, Rev. Thomas H., 147–49, *148*, 153, 267
Jones, Wesley, 70
Jones-Rogers, Stephanie E., 279n28, 283n23
"jumping the broomstick," 281n59, 281n60

Kansas Exodusters, 259
A Key to Uncle Tom's Cabin (Stowe), 120, 296–97n40
Ku Klux Klan (KKK), 221–22, 315n8

Lane Seminary (Ohio), 105, 294n9
Law, Ann J. English, 9
Law, Elizabeth Wells McKelvin, 22–23, 24
Law, Jared R. McKelvin, 22–24
Law family of South Carolina, 22–24, 87, 227, 282n63, 282n66
leather industry of Salem, Massachusetts, 76–78, 91, *93*
Lee Correctional Institution (Bishopville, South Carolina), *217*, 217–18, 278n15
Lee County, South Carolina, 9, 281n53
Lewis, John, 250
The Liberator (antislavery newspaper), 71, *73*, 74, 83, 84, 149, 288n11
Liberty Party (antislavery), 125, *126*, 157
Life on the Old Plantation in Ante-Bellum Days, or a Story Based on Facts (Lowery), *26*, 29, 34–37, 283n15
Lincoln, Abraham, 106, 304n1
literacy
John Andrew Jackson, 122, 136, 146, 188, 207, 216, 242, 265, 318n42
Julia Jackson, 146, 188, 242, 318n42
Liverpool, England, 164–67
Abercromby Square, 166
antislavery activists, 167
Black lecturers' circuit, 166–67
Black seamen, 165, 167
and global slave economy, *165*, 165–66
Jackson and Julia's arrival, 164–67, 304n63
Jackson and Julia's departure from Halifax and journey to, 155, 158–59, 163–64, 303n51, 304n63
population, 164, 305n7
London, England
antislavery movement, 180
Jackson and Julia's home in Finsbury neighborhood, 184–85, *185*, 187
Spurgeon's Metropolitan Tabernacle, *186*, 186–87, 196, 208–10, *209*
Longfellow, Henry Wadsworth, *106*
Louisa (first wife), x, 20–25, 29, 40, 76–91, 113, 141, 226, 250, 267
daughter Jinny, x, 22–24, 29, 40, 76–91, 113, 226–27, 282n66
forced marriage to another slave (Enoch), 24, 87, 227, 264, 291n53, 292n60
Jackson's efforts to liberate, 76–91, 226–28
life as enslaved person, 21–24, 282n66
marriage to Jackson, 20–25, 87, 264, 281–82n61, 292n60
possible survival, 226–28
reported death, 141, 226–27, 292n60
taken to Georgia by the Law family, 24, 29, 33, 48, 227, 282n63
Lovejoy, Joseph, 293n1
Lowery, Rev. Irving E., *26*, 29, 34–37, *35*, 42, 212
on camp meetings, 28–29, 34–36
on the Christmas holiday for enslaved people, 42
memoir (1911), *26*, 29, 34–37, 283n15
Lumpkin, Amie, 41–42
Lynch, Francis, 295n20
Lynchburg, South Carolina, 2–25, 26–43

camp revival meetings, 28–36, 40, 84
census of 1870, 10
Clavon Street, *16*
early town names, 2, 6, 9, 278n18
and the end of the Civil War, 212–13, 235
Jackson's postwar efforts to purchase land and supplies for freed people, 260–63, 265–66
Jackson's transfer of property to Wesley Abraham (1898), 265, 322n31
legacy of white supremacy, 10–11, 315n8
postwar violence and white supremacist backlash, 221–22, 315n8
slaves' "neighborhoods," 20, 35–36
today, 9–10, *16*
white church culture, 31–33
See also English family

Maine
and the Fugitive Slave Act, 100–102, 105–14
Jackson's passage to Canada through, 99–131, 136–37, 293n1, 298n47, 299n6
See also Bath, Maine; Brunswick, Maine; Portland, Maine
Manchester Union and Emancipation Society, 198
Mancini, Matthew, 257, 320n11
Mann, Eldridge, 90
Mariner's Church (Portland, Maine), 128
Massachusetts
Fessenden and the state Senate and House, 125
Fugitive Slave Act and various "personal liberty" laws, 93–94
Jackson fleeing after passage of the Fugitive Slave Act, 94–95, 98–100, 293n1
See also Boston, Massachusetts; Salem, Massachusetts; Springfield, Massachusetts
Matthews, James, 42, 284n30, 286n24, 293n1
McCloud, Lymus, 222, 240
McCoy, Tyre, *xxii*, 2–4, 8
McFaddin, John Gamble, 11–12, 19
McFaddin, Martha English, 11–12, 19
McIntosh, Philis, 248–50, 319n56
McIntosh, Waters, 221, 315n8
McLeod, Jake, xviii–xxi, 250, 253, 265, 266
WPA interview (1936), xviii–xxi, 265
McLeod, Lymus, 222, 240
McLeod, Thomas G., 10
Methodist Episcopal Church, 34
Metropolitan Tabernacle (London), *186*, 186–87, 196, 208–10, *209*
Middletown, Connecticut, 245
Missouri Compromise, 125
Moïse, Marion "Major," 261, 262
Morning News (Saint John, New Brunswick), 151, *152*
Müller, Viola Franziska, 285n17
music. *See* slave songs and "antislavery songs"

Narrative of the Life of Frederick Douglass, An American Slave (1845), 41, 162, 189, 284n27
Narrative of William W. Brown, a Fugitive Slave, Written by Himself (1862), 119, 162, 310–11n81, 313n24
National Era (antislavery newspaper), 106, 115, 117, 120
Nelson family (Sumter County), 50–51, 285n10
New Brunswick census of 1851, *132*, 134–35, 137, *149*, 149–50, 298n2, 299n7. *See also* Saint John, New Brunswick, Canada
New Brunswick Courier, 141
Newell Carriage Company, 245
New England Freedom Association, 74

New Haven, Connecticut, 242–47
census of 1870, 242–44, *243*, 318n42, 318n44
colored freedmen's relief group, 245
desegregated public schools, 245
free Black community, 242–47
Jackson and Julia's home in, 242–47
Winter Street neighborhood's free Black community, 242–45, 267, 318n44
New Haven and Northampton Railroad, 245
New Haven Board of Education, 245
New Haven Register, 260, 321n27
New Park Street Chapel (London), 182–84, *209*
New York Committee of Vigilance, 143–44
New York Times, 260
Niagara (ship), 67
Northampton, Massachusetts, 85, 88, 218–19
Northampton Association of Education and Industry, 85, 218–19
Northampton Lunatic Asylum, 240–41, 242, 246–48
North Carolina
Julia Jackson's escape from slavery in, 142–46, 247
State vs. John Andrew Jackson and sentencing to convict work gang, *252*, 254–57

Ofley, Rev. G. W., 89, 292n57
"Old Carolina State" (minstrel tune), 112, 264
Olney, James, 309n71
Osgood, Rev. Samuel, 88–90, 231
"Osnaburg" cloth, 201
Ottoman (ship), 66–67

Parry, Tyler D., 281n59
Passmore, Joseph, 187, 188–89, 233, 313n24
Patterson, Robert J., 140–41
Paul, Archibald, 203–5
Pennington, James, 162
"personal liberty" laws, 93–94
Phillips, Wendell, 67
Pittman, Samuel, 77
Place, Captain (Freedmen's Bureau representative in Sumter County), 216, 237–40, 266
Player, Ransom, 36–40
Portland, Maine, 100–101, 124–31
antislavery movement, 101, 125–31
Black community and assistance to fugitives, 124, 125, 126–31, 137, 267
census of 1850, 127
Jackson's winter waiting to find passage to Canada (1850–1851), 124–31, 137, 298n47
proslavery activities and riots, 130
shipping industry and Black mariners, 127, 129
Portland Congregational Church (Maine), 130
Portland Daily Press (Maine), 246
post–Civil War era
Black congregants leaving Salem Black River Church, 32
Black migration to Kansas, 259
convict lease system, 254–57
the English family, 213, 217–38, *219*, 228–29, 234–36
Freedmen's Bureau, xxi, 216–22, 224–26, 234, 236–40, 258
Jackson and Julia's home in New Haven, 242–47
Jackson and Julia's home in Springfield, 231–42
Jackson and Julia's return to the U.S., x, xx–xxi, 206–7, 213, 215, 216–51
Jackson and Julia's travel to the South, 213, 223–29
Jackson's attempt to reconnect with family, 226–29

Jackson's collection of donations and relief supplies for freemen in South Carolina, xxi, 232–36, *233*, 238–40, 260–63, 265–66, *266*
Jackson's collection of donations to purchase land in Lynchburg, 260–63
Jackson's scheme to buy the English family's plantation, x, *214*, 216–22, 234–36, 241
Jackson's scheme to start a "colony" in Cheraw, South Carolina, 241–42
Klan and white supremacists, 221–22, 315n8
landownership by freed people in the South, 220, 235, 260–63, 316n24
Republican Party, 220, 232, 317n31
Southern backlash and violent racism, xix, 221–22, 229–30, 237, 315n8
Southern resistance to Reconstruction, xix, 221
"Potter's Raid," 212
Power, James, 295n20
Presbyterians, white Southern, 31–32
Preston Guardian, 169
print culture, 311n88
Putnam, Joseph, 77

Quaker meeting house (Portland, Maine), 130

Ray, Charles, 144
Reconstruction, xix, 221. *See also* post–Civil War era
Remond, Charles, 79
Remond, Charles Lenox, 79, 80, 81, 86, 130, 175, 298n53
Remond, Sarah, 79, 80, 306n26
Remond family, 78–79, 80, 81
Republican Party, 220, 232, 317n31
Reynolds, David S., 118
Rice, John Andrew, 10
Robinson, Charles, 250
Rowers Paper Company (Springfield, Massachusetts), 232
Ruggles, David, 143
runaway slave advertisements
the English family's advertisement for Jackson, xiv–xv, 14, *44*, 45–49, 284n4, 299n7, 308n53
racist language and assumptions about character, xiv, 49
rewards, *44*, 48, 284n4

Sadberry, Larry, 263
Saint John, New Brunswick, Canada, 131, 132–54
and the American Revolution, 137–39
antislavery activists, 136, 140–41, 147–54, 158
Black community, 136, 137–41, 147–54, 259–60
Black refugees following Fugitive Slave Act, 139–41, 150–51, 153
Black schools, 146
Black voter registration and civic identity, 146–47, 151
census of 1851 naming Jackson, *132*, 134–35, 137, *149*, 149–50, 298n2, 299n7
Charter (1785), 139
descendants of Black Loyalists, 138–39
the 1877 fire and changes to, 259–60
Irish immigrants, 134, 139–40
Jackson's decision to leave, 154–55, 158
Jackson's marriage to Julia Jackson, 135, 141–47, 154–55, 158
Jackson's return to deliver lectures (1880s), 259–60
Jackson's work as a whitewasher, 152, 303n49
and racism in Canada, 140
Sparrow and, *149*, 149–54, *152*, *153*, 158, 260, 303n49
Saint John Emancipation Society (New Brunswick), 140–41, 158

Salem, Massachusetts, 76–81, 91–92, 149, 223
  antislavery movement, 76–81, 91–92, 223
  free Black community, 76, 78–80, 149, 223, 289n26
  Irish immigrants, 77
  Jackson's campaign to liberate Louisa and Jinny, 76–80
  Jackson's return to, 223
  Jackson's self-reinvention, 79–80
  leather industry and tanneries, 76–78, 91, *93*
  Remond family, 78–79, 80, 81
Salem Baptist Church (Massachusetts), 78
Salem Black River Presbyterian Church, 7, 31–32, *32*
Salem Directory (1850), 77
Sandy Hook, New Jersey, 142–44
Saturday Review (London), 142
Scott, Capt. George, 59–61, 64–67
Shipman, Mr. (H. Schipman), 52, 285n13
Siebert, Wilbur, 299n6
Sierra Leone, 202
Skinner, Rev. Richard, 179, 180
"slave badge" system, 45, 53–56, *55*, 286n19, 286n22
slave narratives
  activist abolitionist narrative tradition, *26*
  circulation and popularity in England, 162, 187, 193, 309n65
  Douglass, 41, 162, 189, 284n27
  Henson, 119, 162, 275n1, 296–97n40
  Lowery, *26*, 29, 34–37, 283n15
  patterns and characteristics of, 189, 190, 309n71
  Stowe's reading of, 119, 275n1
  William Wells Brown, 119, 162, 310–11n81, 313n24
  WPA's slave narrative project during the Depression, xviii–xxi, 265
  See also *The Experience of a Slave in South Carolina* (Jackson's 1862 memoir)
slavery
  abolished in England (1808), 41, 165
  American slaveholders' attack on Spurgeon for criticism of, 182–83
  Christmas holiday for enslaved people, 42–43, 50–51, 284n32
  cotton trade and, 6–7, 8, 9–10, 13, 24–25, 37, *53*, 59, 102, 123–24, 165–66, 201
  Dundee and global slave economy, 201
  enslaved women without children, 145
  forced and chosen marriages, 20–25, 87, 281n59, 281n60, 291n53
  Jackson on the English family's cruelty, 11–13, 16–19, 23–24, 37, 91–92, 263–64
  Liverpool and global slave economy, *165*, 165–66
  "slave badge" system in South Carolina, 45, 53–56, *55*, 286n19, 286n22
  Slave Schedule of Elizabeth English (1860), 46–47, *47*, 180–81, 308n53
  "soul value" and self-worth of enslaved people, 4, 277n6
  Southern slave laws and *The Slave Code* (1853), 313n24
  white church culture and coerced participation of enslaved people, 31–33
  women slave-owners' cruelty and punishments, 12, 17–18, 36, 39–40, 279n28, 283n23
  See also escapes from enslavement; Fugitive Slave Act of 1850; slave narratives; slave songs and "antislavery songs"

slave songs and "antislavery songs," 111–12, 191–92, 310n77
and British interests in Black music, 310n77
closing chapter of Jackson's memoir, 191–92, 310n77
"Dearest Mae" ("A Slave Song"), 111–12, 192, 264, 295n20, 295n22, 311n82
"The Flight of the Bondman," 192, 310–11n81
Jackson's pamphlet against Spurgeon and final chapter of "Negro Songs," 210
Jackson's singing with Stowe's children, 111–12, 192, 264, 295n20, 295n22, 311n82
Jackson's song lyrics, 111, 191–92, 210, 264, 295n22, 310n77
Liberty Minstrel (1844 songbook), 310n77
"Old Carolina State," 112, 264
William Wells Brown's songbook (*The Anti-Slavery Harp*), 310n77
Smalls, Robert, 235, 316n19
Smith, Ellison D. ("Cotton Ed"), 10
Smith, Jane, 216, 226, 237–39, 266
Smith, William H., 251
Smyrna (barque), 59–61, 64–68, 69–70, 125, 287–88n2
Smyth, Harriet Porter Coffin, 102, 294n7
Smyth, William, 102–4, *103*, 113, 294n7
South Carolina
Black families' acquisition of small farms (1868–71), 220
cotton growing, 6–7, 8, 10
Freedmen's Bureau, 216, 225–26, 234, 236–40, 266, 314n2
Jackson's collection of donations and relief supplies for freemen in, xxi, 232–36, *233*, 238–40, 260–63, 265–66, *266*
"slave badge" system, 45, 53–56, *55*, 286n19, 286n22
See also Charleston, South Carolina; Lynchburg, South Carolina; Sumter County, South Carolina
South Carolina Constitutional Convention, 220
Sparrow, Cornelius, *149*, 149–54, *153*, 158, 260, 267, 303n49
and New Brunswick census of 1851, *149*, 149–50
"White-washing" business in Saint John, 151–52, *152*, 303n49
Sparrow, Martha Jane, *149*, 150–51
Springfield, Massachusetts, 85, 231–42, 248–51
assault on Jackson at home, 250–51
census of 1880, 248, 319n56
Jackson and Ella's home in, 247, 248–51
Jackson and Julia's home in, 231, 236–42
St. John's Congregational Church, 231, 316n19
Willow Street neighborhood, 248–49
See also Springfield Republican
Springfield Republican, *219*, 231–32, 240, 241–42, 250–51, 258
antislavery messaging and activism, 231–32
August 1881 article about Jackson's life, 258
Jackson's connection to, 232, 235–36, 249, 251, 258, 317n31
notice of Jackson's scheme to purchase the English family plantation, 235–36
notice of Jackson's scheme to start a colony in Cheraw, South Carolina, 241–42
notices about Jackson's scheme to collect donations for freemen in South Carolina, 232, 235–36

Springfield Republican (*continued*)
and the postbellum Republican Party, 232, 317n31
reporting 1880 attack on Jackson, 250–51
Spurgeon, Charles Haddon, 181–87, 196–97, 205–11, 305n16
attacked by American slaveholders for criticism of slavery, 182–83
Jackson's association with, 181–87, 193, 196–97, 205–11
and Jackson's efforts to purchase his family, 208–10
Jackson's letter to a local newspaper denouncing, 206–7
Jackson's pamphlet airing his grievances against, *194*, 194–96, 208–11, 313n24
and London's Metropolitan Tabernacle, *186*, 186–87, 196, 208–10, *209*
testimonial included in Jackson's memoir, 193
withdrawn patronage and Jackson's sense of betrayal, 196–97, 205–11
Spurgeon and Jackson, or, the White Preacher and the Black Slave Lecturer (1865 Jackson pamphlet), *194*, 194–96, 208–11, 313n24
final chapter of "Negro Songs" and lyrics, 210
unknown printer for, 208, 313n24
State of North Carolina vs. John Andrew Jackson, *252*, 254
Stein, Jordan, 311n88
St. John's Congregational Church (Springfield, Massachusetts), 231, 316n19
Stowe, Calvin, 105, 107–8, 113–14, 115, 246, 294n7, 294n9
Stowe, Charles (brother), 118–19, 294n7
Stowe, Charles Edward (son), 105–6, 294n8, 296–97n40
Stowe, Eliza, 110
Stowe, Frederick, 110
Stowe, Georgiana, 110, 121
Stowe, Harriet Beecher, xv–xvi, 96–99, *104*, 104–24, 175–78, 250, 266–67
antislavery cause and reactions to the Fugitive Slave Act, 105–21
Brunswick, Maine family and household, ix, 104–14, *106*, 124
Dred (1856), 157, 176–78, *177*, 296n39
"The Freeman's Dream: A Parable" (1850 sketch), 106
Hartford, Connecticut home, 246
A Key to Uncle Tom's Cabin, 120, 296–97n40
reading slave narratives and antislavery fiction, 119, 275n1
on severe Maine winter (1850–51), 124
speaking tour in England, 175–78
testimonial letter for Jackson, 157, 168, 175, 275n1, 303–4n60, 304n61, 311n84
and William Smyth, 104, 294n7
See also Jackson and Stowe's encounter in Brunswick, Maine (1850); *Uncle Tom's Cabin* (Stowe)
Stowe, Hattie, 110
Stowe, Henry, 110
Stowe, Samuel Charles, 294n8
Stowell, Martin, 82–84, 290n42
Stroyer, Jacob, 201
Sumter Banner (1848 runaway slave advertisement), xiv–xv, 14, *44*, 46–49, 284n4
Sumter County, South Carolina, 4–9, 21, 29, 260–63, 281n53
camp revival meetings, 28–36, 40, 84
Civil War, 212–13
Freedmen's Bureau and Captain Place, 216, 237–40, 266
Jackson's collecting donation for freed people in Lynchburg, 260–63, 265–66

and Jackson's postwar return to South Carolina, 228–29
Nelson family, 50–51, 285n10
short-staple cotton growing, 6–7
See also English family; Lynchburg, South Carolina
Surrey Comet, 178–79
Surry County, North Carolina
Cape Fear and Yadkin Valley Railroad, 254–57
Jackson's arrest and sentencing to convict work gang, x, *252*, 254–57

Tabernacle Camp Ground (Lynchburg, South Carolina), 30, 40
Temperance Chronicle, 306n20
Thackeray, William Makepeace, 163
Toronto, Ontario, Canada, 144–45, 302n35
Truth, Sojourner, 86, 313n24
Turner, Nat, 176
Tyre McCoy vs. Robert English (1821), 2–4, 8xxii

Uncle Tom's Cabin (Stowe), ix, 98–99, 104, 114–23, 157, 176, 266–67
array of influences on, 118–19, 275n1, 296–97n40
Jackson as inspiration for, ix, 98–99, 104, 110–23, 176, 267, 275n1, 296–97n40
publication as serial in the *National Era*, 115, 117, 120, 157
publication in book form, 117–18, 157
reception and impact, 114, 117–18, 267
story/plot, 115–17
Stowe's pay for, 115, 118, 176
the "Uncle Tom" model as cultural trope, xvi, 276n8
Underground Railroad (UGRR), 80, 101, *106*, *126*, 143
Underwood, W. L., 203
Union and Advertiser (Rochester, New York), 263–64, 321n29
Upham, Phebe, 107, 108, 114
Upham, Thomas C., *107*, 107–10, 123
Upham family, 103–4, 107–10, 114, 117, 123
U.S. Census
Bath/Brunswick area of Maine (1850), 124
Black seamen residing at Foreman's Boston boarding house (1850), 14, *62*, 68–71, *70*, 90–91
Hallowell, Maine (1850), 293n1
interpreting census data, 242–44, 318n43
Jackson named in the Boston census (1850), 14, *62*, 65, 68–71, 90–91, 293n1
Lynchburg, South Carolina (1870), 10
New Haven, Connecticut (1870), 242–44, *243*, 318n42, 318n44
Portland, Maine (1850), 127
Slave Schedule of Elizabeth English (1860), 46–47, *47*, 180–81, 308n53
Springfield, Massachusetts (1880), 248, 319n56
See also New Brunswick census of 1851

War of 1812, 138
Watchman and Southron (newspaper), 262, 263
Watson, Henry, 313n24
Watson, Julia A. *See* Jackson, Julia A. (second wife)
Wells, Elizabeth. *See* Law, Elizabeth Wells McKelvin
Wells, Ida Mae, 165
Wells, Igby, 83
Wells, Margaret, 22
Wells, Thomas, 22
Wells family, 20, 22, 83, 86, 291n43
Wesleyan Academy (Springfield, Massachusetts), 238

Wesleyan Church (Salem, Massachusetts), 149
Western Sentinel (Surry County, North Carolina), *254*
Western Times, 142, 197
whitewashing work ("rough painting"), 135, 136, 146, 151–53, 184, 206, 213, 303n49, 309n61
Wilson, Elizabeth. *See* English, Elizabeth Wilson
Wilson, Jenny, 20–21
Wilson, John Leighton, 11
Wilson, Rose, 20–21
Winchester Repeating Arms Company, 245
Woodstock, Vermont, 258
Worcester, Massachusetts, 81, 82–83, 84–85, 86, 88–91, 315–16n18
Works Progress Administration (WPA) and slave narrative project (1936–1938), xviii–xxi, 265

Yale College (New Haven, Connecticut), 244
Young, Dennis, 69–70
Young, Lucile, xix

ABOUT THE AUTHOR

Susanna Ashton is professor of English at Clemson University. An expert on slavery and freedom narratives, she was a Du Bois fellow at Harvard's Hutchins Center, a fellow with Yale's Gilder Lehrman Center, and a Fulbright scholar. She lives in Clemson, South Carolina.

PUBLISHING IN THE PUBLIC INTEREST

Thank you for reading this book published by The New Press; we hope you enjoyed it. New Press books and authors play a crucial role in sparking conversations about the key political and social issues of our day.

We hope that you will stay in touch with us. Here are a few ways to keep up to date with our books, events, and the issues we cover:

- Sign up at www.thenewpress.com/subscribe to receive updates on New Press authors and issues and to be notified about local events
- www.facebook.com/newpressbooks
- www.twitter.com/thenewpress
- www.instagram.com/thenewpress

Please consider buying New Press books not only for yourself, but also for friends and family and to donate to schools, libraries, community centers, prison libraries, and other organizations involved with the issues our authors write about.

The New Press is a 501(c)(3) nonprofit organization; if you wish to support our work with a tax-deductible gift please visit www.thenewpress.com/donate or use the QR code below.